Financial Management and Real Options

Jack Broyles

WILEY

Other Wiley Editorial Offices

John Wiley & Sons Inc., 111 River Street, Hoboken, NJ 07030, USA

Jossey-Bass, 989 Market Street, San Francisco, CA 94103-1741, USA

Wiley-VCH Verlag GmbH, Boschstr. 12, D-69469 Weinheim, Germany

John Wiley & Sons Australia Ltd, 33 Park Road, Milton, Queensland 4064, Australia

John Wiley & Sons (Asia) Pte Ltd, 2 Clementi Loop #02-01, Jin Xing Distripark, Singapore 129809

John Wiley & Sons Canada Ltd, 22 Worcester Road, Etobicoke, Ontario, Canada M9W 1L1

British Library Cataloguing in Publication Data
A catalogue record for this book is available from the British Library

ISBN 0-471-89934-8

Project management by Originator, Gt Yarmouth, Norfolk (typeset in 9/13pt Gill Sans Light and Times)
Printed and bound in Great Britain by Ashford Colour Press Ltd, Gosport, Hampshire
This book is printed on acid-free paper responsibly manufactured from sustainable forestry
in which at least two trees are planted for each one used for paper production.

Contents

13   Calculating the Cost of Capital   246

14   Long-term Financing   264

Preface

Readers under pressure such as MBA students and executives want short chapters rich in essential insights. In writing this book, I kept five principles constantly in mind. First, individual chapters must be short. Second, the book must put insight before unnecessary mathematics. Third, each topic should nevertheless reflect the state of the art. Fourth, the book should not distract the reader with nonessentials. Most importantly, the book should be useful throughout. Writing to these tight specifications is both arduous and rewarding. One has to believe that the reader will benefit.

The book primarily is about financial management and, as its title implies, real options are an integral, subsidiary theme. Real options are opportunities available to management permitting them to adapt the enterprise to changing needs. Understanding the value of real options is essential to corporate financial management. Examples in several chapters demonstrate why failure to assess the value of real options leads to mistaken investment decisions. A distinctive feature of this book is showing how to conduct real options analysis without higher mathematics.

Most of the individual chapters were distilled from postgraduate and executive teaching materials used by the author and colleagues in leading European business schools, universities, major companies, international banks, training organizations, and management consultants. These included the London Business School, Templeton College (Oxford), Cranfield School of Management, Warwick Business School, the University of Buckingham, the University of Notre Dame, and the University of Orleans. Training programs at Shell International Petroleum, Imperial Group, Ford of Europe, ICI, ITT, EMI, Expamet, Lucas CAV, Burmah Oil, Citibank, Bank of America, Continental Bank, Morgan Guaranty Trust, Bankers Trust, PricewaterhouseCoopers, London Society of Chartered Accountants, Euroforum, and the Boston Consulting Group also used the materials.

I have had the privilege of working with distinguished colleagues, and I wish to acknowledge their influence on this book. First, I must mention Julian Franks, Willard Carleton, Ian Cooper, and Simon Archer with whom I co-authored earlier books. I can trace the approach adopted in many parts of the book to the thinking of other distinguished former colleagues as well. Prominent among them were Harold Rose, Peter Moore, David Chambers, Howard Thomas, Richard Brealey, Stewart Hodges, Paul Marsh, Elroy Dimson, Stephen Schaefer, Colin Meyer, John McGee, Adrian Buckley, David Myddleton, and Ian Davidson.

In 1981, Ian Cooper and I jointly published one of the first research papers on real options, anticipating results in some of the books and hundreds of papers published subsequently on this subject.

The road from the mathematical beginnings to the less difficult approach to real options advocated here was long. The Financial Options Research Centre (Warwick Business School) workshops and frequent conversations with Stewart Hodges, Les Clewlow, Chris Strickland, Tony Steele, Archie Pitts, Peter Corvi, Elizabeth Whaley, Vicky Henderson, and our postgraduate students provided the environment for such thinking to flourish.

Of particular importance was team teaching at different stages of my academic career, for example, with Julian Franks, Walter Reid, Ian Davidson, Peter Corvi, Mark Freeman, and Archie Pitts. We shared many pedagogical ideas and experiences on how best to explain advanced financial concepts to MBAs and executives. I introduced drafts of chapters and exercises in the more recent courses. Students invariably were enthusiastic; and their feedback, as always, was invaluable.

I owe thanks also to the publisher's referees, Lance Moir, Winfried G. Hallerbach, Stewart Hodges, André Farber, Steve Toms, Edward Sprokholt, Lesley Franklin, Andrew Marshall, Seth Armitage, and other anonymous referees who were generous with their time and insightful with suggestions, many of which made a significant difference to particular chapters. If the book retains flaws, it will not be due to lack of effort and advice from referees.

The book divides into five parts. The first, **Introduction to Financial Management**, begins by defining the role of financial management in corporate governance. It then introduces the fundamental methods of financial analysis used throughout the book. Finally, it introduces financial securities and securities markets. In this way, the first part builds a foundation and sets the scene for the remainder of the book.

The second part, **Valuation of Investment and Real Options**, introduces the reader to the standard methods of capital project appraisal and then shows how to integrate real options analysis with project appraisal methodology. Building on the resulting approach, it shows how to value companies, particularly those with future investment opportunities. The part ends with a review of perhaps the most challenging project appraisal problem, acquisitions and mergers. Four of the chapters in this part contain new material not yet offered in other books.

The third part, **Financial Structure**, covers the important issues concerning how best to finance a company. Interrelated topics included here are portfolio theory and asset pricing, the cost capital, long-term financing, dividend policy, capital structure, and lease finance. Two chapters in this part contain new material not yet offered by other books.

Arguably, the most essential responsibility for the Chief Financial Officer is to keep the company solvent. The fourth part integrates **Solvency Management**, by bringing together the related topics of financial planning, the management of debtors and inventories, and of interest and exchange rate risks.

The purpose of the chapter in the final part is to translate project appraisal to a global setting involving many foreign currencies. In this way, this part provides a bridge to subsequent study of **International Financial Management**.

I would like to dedicate this book to my sympathetic family, stimulating colleagues, and inquiring students.

PART I

Introduction to Financial Management

Financial Management and Corporate Governance[1]

This introductory chapter paints a broad-brush picture of what finance is about and how financial management helps to steer the firm toward its financial objectives. First, we consider the financial problems of the small firm and then see how the same problems reappear in large corporations. We also describe the way these problems give rise to the functions performed by the principal financial officers of the firm and show how financial managers assist operating managers to make decisions that are more profitable. Finally, we discuss how the Chief Financial Officer draws upon the information, analysis, and advice of financial managers and staff when advising other members of the company's board of directors concerning important issues such as shareholder relations, dividend policy, financial planning and policy, and major capital investments.

TOPICS

The chapter introduces the main concerns of financial management. In particular, we begin by addressing the following topics:

O   the fundamental concerns of financial management;

O   organization of the finance function;

O   the principal financial officers;

O   responsibilities of the principal financial officers;

O   financial objectives;

O   the role of financial management in corporate governance.

1-1   WHAT FINANCIAL MANAGEMENT IS REALLY ABOUT

If you were to start a small business of your own tomorrow, you soon would be involved in financial management problems. Having first conceived of a unique product or service, perhaps in a market niche lacking competition, you must then develop a plan. The plan requires answers to some

---

[1] Adapted by permission of J. R. Franks, J. E. Broyles, and W. T. Carleton (1985) *Corporate Finance Concepts and Applications* (Boston: Kent).

important questions; for instance, what assets will the business require? That is, what premises, equipment and inventories of merchandise and materials will the business need? The purchase of these resources can require substantial funds, particularly in the initial stages before generation of much sales revenue. In other words, you need access to money.

PLANNING

The strategy that you adopt for starting and operating your business will affect the amount of money you will need and when you will need it. If the money is not available at the right time and in the required amounts, you will have to alter your plans. As a result, your problems are those of a financial manager, more specifically, the company **Treasurer**. You have to translate the operating plan of your business into a financial plan that enables you to forecast how much capital you need and when.

FUNDING

At the same time, in your role as acting Treasurer, you have to begin building relationships with sympathetic bankers prepared to lend your business money when needed. Banks do not like to lend more than half the money that a business needs, because bankers do not like to take too many chances with their depositors' money. Consequently, before you can borrow you must be willing to risk much of your own funds. If you do not have enough personal capital, you must try to find relations or other people who might be willing to contribute some money. In exchange for their capital, they will want to be part owners of the business and share in its profits. So, your business will require two kinds of capital: **debt** (the bank's funds) and **equity** (the owners' funds). This is an essential function of financial management: ensuring that your business has adequate funds available to operate efficiently and to exploit its opportunities.

CAPITAL INVESTMENT

When you have secured the capital that you need to acquire the assets required by the business, you face some further choices. Which assets do you need, and how do you choose between competing ones? If two business machines have different revenue-producing capabilities and different operating lives, you need some financial yardsticks to help you make a choice. How much money will each machine make each month, and for how many years? Is this cash income sufficient to justify the price that you would have to pay for each machine? Does the rate of return on the investment in either machine compare favorably with your other investment opportunities? Answers to such questions require analysis, and financial management is concerned in part with providing the techniques for this sort of analysis. A large company would employ financial analysts to make such comparisons for the company Treasurer.

FINANCIAL CONTROL

Once your business is in operation, you will engage in an enormous number of transactions. Sales slips, receipts, and checkbook entries pile up. You cannot rely on memory to handle information in the mounting piles of paper on your desk. Your sympathetic accountant says, "You need a management accounting system." For a fee, he sets up a simple system for you.

The system involves keeping a journal that records all financial transactions each day, and various ledger accounts gathering transactions into meaningful categories. The sums in these accounts help you to get your business under control, or to know whether you are winning the battle between profit and loss. If you are losing, the accounts can provide some clues as to what to do about it. For example, they can show whether your prices cover all your costs.

Such an accounting system proves necessary but requires effort to maintain. When the business starts generating sufficient cash, you hire a bookkeeper to make the actual entries in the accounts. Still, the system requires some of your time because you must supervise the bookkeeper and interpret what the accounts might indicate about the health of your business.

FINANCIAL REPORTING

Now that you are keeping accounts regularly, you have made your outside accountant's job much easier. At the end of the year, the accountant must add up your assets (what you own) and your liabilities (what you owe). Your total assets less your total liabilities represent your "net worth". If your net worth has increased during the year, you have made a profit, and your company will have to pay a tax on the taxable income.

FINANCIAL MANAGEMENT

All this detail requires much help from your accountant. As your business grows, you will be able to hire a full-time accountant, who will keep your accounts, prepare your tax returns and supervise your bookkeepers. A good Chief Accountant can also undertake financial analysis of potential investment decisions and help with financial planning and other treasury functions, including raising funds. Perhaps then your full-time accountant deserves the title of **Chief Financial Officer (CFO)**, because he or she will be performing or supervising all the main functions of finance:

1.   Planning and forecasting needs for outside financing.

2.   Raising capital.

3.   Appraising investment in new assets.

4.   Financial reporting and control, and paying taxes.

Financial management mainly concerns planning, raising funds, analysis of project profitability, and control of cash, as well as the accounting functions relating to reporting profits and taxes. A financial manager is an executive who manages one or more of these functions. As we have seen, financial management plays a role in many facets of any business. That is why financial managers participate in virtually all the major decisions and occupy key positions at the center of all business organizations.

DEFINITIONS
Chief Financial Officer (CFO)   A company's most senior financial manager.

Debt   Sum of money or other assets owed by one party to another. Usually, a legally enforceable obligation to pay agreed interest and to repay the principal of a loan to the lender promptly on schedule.

Equity   Net worth or shareholder's capital represented by common stock (ordinary shares) and preferred stock.

Treasurer   Senior financial manager reporting directly to the Chief Financial Officer. Primarily responsible for funding and cash management.

1-2   HOW FINANCE IS ORGANIZED IN CORPORATIONS

LIMITED LIABILITY

Individual entrepreneurs or a few business partners start most companies. The owners and the managers are thus the same people. Very soon, the owners usually will register the company as a limited liability company. One advantage of the corporate form is that the law treats a corporation as an entity distinct from its owners. This offers the advantage of limited liability. That is, the debt holders cannot force the owners to repay the corporation's debt from the owners' personal financial resources. So, the owners' risk is limited to their money already invested. This feature makes it easier for each of the existing owners to sell his or her share in the ownership of the firm.

SHAREHOLDERS

A share certificate (stock) legally certifies that its registered holder shares in the ownership of the corporation. For example, if the corporation has issued 1 million shares, the registered holder of 100,000 shares owns one-tenth of the company. Share certificates are tradable securities that investors can buy and then sell to other investors and speculators in the stock market. The larger corporations get their shares listed on one or more stock exchanges that provide a liquid securities market for the shares.

MANAGERS

As the original owner-managers retire or leave the company to manage other businesses, recruitment of professional managers who might have little or no investment in the company becomes necessary. Professional managers are supposed to act as agents of the shareholders, who gradually become a diverse and somewhat disinterested population of individuals, pension funds, mutual funds, insurance companies, and other financial institutions. So, we find that in most large corporations the actual managers and the owners are two mostly distinct groups of people and institutions.

In this situation, you can understand how a manager might identify his or her personal interests more with the corporation than would any one individual shareholder, and how at times there can be conflicts of interest between managers and shareholders. Such conflicts of interest are the agency problem.

BOARD OF DIRECTORS

Company law entrusts the interests of the shareholders to a board of directors appointed at an Annual General Meeting of the shareholders. The board is responsible for governing the company in accord with the company's Articles of Association within the framework of statutes and regulations established in the company law of the relevant country or jurisdiction. The board meets periodically to review company affairs and has the ultimate authority to set policy, to authorize major decisions, and to appoint top managers.

ANNUAL GENERAL MEETING

At the Annual General Meeting, the shareholders elect or reelect directors to the board. The outside directors usually come from the top ranks of other companies, financial institutions and professional and academic bodies. The CFO, the Chief Executive Officer, and some other key officers of the company will be among the inside directors on the board in countries that permit inside directors. Boards also include employee representatives in some countries.

PRINCIPAL FINANCIAL OFFICERS

The CFO is the senior executive who is responsible to the board for all the financial aspects of the company's activities. Because of the scope and complexity of finance, typically he or she will delegate major responsibilities to the Chief Accountant (Controller) and the Treasurer. Although their functions can overlap, the Chief Accountant tends to concentrate on those activities requiring accountants, and the Treasurer specializes in maintaining active relationships with investment and commercial bankers and other providers of funds in the capital market including the shareholders. The capital market consists of the banks, insurance companies and other financial institutions (including the stock market) that compete to supply companies with financial capital.

DEFINITIONS

Agency problem   Conflicts of interest between professional managers and shareholders.

Capital market   Market for long-term securities. Consists of the banks, insurance companies, and other financial intermediaries (including the stock market) competing to supply companies with financial capital.

Chief Accountant (Controller)   The most senior accounting manager. Reports directly to the Chief Financial Officer.

Limited liability   Restriction of a business owner's financial loss to no more than the owner's investment in the business.

Share (stock)   Security legally certifying that its registered holder is a part-owner of the company.

1-3   THE CHIEF FINANCIAL OFFICER

RESPONSIBILITY TO THE BOARD

As many directors on the board frequently lack financial expertise, the CFO often occupies a strong position of influence. The board relies on the CFO for advice concerning the payment of dividends to shareholders, major capital expenditures for new assets, the acquisition of other companies, and the resale of existing assets. The board may also rely on the finance department for interpretation of economic and financial developments, including the implications of government regulation, economic and monetary policies, and tax legislation.

RESPONSIBILITIES

The board requires that the CFO prepare long-term budgets linking expenditures on fixed assets and financing requirements to strategic plans. Advising the board on investments in new assets can require the CFO to head a capital appropriations committee. In this capacity, the CFO oversees the budgeting of funds for investment, screening investment proposals and the preparation and updating of the capital expenditure proposals manual for operating managers. Ultimately, the CFO is responsible for all activities delegated to the Chief Accountant or to the Treasurer. Figure 1.1 illustrates a typical organization chart for the financial management function.

1-4   THE CHIEF ACCOUNTANT

RESPONSIBILITIES

Primarily, the Chief Accountant (Controller) is responsible to the CFO for establishing, maintaining, and auditing the company's information systems and procedures, and preparing financial statements and reports for management, the board, the shareholders and the tax authorities. Partly because of the data collection required for management accounting and financial reporting activities, the Chief Accountant acquires information that makes his or her participation and advice

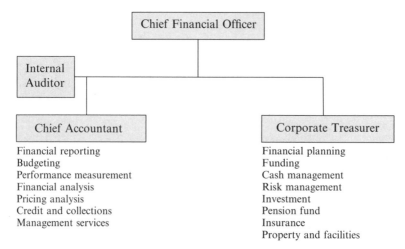

Figure 1.1   Typical organization of financial management.

useful to many decisions throughout the firm. The Chief Accountant might also be responsible for computer facilities and information management.

The Chief Accountant oversees cost control throughout the company. He or she participates in major product pricing and credit decisions, and often supervises collections from customers. Together with staff, the Chief Accountant consolidates forecasts and related financial analyses and prepares budgets for operating departments. This person might also be responsible to the CFO for all matters relating to taxes, although some companies have a separate tax department reporting directly to the CFO. In some firms, the Chief Accountant also performs many of the treasury functions described below.

1-5   THE TREASURER

RESPONSIBILITIES

The main functions of the Treasurer are to invest surplus funds daily and to provide sufficient financing to meet all likely contingencies. For this purpose, the Treasurer puts together a forecast of the financial needs of the firm and manages its cash. The Treasurer must maintain effective business and personal relationships with the firm's commercial bankers and investment bankers, because he or she is responsible for arranging the external financing requirements indicated by the financial plan. The Treasurer also is responsible for issuing the firm's securities and for borrowing, paying interest on, and repaying outstanding corporate debt.

The Treasurer is the custodian of the company's cash balances and oversees all cashier and payroll activities. He or she therefore is in charge of the company's investments in the financial market and arranges for the management of employee pension funds. The Treasurer manages the firm's overseas transactions, taking such measures as required to prevent losses due to changes in foreign exchange rates.

The Treasurer's department might also manage the company's investment in real estate holdings and negotiate its insurance. The Treasurer's staff can advise on customer credit based on information from banks and credit agencies. Finally, the Treasurer's department is often the center for financial analytical expertise in the firm. The Treasurer's staff often engage in special projects analyzing, for example, the firm's overall corporate financial plan, proposed major capital expenditures, takeovers and mergers, and different ways of raising new funds. Financial analysts in the Treasurer's department often participate in training programs making methods of financial analysis more widely known to operating managers.

In summary, the Treasurer is the company's main contact with the financial community. He or she plans long-term financing and manages short-term borrowing and lending. The Treasurer's prime responsibility is to make certain that there are sufficient funds available to meet all likely needs of the company, both domestically and overseas, and to manage risks due to changes in interest and foreign exchange rates.

SOURCES OF FUNDS

Each year the company pays out a part of its after-tax earnings to the shareholders as dividends, with the remainder retained by the firm for reinvestment. In fact, most funds used by companies are the retained earnings together with funds that were set aside for depreciation. Retained earnings are equity because they still belong to the shareholders.

Frequently, however, additional funds are required, and the treasurer looks to various outside sources of capital to meet the balance of the company's needs. Borrowing has tax advantages, and bank borrowing is the largest single source of external financing for companies because it is comparatively easy to arrange.

SHORT-TERM DEBT

Corporate Treasurers like to finance their working capital investments in inventories and debtors (accounts receivable) with short-term bank loans for up to one year. Treasurers also negotiate intermediate-term loans from banks but borrow longer term from other financial institutions such as insurance companies. As short-term requirements for cash change constantly, the Treasurer must maintain close and continuing relationships with the company's bankers.

LONG-TERM DEBT

Next in importance to bank borrowing is the issue of long-term debt with, say, 10 or more years to repay. Long-term debt may take the form of bonds sold publicly in the financial market or placed privately with large financial institutions. Publicly issued debt and equity securities entail higher transaction costs. Therefore, most borrowing takes place privately with banks and insurance companies.

EQUITY VERSUS DEBT

As dividend payments are not tax-deductible, and new issues of equity involve high transaction costs, equity issues are a less significant source of external financing than debt. By law, debt holders have a prior claim on the company's assets, and shareholders can claim only what is left after lenders' claims have been satisfied. This makes borrowing more risky than equity from the company's standpoint. Although moderate borrowing can be less costly than new equity, the company must limit borrowing to control risk and to maintain a favorable credit rating with lenders.

INITIAL PUBLIC OFFERING

When a private company becomes a public corporation, it makes an initial public offering (IPO) of some of its shares with the help of investment bankers. Often, the investment bankers buy the entire issue at a discount to the issue price and resell the shares to pension funds, mutual funds, insurance companies, and other financial institutions, or to the general public through stockbrokers.

RIGHTS ISSUES

Once the shares are issued and begin trading, the treasurer can raise further equity capital from existing shareholders or from the public, depending in part on what is permitted in the company's Articles of Association. A rights issue is an offer of additional shares at a discounted price to existing shareholders. Each shareholder's entitlement depends upon the number of shares already owned. The offer allows shareholders several weeks to exercise their rights to the new shares before a specified date. A shareholder who does not wish to exercise the rights may sell them to someone else. Usually, financial institutions acting as underwriters guarantee the rights issue. That is, they buy any shares that remain unsold to the existing shareholders. They do so at a price agreed beforehand in the underwriting agreement. Rights issues are less frequent in the USA than in Europe. In the USA, corporations sell most equity issues to ("place" them with) financial institutions rather than directly to their existing shareholders.

MARKET CAPITALIZATION

The owners' stake in the company is the equity or net worth. The net worth is the value of all the assets minus the value of the company's liabilities (mostly borrowing and trade credit from suppliers). The stock market makes its own assessment of the values of the assets and liabilities and consequently determines what the net value of the equity is really worth. Typically, this will be very different from the corresponding "book value" in the balance sheet. This stock market value of the equity is the company's market capitalization. The resulting share price equals the market capitalization divided by the number of shares issued.

CAPITAL STRUCTURE

With sufficient equity capital, the company is in a position to borrow. Lenders wish to be relatively certain of getting their money back, however. Therefore, debt typically represents a smaller proportion of the total financing employed by the firm than does equity. These proportions constitute the company's capital structure.

DEFINITIONS

Capital structure   The proportions of different forms of debt and equity constituting a company's total capital.

Initial public offering (IPO)   A limited company's first public issue of common stock (ordinary shares).

Market capitalization   The stock market value of a company's equity. The market price per share multiplied by the number of shares issued.

Rights issue   An offer of new shares by a public company to each of its existing shareholders in proportion to the number the shareholder already holds.

Underwriter   Investment bank or stockbroker undertaking to manage the issuance of securities for a corporate client, often buying the entire issue and reselling it to institutional clients and other investors.

1-6   CORPORATE FINANCIAL OBJECTIVES

SHAREHOLDERS' AND STAKEHOLDERS' INTERESTS

Most authorities agree that maximizing the market value of the shareholders' stake in the company is the appropriate financial objective of management, but this also involves the protection of debt holders' interests and those of other stakeholders such as customers and employees. The share-holders' main concern normally is the preservation and increase of the market value of their investment in the company. The debt holders' main interest is that the company honors its obligations to pay interest and repay the loan on the agreed timetable. Failing to do so can jeopardize the company's access to debt capital at a reasonable cost. Therefore, it is an important objective for management to maximize the value of the company's assets in such a way that it increases the wealth of the shareholders, without detriment to the debt holders and other stake-holders necessary for the long-term survival of the firm.

CONFLICTS OF INTEREST WITH DEBT HOLDERS

Conflicts of interest can arise between shareholders and debt holders. Management can invest in speculative ventures that might result in large losses. These investments might be acceptable to shareholders who are willing to accept higher risk with the expectation of higher reward. Compensation to lenders, however, is just the interest payments; and they require repayment of their loans. Interest payments do not increase when the corporation performs unexpectedly well, but lenders can lose their loans if the borrower becomes bankrupt. Given this asymmetry of rewards for lenders, they would like to prevent managers from making the company more risky. Covenants in loan agreements attempt to restrict management's room for maneuver in this regard but cannot do so very effectively. Competent corporate treasurers try to establish and maintain a satisfactory **credit rating**, and this behavior is the lenders' best protection.

RISK AND REQUIRED RATES OF RETURN

The expected cash flows generated by an asset together with its cost determine the expected rate of return from investing in the asset. In the financial market, different securities have different risks, and investors demand higher rates of return on securities with higher risk. As a result, investors expect managers in a corporation to try to obtain higher rates of return from its investments in commercial activities when the associated risks are greater for the shareholders.

PRESENT VALUE

In principle, shareholders can estimate the worth of the company's investment in an asset by comparing the investment to alternative investments in the financial market. A shareholder would want to know how much it would cost now to buy a portfolio of securities with the same expected future cash flows and the same risk as the asset. The cost of such a portfolio indicates the **present value (PV)** of the asset to the shareholders. If the cost of the asset is less than its PV, the investment is favorable for the shareholders.

In practice, a financial analyst estimates the PV of the asset by estimating the PV of each of its expected future cash flows separately (using the method to be described in Section 2.4) and adding up these PVs. Unless the total PV exceeds the cost of the asset, investment in the asset would not increase the PV of the firm.

EFFICIENCY OF THE FINANCIAL MARKET

In developed economies, financial markets are very competitive. Competition makes financial markets efficient. The meaning of an **efficient financial market** is that the prices of securities reflect all price-sensitive information as it becomes available to market participants. One result of market efficiency is that management normally cannot expect to increase the value of the corporation by raising funds in the financial market and then simply reinvesting the money back into the financial market.

VALUE MAXIMIZATION

The way that management increases the value of the corporation is to raise funds at competitive rates in an efficient financial market and then reinvest the funds in products and services that sell in markets that are less competitive and where higher rates of return are obtainable. Managers must seek profitable ventures in product markets where they can expect to enjoy some advantage over competitors. Competitive advantage can derive from patents and technologies, superior research, respected brands, established channels of distribution, superior locations, and economies of scale. Value-maximizing investment requires the identification, analysis, and exploitation of such opportunities for competitive advantage.

THE COST OF CAPITAL

When management selects investments it hopes will increase the value of the company, it must find activities expected to earn a higher rate of return than the **cost of capital**. The costs of capital include after-tax interest payments on debt and the level of dividends and capital gains that are required to satisfy the shareholders. The cost of capital is a variable that depends upon the risk of the investment. Therefore, an essential element in the search for value-maximizing investment is estimation of the risks of different investments. Without risk estimation, management cannot ascertain the cost of capital and would not know whether the rate of return expected from an activity can justify the use of capital. For these reasons, part of this book concerns measuring risk and the relationship between the cost of capital and risk.

DEFINITIONS

Cost of capital   Cost of funds used by a company for investment.

Credit rating   Classification of a company by a credit rating agency according to its likelihood of defaulting on its obligations to creditors.

Efficient financial market   A securities market in which prices rapidly reflect in an unbiased way all price-sensitive information available to market participants.

Present value (PV)   Value of an investment now as the cost of a comparable investment in the financial market (calculated by multiplying the investment's expected after-tax cash income by the appropriate discount factors).

1-7 CORPORATE GOVERNANCE

AGENCY PROBLEMS

Corporate governance concerns management at board level and the agency relationship between managers and owners.[2] In public companies managers are hired to act as agents for the owners, who are the shareholders in the company. The essence of the resulting agency problem is the potential for conflicts of interest between managers and shareholders. Opportunities for personal empire building, excessive remuneration, overly generous stock options, and extravagant perquisites abound. The problem is how to ensure that managers do not sequester the company's assets in such ways. Quite a different agency problem is that managers interested in job security often are more timid than shareholders (who can diversify away most of the risk) and fail to pursue profitable, risky strategies that would be valuable for shareholders. Responsible corporate governance and the existence of legal and regulatory structures that protect investors and lenders explain many of the responsibilities and functions of financial managers.

CONTROL-ORIENTED FINANCE

Broadly speaking, there are two systems affecting the conduct of corporate governance that operate in different countries: control-oriented finance and arm's length finance.[3] Under control-oriented finance, key investors such as large shareholders and bank lenders protect their own interests by having representatives on the board influencing strategic decisions. Germany, France, and Japan practice control-oriented corporate governance and finance characterized by a high concentration of ownership and a relatively low importance for financial markets.

ARM'S LENGTH FINANCE

In contrast, the USA, the UK, and other countries with Anglo-Saxon legal traditions practice arm's length finance and governance in which ownership is dispersed between a large number of individuals and institutions, and financial market performance is a significant influence on board-level decision-making. With arm's length finance, investors and lenders do not intervene in the decision-making process as long as, for example, the company meets its debt payment obligations. Some individual board members do not always see their duties in terms of safeguarding shareholders' interests, however. The most important legal right shareholders have is to vote on particular corporate matters such as mergers, liquidations, and elections of directors. Voting rights, however, are expensive to enforce and to exercise.

PROTECTION FOR SHAREHOLDERS

Dispersed ownership, large and liquid capital markets, an active market for corporate control (mergers and acquisitions), and extensive legal protection for small shareholders characterize the

[2] See M. Jensen and M. Meckling (1976) "Theory of the firm: Managerial behaviour, agency costs and ownership structure," *Journal of Financial Economics*, October, 305–360.
[3] For an excellent summary of European corporate governance and related financing implications, see Chapter 1 in A. Buckley, S. A. Ross, R. W. Westerfield, and J. F. Jaffe (1998) *Corporate Finance Europe* (Maidenhead, UK: McGraw-Hill).

UK and US arm's length financial systems. A strong unitary board led by a chairperson (who might also be the Chief Executive Officer) governs a corporation in these countries. Banking relationships must be at arm's length, and thus bankers cannot sit on the boards of UK public limited liability companies and US corporations. So, in the Anglo-Saxon framework the CFO has an even greater professional responsibility for the interests of shareholders and debt holders.

The growing importance of stock markets and increasingly dispersed ownership of public companies throughout the world underlie the increasing governmental interest in shareholder protection and better standards of corporate governance. The regulatory frameworks already adopted in the USA and the UK are increasingly the models for systems evolving in other countries. Financial managers are the principal agents for compliance with these systems.

DEFINITIONS

Corporate governance   Customs, rules, regulations and laws defining the way in which stake-holders and their agents (managers) govern the company.

1-8   CONCLUSIONS

Professional financial management can assist operating managers to achieve the financial objectives of the firm and report financial results to the owners, creditors, and employees. For this purpose, the Chief Accountant's department maintains the financial reporting and control system, and the Treasurer's department raises and manages funds and maintains active relationships with institutions in the financial community that are potential sources of capital.

The CFO draws upon the information, analysis, and advice of both financial departments in advising the board of directors concerning such important issues as shareholder relations, dividend policy, financial planning and policy, and major capital investments. The overriding responsibility of the CFO is to increase the value of the firm to its shareholders while also protecting the legitimate interests of debt holders, employees, and other essential stakeholders.

FURTHER READING

Chapter 1 in A. Buckley, S. A. Ross, R. W. Westerfield, and J. F. Jaffe (1998) *Corporate Finance Europe* (Maidenhead, UK: McGraw-Hill).

Colin Mayer and Julian Franks (1988) "Corporate ownership and control in the UK, Germany and France," *Bank of America Journal of Applied Corporate Finance*, Vol. 9, No. 4, 30–45.

QUESTIONS AND PROBLEMS

1   What are the major responsibilities of a company's CFO?

2   What kinds of competitive condition in the marketplace for the firm's products are most likely to increase the wealth of shareholders?

3   Why is maximizing the value of the firm not necessarily the same as maximizing the value of the shareholders' investment?

4   Should managers try to maximize market value of equity or to maximize the accounting value of equity in the balance sheet? Why?

5   Describe the different methods of financing the firm and characteristics of the main sources of finance.

6   Why might conflicts arise between shareholders and lenders?

7   What is your understanding of the relationship between risk and the cost of funds available for investment by managers?

8   If management thinks that it can increase shareholder wealth to the detriment of debt holders, employees, or suppliers, is it duty bound to do so?

9   To what extent can senior managers justify becoming very wealthy by granting themselves high salaries, bonuses, and stock options?

2 Fundamental Methods of Financial Analysis

The engine of the financial market is the flow of funds from savings. People need to provide for their retirement through investment in real property, investment plans, and pension funds. Once retired, these savers need investment income to pay for consumption. They depend, at least in part, on dividend income and realized capital gains from shares in companies in which they and their pension funds invested. Shareholders expect the managers of their companies to invest at rates of return commensurate with the risk of the investments. Managers can often obtain abnormally high rates of return by investing in new products and operations that are more efficient. By investing in such projects, managers add value for their shareholders.

Because savers can invest in the securities market for themselves, they expect their corporate managers to find better investments elsewhere in commercial product markets. In order to add any value for shareholders, these commercial investments must promise higher rates of return than from simply investing in securities of other companies. Therefore, the securities market represents the opportunity cost of capital, providing the benchmark rates for investment in commercial projects.

Financial analysis involves estimating the value of the company's commercial investments by comparing them with alternative investments in the securities market of equivalent risk. In this chapter, we learn the fundamental methods of investment analysis used to appraise capital projects.

TOPICS

Consequently, we cover the following:

○   *what a rate of return is;*

○   *what risk is;*

○   *how to relate required rates of return to risk;*

○   *discounted cash flow and net value for shareholders;*

○   *precision discounting;*

○   *the internal rate of return;*

○   *the present value of a perpetuity;*

○   *the present value of an annuity;*

○   *the loan balance method;*

○   *the value of growth;*

○   *why flexibility and choice have value.*

2-1   WHAT IS A RATE OF RETURN?

Let us start with the basics. What is the distinction between a return and a rate of return? This question is not as trivial as it seems.

RETURN

A return is simply an after-tax cash flow generated by an investment. For example, an investment in a machine can generate after-tax cost savings in each of the several years of its operating life. These after-tax savings are returns.

RATE OF RETURN

It is less easy to define the *rate* of return on the machine. The machine must be able to generate returns that repay the original investment plus a surplus. In principle, the rate of return on the machine is some average of the *annual surplus* per unit of investment. For example, the machine might generate a rate of return of 20%. This means that in addition to repaying the investment, the machine generates an annual surplus averaging 20% of the unrepaid balance of the funds invested.

ACCOUNTING RATE OF RETURN

Accountants like to measure surplus by subtracting annual depreciation to obtain a measure of profit. In this way, they can calculate the rate of Return on Capital Employed (ROCE) or Accounting Rate of Return (ARR). Unfortunately, the choice of depreciation method affects the value of the ARR somewhat. Consequently, financial managers often prefer to use the internal rate of return (IRR) discussed in Section 2-6. The IRR method has its weaknesses, but sensitivity to depreciation methods is not one of them.[1]

HOLDING PERIOD RATE OF RETURN

Defining the rate of return on a security is easier. This is because a security's market prices enable us to measure its returns one period at a time.

---

[1] For a rigorous comparison between the Accounting Rate of Return and the Internal Rate of Return, see John A. Kay (1976) "Accountants, too, could be happy in a golden age: The accountant's rate of profit and the internal rate of return," *Oxford Economic Papers*, Vol. 28, No. 3, 447–460.

EXAMPLE 2.1

For example, a share's price at the end of a year was 110 cents but only 100 cents at the beginning of the year. The company paid a 2-cent dividend near the end of the year. The holding period rate of return on the share for that year was:

$$Holding\ Period\ Rate\ of\ Return = \frac{Capital\ Gain + Dividend}{Initial\ Price}$$

$$R_t = \frac{P_t - P_{t-1} + D_t}{P_{t-1}}$$

$$= \frac{110 - 100 + 2}{100} = 0.12 \quad or \quad 12\%$$

This is the true holding period rate of return on the share for the year because it represents the surplus per unit of investment. The surplus is the capital gain 100 − 100 cents plus the dividend of 2 cents, and the investment clearly is the 100 cents invested at the beginning of the year.

DEFINITIONS

Accounting Rate of Return (ARR)   Rate of return as accounting income divided by the book value of all assets employed to generate the income.

Holding period rate of return   Dividends and capital gain for the period divided by the required investment at the beginning of the period.

Internal rate of return (IRR)   Discount rate that would make the net present value for an investment equal to zero.

Rate of return   After-tax cash income and capital gain divided by the investment.

Return   After-tax cash income and capital gain, if any.

Return on Capital Employed (ROCE)   Accounting rate of return before interest changes on the book value of all assets employed to generate the return.

Return on Investment (ROI)   Accounting Rate of return net of interest on the book value of the shareholders' investment in the asset (excludes liabilities).

2-2   WHAT IS RISK?

Mathematicians and statisticians measure risk in terms of variation from the mean or expected return, that is, 'How wrong could our best estimate be?' Psychologists say that investors think of risk as the probability of having to take an unacceptable loss. These two aspects of risk are closely related.

PROBABILITY

Probability can measure the likelihood of an event in the future. For example, the most likely annual rate of return on an investment might be in the range 9–10%. Suppose management expects the probability of realizing a figure in this range to be three chances out of ten or 0.30. Rates of return

Table 2.1 Probability distribution.

Range of rate of return	Likelihood (chances out of 20)	Probability* (%)
5–6	1	0.05
7–8	2	0.10
9–10	6	0.30
11–12	5	0.20
13–14	3	0.15
15–16	2	0.10
17–18	1	0.05
	20	1.00

*The likelihood of 2 chances out of 20 is the probability 2/20 or 0.10. Figure 2.1 shows the probability distribution graphically as a "histogram".

below 9% and above 10% are less likely and diminish according to a probability distribution, as in Table 2.1.

NORMAL PROBABILITY DISTRIBUTION

Figure 2.1 illustrates use of the Normal Probability Distribution to characterize the dispersion of rates of return. Under this distribution, roughly 68% of all outcomes would fall within a range of plus or minus one standard deviation from the average or mean. Suppose the mean is 11% and the standard deviation is 4%. The probability that the actual return would fall in the range 7–15% would be a 68% (11 plus or minus 4%). Therefore, the statistician's measure of risk can give a good indication of how far actual returns might exceed or fall short of the mean or best estimate.

Because minimizing the standard deviation minimizes the probability of loss in the normal distribution, the standard deviation is a very useful measure of risk in financial analysis.[2]

PORTFOLIO DIVERSIFICATION OF RISK

The standard deviation of the rate of return on an individual investment usually overstates its actual risk because diversification can reduce the risk. Diversification means holding a portfolio of many different investments. Portfolio theory shows how diversification reduces risk.[3] Chapter 12 tells more of portfolio theory, but all we need to know at this stage is that:

1.   Shareholders reduce risk by holding many different investments in a portfolio. Less-than-perfect correlation between the rates of return on the securities in a portfolio reduces the portfolio's risk.

---

[2] Because prices are nonnegative and returns cannot be less than −100%, the normal distribution is increasingly inaccurate with larger standard deviations. The lognormal distribution provides a better representation of probability for this application.
[3] For the seminal text, see Harry M. Markowitz (1959) *Portfolio Selection: Efficient Diversification of Investments* (New York: John Wiley & Sons).

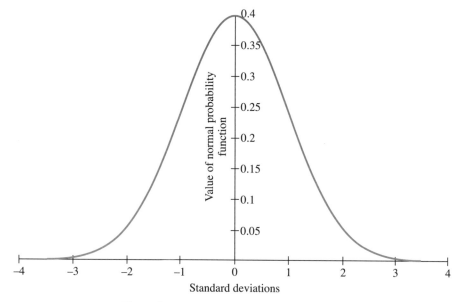

Figure 2.1 Normal probability distribution.

2.   Efficient diversification eliminates diversifiable risk.

3.   Diversification cannot eliminate systematic risk or market risk. A very large portfolio of stocks resembles the stock market as a whole, and thus its risk becomes the same as the risk of the market.

Portfolio theory suggests that diversified investors would not worry about diversifiable risk because an efficiently diversified portfolio eliminates this risk. They worry about the remaining systematic risk, however. Investors need a reward for systematic risk because they have the alternative of investing in safe short-term Government securities.

DEFINITIONS

Diversifiable risk   Risk eliminated in a well-diversified portfolio.

Diversification   Reduction of a portfolio's risk by holding a collection of assets having returns that are not perfectly positively correlated.

Market risk   Risk that portfolio diversification cannot eliminate.

Normal probability distribution   Symmetric bell-shaped probability distribution completely defined by its mean and standard deviation.

Portfolio   Collection of investments in financial securities and other assets.

Probability distribution   The probabilities associated with the set of possible outcomes.

Risk   Probability of an unacceptable loss. In portfolio theory, the standard deviation of holding period returns.

Standard deviation   Square root of the variance.

Systematic risk   See Market Risk.

Variance   Mean squared deviation.

2-3   HOW TO RELATE REQUIRED RATES OF RETURN TO RISK

OPPORTUNITY COSTS

Alternative investment in financial securities represents the opportunity cost of investing in capital projects. So, a manager needs the expected return on a proposed new project to be at least as great as on an equivalent investment in financial securities. To be equivalent, the securities must have the same systematic risk as the project. By systematic risk, we mean the risk that a shareholder cannot eliminate by diversifying his or her portfolio of securities.

EXPECTED RATES OF RETURN

Figure 2.2 shows the relationship supposed to exist between expected rates of return on securities and their systematic risk. The systematic risk on the horizontal axis determines the expected rate of return on the vertical axis. The line begins on the far left with the risk-free rate R_F on short-term Treasury bills. Moving to the right, the line slopes upward to the stock market index at point M, and beyond to even greater risk. Individual companies' securities lie on the line on both sides of M.

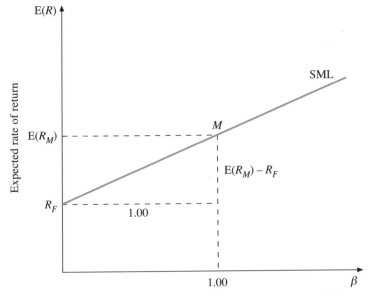

Figure 2.2   The Securities Market Line (SML) relating expected returns E(R) to systematic risk (beta).

BETA AND SYSTEMATIC RISK

As will be explained in Chapter 12, the beta factor on the horizontal axis measures the systematic risk. Note that the beta factor for the market index at M equals 1.00. The beta factor scales the risk of the market index. For example, if the beta value for an investment equals 2.00, then the investment is twice as risky as the market index and lies to the right of M.

RISK PREMIUM ON THE MARKET

The large triangle in the figure indicates the slope of the line. The base of the triangle is of length beta $= 1.00$. The height of the triangle is the difference $E(R_M) - R_F$ between the expected rate of return $E(R_M)$ on the market index at M and the risk-free rate R_F. We obtain the slope of the line by dividing the height of the triangle by its base:

$$\frac{E(R_M) - R_F}{1.00} = E(R_M) - R_F$$

The slope of the Securities Market Line represents the risk premium on the Market Portfolio.

CAPITAL ASSET PRICING MODEL

So, the equation for the Securities Market Line is:

$$Expected\ Rate\ of\ Return = Intercept + Beta \times Slope$$
$$E(R) = R_F + \beta[E(R_M) - R_F]$$

This equation is the Capital Asset Pricing Model (CAPM).[4] The CAPM is easy to use.

EXAMPLE 2.2

Suppose, for example, management considers investment in a new product with beta equal to 1.50. Suppose also that the 90-day Treasury bill rate is 5%, and the expected risk premium on the market index is 8%. Then we have simply:

$$E(R) = 5 + 1.50 \times 8 = 17\%$$

Chapter 13 explains how to measure asset betas. The shareholders' required rate of return determined in this way is the discount rate that we shall use in the discounted cash flow method.

---

[4] The Nobel Prize-winning paper on this subject is, William F. Sharpe (1964) "A theory of market equilibrium under conditions of risk," *Journal of Finance*, Vol. 19, No. 3 (September), 425–442.

OPPORTUNITY COST OF CAPITAL

The Securities Market Line provides the benchmark for managers investing in capital projects. If they cannot find commercial investments that would lie above the Securities Market Line, they cannot add any value for shareholders. They might as well pay the funds out as dividends and let the shareholders invest for themselves on the Securities Market Line. Therefore, the expected rates of return on this line represent the securities market opportunity cost of capital for investment by the firm. We use the opportunity costs on the Securities Market Line as the discount rates in the calculation of a project's net present value.

DEFINITIONS

Beta factor   A measure of the market risk of an asset. The factor by which mean returns on the asset reflect returns on the market portfolio.

Capital Asset Pricing Model (CAPM)   Linear model attempting to explain the expected return on a risky asset in terms of the risk-free rate, its Beta factor (market risk) and the risk premium on the market portfolio.

Expected rate of return   Probability-weighted average of all possible outcomes for the rate of return.

Market portfolio   Portfolio of all risky assets.

Opportunity cost of capital   Return forgone when investing in a project instead of the securities market.

Risk premium on the market portfolio   Extra return necessary to persuade investors to invest in the market portfolio.

Systematic risk   Risk that cannot be eliminated by portfolio diversification.

2-4   DISCOUNTED CASH FLOW AND NET VALUE FOR SHAREHOLDERS

TIME VALUE OF MONEY

The expected rate of return for a capital investment obtained from the Securities Market Line represents the risk-adjusted time value of money for the investment's cash flows.

EXAMPLE 2.3

For example, suppose that the expected rate of return $E(R)$ for a return of €110 received after one year is 10%. It should be clear that this requires an investment of €100 in the securities market now: $100 \times (1 + 0.10) = €110$.

FUTURE VALUE OF A CASH FLOW

Thus, the future value (FV) of the €100 is €110, and the present value (PV) of the €110 is €100. In symbols the above becomes:

$$PV[1 + E(R)]^1 = FV_1$$

It follows that we must invest €100 now in the securities market at 10% to generate €121 two years from now:

$$100 \times (1 + 0.10)^2 = €121$$

That is,[5]

$$PV[1 + E(R)]^2 = FV_2$$

Here we see the effect of the compounding of reinvested returns. Failing to reinvest would leave us with only €120 rather than €121.

PRESENT VALUE OF A CASH FLOW

Suppose now that we will receive only €100 in two years time. What PV must we invest at 10% to give this cash flow two years hence?

$$PV(1 + 0.10)^2 = €100$$

Therefore,

$$PV = \frac{100}{(1 + 0.10)^2} = €82.64$$

We would have to invest just €82.64 at 10% compounded to have €100 in two years time. In other words, the PV of €100 two years later is only €82.64 if the expected rate of return on securities of equivalent risk is 10%.

DISCOUNT FACTOR

Using symbols, the present value of 1 euro received in t years is the discount factor:

$$\frac{1}{1 + [E(R)]^t}$$

We obtain the PV of a future cash flow simply by multiplying it by its discount factor.

DISCOUNT RATE

The rate E(R) used in the formula is the discount rate. PV tables found at the back of finance textbooks, including this one, tabulate discount factors. Frankly, you can find discount factors more easily and more accurately with the above formula than by copying them out of the tables.

---

[5] This widely used equation is not strictly true when the expected returns are uncertain. For example, spot and forward rates of interest in the Government bond market usually are virtually certain. The expected returns used as discount rates for project cash flows, however, are subject to uncertainty. The effect has not been sufficient to persuade practitioners to use a more elaborate formula.

More generally, if the discount rate changes in each future period, the discount factor becomes:

$$\frac{1}{[1 + E(R_1)][1 + E(R_2)] \cdots [1 + E(R_t)]}$$

PRESENT VALUE OF A PROJECT

Typically, a firm invests in projects that have after-tax cash income each year for perhaps many future years. One must multiply each such future cash flow by its discount factor before adding it to the rest. The resulting sum of PVs is the present value of the project.[6]

NET PRESENT VALUE OF A PROJECT

If we subtract the PV of the project's *investment* cash flows from the PV of its *income* cash flows, we obtain the project's net present value (NPV). The NPV tells us something very important, whether or not the project is worth more than it costs. Furthermore, it gives us an estimate of how much value the project would add for shareholders.

NET PRESENT VALUE RULE

Therefore, we have the so-called net present value rule: management should invest only in projects that have positive NPVs. (Chapter 6 gives some exceptions to this rule.) The net present value rule is quite easy to implement, as demonstrated in Example 2.4.

EXAMPLE 2.4

Netron International is a leading European Internet products company considering investing €12 million in a new product. Management expects the product to generate incremental after-tax cash flows of €5 million each year for five years, starting in one year's time. The company's finance director estimates that the product's asset beta equals 1.50 and that the Treasury bill rate will be 5% during the life of the product. From the Securities Market Line, he calculates that the required rate of return for the product would be 17% (as in Example 2-2). Table 2.2 gives the forecasts of the incremental after-tax cash flows for the product and their PVs.

Row 1　of Table 2.2 shows the investment of €12 million in the Year 0 column signifying immediate investment.

Row 2　shows the annual cash flow of €5 million beginning at the end of Year 1.

Row 3　contains the discount factor at 17% for each future year.

Row 4　gives the PV of each cash flow obtained by multiplying the cash flows in Row 2 by the corresponding discount factors in Row 3.

Row 5　shows the PV of the product as at Year 0, obtained by summing the PVs in Row 4 of the cash income in Years 1 to 5.

---

[6] Discounted cash flow was already being used to value projects in the UK coal industry in the 19th century.

Table 2.2 Net present value of the new Internet product (million euro).

		Year Ending					
		0	1	2	3	4	5
1	Investment	−12					
2	Incremental cash income		5	5	5	5	5
3	Discount factor at 17%	1.0000	0.8547	0.7305	0.6244	0.5337	0.4561
4	Present values	−12.00	4.27	3.65	3.12	2.67	2.28
5	Present value of product	16.00					
6	Present value of investment	−12.00					
7	Net present value	4.00					
		4.00					

Row 6 contains the PV of the investment of €12 million required for the product (as in Row 1).

Row 7 gives the NPV for the new product, found simply by subtracting the PV of the investment in Row 6 from the PV of the products cash income in Row 5.

The Finance Director felt that the NPV for the product was sufficiently large to consider proposing the project to the board. It would add approximately €4 million of net value for shareholders, and the product evidently earns a higher rate of return than the 17% discount rate.

DEFINITIONS

Compounding   Earning further returns on reinvested returns.

Discount factor   Sum of money invested today that would compound to one unit of the same currency at a specified future date if invested at the appropriate rate of interest or required rate of return.

Discount rate   Required rate of return used in the calculation of a discount factor.

Future value (FV)   Value obtainable from investing a given sum of money for a specified number of years at the required compound rate of return.

Net present value (NPV)   Difference between the present value of a project's expected after-tax operating cash flows and the present value of its expected after-tax investment expenditures.

Net present value rule   Rule suggesting that investment in a project should take place if its net present value (NPV) is greater than zero because the project would contribute net positive value for shareholders.

Present value (PV)   Value of an investment now as the cost of a comparable investment in the financial market (calculated by multiplying the investment's after-tax cash income by the appropriate discount factors.

Time value of money   Rate of return obtainable from comparable alternative investment in the financial market.

2-5 PRECISION DISCOUNTING

In big corporate transactions with banks, precision discounting is "the name of the game." We need to know how to discount cash flows to the very day.

INTRA-YEAR DISCOUNTING

You can use the annual rate to discount cash flows that occur at points of time within years as well as beyond.

EXAMPLE 2.5

For example, let us suppose that you want to discount a cash flow expected 500 days from now. We know that 500 days is $500/365 = 1.37$ years (rounded). Simply raise the discount factor to the 1.37 power:

$$\frac{1}{[1 + E(R)]^{1.37}}$$

Raising the discount factor to a fractional power is no problem in a spreadsheet or if your calculator has the x^y function.

SIMPLE VERSUS EFFECTIVE INTEREST RATES

Let R be the equivalent annual rate and r_q be the corresponding quarterly rate. For both to give the same return at the end of one year, we must have:

$$(1 + R) = (1 + r_q)^4$$

EXAMPLE 2.6

For example, if the interest on a bank loan is 3% per quarter, what is the equivalent annual interest rate on the loan?

$$1 + R = (1 + 0.03)^4 = 1.1255 \quad \text{or} \quad R = 1.1255 - 1 = 12.55\%$$

This loan provides a simple rate interest of only:

$$4 \times 3\% = 12\%$$

but the effective rate of interest is actually 12.55%. The more frequent the number of interest payments in a year, the more the equivalent rate exceeds the simple rate.

CONTINUOUSLY COMPOUNDED RATES

If R_m is the simple rate when there are m interest payments per year, then:

$$(1 + R) = \left(1 + \frac{R_m}{m}\right)^m$$

This formula holds for any payment frequency m, whether it is quarterly, monthly, daily, or continuous (m goes to infinity).

When we let the number m of payments in the above formula go to infinity $R_m \rightarrow r$ compounded continuously. Mathematically the annual rate R that is equivalent to compounding continuously at the rate r is:

$$(1 + R) = e^r$$

where e is Euler's constant 2.71828.

With continuous compounding, the future value FV of an investment I paying the continuously compounded rate r for t years is:

$$FV = PVe^{rt}$$

EXAMPLE 2.7

For example, if the continuously compounded rate is 5%, then after two years €100 will have compounded to:

$$FV = €100 \times 2.71828^{0.05 \times 2} = €110.517$$

CONTINUOUS DISCOUNTING

Solving for the present value PV, we have:

$$PV = \frac{FV}{e^{rt}} = FVe^{-rt}$$

Suppose we want to know the present value of €110 paid two years from now. If the continuously compounded rate is 5%, the present value is:

$$PV = \frac{110}{2.71828^{0.05 \times 2}} = 110 \times 2.71828^{-0.05 \times 2} = €99.53$$

We encounter continuous compounding in the context of financial options pricing.

DEFINITIONS

Effective rate of interest   Annualized rate of interest reflecting reinvestment of intra-year interest payments.

Simple rate of interest   Annualized rate of interest reflecting merely the sum of intra-year interest payments without reinvestment.

2-6   THE INTERNAL RATE OF RETURN

Senior managers like to know the rate of return that a capital project earns on its investment. They attempt to estimate a project's rate of return by calculating its internal rate of return.

INTERNAL RATE OF RETURN

The internal rate of return (IRR) is the discount rate that forces the NPV of the project to zero. It really answers the question as to how high the shareholders' required rate of return for the project would have to be to make the project just break even.

Figure 2.3 illustrates the relationship between the NPV and different discount rates for the capital project in Example 2.4. On the horizontal axis, we see discount rates ranging from 0 to 60%. The NPV on the vertical axis corresponds to each of the discount rates on the horizontal axis. The shape of the NPV curve in the figure is typical of a simple project but can be radically different in some cases, depending on the way in which the cash flows change over time. Point A indicates the NPV of the project at the 17% rate used in Example 2.4. The IRR is the discount rate at which the NPV equals zero, so the point where the curve crosses the horizontal axis (at just over 30%) identifies the IRR in the figure.

If the project's NPV is greater than zero, we normally find that its IRR is greater than its required rate of return. Chapter 6 discusses exceptions to this rule. There is no formula for finding the value of the IRR. We have to calculate the IRR using a procedure.

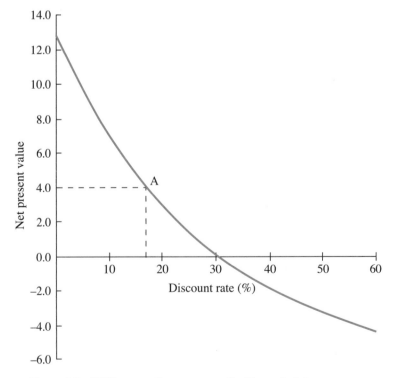

Figure 2.3   NPV versus discount rates for Example 2.4.

CALCULATING THE INTERNAL RATE OF RETURN

Calculation of the IRR requires a process of trial and error as follows:

1.   Guess a moderately high discount rate that makes the NPV negative.

2.   Guess a moderately low discount rate that makes the NPV positive.

3.   Interpolate.

4.   Use the interpolated value as the next guess and repeat. Keep repeating until the successive changes in the calculated IRR are sufficiently small to satisfy the accuracy required.

EXAMPLE 2.8

For example, the procedure to obtain the IRR of the net cash flow in Rows 1 and 2 of Table 2.2 is as follows:

1.   At 17%, we know the NPV is plus €4 million (Point A in Figure 2.4).

2.   Recalculating the NPV at 50%, we obtain an NPV of − €3.32 million (Point B in Figure 2.4).

3.   Interpolating as follows, we obtain a first value at Point C of 35% for the IRR that we can use as our next guess:

$$IRR_1 = 17 + \left(\frac{4}{4 + 3.32} \right) \times (50 - 17) = 35\%$$

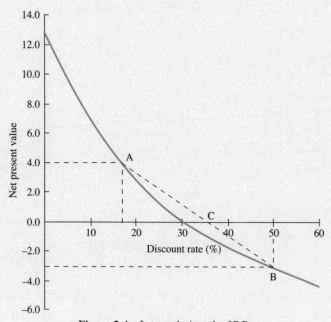

Figure 2.4 Interpolating the IRR.

This interpolation is the straight line joining Points A and B in the figure. The straight line crosses the horizontal axis at 35%. Because the NPV line is not straight, the actual value of the IRR is less than the interpolated value.

4. If we repeat this process several times, we find that the interpolated IRR settles down to 30.77%.

The IRR function in any popular spreadsheet software package also obtains this result. Now that you understand the interpolation process by which the software gets the solution, you can use your computer, rather than doing this tedious task manually.

In order for this practice to work well, the IRR must be a good approximation to the project's true rate of return. In addition, the hurdle rate must equal the shareholders' required rate of return as found on the securities market line. Chapter 6 reveals when the IRR provides a good approximation to the rate of return and when it does not.

DEFINITIONS

Internal rate of return (IRR) Discount rate that would make the net present value for an investment equal to zero.

2-7 THE PRESENT VALUE OF A PERPETUITY

A perpetuity is an equal sum of money paid in each period for ever. Examples of perpetuities are Government securities called Consols that pay a fixed payment of interest every year, for ever.

EXAMPLE 2.9

The following is an example of the income from a perpetuity contracted now and paying 1 euro per year for ever:

Year	0	1	2	3	4	5	6	7	⋯
Perpetuity	0	1	1	1	1	1	1	1	⋯

Note that the first payment comes one period after the start of the perpetuity contract. The PV of the annuity of €1 per year discounted at the rate R is just:

$$A_R = \frac{1}{(1+R)^1} + \frac{1}{(1+R)^2} + \frac{1}{(1+R)^3} + \cdots$$

This is the sum of an infinite geometric series, which has an exact solution. The solution is simply:

$$A_R = \frac{1}{R}$$

Perpetuities are easy to value. Just divide the annual cash flow by the discount rate R expressed as a decimal fraction.

EXAMPLE 2.10

For example, what is the PV of a €100 annual payment received as a perpetuity for ever and discounted at 10%?

$$PV = A_R \times 100 = \left(\frac{1}{0.10}\right) \times 100 = 10 \times 100 = €1,000$$

To see why this is so, consider the answer to the following question. If the interest rate R is 10%, how much income would I receive every year from a perpetuity costing €1,000? The answer obviously is €100:

$$R \times 1000 = 0.10 \times 1000 = €100 \text{ per year}$$

DEFINITION

Perpetuity   Equal sum of money paid in each period for ever.

2-8   THE PRESENT VALUE OF AN ANNUITY

An annuity is a sequence of equal cash flows paid each period for a specified number of periods. The payments on loan contracts, mortgages, and leases often are annuities. So, it will be useful to have an efficient method of determining the value of an annuity. Of course, we could just discount the cash flows the usual way; but because annuity cash flows are all equal, we can exploit a short cut. In order to obtain the value of an annuity, we need to know just three things: the cash flow, the life of the annuity, and the discount rate.

EXAMPLE 2.11

To see how the short cut works, consider the example in Table 2.3 concerning a five-year annuity of just 1 euro per year.

Column 1   of the table indicates the 5 annual payment periods.

Column 2   shows the equal annual payment of 1 euro each starting at the end of the first year.

Column 3   contains the discount factors at 10% for each year. At the bottom of the column, we have the sum of the five discount factors.

Column 4   shows the present value of each annuity payment obtained by multiplying the annuity payment in Column 2 by its corresponding discount factor in Column 3. At the bottom of the column, we have the sum of all the PVs. This sum is the PV of the annuity.

Table 2.3 Five-year annuity of 1 euro per year.

Year ending (1)	Annuity payments (2)	Discount factors (10%) (3)	Present values (4)
1	1	0.9091	0.909 09
2	1	0.8264	0.826 45
3	1	0.7513	0.751 31
4	1	0.6830	0.683 01
5	1	0.6209	0.620 92
		3.7907	3.790 7

ANNUITY FACTOR

Unsurprisingly, the sum of all the discount factors at the bottom of Column 3 equals the PV of the annuity at the bottom of Column 4. The reason is that the payments are only 1 euro per year. The sum of all the discount factors equals the annuity factor.

We could have found the PV of this annuity by just multiplying the annuity factor by 1 euro. In this way, we can find the PV of *any* equal annual payment C by multiplying it by the annuity factor:

$$PV = C \times A_{N,R}$$

where C represents one of the equal payments, and $A_{N,R}$ is the annuity factor for N periods when the discount rate is R per period.

In Table 2.3, this short cut could have eliminated five multiplications. We can also eliminate the addition of the discount factors because Annuity Tables in the back of all finance texts, including this one, tabulate these values. Actually, it is easier and more accurate to calculate an annuity factor than to copy it from the tables, using the following formula:

$$A_{N,R} = \frac{1}{R}\left[1 - \frac{1}{(1+R)^N}\right]$$

In this formula, we just calculate the final discount factor at time N, subtract it from 1 and then divide the result by the discount rate, expressed as a decimal fraction. If you learn these simple operations, you can remember the formula.[7]

EXAMPLE 2.12

Table 2.2 calculated the PV to be €16 million at 17% in Example 2.1. As the project cash flows were really an annuity (€5 million per year for 5 years), we could have used the annuity factor to get the same result.

---

[7] The annuity formula reflects that an annuity is just the difference between two perpetuities. The first perpetuity begins in the next period. From this subtract the perpetuity beginning N periods later. The remainder is the desired annuity. The PV of the first perpetuity is $1/R$. The PV of the second perpetuity beginning N periods later is $(1/R)/(1+R)^N$. The difference between these two PVs gives the annuity formula.

$$A_{5,0.17} = \frac{1}{0.17}\left[1 - \frac{1}{(1+0.17)^5}\right]$$

$$= 3.1993$$

$$PV = C \times A_{N,R}$$

$$= 5 \times 3.1993 = €16 \text{ million}$$

Whenever you encounter fixed annual payments as in bonds, loans, mortgages, and leasing contracts, "think annuity." Recognizing an annuity when you see one puts the power of the annuity method at your disposal. Example 2.13 demonstrates a very useful application of the annuity method.

EXAMPLE 2.13

A bank offers you a five-year loan of €10,000 at 10% interest, compounded annually. The loan contract requires five equal annual payments to the bank. These payments incorporate both interest and repayments of the loan, beginning one year after the bank advances the €10,000. How much should the annual payment be if the bank really is charging 10% interest?

There are five equal annual payments, so you should recognize that this is a five-year annuity at 10%. The following formula gives the required value for the annuity factor:

$$A_{N,R} = \frac{1}{R}\left[1 - \frac{1}{(1+R)^N}\right]$$

$$= \frac{1}{0.10}\left[1 - \frac{1}{(1+0.10)^5}\right] = 3.7908$$

We also need to recognize that the PV to the bank of the five equal payments must equal the €10,000 that they are willing to lend now:

$$PV = C \times A_{N,R}$$

$$10,000 = C \times 3.7908$$

So, the equal annual instalments that you must pay the bank would be:

$$C = 10,000/3.7908 = €2,637.97 \text{ per year}$$

Of course, the five equal instalments add up to more than €10,000 because they include compound interest.

DEFINITIONS

Annuity   Investment generating equal cash flows each period for a specified number of periods.

Annuity factor   PV of one unit of currency paid in each of a specified number of periods. Equals the sum of the corresponding discount factors.

2-9   THE LOAN BALANCE METHOD

In Example 2.13, we were able to use the annuity method to ascertain the five equal payments required from a bank on a €10,000 loan at an interest rate of 10% compounded annually. We might need to know (for tax reasons) how much of each annual instalment is interest and how much of it reduces the outstanding balance owed to the bank. We can determine the annual interest and repayments on any loan (regardless of whether or not the annual payments are an annuity) using the loan balance method.

The loan balance method recognizes that an instalment is a combined payment of interest and part repayment of the loan. When the bank receives an instalment, it takes the interest owed on the previous loan balance and uses the remainder to reduce the balance owed. In the following period, the interest payable on the smaller balance is less and the part repayment is correspondingly greater.

EXAMPLE 2.14

Table 2.4 shows the calculation used in the loan balance method.

The rows in Table 2.4 correspond to the timing of the relevant cash flows. The columns show timing, instalments, interest payments, repayments, and the resulting loan balance at the end of each period.

Row 0   contains the initial balance of €10,000 on the loan.

Row 1   shows the first instalment of €2,637.97. From this, we deduct €1,000 interest in the third column, leaving a repayment of €1,637.97 in the fourth column. This repayment reduces the loan balance in the final column from €10,000 to €8,362.03.

Row 2   shows the loan balance reduced to €8,362.03, and the interest at 10% reduced to €836.20. This lower amount of interest permits a larger loan repayment of €1,801.77. Therefore, the balance of the loan in the final column is now only €6,560.25.

Table 2.4   The loan balance method.

Year ending	Instalment	Interest	Repayment	Loan balance
0				10,000
1	2,637.97	1,000	1,637.97	8,362.03
2	2,637.97	836.20	1,801.77	6,560.25
3	2,637.97	656.03	1,981.95	4,578.30
4	2,637.97	457.83	2,180.14	2,398.16
5	2,637.97	239.82	2,398.16	0.00

Implementing this repetitive procedure on a spreadsheet is easy. An advantage of the loan balance method is that you can see the actual interest and repayments. This facilitates claiming tax deductions for the interest payments.

Note that the equal annual payment of €2,637.97 obtained using the annuity factor is exactly the right annual instalment to cover the compound interest and loan repayments in Table 2.4. What the annuity formula cannot do is tell us the amounts of money paid as interest. For that, we need the loan balance method.

Furthermore, we can use the loan balance method with *any* payment schedule. The instalments do not have to be an annuity. So, we can use the loan balance method to calculate the PV of the payment schedule. The PV equals the initial loan balance that leaves a zero balance after the final payment.

> **DEFINITION**
>
> **Loan balance method**   Alternative method of obtaining the present value of a schedule of payments or cash flow. The present value is the initial balance of the equivalent loan leaving a zero balance after the final payment.

2-10   THE VALUE OF GROWTH

Let us now consider a perpetual cash flow that grows (or declines) for ever. An example would be a share price equal to the PV of a steadily growing stream of expected dividends. What would be the PV of such a perpetual cash flow if you expect it to grow at a constant compound rate of growth G?

$$PV_0 = \frac{C_1}{(1+R)^1} + \frac{C_2}{(1+R)^2} + \frac{C_3}{(1+R)^3} + \cdots$$

where

$$C_t = C_0(1+G)^t.$$

Thus,

$$PV_0 = \frac{C_0(1+G)}{(1+R)} + \frac{C_0(1+G)^2}{(1+R)^2} + \frac{C_0(1+G)^3}{(1+R)^3} + \cdots$$

This is the sum of an infinite geometric series. If G is less than R, the sum is less than infinity. The sum equals the PV:

$$PV_0 = \frac{C_0(1+G)}{R-G} \qquad (G < R)$$

This equation is the well-known Gordon–Williams formula frequently used to discount expected dividends to value a company's shares.

2-11   WHY FLEXIBILITY AND CHOICE HAVE VALUE

PROJECT FLEXIBILITY AND REAL OPTIONS

The discounted cash flow method treats capital projects as if they were investments in securities such as bonds. Unlike a capital project, you usually cannot change a bond before it matures.[8]

---

[8] An exception is the convertible bond. A convertible bond permits the bondholder to exchange the bond for a specified number of shares in the company issuing the convertible bond.

The potential to improve an existing project in response to changes in the business environment is valuable. Therefore, conventional discounted cash flow analysis does not permit estimating the full value of a project. Opportunities to adapt real investments to changing circumstances are real options.

EXAMPLE 2.15

Consider the example of a company creating an opportunity to invest in a new product in two years' time by engaging in research and development now. If the market is very competitive, the NPV need not still be positive after two years. Suppose that management expects that potential competition could make the NPV fall to zero on average. Is it worth continuing with the R&D?

For example, suppose that the probability is 0.5 that the NPV will be €10 million and 0.5 that it will be minus −€10 million. The expected NPV would appear to be equal to zero:

$$0.5 \times 10m + 0.5 \times (-10m) = 0$$

One might be tempted to stop "wasting" money on the R&D immediately.

This conclusion would be wrong because it ignores the fact that management has a choice. Nothing forces management to invest in the project if the NPV becomes negative. If it rejects the investment when the time comes, the NPV will be zero instead of negative. Therefore, the correct analysis is:

$$0.5 \times 10m + 0.5 \times 0 = €5 \text{ million}$$

Obviously, being able to make the choice is valuable, and the expected value of this real option is €5 million. So, it would be worth continuing to spend on the R&D as long as the additional expenditure (including compound interest) is less than the €5 million by that time.

RISK INCREASES THE VALUE OF A REAL OPTION

Now suppose the business environment in our example becomes twice as risky and uncertain. Management now thinks that the NPV on the new product could be either +20 million or −€20 million, each with equal probability of 0.5. Management will not invest if the NPV becomes negative, so the analysis is:

$$0.5 \times 20m + 0.5 \times 0 = €10 \text{ million}$$

Doubling the risk has doubled the value of this real option, and thus spending more on the R&D is justifiable.

Can this be right? Yes! The reason is that management does not have to invest on the downside, and the upside risk works entirely in the company's favor. If the future investment is optional, the more risk the better. That risk increases the value of options is a known fact in the traded financial options markets. We will have much more to say about what affects the value of an option and how to calculate its NPV.

DEFINITION

Real option   Right to make favorable future choices regarding real asset investments. More precisely, a real option is an opportunity for voluntary future investment in a nonfinancial asset when at least a part of the required investment expenditure is certain or, alternatively, when at least a part of the required investment expenditure is not perfectly positively correlated with the project's present value.

2-12 CONCLUSIONS

In order to add any value for shareholders, managers must find commercial investments that promise a higher rate of return than the alternative of simply investing in the securities market. Therefore, the shareholders' required rate of return for the company's commercial investments equals the rate of return expected from alternative investment in securities with equivalent risk.

Financial analysis involves comparing corporate capital investments with equivalent investments in the securities market. We have shown ways to use discounted cash flow methodology to make this comparison. We have also considered briefly the additional value that real options can add to projects. In subsequent chapters, we shall show how to implement these fundamentals.

FURTHER READING

Simon Benninga (2000) *Financial Modeling*, 2nd edn (London, UK: The MIT Press).

QUESTIONS AND PROBLEMS

1   A company bought a machine two years ago for €100,000. The machine's accounting depreciation is €20,000 per year. The machine's second-hand market value currently is only €55,000. The expected second-hand market value one year from now is €40,000. The expected after-tax profit attributable to the machine in the coming year is €25,000.

        (a)   What is the expected ARR on the machine for the coming year?

        (b)   What is the expected true rate of return (after-tax cash income divided by the investment) on the machine in the coming year?

2   The following table lists different cash flows that management believes a project might earn in the fifth year of its life. Listed also in the table is management's estimate of the probability associated with each of the alternative possible cash flows the project might generate in that year.

Cash flow	Probability
20	0.04
17.5	0.06
15	0.12
12.5	0.18
10	0.20
7.5	0.18
5	0.12
2.5	0.06
0	0.04

(a)   What is the expected cash flow in Year 5?

(b)   Each of the possible cash flows is different from the expected cash flow. If we square each of the differences from the expected cash flow and calculate the probability-weighted average of these squared differences, we obtain the variance of the cash flow. Calculate the variance of the Year 5 cash flow.

(c)   The standard deviation is the square root of the variance. Calculate the standard deviation of the Year 5 cash flow.

3   The Securities Market Line gives the opportunity cost of investing in capital projects. Management considers investing in a capital project with an estimated beta value of only 0.50. The expected risk-free rate during the life of the project is 5%, and the expected market risk premium is 6%.

(a)   What is the value of the project's risk premium?

(b)   What is the minimum acceptable rate of return on the project?

(c)   Suppose that the revised estimate for the project's beta is 1.20. What would be the revised minimum acceptable rate of return for the project?

4   The table below gives the expected after-tax cash flows for a capital project. If the Securities Market Line indicates the opportunity cost of capital for this project is only 10%, what is the project's NPV?

	End of year			
0	1	2	3	4
−10,000	2,000	3,000	4,000	5,000

5   An investment of €1,000 is to return an expected €1,150 in 1.5 years' time. The opportunity cost of capital is 15%.

(a)   What is the NPV of this investment?

(b)   What annual rate of return does the investment earn?

6   An investment of €1,000 will return €1,025 in 0.25 years' time. The required rate of return on the investment is 10% per year.

(a)   What is the NPV of this investment?

(b)   What annualised rate of return does the investment earn?

7   A loan requires quarterly interest payments of 1.25 cents for each euro borrowed. That is, the interest rate on the loan is "5% per year compounded quarterly."

(a)   What is the effective annual rate of interest payable on the loan?

(b)   If the rate quoted is 5% per year compounded continuously instead, what would be the effective annual rate of interest on the loan?

8   Calculate the IRR on the project in Problem 4.

9   Your bank offers you a five-year loan of €10,000 at 8% interest. The loan contract requires five equal annual payments. Each of these annual instalments includes interest and repayment of principal and is payable at the end of the year.

(a)   How much is the instalment?

(b)   How much of each instalment represents interest and how much goes to repaying the principal of the loan?

[*Hint:* Use the loan balance method.]

10   An investment requires €90,000 and its expected cash flow is €10,000 per year in perpetuity. The opportunity cost of capital for the investment is 10%.

(a)   What is the PV of the investment, and what is its NPV?

(b)   If the expected growth rate of the cash flow is 5% per year, what are the PV and the NPV of the investment?

(c)   Suppose the expected life of the income is only 10 years, and will not grow at all. What are the PV and the NPV of the investment?

11   The XTRON product requires a €1 million investment in one year's time if management should decide to launch the product. The project sponsor thinks that the NPV will be €200,000, but the probability is 20% that the NPV will be −€100,000 instead. How much value can management expect this investment to add for shareholders at that time?

3 An Introduction to Corporate Debt and Equity

Company financing falls into two broad categories, equity and debt. Equity is the owners' initial and subsequent investment in the company. Ordinary shares (common stocks) are securities certifying the proportionate ownership of the company by each shareholder. Retained earnings, which are after-tax profits reinvested in the company, increase the owners' collective stake in the company. The issuance and sale of additional shares provide more equity capital for long-term growth.

Debt consists mainly of various forms of short-term and long-term borrowing. Banks provide mostly short-term debt. Long-term debt repayable after say 10 years is obtainable by issuing corporate bonds to institutions such as insurance companies. Interest rates on the debt can be either fixed or floating (variable). Floating rates change in response to changes in a relevant index of prevailing market rates of interest.

Companies can deduct interest payments from taxable income, thereby saving taxes. They cannot deduct dividends paid to their shareholders, however.

A company can choose not to pay a dividend to its equity shareholders, but risks their displeasure if it reduces dividends. The company is contractually obliged to pay agreed interest and repayments on debt, however. Failing to do so can lead to bankruptcy.

TOPICS

In this chapter we discuss how to value debt and equity securities. We also introduce the concept of financial options because most securities incorporate valuable options. The themes introduced in this chapter continue in subsequent chapters:

○ *how much an investor should pay for a corporate bond;*

○ *how much an investor should pay for shares in a company's equity;*

○ *how limited liability affects the relative values of equity and debt;*

○ *executive stock options;*

○ *equity warrants;*

○ *other corporate securities;*

○ *traded equity options.*

3-1   HOW MUCH SHOULD AN INVESTOR PAY FOR A CORPORATE BOND?

For both companies and their investors the correct valuation of securities is a matter of the utmost importance.

SECURITIES

A security is a certificate granting the security holder a legal claim on a company. Therefore, the value of the security depends upon the worth of the cash flow or assets to which the security grants a defined claim.

CORPORATE BONDS

For example, outstanding bonds represent a part of the debt of many companies. The holder of a corporate bond has a legal right to prompt payment of contractually agreed interest payments and repayments on the bond. The bond indenture specifies a payment schedule enforced by trustees acting on behalf of the bondholders. A company failing to pay on time is in default on its obligations to bondholders, who then have a high-priority claim on any remaining assets in the company.

VALUING A CORPORATE BOND

The value of a risk-free corporate bond would equal the present value (PV) of its interest and repayment cash flow discounted at the risk-free rate of interest. Unlike some government bonds, corporate bonds are not risk-free, however. The actual market price of a corporate bond depends on such factors as the credit risk of the particular corporate borrower and how easily bondholders can resell the bond in the financial market. Consequently, discount rates for corporate bonds exceed the risk-free rate by a spread of up to several percent depending on the credit rating of the issuer.

A corporate bond certifies that the company issuing the bond owes money to the bondholder. The amount owed, shown on the face of the bond, is the bond's face value (par value). Also indicated on the face of the bond is its maturity. The maturity is the final date for repayment of the bond.[1] The bond certificate also specifies the interest payments, called coupons. Typically, coupon payments occur every six months until the bond matures. Therefore, the value of a bond must equal the PV of the coupons and of the eventual repayment of its face value:

Bond Value Now = [Present Value of Coupons] + Present Value of Face Value

$$B_0 = \left[\frac{c_1}{(1+r)^1} + \frac{c_2}{(1+r)^2} + \frac{c_3}{(1+r)^3} + \cdots + \frac{c_N}{(1+r)^N} \right] + \frac{B_N}{(1+r)^N}$$

---

[1] In practice, companies redeem their bonds by making regular payments to the bond's sinking fund operated by the trustees for the bondholders. The trustees use the cash to buy back the bonds in the bond market or directly from the bondholders. In the latter case, bondholders, chosen by lottery, are obliged to accept face value for their bonds.

Because the issuer of the bond pays the coupons twice yearly, we value the bond using six-monthly periods. Consequently, the number N of six-monthly periods to maturity in the formula equals twice the number of years before the bond matures.[2]

EXAMPLE 3.1

For example, a corporate bond with exactly five years left to maturity pays interest at 10% of face value. This implies that if the face value equals €100, the bond pays two coupons per year of €5 each for five years.

Suppose that the annualized interest rate on securities of the same risk is currently only 7%. What is the PV for the bond? In order to discount the six-monthly coupons in the above formula, we need the corresponding semiannual discount rate:[3]

$$r = (1 + 0.07)^{0.5} - 1 = 0.0344 \quad \text{or} \quad 3.44\%$$

Discounting the bond payments at 3.44%, we obtain:

$$B_0 = \left[\frac{5}{(1.0344)^1} + \frac{5}{(1.0344)^2} + \frac{5}{(1.0344)^3} + \cdots + \frac{5}{(1.0344)^{10}} \right] + \frac{100}{(1.0344)^{10}}$$

$$= €113.01.$$

INTEREST RATES AND BOND PRICES

When the market rates of interest fall, many fixed-rate bonds like this sell for more than their face value. When the rates rise, many such bonds sell for less than face value. The reason is that the market uses the most up-to-date interest rates when discounting the cash flows on existing bonds. When the market price of the bond is less than its face value, the investor enjoys a capital gain from holding the bond until its maturity.

If instead a company's bond price becomes greater than its face value, the company could gain an advantage for its shareholders by redeeming the bond early and replacing it with a new bond at the lower rate of interest. Indeed, the bond indenture agreement often gives the borrower an option to redeem early (call the bond).

A BOND'S REDEMPTION YIELD

The bond market actually quotes a bond's redemption yield rather than its price. The redemption yield on a bond is merely the discount rate that makes the PV of the bond in the above formula

[2] Ordinarily, the date when we value a bond will fall between two coupon payment dates. Therefore, the next coupon comes after just a fraction of six months. The next following coupon payment comes six months after that, and so on. Consequently, accurate pricing requires the precision discounting described in the previous chapter. Normally, market rates of interest vary for different maturities. So, accurate pricing also requires the use of slightly different discount rates for each coupon.
[3] When using a quoted bond yield as a surrogate for the annual interest rate, simply divide the yield by 2 instead of using the formula to obtain an estimate of the semiannual rate.

equal to the bond's market price. Therefore, the bond's semiannual redemption yield equals its internal rate of return. Consequently, the redemption yield reflects both the coupons and any capital gain (or loss) for bondholders who hold the bond to maturity.

When we calculate the redemption yield on a bond, we use the six-monthly coupon payment periods. Consequently, the resulting internal rate of return (IRR) is a semiannual rate. The redemption yield quoted in the financial press is this six-monthly rate multiplied by two, however. For example, the semiannual redemption yield on the above bond is 3.44%. Therefore, the quoted annual yield is $2 \times 3.44 = 6.88\%$. This crude method of annualizing the yield ignores compounding. Consequently, the quoted yield is less than the true annualized rate of interest, which in our particular example is 7% rather than only 6.88%.

DEFINITIONS

Claims   Refers to financial claims on the company by governments and by other creditors including lenders, bondholders, trade creditors, employees, and the company's shareholders.

Bond   An interest-bearing security with usually long-term maturity. Interest payments may be fixed or variable (floating).

Coupon   When detached from a bond, a coupon serves as evidence of entitlement to an interest payment. The word coupon more usually refers to the rate of interest on an interest-bearing security, however.

Default   Failure to make a payment of interest or a repayment of principal on the due date.

Face value (Par value)   Redemption value printed on a bond or share certificate. The actual market price for the security need not equal its face value.

Indenture   Formal agreement. Formally agreed terms of a bond issue.

Internal rate of return (IRR)   Discount rate that would make the net present value for an investment equal to zero.

Maturity   Period between the creation of a financial claim and the date on which it is to be paid. The date when a bond is due for repayment.

Par value   See face value.

Present value (PV)   Value of an investment now as the cost of a comparable investment in the financial market (calculated by multiplying the investment's expected after-tax cash income by the appropriate discount factors).

Redemption yield   Internal rate of return on a bond's interest and redemption payments.

Security   Bond or a share certifying legal ownership of a financial asset or a claim on the assets or cash flow of a company. Also denotes collateral for a loan.

Trustee (for a bond)   Trustee department of a bank, acting on behalf of the bondholders, for example, by administering the bond's sinking fund.

3-2   HOW MUCH SHOULD AN INVESTOR PAY FOR SHARES IN A COMPANY'S EQUITY?

Limited liability companies obtain much of their finance by issuing shares in the company's equity.

EQUITY AND LIMITED LIABILITY

Equity is the owners' stake in the company. Limited liability means that the equity shareholders are not personally liable for the company's debts. An equity share (ordinary share or a common stock) is a security certifying that the shareholder owns a proportion of the company's equity. For example, if the company issued only 100 shares to date, each share would represent 1/100th of the ownership of the equity.

DIVIDENDS

Well-established companies make regular dividend payments to shareholders, usually once or twice a year. The company's board decides whether to pay each dividend, how much to pay, and when to pay it. A company is not obliged to pay dividends or to repay its equity. This means that investors must base their share-value assessment on their expectations of dividend payments rather than on a legally binding agreement.

VALUING A COMPANY'S EQUITY

Consequently, the value of a share equals the PV of its expected dividends:

Share Value Now = Present Value of Expected Dividends

$$S_0 = \frac{E(d_1)}{(1 + R_E)^1} + \frac{E(d_2)}{(1 + R_E)^2} + \frac{E(d_3)}{(1 + R_E)^3} + \cdots$$

The discount rate R_E equals the cost of equity for the particular company. The capital asset pricing model can give an estimate for this rate. Note that an equity share has no maturity. That is, the company is not obliged to buy back the shares on any particular date. In principle, the dividend payments could continue for ever, as implied by the formula. The owner of the share, however, does not expect to keep it for ever. Eventually, at some time N periods hence, the shareholder will sell the share in the stock market at some expected price $E(S_N)$. So, from the standpoint of the shareholder, the value of the share is:

$$S_0 = \left[\frac{E(d_1)}{(1 + R_E)^1} + \frac{E(d_2)}{(1 + R_E)^2} + \cdots + \frac{E(d_N)}{(1 + R_E)^N} \right] + \frac{E(S_N)}{(1 + R_E)^N}$$

The form of this equation, known as the Malkiel model, is the same as we used to value a bond.[4] The difference is that dividend payments to shareholders and the eventual price of the share are uncertain, and we have to discount expected rather than known values. The other difference is that we use the company's cost of equity as the discount rate instead of an interest rate.

---

[4] B. G. Malkiel (1963) "Equity yields, growth and the structure of share prices," *American Economic Review*, Vol. 53, 1004–1031.

Each investor has a different set of expectations regarding dividends, future prices, and the cost of equity. So, the actual stock market price of a share reflects a resolution of investors' differing expectations.

GROWTH AND THE VALUE OF EQUITY

Individual investors frequently do not feel able to forecast individual future dividends. They often have expectations about the rate at which dividends will grow, however. If an investor expects dividends to grow for ever at the compound rate G, then the implied expected dividend at future time t is:

Expected Annual Dividend = Current Annual Dividend × Compound Growth Factor

$$E(d_t) = d_0(1 + G)^t$$

The resulting formula for the PV of all future dividends becomes the sum of an infinite geometric series. If G is less than R_E the sum is equal to:

$$S_0 = \frac{d_0(1 + G)}{R_E - G} \qquad (G < R_E)$$

This equation is the well-known Gordon–Williams formula, intended for use in valuing the shares of growth companies.[5]

EXAMPLE 3.2

For example, an investor expects a company to enjoy 10% compound annual growth for ever, and she thinks that the appropriate rate for discounting the company's dividends would be 12%. She knows that the company's most recent annual dividend was 2 cents. If she had no other information, she still could use the Gordon–Williams formula to estimate a value for the share. That is:

$$S_0 = \frac{2 \times (1 + 0.10)}{0.12 - 0.10} = €1.10 \text{ per share}$$

ASSET VALUE, DEBT, AND THE VALUE OF EQUITY

We should also consider a theoretically equivalent approach that we shall often use in this book for valuing equity. Readers will be aware of the balance sheet equation:

Equity + Debt = Assets

Rearranging the equation we have:

Equity = Assets − Debt

---

[5] J. B. Williams (1938) *The Theory of Investment Value* (Cambridge, MA: Harvard University Press) and M. J. Gordon (1959) "Dividends, earnings and stock prices," *Review of Economics and Statistics*, Vol. 41, 99–105.

In terms of economic value, this equation becomes:

$$Present\ Value\ of\ Equity = Present\ Value\ of\ Assets - Present\ Value\ of\ Debt$$

Thus,

$$Share\ Value\ Now = \frac{Present\ Value\ of\ Equity}{Number\ of\ Shares\ Issued}$$

$$= \frac{Present\ Value\ of\ Assets - Present\ Value\ of\ Debt}{Number\ of\ Shares\ Issued}$$

We can easily obtain the number of issued shares from the company's published accounts. In order to estimate the economic value for a share with this formula, we have also to determine the PV of the company's assets and of its debt. In the section above, we showed how to obtain the PV of a company's debt. Estimating the PV of the company's assets is a major theme of this book that we leave to subsequent chapters.

EXAMPLE 3.3

For example, Company A would like to buy Company B and needs to know how much it should be willing to pay. Company A has potential uses for Company B's assets that would make the assets worth €10 million to Company A. The PV of Company B's debt is €5 million. The number of issued shares in B is 2 million. How much should Company A be willing to pay per share for Company B?

$$Share\ Value\ Now = \frac{Present\ Value\ of\ Assets - Present\ Value\ of\ Debt}{Number\ of\ Shares\ Issued}$$

$$= \frac{10,000,000 - 5,000,000}{2,000,000} = €2.50\ per\ share$$

Therefore, if the stock market price were somewhat less than €2.50 per share, Company A would be in a position to make an attractive bid for the shares of Company B.

DEFINITIONS

Debt Sum of money or other assets owed by one party to another. Usually, a legally enforceable obligation to pay agreed interest and to repay the principal of a loan to the lender promptly on schedule.

Equity Net worth or shareholder's capital represented by common stock (ordinary shares) and preferred stock.

Limited liability Restriction of a business owner's financial loss to no more than the owner's investment in the business.

Ordinary shares (common stock) UK term for common stock, a security certifying the shareholder's proportionate ownership in a public company (corporation) and proportionate claim on declared dividends.

3-3 HOW LIMITED LIABILITY AFFECTS THE RELATIVE VALUES OF EQUITY AND DEBT

The majority of organizations are either partnerships or limited liability companies (corporations). Examples of partnerships are accounting firms and many management consultancies. Most other firms are limited liability companies. From the lenders' perspective, partnerships and limited companies differ in important ways.

LENDING TO PARTNERSHIPS

The unlimited liability of partners is an advantage for lenders. If a partnership is in financial difficulty, the individual partners have to help pay the interest and repayments on the partnership's debts. This provides the lenders extra security for their loans.

LENDING TO LIMITED LIABILITY COMPANIES

In contrast, shareholders in a limited liability do not have to help pay the company's debts. Lenders are correspondingly worse off because the owners do not have to guarantee repayment of the company's debts.

An implication is that a limited liability company can default on loans without involving the shareholders. Smart bankers charge for this valuable option to default, usually with higher interest rates on loans. Higher corporate bond yields also reflect the implications of limited liability.

We can begin to see how to quantify the advantage of limited liability to borrowers using a simple example.

EXAMPLE 3.4

A company finances the purchase of a machine with a bank loan secured on the machine. The loan agreement requires monthly interest payments and repayments on the loan. Therefore, if the company defaults on any of these payments, the bank can take possession of the machine. By selling the machine in the secondhand market, the bank can try to recoup some of its loss.

Suppose after several months, improved technology makes the machine obsolete and reduces the secondhand market value of the machine to less than the outstanding balance on the loan. The borrower can recoup at least some of this loss by defaulting on the loan.

If the outstanding balance on the loan is €50,000, and this exceeds the €20,000 secondhand market value of the machine, the benefit to the borrower from defaulting would be:

$$50,000 - 20,000 = €30,000$$

The loss to the bank would be the same €30,000. So, the value of the loan to the bank reduces by €30,000 to only €20,000.

CREDIT RATING

When the bank makes its lending decision, it must consider the probability that it might take such a loss. The bank uses the borrower's credit rating as an indirect measure of this probability. A higher credit rating implies a lower probability of default. Consequently, the credit rating influences the bank's willingness to lend and the interest it would charge on the loan.

DIVISION OF ASSET VALUE BETWEEN SHAREHOLDERS AND LENDERS

The following example takes the logic a few steps further.

EXAMPLE 3.5

A limited liability company has only one large, outstanding loan. The loan agreement requires repayment of €10 million at the end of one year. The company's assets are the collateral for the loan. Therefore, if the company defaults, the lender can try to recoup the value of the loan by selling any or all of the company's assets.[6]

By the end of the year, however, the company's asset value will have changed. Figure 3.1 illustrates the situation at that time. The 45° line in the figure represents the following relationship between the value of the company's equity and the value of its assets:

$$Value\ of\ Equity = Asset\ Value - Debt$$

$$= A - €10\ million$$

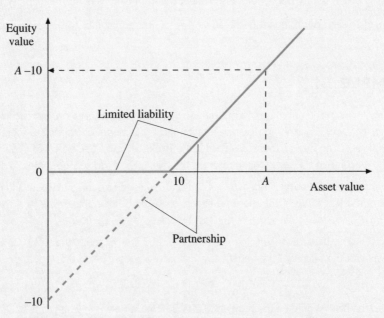

Figure 3.1   Limited liability and the value of equity (millions).

---

[6] A simplification in this example is that it considers only one possibility of default. Actually, a borrower might default on any one of its loan payments. Furthermore, the borrower might have other debts with different maturities also at risk of default.

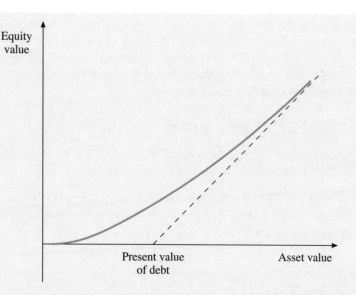

Figure 3.2 Value of equity before repayment of debt.

Obviously, if the asset value falls toward the value of the debt, the value of the equity falls with it. Indeed, if the asset value falls to €10 million, the equity will be worthless.

The important question is: What will happen if the asset value falls below €10 million? If the company were a partnership, the equity value would become negative, as indicated by the dashed portion of the 45° line in Figure 3.1. This is a limited liability company, however, and the equity shareholders are not liable for the company's debt. Therefore, the value of the equity cannot fall below zero. So, the line representing the equity value will become horizontal and equal to zero to the left of €10 million on the horizontal axis.

Figure 3.2 shows the corresponding relationship earlier before the loan repayment date. At such earlier points in time, the function follows a smooth curve starting at zero on the left and approaching the 45° line on the right. As time approaches the date when the company might default, however, the curve in Figure 3.2 sinks toward the heavy, straight lines described earlier in Figure 3.1.

WHY SHARE PRICES ARE NEVER NEGATIVE

Figure 3.2 helps to explain what we see in the stock market. As long as a company is still in business and has a chance of recovery, its share price and therefore the value of its equity stays above zero. The curve remains above the straight lines considered earlier in Figure 3.1 as long as there is any chance that the value of the company's assets will exceed its liabilities in the future.

It is important to realize that, although limited liability affects the value of the company's equity, it does not affect the value of the enterprise. The reason is that the benefit of limited liability to equity shareholders is entirely at the expense of the debt holders. The PV of the equity plus the PV of the debt must still equal the PV of the company's assets.

Furthermore, lenders have to use higher interest or other charges to cover the expected costs of possible default. Consequently, whether shareholders enjoy a positive net present value (NPV) from limited liability depends upon how successfully the company's treasurer negotiates the loan agreements with the lenders. The real attraction of limited liability for shareholders is elimination of the risk of being personally liable for the company's debts.

LIMITED LIABILITY AS AN OPTION TO DEFAULT

As implied earlier, limited liability represents a type of option. The most general definition of an option is the right, without obligation, to exercise a prearranged transaction.[7]

An option is valuable because its holder need not exercise it if there would be no resulting benefit. Indeed, the owners of limited liability companies ordinarily choose not to default on loans because usually it is not in their interests to do so.

DEFINITIONS

Call option   Option giving the holder the right without obligation to buy the option's underlying asset at a specified price on or before a specified date.

Collateral   Security for a loan subject to forfeit if the borrower defaults on an agreed payment to the lender.

Credit rating   Classification of a company by a credit rating agency according to its likelihood of defaulting on its obligations to creditors.

Net present value (NPV)   Difference between the present value of a project's expected after-tax operating cash flows and the present value of its expected after-tax investment expenditures.

Option   Contract granting the right without obligation to engage in a future transaction on terms specified in the contract.

Partnership   Contractual business relationship between two or more people who share in the risks and profits of the business. Each partner has unlimited liability for the actions and debts incurred by the other partners.

Put option   Option giving the holder the right without obligation to sell the option's underlying asset at a specified price on or before a specified date.

3-4   EXECUTIVE STOCK OPTIONS

Options play a prominent role in finance. Executive stock options are especially important. Executive stock options represent a type of bonus for managers. The purpose of these options is to

---

[7] For example, an American call option is a financial contract permitting the option holder the right, but not the obligation, to buy a given number of a company's shares at a specified price before a specified future date. An American put option is a financial contract permitting the option holder the right, but not the obligation, to sell a given number of a company's shares at a specified price before a specified future date.

reward managers when their actions increase the company's share price, thereby benefiting share-holders.

EXAMPLE 3.6

For example, a company's share price currently stands at €1.00. The board of the company grants executive stock options to the senior and middle-ranking managers, giving each of them the right to buy 1,000,000 shares from the company for €1.50 per share. The options are eligible for exercise after five years by managers still employed by the company.

The incentive for these managers is obvious. If they pursue activities that increase the share-holders' equity, and after five years the share price increases to €2.50, exercising the executive option would be worth $2.50 - 1.50 = €1.00$ per share. The resulting payoff on 1,000,000 shares would be €1 million for each manager.

If after five years the share price remains unchanged, the stock options would not be worth exercising. If any of the managers were foolish enough to exercise their options, the loss would equal $1.00 - 1.50 = -€0.50$ per share. Because managers are not obliged to exercise their options, they do not have to take this loss. Instead, they can wait for the possibility of prices exceeding €1.50.

DILUTION EFFECT ON THE SHARE PRICE

When investors estimate the value of a company's shares, they need to consider the executive stock options. Eventually, the company is likely to be selling additional shares to stock holders at prices below market value. This loss dilutes the value of the existing owners' stake in the company and thus reduces the value of their shares.

DEFINITION

Dilution   Increase in the number of a company's shares without a proportionate increase in the company's assets and earnings (more precisely, an increase in the number of shares that reduces shareholder value per share).

3-5   EQUITY WARRANTS

Companies often try to make a bond issue easier to sell by offering equity warrants as a "sweetener" with the issue.

WARRANTS ARE OPTIONS TO BUY A COMPANY'S SHARES

An equity warrant is a security giving the holder the right to buy shares from the company at a pre-determined price or prices during a specified range of dates. So, a warrant is an option contract created and sold by the company. Issuing warrants to purchasers of the company's bonds gives them an opportunity to participate in capital gains on the company's shares.

If the stock market price for the shares rises sufficiently, then the warrant holder can buy the shares from the company at an exercise price lower than their market value. If the share price remains below the exercise price, however, the warrant holder is not obliged to exercise the warrant. Instead, the warrant holder can wait for a better price during the remaining time before the warrant expires.[8] Alternatively, the warrant holder can sell the warrant in the stock market.

VOLATILITY AND THE WARRANT PRICE

Because exercising the warrant is optional, its market price is always greater than zero. Furthermore, the market price virtually always exceeds the value from exercising the warrant. Share price volatility explains this difference. Volatility creates the expectation that the share price could rise, increasing the value of exercising the warrant. If the share price falls instead, the warrant holder need not exercise the warrant. So, the net effect of greater share price volatility is a higher market price for the warrant.

ADVANTAGES AND DISADVANTAGES OF WARRANTS

An advantage for the company offering warrants as sweeteners for a bond issue is that the company usually can get investors to accept the bonds with a lower coupon, thereby reducing the company's cash expenditure on interest payments. A disadvantage for the existing shareholders, however, is that the company could eventually be selling additional shares to the warrant holders at prices below market value. Warrant holders benefiting at the expense of the existing shareholders in this way would affect the share price.

Consequently, when investors estimate the value of a company's shares, they need to consider whether there are outstanding warrants.

DEFINITIONS

Volatility   Standard deviation of percentage changes in the asset price. More precisely, standard deviation of changes in the natural logarithm of the asset price.

Warrants   Securities giving the holder the right to buy shares directly from a company at potentially advantageous prices. Warrant terms specify the number of shares, prices, and dates when the warrant may be exercised.

3-6   OTHER CORPORATE SECURITIES

So far, we have introduced corporate equity (stocks), bonds, and warrants used by limited companies to finance their operations. It would be appropriate at this stage to mention briefly some of the other securities they use to raise capital.

---

[8] Some warrants are perpetual. Perpetual warrants never expire and thus remain valid until actually exercised.

PREFERENCE SHARES

Preference shares (preferred stock) represent another type of equity claim on the company. Unlike ordinary shares (common stock), the preference share certificate specifies the level of the dividend. The company agrees to pay the specified preference dividends before payment of any dividends on the ordinary shares. With cumulative preference shares, the company must pay all preference dividends to date before paying any further dividends to the ordinary shareholders.

CONVERTIBLES

Convertible securities combine the features of both corporate bonds and warrants, or of preference shares and warrants. That is, they are exchangeable for ordinary shares on terms and at times specified by the convertible. Therefore, the value of a convertible bond is the sum of the values of a pure bond and a warrant that is exchangeable for shares on terms equivalent to those specified in the convertible bond contract.

DEFINITIONS

Convertibles   Bonds or preferred stocks that give the holder the option (effectively a warrant) to convert the security into the issuing company's ordinary shares (common stock) according to specified terms during some stated period of years.

Preference shares (preferred stock)   Equity security that pays a (normally fixed) dividend. The issuer must pay the preference dividend before paying any dividends on common stock (ordinary shares). Cumulative preference shares carry forward entitlement to unpaid preference dividends. Participating preference shares also entitle holders to a share of profit.

3-7   TRADED EQUITY OPTIONS

A warrant is really a type of equity call option. The difference is that the company creates its warrants but does not create the options contracts on its equity (stock). In contrast, a traded equity option contract comes into existence when an individual seller and a buyer agree a transaction on the options exchange.

CALLS AND PUTS

A call option is a contract granting the right without obligation to buy the underlying asset, whereas a put option grants the right to sell the underlying asset. A difference between a warrant and an equity option is that exercising the equity option does not involve the company in the transaction. The holder of an equity call option exercises it by buying the underlying stock from a seller of the option, not from the company itself.

TRADED OPTIONS

A traded option is a standardized option contract listed and traded on an options exchange. An American option permits the option holder to exercise the option at any time before it expires.

A European option permits exercise only on the date that the option matures. Most options traded throughout the world are of the American type and exercisable at any time before maturity. The option contract specifies the number of the underlying securities, the exercise price, and the date when the contract matures. Most equity option contracts mature on standardized dates three, six, and nine months apart.

RELATIONSHIP BETWEEN THE VALUE OF AN OPTION AND THE UNDERLYING ASSET

Figure 3.3 illustrates the relationship between the value of an equity call option and the value of the underlying equity (stock). Figure 3.3 is similar to Figure 3.2 as both figures concern types of call option. The axes of Figure 3.3, however, represent different variables. The horizontal axis in Figure 3.3 represents the price of one share of stock. The vertical axis represents the corresponding value of a call option on the share.

The dashed 45° line in Figure 3.3 meets the horizontal axis at the present value $PV(X)$ of the exercise price X discounted at the risk-free rate.[9] The 45° line represents the difference between the share price S and the present value of the exercise price X. So, the height of the line equals the lowest rational call option values corresponding to share prices on the right of $PV(X)$. Option values must also be greater than zero.

The curve in the figure gives the value of the call option for each corresponding value of the share price. On the left of $PV(X)$, the curve approaches zero. On the right of $PV(X)$, it approaches the 45° line. The famous Black–Scholes (and Merton) option–valuation formula gives values for this curve.[10] Appendix 3.1 shows how to use the equation, given values for the share price, the

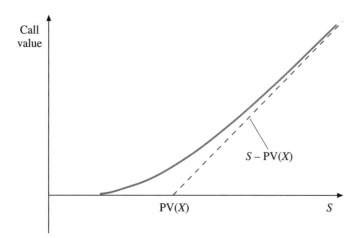

Figure 3.3   Value of a traded call option as a function of the share price.

---

[9] The discount rate is the risk-free rate because the exercise price is contractual and thus known with certainty.
[10] This Nobel Prize-winning work was published in F. Black and M. Scholes (1973) "The pricing of options and corporate liabilities," *Journal of Finance*, Vol. 81, 399–418 and in R. Merton (1973) "Theory of rational option pricing," *The Bell Journal of Economics and Management Science*, Vol. 4, 141–183.

exercise price, the risk-free rate, the volatility of the share price and the maturity of the options contract.

DEFINITIONS

American option   Type of option that may be exercised before its maturity.

Call option   Option giving the holder the right without obligation to buy the option's underlying asset at a specified price on or before a specified date.

European option   Type of option that may be exercised only on its date of maturity.

Put option   Option giving the holder the right without obligation to sell the option's underlying asset at a specified price on or before a specified date.

Traded option   Standardized option contract traded on an options exchange.

Underlying asset   Asset specified for purchase or sale in an option contract.

3-8   CONCLUSIONS

This chapter is an overview of the main sources of corporate finance. It illustrates relationships between the PVs of debt, equity, and assets in limited liability companies. In addition, it briefly describes the debt and equity securities that companies issue to raise capital and how to value them. The chapter also introduces the concept of an option and the factors affecting option values. In this way, the chapter touches on many important financial topics revisited in subsequent chapters.

FURTHER READING

Peter Casson (2001) *Company Share Options* (Chichester, UK: John Wiley & Sons).

Sharpe, W. F. and Alexander, G. J. (1999) *Investments*, 6th edn (Englewood Cliffs, NJ: Prentice Hall).

QUESTIONS AND PROBLEMS

1   A corporate bond with exactly five years left to maturity pays interest at 8% on its €100 face value. The bond pays two coupons per year. The currently quoted redemption yield on an identically rated ten-year bond is 10%. What price for the corporate bond would give it the same redemption yield?

2   A corporate bond with exactly 59 months left to maturity pays interest at 8% on its €100 face value. The bond pays two coupons per year. The currently quoted redemption yield on an identically rated ten-year bond is 10%. What price for the corporate bond would give it the same redemption yield?

3   Suppose that the current market price of the bond in Problem 1 is €95. Calculate the resulting redemption yield.

4   An investor expects a company to enjoy 8% compound annual growth for ever, and she thinks that the appropriate rate for discounting the company's dividends would be 14%. She knows that the company's most recent annual dividend was €1.50. What should be the value of the share?

5   A stockbroker expects XSTREME plc to pay the following annual euro dividend per share during the next five years.

	Year ending			
1	2	3	4	5
1.00	1.20	1.44	1.73	2.07

The broker wants to estimate the value per share for comparison with the current market price. If the value compares favorably with the current price, he will consider recommending purchase of the shares to his clients.

To calculate the value per share, he needs to estimate the price per share at the end of Year 5. The Year-5 price, however, depends upon expected dividends beyond that date. He expects a 7% compound rate of growth for the dividends beyond Year 5. He thinks that the discount rate for all dividends should be 12%.

Estimate the Year 5 price and the Year 0 value per share.

6   Company A would like to buy Company B and needs to know how much it should be willing to pay. Company A has potential uses for Company B's assets that would make the assets worth €20 million to Company A. The present value of Company B's debt is €15 million. The number of issued shares in B is 5 million.

What is the most that Company A should be willing to pay per share for Company B?

7   A partnership operates with assets worth €15 million, but owes €10 million to its bank. The annual interest on the loan is 10%. The €10 million is repayable in one balloon payment at the end of five years. The partners want to change the partnership into a limited liability company. They recognize that limited liability would be less risky for them, and they think that the benefit of limited liability would be worth €1 million. Unfortunately, the bank would want to renegotiate the loan, requiring a higher rate of interest.

How much additional annual interest is the bank likely to charge on the five-year loan?

8   A company issues warrants as sweeteners for its bond issue. With each one of the 1,000 new bonds, the buyer receives a warrant permitting the purchase of 100 shares at €150 each. The company's share price currently is only €100. The warrants are eligible for exercise after five years. The company has already issued 1 million shares. If, at the end of five years, the share price rises to €200 and the warrant holders exercise their options:

(a)   What would be the cost to the existing shareholders?

(b)   What might be the effect on the share price?

9 Instead of issuing warrants with its bond issue, a company issues convertible bonds. Similar bonds without the conversion privilege sell for €75 each. An option pricing formula indicates that the conversion privilege, treated as an option, would be worth €25 each. At what price can the company expect to sell the convertibles?

APPENDIX 3.1 USING THE BLACK AND SCHOLES OPTION PRICING FORMULA

There are several ways of deriving the Black and Scholes option pricing formula, but all require mathematics beyond the scope of this book. It is better for us to learn to use the formula, which is quite easy to do. The method is simply to use a spreadsheet function to represent the probability factors in the formula. The formula for the value of a European call option on a share paying no dividend before the option matures is:

Call Value = Share Price × Probability₁ − Present Value of Exercise Price × Probability₂

That is,[11]

$$Call = S \times Probability_1 - PV(X) \times Probability_2$$
$$= S \times N(d_1) - PV(X) \times N(d_2)$$

in which,

$$PV(X) = Xe^{-rT}$$

r is the risk-free rate, T is the maturity of the option, and $N(d)$ is the normal probability distribution function. The function NORMSDIST(d) in Excel gives values for the two required probabilities.[12] To use this function we just need the values of d_1 and d_2 given by:

$$d_1 = \frac{\ln\left(\frac{S}{X}\right) + (r + 0.5\sigma^2)T}{\sigma\sqrt{T}}$$

$$d_2 = d_1 - \sigma\sqrt{T}$$

in which:

S = Share price

X = Exercise price

r = Continuously compounded risk-free rate

T = Maturity

σ = Standard deviation of $\ln(S)$

---

[11] The first probability $N(d_1)$ gives the value of the Hedge Ratio, which is the number of shares to buy for each call option sold in order to create a risk-free combination. The second probability $N(d_2)$ relates to but does not equal the probability of exercise. It is the probability of exercise in a risk-neutral world.

[12] Of course, one can also use tables for the normal distribution function. This approach, however, is cumbersome when one is plotting the curve relating call option values to corresponding values of the share price.

The following is a copy of part of the spreadsheet used to calculate the values used in Figure 3.3:

$$X_n = 1$$
$$r = 0.05$$
$$T = 1$$
$$PV(X) = 0.9512$$
$$\sigma = 0.5$$

S	Call	d_1	d_2	$N(d_1)$	$N(d_2)$
0		−4.1589	−4.6589	0.0000	0.0000
0.2	0.00	−2.1857	−2.6857	0.0144	0.0036
0.4	0.00	−1.2121	−1.7121	0.1127	0.0434
0.6	0.04	−0.5601	−1.0601	0.2877	0.1446
0.8	0.11	−0.0691	−0.5691	0.4724	0.2846
1	0.22	0.3247	−0.1753	0.6273	0.4304
1.2	0.36	0.6536	0.1536	0.7433	0.5610
1.4	0.52	0.9360	0.4360	0.8254	0.6686
1.6	0.69	1.1834	0.6834	0.8817	0.7528
1.8	0.88	1.4035	0.9035	0.9198	0.8169
2	1.07	1.6018	1.1018	0.9454	0.8647

# Shareholder Value in Efficient Markets[1]

Prices in an **efficient market** (financial) rapidly reflect all relevant information. So, a firm's share price would reflect all available information concerning the value of its assets including the value-generating potential of its existing products and the **net present values (NPVs)** of its expected future investment opportunities. Consequently, share prices would fully reflect profitable new capital projects. Conversely, unwise or unprofitable capital investment decisions would reduce the market value of the firm relative to that of other firms.

The volatility of stock market prices can give the impression, however, that investors are irrational. Nevertheless, it would be surprising if the market were not volatile. The prices of equities change rapidly in response to changes in the market's discount rates. Discount rates for equities are a function of interest rates, risk premiums, and the risk of expected cash flows. In addition, price changes reflect changes in expected future dividends. In a rational stock market, investors seek returns commensurate with risk. Therefore, share price changes reflect changes in risk and the risk premium as well as changes in interest rates and dividend prospects. The important question is: How quickly do share prices respond to new information relevant to the economic value of the firm? The answer to this question is an empirical one. That is, one must use very large samples of share prices, earnings announcements, and other relevant data to measure the market's rate of response to new information.

TOPICS

This chapter considers the following:

○ *conditions conducive to capital market efficiency;*

○ *weak-form tests of market efficiency;*

○ *semistrong-form tests of market efficiency;*

○ *strong-form tests of market efficiency;*

○ *apparent exceptions to market efficiency and their economic significance.*

---

[1] Adapted by permission of J. R. Franks and J. E. Broyles (1979) *Modern Managerial Finance* (Chichester, UK: John Wiley & Sons).

4-1   CONDITIONS CONDUCIVE TO CAPITAL MARKET EFFICIENCY

DEFINITION OF AN EFFICIENT MARKET

A market is efficient if transaction prices fully reflect in an unbiased way all available price-sensitive information.

CONDITIONS CONDUCIVE TO MARKET EFFICIENCY

The strict assumptions that define perfect markets are not necessary for an efficient capital market. It is only necessary that dealing costs are not too high, that the relevant information is available to a sufficient number of investors, and that no individual participant is sufficiently wealthy to dominate market trading. Because such conditions are not very stringent, it should not be surprising if the evidence is consistent with stock market efficiency.

THE EFFICIENT MARKETS HYPOTHESIS

Efficiently priced securities fully reflect the present value (PV) of expected cash benefits to security holders. Of course, individuals can disagree about such expectations, and this disagreement between them generates transactions between buyers and sellers. In an efficient market, the aggregation and resolution of differing expectations results in unbiased prices.

Therefore, we have the Efficient Markets Hypothesis (EMH), which is testable using market price and related data. Statistical tests cannot actually prove a hypothesis. It is possible to reject a hypothesis with a measurable degree of confidence, however, if the data are not consistent with either the hypothesis itself or its major implications.

THE SECURITIES MARKET AS A FAIR GAME

Fama[2] described such a market as a fair game. In a fair game, the average rate of return that an investor can expect from holding a security equals the market's discount rate for the security's expected cash flow. Information emerging subsequent to transactions will usually prove the market's valuation to have been incorrect, and some individual investors will have experienced unusual gains or losses. If the market is a fair game, however, no individual can expect to beat the market systematically.

TESTING THE EFFICIENT MARKETS HYPOTHESIS

Various universities have compiled monthly share price data for all companies listed on the New York, American, and London Stock Exchanges for up to 80 years. Very many published tests of the Efficient Markets Hypothesis have used these data. Researchers have found it difficult to find evidence inconsistent with the Efficient Markets Hypothesis.

---

[2] Eugene F. Fama (1970) "Efficient capital markets: A review of theory and empirical work," *Journal of Finance*, May 1970, 383–417.

The issue of market efficiency is of such fundamental importance in finance that we should consider some of the evidence. Broadly speaking, researchers divide the evidence on market efficiency into three categories of test:

(a)   Weak-form tests of the hypothesis that current prices already reflect all information implied in the sequence of past price changes.

(b)   Semistrong-form tests of the hypothesis that current prices reflect not only the implications of past price changes but indeed all publicly available information relevant to the valuing of a company's securities.

(c)   Strong-form tests of the hypothesis that prices reflect all relevant information including information available only to company insiders or to other privileged groups.

Note that each succeeding test in this list includes all the information in the preceding tests in the list.

These three rough categories classify tests of market efficiency according to the degree and availability of information relevant to share prices. Let us now consider some of the better known tests in each category.

DEFINITIONS

Efficient market   Market in which prices rapidly reflect all relevant information in an unbiased way.

Efficient Markets Hypothesis (EMH)   Hypothesis asserting that prices instantaneously adjust without bias to new, price-sensitive information.

Fair game   Market in which the expected rate of return on a security equals the market's discount rate for the security's expected cash flow.

Net present value (NPV)   Difference between the present value of a project's expected after-tax operating cash flows and the present value of its expected after-tax investment expenditures.

Present value (PV)   Value of an investment now as the cost of a comparable investment in the financial market (calculated by multiplying the investment's expected after-tax cash income by the appropriate discount factors).

Semistrong-form Efficient Markets Hypothesis   That a stock price already reflects all publicly available information relevant to the value of the stock (including price history).

Strong-form Efficient Markets Hypothesis   That a stock's price already reflects inside information not yet made known to the public.

Weak-form Efficient Markets Hypothesis   Hypothesis that a stock price already reflects any information in the past price history of the stock.

4-2 WEAK-FORM TESTS OF MARKET EFFICIENCY

Weak-form tests of market efficiency concern any information implied by patterns of past price changes. If the current price fails to reflect all the information conveyed by past price changes, one could use the remaining information to help predict future price changes. In an efficient market, charting or otherwise analyzing past price patterns for the purposes of prediction would be useless, however. The current price would already reflect all information in the price data.

THE RANDOM WALK HYPOTHESIS

If the current prices already reflect all relevant information, the prices follow (approximately) a **random walk** in which each future price change is a random departure from the last price.[3] Each price deviation reflects the influence of newly arriving information. If changes in share prices follow a random walk, then expected future prices equal the last price, the correlation between successive price changes equals zero, and deviations from the expected price will tend to be proportional to the square root of time. New information changes the price; but, by definition, the market cannot anticipate what is new. For this reason, the resulting price changes would be unrelated to past price changes.

ARE SUCCESSIVE PRICE CHANGES RELATED?

The **serial correlation** coefficient measures linear relationship over time between successive price changes. If share prices follow a trend, and price changes during one period relate positively to price changes in the preceding period, then the serial correlation coefficient would have a value between 0 and +1. If, on the other hand, the market overreacts, and each price change tends to reverse the change in the immediately preceding period, the value of the serial correlation coefficient would be between 0 and −1. Finally, if current prices reflect all available information, the market would exhibit neither trend nor reaction. In this case, the value of the correlation coefficient would not be significantly different from zero.

On this basis, Kendall[4] observed that successive changes in various UK economic indices, including shares and commodities, appeared to be random. Fama reported similar results for New York Stock Exchange price changes.[5] Table 4.1 shows Solnik's evidence for average daily, weekly, and

---

[3] More precisely, a share price series follows a random walk if the price changes are serially independent and identically normally distributed. A slightly better description of share prices is geometric Brownian motion. In geometric Brownian motion, the natural logarithms of the share prices follow a random walk. A more general model is the Martingale model, which simply states that the expected value of the next price is equal to the present price, conditioned on all past prices. If prices follow a Martingale, then the expected return equals zero. A slightly better representation is the sub-Martingale. This type of Martingale permits the expected return to be nonzero and equal to the risk-free rate. The fair game model is less restrictive in that the expected return on any share equals the market capitalization rate for the share. In all these models, actual returns are completely unpredictable outcomes.

[4] Maurice G. Kendall (1953) "The analysis of economic time series, Part I: Prices," *Journal of the Royal Statistical Society*, Vol. 116, 11–25.

[5] Eugene F. Fama (1970) "Efficient capital markets: A review of theory and empirical work," *Journal of Finance*, May 1970, 383–417.

Table 4.1 Average serial correlation.

Country	Daily returns	Weekly returns	Monthly returns
France	−0.019	−0.049	0.012
Italy	−0.023	0.001	−0.027
UK	0.072	−0.055	0.020
Germany	0.078	0.056	0.058
Netherlands	0.031	0.002	−0.011
Belgium	−0.018	−0.088	−0.022
Switzerland	0.012	−0.022	−0.017
Sweden	0.056	0.024	0.140
USA	0.026	−0.038	0.009

Source: Bruno H. Solnik (1973) "Note on the validity of the random walk for European stock prices", *Journal of Finance*, Vol. 28, 1156.

monthly **holding period rate of return** in nine countries.[6] In all cases, the serial correlation coefficients are not sufficiently different from zero to have any economic significance.

All these results are consistent with the weak form of the Efficient Market Hypothesis and with the related **Random Walk Hypothesis (RWH)**.

DO COMPLEX PRICE PATTERNS CONVEY VALUABLE INFORMATION?

Some analysts raise the objection that serial correlation tests are insufficiently sensitive to measure the complex patterns in prices that might convey useful relevant information. In answer to this argument, researchers proposed the ultimate weak-form test. Those who believe that the stock market is inefficient must demonstrate a trading rule, based on historical price patterns, that beats the market systematically. In exhaustive tests, the trading rule must earn a significantly better return after transaction costs than a simple buy-and-hold strategy for shares of equivalent risk.[7] Alexander[8] proposed the following apparently profitable strategy. Buy a share when it rises a specified percentage above a previous trough. Then sell the share and sell it short when it falls by this percentage below a previous peak.[9] Unfortunately, Fama and Blume[10] showed that this strategy is unprofitable after inclusion of all transaction costs and dividends.[11]

---

[6] Holding period returns usually are defined in such tests as the natural log of the ratio of successive prices adjusted for dividends, $R_t = \ln[(P_t + D_t)/P_{t-1}]$.

[7] Beware of "data snooping." It is easy to construct apparently profitable trading rules using historical data. Almost invariably these fail to be profitable when used in real time.

[8] Sydney S. Alexander (1961) "Price movements in speculative markets: Trends or random walks," *Industrial Management Review*, Vol. 2, 7–26.

[9] Selling shares short means selling temporarily borrowed shares. The seller is obliged subsequently to repurchase the shares and repay them to the lender.

[10] Eugene F. Fama and Marshall Blume (1966) "Filter rules and stock market trading profits," *Journal of Business* Vol. 39 (special supplement, January), 226–241.

[11] The short seller is required to pay any dividends declared on the borrowed shares to the lender. See Eugene F. Fama and Marshall Blume (1966) "Filter rules and stock market trading profits," *Journal of Business*, Vol. 39 (special supplement, January), 226–241.

Alexander's trading rule was the first of many such tests. If any of them proved profitable, they remain well-guarded secrets.

DEFINITIONS

Holding period rate of return Dividends and capital gain for the period divided by the required investment at the beginning of the period.

Random Walk Hypothesis (RWH) Hypothesis that successive price changes are identically normally distributed, are uncorrelated, and have an expected value equal to zero.

Random walk Process in which successive changes to the value of a random variable are identically normally distributed, are uncorrelated, and have an expected value equal to zero.

Serial correlation (autocorrelation) Measures the degree of association between successive values of a random variable, for example, between successive holding period returns.

Transaction costs Stockbroker's commission plus the bid-offer spread plus the adverse effect of the transaction on the market price (plus stamp duty on stock purchases in the UK).

4-3 SEMISTRONG-FORM TESTS OF MARKET EFFICIENCY

The hope that one could use limited information about past prices to make profitable predictions appears to have been naive. Information from so many other sources relating to the future of the firm is of more fundamental relevance. For this reason, many thousands of investment analysts employed by financial institutions and their clients comb through company accounts and other economic information about the company, its industry, and the economy. In this way, share prices are likely to reflect this information as well. A stronger definition of stock market efficiency would be that stock prices fully reflect all such publicly available information. Semistrong-form tests measure the timing of market response to such publicly available information.

THE EVENT STUDY METHOD

In their study of the stock market's response to stock splits, Fama et al.[12] devised an ingenious method for measuring the behavior of the prices market before and after publication of new information. Most subsequent semistrong-form tests used their event study methodology. Fama et al. wished to examine the average behavior of equity prices of firms before and after their announcement of a stock split. First, they adjusted the price data for capitalization changes and stock splits. Then they calculated holding period returns for each share and for the market index. They used these returns to calculate the abnormal returns for each company's share. An abnormal return is the difference between the return on an individual share and the risk-adjusted return on the market index for the same holding period. In this way abnormal holding period returns separate

---

[12] Eugene Fama, Lawrence Fisher, Michael Jensen, and Richard Roll (1969) "The adjustment of stock prices to new information," *International Economic Review*, Vol. 10 (February), 1–21.

the price effect of information related to the specific company from the effect of price movements in the stock market as a whole.

Fama et al. averaged the abnormal returns for 940 stock splits between January 1927 and December 1959 and cumulated them over 30 months before and after stock splits. The level pattern observed during the 30 months after the announcement of stock splits indicated virtually no abnormal returns. In other words, the public announcements added no new information not already reflected in the prices of the shares. In the 30 months before stock splits, however, the cumulative average abnormal returns rose significantly. This evidence is consistent with the semistrong form of the EMH. By the time splits occurred, prices already reflected all information attributable to the splits.

Of itself, a stock split has virtually no economic significance. For example, if management declares a two-for-one stock split, the shareholders have twice the number of shares but the resulting share price is only half. The share price would not fall to half, however, if the split somehow conveyed favorable information. Management often splits stock when increasing the dividend. Dividend increases tend to signal favorable information about the firm's prospects. So, we have a possible reason for share prices rising in anticipation of stock splits.

Consequently, Fama et al. divided their sample into companies that increased their dividends and those that did not. Then they reran the tests. The firms that did not increase their dividends suffered a loss in valuation in the 10 months following the stock split announcement. The firms that increased their dividends experienced very little additional gain. Apparently, the market anticipated most of the dividend increases.

Subsequently, other authors adopted the event study method to measure cumulative abnormal returns before and after the announcements of takeovers and mergers between companies. Acquirers usually have to pay a substantial premium over market value to shareholders in the acquired company to induce them to sell their shares. Therefore, one might expect an efficient market to anticipate this windfall. Halpern[13] and Mandelker[14] in the USA found that the market began to anticipate the benefits of mergers up to eight months on average before the merger. Franks et al.[15] found that market prices began to anticipate mergers in the UK at least three months on average before the merger announcement date.

STANDARDIZED UNEXPECTED EARNINGS

A notable exception to the pattern of results reported in most such research is the study by Latané and Jones[16] concerning the stock market's response to Standardized Unexpected Earnings (SUE).

---

[13] P. J. Halpern (1973) "Empirical estimates of the amount and distribution of gains to companies in mergers," Journal of Business, October, 554–575.

[14] G. Mandelker (1974) "The economic consequences of corporate managers," Journal of Business, January, 85–104.

[15] J. R. Franks, J. E. Broyles, and M. J. Hecht (1977) "An industry study of the profitability of mergers in the UK," Journal of Finance, December, 1513–1525.

[16] H. A. Latané and C. P. Jones (1977) "Standardized unexpected earnings—a progress report," Journal of Finance, Vol. 32, No. 5 (December), 457–460.

Latané and Jones compared actual quarterly earnings for US companies with forecast earnings. Their forecasting model was a least-squares extrapolation of earnings in the preceding 20 quarters. Differences between forecast and actual earnings were standardized (by dividing the differences by their standard deviation) to obtain SUE. Then they ranked all 975 of the New York Stock Exchange companies in their sample according to the value of SUE in each quarter. Latané and Jones found significant rank correlations between returns on the portfolios and their deciles. The surprising result was that these correlations persisted after earnings announcements. During a 14-quarter period starting in 1971, one could have obtained abnormal returns averaging over 7% before transactions costs and taxes. The strategy was simply to buy the top 20 SUE companies and sell short the bottom 20. The transactions took place as late as five months after the accounting quarter and held for three months. Subsequent studies using larger samples of more recent data confirmed these results.

One should recognize that these results apply mostly to outliers rather than to the great bulk of companies in the sample. The data collection and computing time required in the early 1970s to implement the SUE strategy was costly. So, these results would have been of interest only to a large institutional investor. If the market is efficient, institutions will by now have exploited the information implicit in SUE and thus will have eliminated any abnormal returns in excess of transactions costs and the required incremental data acquisition and processing costs.

DEFINITIONS

Abnormal return   Difference between actual and expected holding period rates of return. Expected return used in the method generated by, for example, the Capital Asset Pricing Model.

Event study   Empirical method measuring cumulative average abnormal returns during the periods immediately before and after significant company announcements such as stock splits or dividend increases (see abnormal return).

Standardized Unexpected Earnings (SUE)   Deviation of reported earnings per share from expected earnings per share divided by the standard deviation of past earnings per share from expected earnings per share.

4-4   STRONG-FORM TESTS OF MARKET EFFICIENCY

Virtually no one believes the strong-form hypothesis that share prices fully reflect information known only to company insiders or other privileged groups. That is why undisclosed trading of a company's shares by corporate insiders is illegal in the UK and the USA.

SECONDARY DISTRIBUTIONS

Scholes published important evidence concerning the validity of the strong-form hypothesis. Table 4.2 summarizes some of Scholes's results.

Secondary distributions are New York Stock Exchange transactions permitting the sale of very large blocks of existing shares by institutions and other large shareholders. These transactions

Table 4.2 Strong-form test: abnormal performance index for secondary distributions partitioned by seller.

Number of observations	Category	Abnormal returns	
		−10 to +10 days (%)	0 to +10 days (%)
192	Investment companies and mutual funds	−2.5	−1.4
31	Banks and insurance companies	−0.3	−0.0
36	Individuals	−1.1	−0.7
23	Corporation and officers	−2.9	−2.1
50	Estates and trusts	−0.7	−0.5

Source: Myron Scholes (1972) "The market for securities: Substitution vs. price pressure and the effects of information on share prices," *Journal of Business*, Vol. 45 (1972), 179–211.

occur off the floor of the Exchange after hours when normal trading has closed. The purpose of this special procedure is to permit the sale of very large blocks of shares without disrupting an orderly market.

One can imagine that the sellers of very large blocks of shares are more likely to possess inside information. Furthermore, some types of large seller are more likely to have inside information than others do. Table 4.2 partitions sellers into appropriate categories. The table shows the average market response to sales in each category during the 20 days surrounding distributions. Unsurprisingly, the largest response was associated with sales by obvious insiders such as the companies and their officials (directors and senior managers). Response was almost as great when investment companies and mutual funds sold large blocks of a company's shares. Apparently, fund managers in these institutions were also in receipt of privileged information obtained from regular briefings by company officers.

Scholes's results suggest at least two conclusions. The first is that the negative share price response to large block sales by insiders did not support the strong-form hypothesis that share prices already reflect privileged information. The second conclusion is that although prices did not fully reflect insider information, the pricing error was not very large on average compared with the transaction costs paid by most investors at that time.

The results lead naturally to a further question. Is the mispricing of shares sufficiently large that individuals or institutions regularly in receipt of privileged information can expect to benefit?

FUND MANAGEMENT

A portfolio manager has many advantages that would qualify him or her as something of an insider. Besides professionalism, portfolio managers have sources of information not generally available to the public and have the resources to analyze the information adequately. Of course, portfolio managers compete in the market with many other professionals having similar resources. The interesting questions are: Can professional managers expect to outperform the general market index in a market using the high quality of information available to them? Can the private investor hope to improve her investment performance by buying units in unit trusts or mutual funds with outstanding previous performance?

Jensen[17] measured the risk-adjusted performance of 115 mutual funds in the period 1955–1964. Each share holding or unit in such a fund represents a proportion of the underlying assets, consisting of cash and a professionally managed portfolio of securities. The fund agrees to buy back units when required at a price representing a proportion of the current market value of the underlying cash and securities.

Jensen compared the risk and associated returns from investment in each of the 115 US mutual funds with the alternative of holding comparable-risk combinations of a risk-free government security and a portfolio tracking the market index. He found that many funds performed relatively badly and the distribution of relative fund performance was not significantly different from that of randomly selected portfolios.

The average performance of the mutual funds was slightly worse than random selection. Apparently, management expenses and transaction costs dissipated any relative advantages of professionalism. Jensen also found that mutual funds selected for excellent previous performance did not perform significantly differently from average subsequently.

One can expect that financial analysts can identify companies and industries that are innovating and expecting increased future earnings. It is questionable, however, whether one can use this information to make abnormal returns net of transactions costs and taxes.

A number of subsequent studies confirmed Jensen's results. As a result, many index tracker funds now exist that seek merely to match the performance of selected popular market indices while minimizing management overheads and charging lower management fees.

MARKET MAKERS

To be sure, some insiders must be profiting from advantages not available even to the professionals. An excellent example of an insider is the New York Stock Exchange specialist. Specialists are market makers who conduct the market for the shares of various companies on the floor of the Exchange.

The specialist does this by buying and selling shares in the companies for which he or she is the specialist and pays no transaction costs. In this role, he or she has access to information about various kinds of buying and selling orders executed on behalf of brokers. These orders get first priority before any transactions made on the specialist's own behalf. Niederhoffer and Osborne found that the New York Stock Exchange specialists earned a positive return on 82% of their transactions.[18] Most investors who pay transaction costs and who do not have access to such privileged information, however, do not find much comfort in such evidence.

---

[17] M. C. Jensen (1969) "Risk, the pricing of capital assets, and the valuation of investment portfolios," *Journal of Business*, Vol. 42, No. 2 (April), 167–247.
[18] Victor Niederhoffer and M. F. M. Osborne (1966) "Market making and reversal on the stock exchange," *Journal of the American Statistical Association*, Vol. 61 (December), 897–916.

That the market discounts publicly available information is not a new or very strange notion. The relatively long period on average that market prices seem to anticipate various public announcements commands respect, however. The many professional analysts employed by stockbrokers and their institutional clients are contributing to the efficiency of the market. As a body, they appear to anticipate the most likely future developments of economic significance to the firm. The resultant buying and selling behavior of portfolio managers and other investors results in share prices discounting the future in a manner that appears consistent with valuation models and the EMH.

All this may be a little disappointing to those who had hoped to make their fortune by trading in the stock market without actually soiling their hands in industry. Long-term investment in a well-diversified portfolio is almost certainly the better way to invest.

DEFINITIONS

Market maker   Individual standing ready in the Exchange to make a market in particular securities, that is, to supply liquidity to the market by buying or selling the securities at fair prices.

Mutual fund (unit trust)   Open-end fund standing ready to redeem or issue shares (units) at their net asset value, which is the market value of all securities and cash held in the fund divided by the number of the fund's shares (units) outstanding.

Secondary distribution   Special procedure for selling blocks of shares too large for selling on the Exchange in the usual manner.

Specialist   Market maker on the New York Stock Exchange (see market maker).

Tracker fund   Managed fund using statistical techniques to replicate the returns on a market index with a portfolio composed of a subset of the securities in the index.

4-5   APPARENT EXCEPTIONS TO MARKET EFFICIENCY

Mostly in the last two decades, evidence of apparent anomalies has surfaced. An anomaly is an exception to the main body of evidence. The delay in response of abnormal returns to SUE, mentioned in Section 4.3, is one such apparent anomaly. It is not clear that any of the anomalies seriously challenges the EMH, however.

SEASONAL ANOMALIES

Because investment managers tend to adjust their portfolio strategies at the turn of the year, stock markets tend to rise in early January or late December. This effect reflects the price movements mainly of companies that have a small market capitalization.[19] (A company's market capitalization

---

[19] M. R. Reninganum (1983) "The anomalous stock market behaviour of small firms in January: Empirical tests for tax-loss selling effects," *Journal of Financial Economics* (June), 89–104.

is its price per share multiplied by the number of its issued shares.) For the rest of the year the market follows more nearly a random walk. Weak regularities also have occurred at the turn of the month, at the turn of the week, and during the day. Only the **January effect** appears to have been (slightly) profitable net of transaction costs, but institutional investors seem to have been constrained from taking advantage of this curious anomaly. Some recent research suggests that the evidence for calendar anomalies is diminishing.

THE SMALL COMPANIES EFFECT

For most years, returns on shares have been inversely proportional to their market capitalizations. That is, smaller companies enjoy abnormally higher returns. This **small companies effect** attracted much research interest because it appeared to be inconsistent with market efficiency. Berk,[20] however, explained that the small companies effect is a natural consequence of market efficiency if market discount rates reflect risk factors not included in the **Capital Asset Pricing Model (CAPM)**.[21] Companies affected by the additional risk factors require higher discount rates. The higher discount rates result in smaller market capitalizations. If the market is a fair game, expected returns equal the higher discount rates for the small capitalization companies.

Evidence consistent with market efficiency does not prove that stock prices are always unbiased. Quite large deviations of a stock price from fair value can escape detection by existing statistical methods if obscured by the high volatility of share prices. Such deviations from fair value appear not to create profitable trading opportunities, however, because they are so difficult to detect.

DEFINITIONS

Anomaly   Evidence appearing inconsistent with a widely accepted hypothesis.

Capital Asset Pricing Model (CAPM)   Linear model attempting to explain the expected return on a risky asset in terms of the risk-free rate, its Beta factor (systematic risk) and the risk premium on the market portfolio.

January effect   Anomalous evidence that in many countries, the stock market rises more often in January than in other months.

Market capitalization   The stock market value of a company's equity. The market price per share multiplied by the number of shares issued.

Small companies effect   Long-term returns on small companies have been higher than for large companies even after allowing for differences in systematic risk.

---

[20] J. B. Berk (1995) "A critique of size-related anomalies," *Review of Financial Studies*, Vol. 8, 275–286.
[21] The Capital Asset Pricing Model, encountered frequently in this book, provides a means of adjusting the market index for risk in the calculation of abnormal returns.

4-6 CONCLUSIONS

Reported here are only selected highlights of the seminal research stimulating very many further studies of market efficiency during the last four decades. The results have shown a substantial consistency: little evidence emerged casting any serious doubt that capital markets are efficient. The evidence highlighted the ability of the market to alter quickly the valuations of shares relative to other shares, often before public announcements of the relevant information.

Of course, some individuals can gain an unfair advantage exploiting inside information. No recognizable group other than the market makers on the exchange appear to profit in any systematic way from privileged information, however. Although studies based on SUE suggest that prices might not always respond immediately to new information, we have no evidence that anyone can profit systematically using this approach.

Most evidence supports the assertion that the major capital markets of the world are at least reasonably efficient. An efficient stock market provides a valuation mechanism discounting forecasts of expected cash flows in the corporate sector. An unbiased market valuation mechanism helps to ensure that market-traded companies can finance profitable capital investments. Such firms should not normally face **capital rationing** if the market can value the firm's investment opportunities. Finally, managements communicating timely and reliable information to the market about significant company developments can be confident that equity prices will rapidly reflect news relevant to the company's share price.

DEFINITION

Capital rationing   Insufficient funds for investment in all acceptable capital projects.

FURTHER READING

J. B. Berk (1995) "A critique of size-related anomalies," *Review of Financial Studies*, Vol. 8, 275–286.

Elroy Dimson (ed.) (1988) *Stock Market Anomalies* (Cambridge, UK: Cambridge University Press).

Eugene F. Fama (1970) "Efficient capital markets: A review of theory and empirical work," *Journal of Finance*, May 1970, 383–417.

QUESTIONS AND PROBLEMS

1   Suppose that the serial correlation coefficient for weekly returns on a stock is equal to +0.2 and statistically significant. What would this imply for your trading strategy for this stock? Would your trading strategy be any different if this serial correlation coefficient were negative instead of positive? If so, in what way?

2   Is it possible for the serial correlation coefficient for a stock's prices to equal, say, 0.80 while the value of the serial correlation coefficient for the stock's price changes to be negative, say −0.10? Explain.

3   Two stocks appear to be identical in all important respects at time 0 when they have the same price. After a year, Stock A's price has gone down 25% and Stock B's has risen 25%. Is there an incentive to buy one stock and sell the other? Why or why not?

4   (a)   For a coin flipped 500 times, the score so far is +50 heads (i.e., there are $275 - 225 = 50$ more heads than tails). If you were to continue flipping this coin 500 more times, what would be the expected score for the total 1,000 trials?

             (b)   What do coin flipping and stock price forecasting have in common?

5   A stock has an expected return of 1% per month. The annualized standard deviation of its price changes is 20%. If the stock is held for 10 years:

             (a)   How would its expected arithmetic average annual return for the 10 years compare with 1% per month compounded?

             (b)   In what way would the price tend to deviate from the expected price for the 10 years?

PART 2

Valuation of Investment and Real Options

5 An Introduction to the Appraisal of Capital Projects

Capital project appraisal is the financial analytical process of strategy implementation. The object of project appraisal is to assess whether strategies, as implemented by projects, add value for the company's shareholders. Capital projects are investments that frequently involve the purchase of a physical asset, such as a machine or a new factory. A capital project can also involve investment in a less tangible asset, such as a new product or service or an advertizing campaign. Usually, a capital project entails paying cash now or in the near term in order to obtain a return of more cash later. In this chapter, we shall show how financial managers estimate the present value (PV) of a project's future cash flows for its shareholders. Using discounted cash flow methods, we show how to decide whether a project is worth more than it costs, and we compare discounted cash flow with other methods that are in use. In this chapter, we focus mostly on standard industrial practice, leaving consideration of the inherent pitfalls and advanced practice to subsequent chapters.

TOPICS

The issues considered are:

- *capital budgeting;*
- *competitive advantage and value creation;*
- *project appraisal;*
- *incremental cash flow and incremental value;*
- *net present value (NPV);*
- *the rate of return on a project;*
- *project liquidity;*
- *related issues;*
- *taxes;*
- *project risk and the discount rate;*
- *real options.*

5-1 CAPITAL BUDGETING

BUDGETS

Companies usually follow a capital budgeting procedure for allocating funds to capital projects. Each division of a company may have its own capital budget. In large companies a high-level capital appropriations committee proposes the budgetary allocations for approval by the board of directors. The allocations reflect the board's strategic priorities regarding growth in different markets, new products, and greater efficiency.

Budgets often anticipate likely expenditure on larger projects such as chemical plants or important new products by as much as five or more years. Budgets also anticipate the need to fund smaller investments (machine tools, for example).

SPENDING PROPOSALS

A formal capital expenditure proposal includes analysis of the project in terms of specified financial criteria. It should also indicate how the project fits into the company's overall commercial strategy and other relevant qualitative considerations.

AUTHORIZATION

No one can spend the budgeted funds until the appropriate level of management formally approves the project. For example, one company might permit certain middle managers to approve projects costing up to €10,000. More costly projects must go to the divisional manager for final approval. Projects costing €50,000 or more must also get board approval.

DEFINITIONS

Capital budgeting   Procedure for allocating funds to capital projects.

Capital expenditure proposal   Formal application for allocation funds to investment in a proposed capital project including a detailed justification of the project.

Capital project   Investment in a nonfinancial asset.

Present value (PV)   Value of an investment now as the cost of a comparable investment in the financial market (calculated by multiplying the investment's expected after-tax cash income by the appropriate discount factors).

Net present value (NPV)   Difference between the present value of a project's expected after-tax operating cash flows and the present value of its expected after-tax investment expenditures.

5-2 COMPETITIVE ADVANTAGE AND VALUE CREATION

EXPLOITING COMPETITIVE ADVANTAGE

Successful strategies usually require investment in capital projects. A principal financial objective of strategy is to exploit competitive advantage in order to maximize the value of the firm to its investors. Accordingly, the board seeks projects expected to be worth more to the company than they actually cost.

EXPLOITING UNCERTAINTY

If the product markets were perfectly competitive and certain, then price competition would reduce NPVs to zero. In reality, markets are imperfect and uncertain, and thus one can exploit market imperfections and the uncertainty of competitors. For example, find a niche in the market where currently there is little or no competition and exploit it before competitors perceive the opportunity. Create new or better products or services and exploit them before competitors can. Use and create barriers to entry, if legally possible. Keep options open, permitting change in response to unexpected commercial developments.

VALUE FOR SHAREHOLDERS

Financial appraisal methodology must measure the net value for shareholders generated by the market strategy, the product technology, and the price and cost structure of investments. The discounted cash flow methodology helps do this because it calculates the NPV of a project.

DEFINITIONS

Competitive advantage   Comparative advantage permitting a firm to earn economic rents in an imperfect product market.

Uncertainty   Risk not measurable with historical data.

5-3   PROJECT APPRAISAL

OBJECTIVE

Project appraisal is the analytical process for ascertaining the financial and strategic value of a proposed investment in the business. To increase shareholder value a project's PV must be greater than the cost of investing in it.

METHODOLOGIES

Large, financially sophisticated companies use several methods to appraise a project, whereas smaller companies use only a few. For example, a large company analyzing an important project proposal is quite likely to use the NPV, internal rate of return (IRR), accounting rate of return (ARR), and payback methods simultaneously. Smaller companies often use the payback method only. In the context of Example 5.1, we shall consider how managers often use a combination of the four methods to assess a project.

First, however, we must be clear how to construct a project's net incremental after-tax cash flow, which is the foundation of three out of four of these methods.

DEFINITIONS

Accounting Rate of Return (ARR)   Rate of return as accounting income divided by the book value of all assets employed to generate the income.

Internal rate of return (IRR)   Discount rate that would make the net present value for an investment equal to zero.

Shareholder value   Economic value of the shareholders' financial claim on the business.

5-4   INCREMENTAL CASH FLOW AND INCREMENTAL VALUE

In order to determine whether a project can add value for shareholders, it is necessary to forecast its expected incremental impact on the company's after-tax cash flow. Net incremental cash flow is the *difference* between the relevant expected after-tax cash flows associated with two mutually exclusive scenarios:

1.   *With* the project (the project goes ahead).

2.   *Without* the project (the project does not go ahead).

For example, tax cash flows can be quite different in the two mutually exclusive scenarios. The relevant cash flows are those affected by the project if it goes ahead:

(a)   new cash flows that occur only if the project goes ahead;

(b)   existing cash flows that *change* if the project goes ahead.

We cannot estimate the value that a project adds for shareholders without knowing its net impact on the company's after-tax cash flow. The crucial concept of net incremental cash flow is best understood in the context of a realistic example.

EXAMPLE 5.I

DIGITAL DYNAMICS PLC produces a variety of computer-based electronic products sold throughout Europe and exported, mainly to the USA. The company employs financial analysts to help prepare and to assess the many project proposals put forward by its creative and highly motivated technical staff.

The Advanced Synthesizer is a project being prepared for proposal to the board. This electronic product is designed to translate a human voice into the sampled sounds of musical instruments and back again at will, thus creating exciting effects with special appeal in the music business.

A four-person project team prepared an initial project proposal. The technical originator, the production engineer, and the product manager specified the technical characteristics of the product. The production engineer defined the processes and capital equipment required to produce it. The management accountant costed the required facilities and equipment and

Table 5.1 Preliminary net incremental after-tax cash flow analysis of the Advanced Synthesizer product.

				Year ending			
		0	1	2	3	4	5
	With						
1	Investment	−1,000					200
2	Contribution (advanced product)		2,000	2,400	2,640	2,400	2,000
3	Fixed operating expenditure		−50	−50	−50	−50	−50
4	Marketing expenditure		−1,000	−1,200	−1,320	−1,200	−1,000
5	Contribution (existing products)		1,600	1,600	1,600	1,600	1,600
6	Taxes		−810	−870	−906	−870	−810
7	*Total with*	−1,000	1,740	1,880	1,964	1,880	1,940
	Without						
8	Factory space	200					
9	Contribution (existing products)		2,000	2,000	2,000	2,000	2,000
10	Taxes		−600	−600	−600	−600	−600
11	*Total without*	200	1,400	1,400	1,400	1,400	1,400
12	*Net incremental*	−1,200	340	480	564	480	540
13	PV @ 20%	−1,200.00	283.33	333.33	326.39	231.48	217.01
14	NPV	191.55					
15	IRR	26.6%					
16	Comulative cash flow	−1,200	−860	−380	184		
17	Payback					2.7 years	

estimated the fixed and variable costs of production. The synthesizer product manager defined the market and, together with the management accountant, considered feasible prices and resulting sales volumes in the intended markets.

A financial analyst joined the team to help them prepare a formal proposal for consideration by the board. Her first task was to translate the data produced by the team into a net incremental after-tax cash flow forecast. Using this, she had to ascertain whether the project could add value for shareholders and satisfy several other financial and strategic criteria. For example, at DIGITAL DYNAMICS formal proposals must include estimates of the project's NPV, IRR, ARR, and the payback period.

She was well aware that defining the project's net incremental after-tax cash flow correctly was essential and could require several drafts. Table 5.1 shows a simplified version of her preliminary net incremental cash flow forecast. We explain and analyze the table below.

Table 5.1 divides into three sections. The uppermost section shows the relevant after-tax cash flows for the company assuming that the project goes forward—the *with* project scenario. The middle section of the table shows the relevant expected after-tax cash flows for the company if the project does not go forward—the *without* project scenario. The bottom section gives the resulting *net* incremental cash flow—*net*, which is merely the difference between the cash flows in the first two sections of the table.

The upper section of the table contains the relevant cash flows for the *with* project scenario:

Row 1   shows the estimated investment expenditure of €1 million. This includes the costs of capital equipment and investment in net working capital, that is, cash, inventories, and debtors minus creditors. This initial investment is immediate and therefore appears in the Year 0 column. In the Year 5 column, the expected release of cash from working capital and the residual value of equipment when the project ends totals €200,000.

Row 2   shows the expected cash flow contributions from the new product, representing sales revenues net of direct (variable) manufacturing expenditure. These begin in the Year 1 column representing the first year of operations.

Row 3   contains the fixed annual operating expenditures (excluding depreciation, which is not a cash expenditure).

Row 4   contains the substantial expected annual marketing expenditure required to promote this innovative product and to combat competition.

Row 5   shows the total contribution from existing synthesizer products that would be affected by some customers buying the new product instead of the existing ones. This compares with the greater level of contributions in Row 9 if the project does not go ahead.

Row 6   contains the analyst's preliminary estimate of taxes related to the transactions generating the cash flows in this section of the table.

Row 7   is just the column totals for the *with* project scenario in the upper section of the table. From these will be subtracted the corresponding totals for the *without* project scenario in Row 11.

The middle section of the table contains the relevant cash flows for the *without* project scenario:

Row 8   in the Year 0 column shows the €200,000 PV of the space not available for other products if used for production of the Advanced Synthesizer instead.

Row 9   contains the contributions from the existing synthesizer products at the higher level that would continue if the proposed new product were not going to draw customers away from them.

Row 10   shows the analyst's estimate of the taxes associated with the contributions in Row 9.

Row 11   is just the column totals for the *without* project scenario in the lower section of the table.

Row 12   contains the net incremental after-cash flow for the project obtained by subtracting Row 11 from Row 7.

Because net incremental cash flow measures the difference that the project makes to the company's after-tax cash flow, it provides the basis for assessing the net value the project adds for shareholders. Therefore, the next task for the financial analyst was to estimate this net value for shareholders by using the discounted cash flow method.

Row 13   gives the PVs of the net incremental cash flows in Row 12, discounted at 20%.

Row 14   shows the resulting NPV for the Advanced Synthesizer project, obtained by summing all the values in Row 13.

Row 15   shows the project's IRR.

Row 16   cumulates the net incremental cash flow to the end of Year 3 for calculating the payback period given in Row 17.

The analyst was pleased to see that the resulting NPV of €191,550 was positive. This implied that the expected return on the project was attractive. The expected IRR was greater than the 20% that the Finance Director considered obtainable in the financial market on investment in securities of equivalent risk. So, the project appeared to be worthy of further analysis based on these preliminary results.

DIGITAL DYNAMICS' board usually considered only those projects that promise NPVs greater than zero. The exceptions were when a project created sufficiently valuable indirect benefits that were not in the net incremental cash flow analysis. These included strategic considerations, such as the potential to change the project during its life. Another was the possibility that the existence of the product in the marketplace might generate subsequent future investment opportunities with positive NPVs.

DEFINITION

Incremental cash flow   Difference between the relevant expected after-tax cash flows of the firm if the project goes forward and if it does not go forward.

5-5   NET PRESENT VALUE

The net present value method is the means of estimating the net value that a project adds for shareholders. The principle is that the value of a project is equal to the amount shareholders would have to invest in the securities market to generate the same expected cash flow at the same systematic risk.

In Table 5.1, the figures in Row 13 are the result of multiplying the net incremental cash flows in Row 12 by corresponding PV factors. The NPV in Row 14 is simply the sum of the figures in Row 13. The positive NPV indicates that investment in the project would generate more value for shareholders than comparable investment in securities.

DEFINITION

Net present value method   Method using positive net present value as the selection criterion for capital projects.

5-6   THE RATE OF RETURN ON A PROJECT

Most boards want to know the expected rate of return on the investment in a proposed project. They like to compare a proposed project's expected rate of return with a prespecified minimum required rate of return or hurdle rate.

In principle, the hurdle rate should be high for risky projects and low for safe investments and should compare favorably with expected returns from alternative investment in securities of comparable systematic risk. Many companies do not change hurdle rates very often, however, and thus the rates do not reflect current securities market rates.

The rate of return criterion becomes more appropriate for selecting projects when the funds available for projects are limited. The reason is that the rate of return measures the return per unit of scarce funds invested in the project.

Two popular methods for attempting to estimate the rate of return on a project are the internal rate of return and the accounting rate of return.

INTERNAL RATE OF RETURN

The definition of the internal rate of return (IRR) is the discount rate that makes the NPV equal to zero. Many describe the IRR as the break-even discount rate.[1] It answers the question as to how high the shareholders' required rate of return for the project would have to be to make the project's NPV equal zero.

If the project's NPV is greater than zero, we normally find that its IRR is greater than the discount rate. The next chapter discusses exceptions to this rule.

ACCOUNTING RATE OF RETURN

Many boards also want to see the proposed project's Accounting Rate of Return (ARR). The most useful definition of the ARR is accounting profit after tax divided by the average book value (balance sheet value including net working capital) of the investment during its life:

$$ARR = \frac{Average\ Annual\ Profit\ After\ Tax}{Average\ Annual\ Capital\ Employed}$$

A project's ARR must exceed the board's ARR hurdle rate to be acceptable. While it is true that the value of the ARR depends to some extent on the method of depreciation used, the method's fatal flaw is that it is not an incremental concept. If the ARR does not reflect the impact of the project on the profitability of the firm's other assets, then it can be very misleading indeed.

DEFINITIONS

Accounting Rate of Return (ARR) Rate of return as accounting income divided by the book value of all assets employed to generate the income.

Hurdle rate Minimum acceptable rate of return for proposed capital projects.

---

[1] The IRR is not a proper break-even rate. By definition, a high IRR equates to a high discount rate. A high discount rate reflects either high risk or a high rate of inflation, or both. Unless the risk and the rate of inflation implied by the value of the IRR happen to be equal to the assumptions about risk and inflation in the project's expected cash flow, the value of the IRR cannot equal the break-even rate for the project. See A. A. Alchian (1955) "The rate of interest, Fisher's rate of return over cost and Keynes' internal rate of return," *American Economic Review*, Vol. 45 (December), 938–942.

Internal rate of return   Discount rate making the net present value for an investment equal to zero.

Rate of return   After tax income and capital gain divided by the investment.

5-7   PROJECT LIQUIDITY

Liquidity is a concern of smaller companies that do not have ready access to the financial market. They depend largely on their projects to generate the necessary cash flow to fund further investment. Even large companies usually want to know how quickly a project will repay its initial investment. The definition of a project's payback period is the time required for the project's expected after-tax incremental cash flow to repay the entire initial investment in the project. Therefore, the payback period is a measure of a project's liquidity in the short term. Acceptability requires a project to have a payback that is shorter than the target level set by the board.

Many companies also consider the payback period to be a measure of exposure to risk. For example, innovative companies with new products naturally like to get their money back on a project before competition enters the same market. When there are short-term competitive threats, projects with short payback periods generally are less risky. Short payback periods are also favored for projects in countries with high political risks.

For these various reasons the payback method is the most widely used method in project appraisal, even though most financial managers are aware of the superiority of the NPV method.

The payback method does not directly reflect the time value of money, although some companies discount the cash flows used in calculating payback. The method ignores the often very significant cash flows beyond the payback period. Furthermore, it takes no account of the timing of the cash flows within the payback period. So, payback does not measure liquidity very accurately.

EXAMPLE 5.1 (continued)

As specified in the company's Project Appraisal Manual, DIGITAL DYNAMICS' board wanted to compare four measures of the Advanced Synthesizer's financial viability. The four measures were NPV, ARR, IRR, and the project's payback period.

The members of DIGITAL DYNAMICS' board always wanted to know the expected rate of return on a proposed project. They liked to compare a project's rate of return to a minimum required rate of return or hurdle rate.

The analyst used the two required methods to estimate the rate of return on the Advanced Synthesizer project, the IRR and the ARR.

Because the NPV of the Advanced Synthesizer product appeared to be positive, the analyst expected that the corresponding IRR would be greater than 20%. Using the IRR function in the same spreadsheet that she used to prepare the incremental cash flow figures, she found the value of the IRR for the project to be 26.6%. As it was likely that the hurdle rate would be 20%, this IRR was satisfactory though not exceptional.

Table 5.2 Preliminary estimate of the ARR for the Advanced Synthesizer product.

	Year ending				
	1	2	3	4	5
Contribution	2,000	2,400	2,640	2,400	2,000
Fixed operating cost including depreciation	−200	−200	−200	−200	−200
Marketing expenditure	−1,000	−1,200	−1,320	−1,200	−1,000
Taxes	−240	−300	−336	−300	−240
Profit after tax	560	700	784	700	560
Capital employed	1,000	840	680	520	360
Average profit after tax	660.8				
Average capital employed	680				
ARR =	97.2%				

The board also wanted to see the proposed project's ARR. The company's Project Appraisal Manual defined the ARR as the project's average annual accounting profit after tax divided by the average book value (balance sheet value including net working capital) of the investment during its life.

The analyst was well aware, however, that this method did not take into account the negative effects of the new product on the cash flows of the existing products. Accordingly, she knew that the calculated 97.2% ARR (Table 5.2) on the project would be misleading. It needed explanation and comparison with the IRR of only 26.6%.

Finding the payback period required cumulating the incremental cash flows in Row 12 of Table 5.1 from left to right until the cumulative cash flow turns positive. The cumulative cash flow turns positive during Year 3. By interpolation, the estimated payback period was 2.7 years. As the board was looking for a minimum payback of three years, the estimated payback period for the Advanced Synthesizer would be satisfactory.

In summary, the values of the four criteria were:

$$NPV \text{ (at 20\%)} = €22,260$$

$$IRR = 27.2\%$$

$$ARR = 97.2\%$$

$$Payback = 2.7 \text{ years}$$

The project appeared to be reasonably attractive on all four measures assuming a hurdle rate of 20%. The payback period of less than three years was a desirable feature because the company was cash-constrained, and the rate of product obsolescence was high in this industry.

It was obvious to the analyst that the profitability of the project would be particularly sensitive to the large marketing expenditure included in the net incremental cash flow analysis in Table 5.1. This item in particular would require careful further examination before she could complete the formal project proposal for the Advanced Synthesizer. She was also concerned that the cash flows needed adjustment for inflation.[2]

DEFINITION

Payback period   Time required for the project's expected after-tax incremental cash flow to repay the entire initial investment in the project.

5-8   SOME RELATED ISSUES

Three related issues that often require consideration are the precise timing of cash flows, mutually exclusive projects, and capital rationing.

THE PRECISE TIMING OF CASH FLOWS

Precision regarding the timing of cash flows can make the difference between a calculated positive or negative NPV for a project.

There are two ways of treating the timing of cash flows more accurately. One way is to use monthly or weekly cash flows and discount rates. A less cumbersome method for the discount rates would be to use *annual* discount rates as usual but to define time in terms of decimal *fractions* of a year.

If the expected cash flow spreads evenly throughout the year, we can approximate this with the assumption that the entire annual cash flow occurs at the middle of the year. For example, if we want to discount a cash flow at 20% from the middle of Year 2, we would multiply it by the discount factor:

$$1/1.20^{1.5} = 0.760\,73$$

For comparison, the *end* of Year 2 factor used in Table 5.1 was:

$$1/1.20^2 = 0.694\,44$$

which is nearly 9% smaller. Clearly, year-end discounting of the positive cash flows can be quite conservative, thus negatively biasing the NPV. This bias becomes particularly significant when the discount rate is large due to risk or inflation.

When the expected cash flows are seasonal, mid-year discounting might not be sufficiently accurate. For example, a Christmas seasonal effect might suggest treating the cash flows as though they occur at a chosen point in the latter half of the year but before the year-end.

Banks use the exact dates of contractual payments to evaluate deals with corporate customers.

---

[2] In many economies, inflation is still a significant issue for project appraisals. Chapter 6 deals with inflation along with some other troublesome issues.

MUTUALLY EXCLUSIVE PROJECTS

Mutually exclusive projects usually represent either alternative means of achieving the same objective, or two different ways of using the same asset. The choice of one of a pair of projects implies rejection of the other if the projects are mutually exclusive. The NPV rule makes the choice easy: just select the project with the larger NPV.

Unfortunately, one cannot just compare the IRRs of two mutually exclusive projects in this way. The reason is that the projects might require different levels of investment, and their different cash flow profiles can bias the IRR values differently. Nevertheless, the IRR procedure usually can help choose between alternative projects by using the right procedure.

The right procedure is to treat the smaller of the two projects as the **opportunity cost** of investing in the larger one:

1.   Subtract the cash flows of the smaller project from the cash flows of the larger project.

2.   Calculate the IRR for the resulting difference, thus obtaining the IRR on the *extra* investment required by the larger project.

If the IRR on the extra investment is less than the hurdle rate, then the company could do better. It could invest in the smaller project and use the funds left over to invest in comparable securities or in other more attractive projects.[3]

CAPITAL RATIONING

Capital rationing occurs when a company does not expect to have sufficient funds to take advantage of all its investment opportunities. The required funds normally come from reinvested earnings, supplemented by a proportion of additional borrowing. When the company is growing rapidly or earnings are insufficient, these sources can be inadequate. Then the company would need to turn to the financial market for funds. Issuing securities can be expensive, however, especially for smaller companies, and it is out of the question for the smallest. Therefore, capital rationing can be a reality for very many companies.

Constrained by capital rationing, a company must set priorities and choose the projects that make the best use of the limited funds available. The objective is to maximize value per unit of scarce funds. A natural way to choose projects subject to capital rationing is to rank them in the descending order of their **Profitability Index (PI)** values:

$$Profitability\ Index = Present\ Value/Investment$$

$$PI = \frac{PV}{I}$$

in which we let *I* represent the required investment during the capital-rationed period. So, the projects with higher *PI* make better use of the available capital, creating value for the shareholders.

---

[3] Although this is the right procedure, it is not foolproof. If the net of the two cash flows changes sign more than once, it can have more than one value for the IRR. In this case, the better procedure is simply to compare project NPVs.

The choice becomes more complex when we consider several capital-rationed years at once because we must then take account of the degree to which earlier projects can generate funds for investment in later ones. Large companies that need to plan investments more than one year at a time and have scores of projects to select often use mathematical programming methodology. These operational research techniques aid in selecting the combination of competing projects that make the best use of the available capital. Mathematical programming is too large a topic for us to cover adequately in this chapter.

DEFINITIONS

Capital rationing   Insufficient funds for investment in all acceptable capital projects.

Mutually exclusive projects   The choice of one of a pair of mutually exclusive projects implies rejection of the other.

Opportunity cost of capital   Rate of return forgone when investing in a project instead of the securities market.

Profitability index (PI)   Present value of a project divided by the required investment.

5-9   ABOUT TAXES

Corporate taxes have a major impact on cash flow. Attempting to appraise capital projects without looking at the tax implications is misleading if not fruitless. Capital projects require evaluation in terms of their after-tax incremental cash flows. The details of tax assessment differ between countries but certain principles apply to most of them.

Corporate taxes are on taxable income, which resembles profit but with important differences. The Government specifies the type of fiscal depreciation for each category of asset used in the calculation of taxable income. The Government will also specify whether the company can choose between first-in-first-out (FIFO) and last-in-first-out (LIFO) in the calculation of cost of goods sold. During periods of inflation, companies could reduce corporate taxes by using LIFO to calculate the cost of goods sold. When prices are falling, however, FIFO saves taxes. The required tax cash flow is simply the taxable income for the year multiplied by the company's corporate tax rate.

The tax payment cash flow does not necessarily occur in the same year in which the tax liability is accrued. Most countries permit carrying losses forward to net against future profits. This delays the effect of the tax on the cash flow until the company is again in a tax-paying position. Of course, such delays in tax payment are valuable because they reduce the PV of the taxes.

5-10   MEASURING PROJECT RISK AND DETERMINING THE DISCOUNT RATE

The value of the discount rate is set quite arbitrarily in many companies, usually at board level. Wrong discount rates can lead to wrong investment decisions.

RISK CLASS

A better approach is to group projects into several risk classes and to set a different discount rate or hurdle rate for each class. The rate for each class is set equal to the required rate of return for the average risk of the projects in the risk class. The Securities Market Line (SML) provides the benchmark-required rate of return for each risk class. So, risk measurement is central to determining discount rates.

SENSITIVITY ANALYSIS

Projects are subject both to inherent risk and risk due to estimation error. Inherent risk is the risk of the project attributable to such factors as unexpected changes in product markets and the economy. Risk also arises from estimation error, however. Under uncertainty, managers cannot accurately forecast either the expected cash flows or their standard deviations. Sensitivity analysis is quite widely used by companies to explore the effects of such risks on large capital projects. The analyst changes one variable at a time (for example, price, volume, direct costs, etc.) to ascertain where the project's NPV is most vulnerable. The analyst must judge how much to change each variable. In principle, the degree of change should reflect the analyst's view of the combined effect of both inherent risk and estimation error on its variance. In practice, such judgments are largely subjective and involve their own estimation error. The strength of this approach is that it enables consideration of specific ways to alter the project to reduce its risk, but it does not provide a basis for determining the discount rate.

SCENARIO ANALYSIS

Scenario analysis is a more refined method that changes the different variables simultaneously to reflect alternative assumptions about future economic and business conditions. Whereas sensitivity analysis highlights risks that are unique to the company and the project, scenario analysis focuses on systematic macroeconomic risks that also affect shareholders' diversified portfolios. Used properly, scenario analysis can help to estimate the systematic risk that determines discount rates for projects.

SECURITIES MARKET LINE

The SML determines the appropriate discount rate for a project or for its risk class. As discussed in Chapter 2, it is necessary to determine the project's risk premium in the following formula describing the SML:

$$Discount\ Rate = Risk\text{-}free\ Rate + Risk\ Premium$$

For example, suppose the currently expected risk premium on the market index is 6%. The systematic risk of the market index by definition is average (beta = 1.00). If the systematic risk of the project in question is twice the average (beta = 2.00), then its risk premium would be $2.00 \times 6 = 12\%$.

Therefore, if the risk-free rate is expected to be 5% during the life of the project, then the discount rate for the project would be:

$$Discount\ Rate = 5 + 2.00 \times 6 = 17\%$$

Chapter 13 shows how to obtain the shareholders' required rates of return for projects in different risk classes.

DEFINITIONS

Risk class   Class of capital projects having insignificantly different systematic risk.

Scenario   Plausible sequence of future events.

Securities Market Line (SML)   Hypothesized linear relationship in the Capital Asset Pricing Model between the expected return on a security and its systematic risk.

Sensitivity analysis   Testing the effect of changes to individual variables on a project's net present value.

5-11 REAL OPTIONS

Real options are features of a project that provide flexibility. Contemporary corporate project appraisal procedures frequently do not include a formal valuation of real options. This can be a serious oversight because real options can affect significantly a project's NPV. Examples of real options are the choice of a project's capacity, the potential to abandon or sell a project, to change its use or to extend its life. Strategically minded managers attempt to incorporate in a project all the flexibility that they think would have positive NPV. Unfortunately, it is not possible to measure the value of options using conventional discounted cash flow methodology. Accordingly, it is difficult for them to know how much they can spend on desirable real options in a project. In Chapters 8 and 9, we show how to value some of the real options commonly found in projects.

DEFINITION

Real option   Right to make favorable future choices regarding real asset investments. More precisely, a real option is an opportunity for voluntary future investment in a nonfinancial asset when at least a part of the required investment expenditure is certain or, alternatively, when at least a part of the required investment expenditure is not perfectly positively correlated with the project's present value.

5-12 CONCLUSIONS

Ultimately, strategic decisions require investment in capital projects. A principal financial objective of strategy is to exploit competitive advantage in order to maximize the value of the firm to its investors. Therefore, we try to invest in projects that create net value, that is, the projects expected to be worth more to the company than they actually cost.

The concept of expected incremental cash flow is crucial. It is the difference (hence, incremental) between the relevant expected after-tax cash flows associated with two mutually exclusive scenarios: (1) the project goes ahead, (2) the project does not go ahead.

The objective of the NPV method is to put a value on a project's net incremental cash flow. The principle is that the value shareholders would attach to an expected cash flow from a project is equal to the amount that they would have to invest in equivalent financial securities. The equivalent securities generate the same expected cash flow at the same systematic risk. So, the method is to discount a project's net incremental cash flows at the market rate for an equivalent investment in securities.

A related method is to select projects by comparing their IRR to a hurdle rate. A project's IRR is the discount rate that would make the project's NPV equal to zero. The hurdle rate often is set somewhat higher than the shareholders' required rate of return in quite an arbitrary way. Arbitrary hurdle rates usually fail to allow for differences in project risk or for changes in the rate of inflation.

Correct application of discounted cash flow requires financial education. A simpler procedure is the payback method. A project's payback period is the length of time it takes for the project's after-tax incremental cash flows to repay the entire initial investment. In this way, the payback period is a rough measure of a project's liquidity.

Many companies also consider the project's ARR. The ARR is the project's average annual accounting profit after tax divided by the average book value (balance sheet value including net working capital) of the investment in the project during its life. Acceptability to the board requires that a project's ARR exceeds the board's hurdle rate for the ARR. The ARR can be sensitive to the depreciation method used and fails to reflect the time value of money. More seriously, the ARR does not reflect the opportunity costs of investing in the project.

Surveys have revealed that large companies tend to use up to three methods in conjunction. In order of frequency of use, these would be payback, IRR (or ARR), and NPV. The use of NPV is growing but probably has not quite overtaken IRR as the foremost criterion in large companies. Payback tends to be the primary if not the only criterion in small companies but usually plays a more subsidiary role in large companies.

Boards looking to create value for shareholders tend to favor the NPV approach because NPV represents estimated value for shareholders. A calculated NPV that merely reflects an optimistic cash flow forecast is meaningless, however. Identifying the competitive advantages exploited by a project is essential. Project sponsors need to explain in each case how the company's relative strengths can justify the assumed price, volume or cost advantages that generate the calculated positive NPV.

DEFINITIONS

Discounted cash flow (DCF)   Method of determining the present value of a cash flow expected to be received on a specific future date.

Net incremental cash flow   Difference between a company's expected after-tax cash flows with or without a proposed investment.

Security   Bond or a share certifying legal ownership of a financial asset or a claim on the assets or cash flow of a company. Also denotes collateral for a loan.

Systematic risk   Risk that portfolio diversification cannot eliminate.

Time value of money   Rate of return obtainable from comparable alternative investment in the financial market.

FURTHER READING

H. Bierman and S. Smidt (1992) *The Capital Budgeting Decision*, 8th edn (New York: Macmillan).

QUESTIONS AND PROBLEMS

1   The expected after-tax cost of an advertizing campaign is €1 million per month for the coming year. The advertizing will enable the company to maintain sales and the resulting cash flow at the current level. Without the campaign, the expected sales are lower, resulting in €1.5 million less cash after-tax for the company. Advertizing has a delayed impact on sales and cash flow. The delay is approximately one month.

   (a)   Show the monthly net incremental cash flow associated with the advertizing campaign.
   (b)   Calculate the PV of this advertizing project at 1% per month.
   (c)   Calculate its NPV.
   (d)   What is the rate of return on the advertizing?

2   Spacemonitor plc is building a factory on a site that it already owns. The total investment in the factory (excluding the site) will be €10 million. Management expects the factory to generate new net cash flows worth €3 million per year after tax for five years. The factory's expected residual value at the end of its life is €8 million. The company bought the site 10 years earlier for the equivalent of only €1 million. Selling the site today would realize about €2 million, and the expectation is that selling it would realize €2 million at the end of the factory's life.

   (a)   What is the incremental investment cash flow for this project?
   (b)   What is the net incremental cash flow for the factory in the last year of its life?

3   Spacemonitor plc is considering investing in a machine costing €2 million for its new factory. One million euros per year of the factory's after-tax incremental cash flow would be attributable to the capacity provided by this one machine in each of the five years of operation. The accountants will depreciate the machine at 10% per year straight line, and the expected residual value of the machine at the end of Year 5 is €1 million.

   (a)   What is the ARR on the investment in the machine?
   (b)   What is the value of its IRR?
   (c)   Explain the difference between these two calculated rates of return.

4   What is the value of the payback period for Spacemonitor's new machine in Problem 3?

5   The table below provides the expected after-tax net incremental cash flow for one of the machines to be installed in Spacemonitor's new factory:

End of year						
0	1	2	3	4	5	6
0	−400	130	130	130	130	130

The company's financial analyst was unhappy with the company's conventional procedure of treating all cash flows as though they occur at the end of each year. Completing the factory would take approximately one year, and investment in machinery will not take place until completion. So, operations cannot start until the beginning of the second year. He was also aware that cash income spreads quite evenly over each year of operation and certainly not concentrated at the end of each year. He felt it would be a better approximation to treat the cash income as though it occurred at the middle of each year.

(a)   What is the NPV of the machine based on end-of-year discounting?
(b)   What is the NPV of the machine based on mid-year discounting?
(c)   What is the financial reason for the difference between your results in (a) and (b)?

6   Spacemonitor's analyst is helping the company's chief industrial engineer to choose between two machines for the new factory. The machines are capable of much the same functions, but they have very different expected cash flows. The table below gives the expected net incremental after-tax cash flows for both machines. (The table assumes that operations begin in Year 2 after completion of the factory.)

	End of year							
Project	0	1	2	3	4	5	6	IRR
Machine A	0	−400	130	130	130	130	130	18.7%
Machine B	0	−200	70	70	70	70	70	22.1%

(a)   Show how to use the IRR method to choose between the two machines if the hurdle rate is 10%.
(b)   Show how to use the NPV rule to choose between the two machines if the discount rate is 10%.
(c)   Discuss the relative advantages or disadvantages of the two methods for this purpose. For simplicity, use end-of-year discounting.

7   Toward the end of the first year, Spacemonitor's factory construction costs were higher than expected. The company had already used external financing and the company's Treasurer felt he could not approach the banks or the financial market again for the next two years. These factors limited the remaining budget for machinery and equipment. The chief engineer called upon the financial analyst again to help him choose machines that made the best use of the limited funds available. The financial analyst decided to rank the less essential machines in the descending order of their PI values. This would help to make choices that would maximize the PV per unit of investment in the machinery. Given below are data for two of the machines.

Machine	A	B
PV	120	300
NPV	20	30
Initial investment	100	270

(a)   What is the PI for each machine?

(b)   Which machine would generate the most value for shareholders?

(c)   Could we not simply choose the machine with the largest NPV?

8   Given below are expected annual data (€1,000s) for a project. The company pays taxes at 30%.

Sales	1,000	Selling, general and administrative expenses	200
Raw materials	250	Fiscal depreciation	100
Labor	200		

(a)   What is the annual after-tax cost of labor for the project?

(b)   What is the project's expected annual taxable income?

(c)   What are the expected incremental taxes if the project goes ahead?

(d)   What is the project's expected annual after-tax cash flow?

(e)   The project's expected life is five years, and its expected residual value is zero (the asset will be valueless at the end of its life). Use the appropriate formula to determine the PV of these equal annual cash flows if the discount rate is 10%.

9   The company's treasury staff estimated that the beta factor for the average asset in the company was equal to 0.7. The expected risk-free rate for the following five years was 5%. The expected risk premium in the securities market for the same period was 6% for the same period.

(a)   The expected systematic risk for a proposed project was 50% greater than for the average asset in the company. What discount rate would be appropriate for calculating the project's NPV?

(b)   Let F be a factor representing the ratio of a project's systematic risk to the average systematic risk of a company's assets. Write an equation for project discount rates in terms of the risk-free rate, of F, of the company's average asset beta and of the securities market risk premium.

10   A project has an expected life of five years. Its NPV is €1 million. The chief industrial engineer says that spending a little more on the project now would create the option to overhaul the project five years from now and extend its life for five more years. Taking into account the expected cost of the overhaul, the project's NPV for the 10 years would increase by €1.5 million. The probability that the extra life will be needed is only 0.20, however. What is the most that management can justify spending now to create the option to overhaul the project?

6 Pitfalls in Project Appraisal

Correctly appraising capital projects requires knowledge, practice, and acute awareness of potentially serious pitfalls. In this chapter, we outline many of the common errors in project appraisal and suggest ways of avoiding them. The object is to have at one's fingertips all the methodology necessary for correct capital investment decisions.

TOPICS

We shall consider project appraisal pitfalls in the following areas:

- *specifying a project's incremental cash flow requires care;*
- *the internal rate of return is biased;*
- *the payback period is often ambiguous;*
- *discount rates frequently are wrong;*
- *rising rates of inflation are dangerous;*
- *the precise timing of cash flows is important;*
- *forecasting is often untruthful;*
- *risk adds value to real options;*
- *real options affect the net present value rule.*

6-1 SPECIFYING A PROJECT'S INCREMENTAL CASH FLOW REQUIRES CARE

Making unbiased forecasts of project cash flows is obviously difficult, but actually specifying *which* cash flows to include in the analysis presents greater pitfalls for the inexperienced financial analyst.

INCREMENTAL CASH FLOW

The correct definition of **incremental cash flow** is crucial. It is the *difference* between the relevant expected after-tax cash flows associated with two mutually exclusive **scenarios**: (1) the project goes ahead, and (2) the project does not go ahead.

COMPARING SCENARIOS

More specifically, the scenarios we compare are:

1.   Scenario 1: *with* the project. In this scenario we identify the expected values of the relevant cash flows assuming that the project goes ahead, for example:

> Revenues or cost savings reflecting expected prices, volumes, and technology
> New levels of existing cash flows changed by the project

Less:

> Direct labor and materials
> Incremental fixed expenditure
> Incremental overheads
> Investment in capital assets including legal, transport and other acquisition costs
> Investment in working capital
> Related tax effects.

Proceeds from the sale of an existing asset do *not* reduce investment in a particular project; it merely helps to finance the investment. Residual values of earlier investments must not be double-counted in this way.

The cash flow must reflect not only the expected changes of prices and costs due to inflation but also the expected additional investments in working capital necessary to keep abreast of inflation.[1] The tax effect of stock appreciation must also be included when the Government requires use of first-in-first-out (FIFO) accounting in the calculation of taxable income.

2.   Scenario 2: *without* the project. In this scenario, we identify which of the company's expected levels of assets or cash flows that would be changed or preempted by the project. For example, levels of working capital that will not be the same under Scenario 1. Other examples are revenues that would be increased by a proposed marketing project, or existing sales that would be cannibalized by a proposed new product. Identify also the market values of the company's land, buildings, or other assets needed by the project. Expected taxes or tax benefits that the project would change also are relevant.

The most common pitfall is to omit items in the second scenario when subtracting their values from those in the first scenario to obtain the net incremental cash flow.

RELEVANCE OF OVERHEADS

Many textbooks assert that an accounting allocation of general overheads is not an incremental cash flow to the project and therefore should not be included. This narrow, short-term definition of cash flow is bad economics. Finance directors are unwilling to let the company transform itself into a set of projects that collectively could not cover the company's general overheads.

With the possible exception of some cost-saving projects, each new project eventually will have its

---

[1] This applies to working capital other than inventory. The increase in costs of goods sold due to inflation already accounts for the additional cash required for inventory and must not be double-counted.

effect on overheads. Even if excess overhead leaves room for growth, we still need to forecast when growth will increase overhead expenditure. The part of the additional overhead expenditure attributable to the project becomes an incremental after-tax cash flow of the project.

While the incremental effect of an individual project on overheads usually cannot be determined precisely, the eventual incremental overhead cost rarely is zero. A reasoned overhead allocation is less biased than a zero allocation.

EXPECTED VERSUS MOST LIKELY CASH FLOWS

Financial economists intend that project appraisal methodology should value expected incremental after-tax cash flows. The expected cash flow is the probability-weighted average of the different possible cash flow outcomes. That is, an expected cash flow is the mean of the probability distribution of all its possible values. Most managers, however, forecast what they perceive to be the *most likely* cash flows, or the mode of the distribution. For symmetrically distributed cash flows, the mean and the mode are equal, and the distinction makes no difference. Unfortunately, the distribution is rarely symmetrical.

LIMITED CAPACITY

For example, the most likely scenario usually involves operating at or near a project's capacity. Without additional capacity, actual volume cannot go up, but it can go down. So, on balance, the expected cash flow is less than the most likely one. Consequently, the most likely cash flow forecast gives an overly optimistic result.

A difference also arises if there are no capacity restrictions. The most likely scenario is too conservative in this case because volume could be very much better. If it should turn out to be worse, management can try to cut costs, or even abandon the project.

DEFINITIONS

Incremental cash flow   Difference between the relevant expected after-tax cash flows of the firm if the project goes forward and if it does not go forward.

Scenario   Plausible sequence of events.

Expected rate of return (mean)   Probability-weighted average of all possible outcomes for a random variable.

Mode   The most probable outcome for a random variable.

6-2   THE INTERNAL RATE OF RETURN IS BIASED

Here is a nice examination question: "The internal rate of return was a brain child of J. M. Keynes that might better have been stillborn." Comment on this.

PROBLEM OF DEFINITION

This assertion contains an element of truth. The reason is matter of definition: An internal rate of return (IRR) for an investment is a discount rate that makes its net present value (NPV) equal to zero. The IRR does not therefore measure directly the rate of return for an investment. As a result, the IRR is an unbiased measure of a project's rate of return only in a very limited set of circumstances and often is misleading. In extreme cases, a project can have more than one IRR. In such cases, the IRR becomes useless as a measure of a project's rate of return. We can demonstrate these points with three simple examples.

EXAMPLE 6.1

As our base case, consider the following cash flow:

		Year ending			
0	1	2	3	4	5
−100	20	20	20	20	120

This cash flow profile makes a suitable base case because it resembles the cash flow on a bond priced at its face value. That is, it costs €100, pays an annual annuity of €20 for the five-year life of the investment plus an additional €100 in the final year repaying the original investment. Clearly, this project earns 20% annually on its investment of €100. In this instance, the IRR gives the correct result, 20%, as illustrated in Figure 6.1.

In Figure 6.1, the vertical axis gives the project's NPV for each of the discount rates shown on the horizontal axis. The project's NPV at 10% equals €37.91 as illustrated in the figure. The curve falls to 0 at the 20% discount rate on the horizontal axis. Therefore, the IRR equals 20%.

The IRR gives an accurate estimate of the rate of return for this particular project because it has a bond-like cash flow profile. Unfortunately, very few capital projects have this profile.

EXAMPLE 6.2

Given below is the cash flow for the second example. In this example, the initial investment of €100 yields an annuity of €33.44 per year for five years. Unlike the previous example, there is no capital repayment at the end. The annuity has to repay the initial investment as well as provide a return.

		Year ending			
0	1	2	3	4	5
−100	33.44	33.44	33.44	33.44	33.44

In Figure 6.2, the vertical axis gives the project's NPV for each of the discount rates shown on the

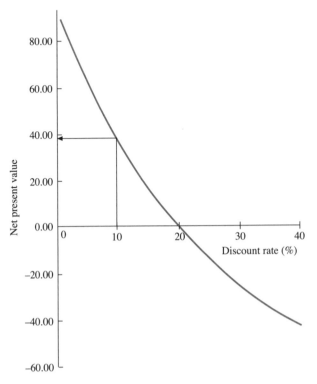

Figure 6.1 NPV versus discount rate for bond-like cash flow profile.

horizontal axis. The curve falls to 0 at the 20% discount rate on the horizontal axis, as in the previous example. Therefore, the IRR equals 20%.

Because this project does not have a bond-like cash flow profile, however, we cannot be certain that the IRR is a correct estimate of the actual rate of return on the project. We cannot conclude, for example, that this project is as attractive as the one in the previous example just because it also has a 20% IRR. Indeed, the NPV at 10% for this project is only €26.76 compared with €37.91 for the previous project. This tells us that the actual rate of return for this second project must be less than 20%.

EXAMPLE 6.3

Given below is the cash flow for the third example. In this case, the initial investment of €100 yields a four-year annuity of €85.22 followed by a large negative cash flow of €300 in the fifth year.

<table>
<tr><th colspan="6">Year ending</th></tr>
<tr><th>0</th><th>1</th><th>2</th><th>3</th><th>4</th><th>5</th></tr>
<tr><td>−100</td><td>85.22</td><td>85.22</td><td>85.22</td><td>85.22</td><td>−300.00</td></tr>
</table>

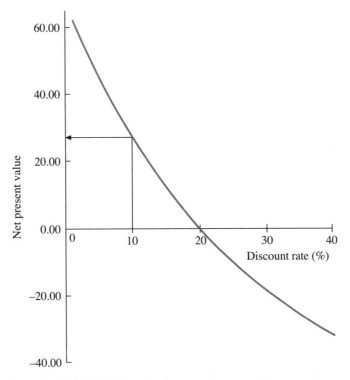

Figure 6.2   NPV versus discount rate for annuity cash flow profile.

In Figure 6.3, the vertical axis gives the project's NPV for each of the discount rates shown on the horizontal axis. The figure reveals that the curve cuts the horizontal axis at two discount rates, 19.94% and 44.42%.

Therefore, the project has two IRRs, and we now have no reliable indication of what the actual rate of return on the project might be. The NPV can give us a clue, however. As illustrated in Figure 6.3, the NPV at the 10% discount rate is −€16.14. The fact that the NPV is negative implies that the project's actual rate of return must be less than the 10% discount rate.

Projects such as marginal North Sea oil platforms that involve repairing environmental damage can have a cash flow looking like this, with a large expenditure at the final stage.

In principle, a project can have as many different values for the IRR as there are changes in sign for the cash flow sequence. There can be fewer IRRs than this, however. The number of IRRs depends on how often the NPV curve actually crosses the horizontal axis.[2]

OVERVIEW

The small table overleaf summarizes the results of our three examples.

---

[2] J. Hirschleifer (1969) *Investment, Interest and Capital* (Englewood Cliffs, NJ: Prentice Hall).

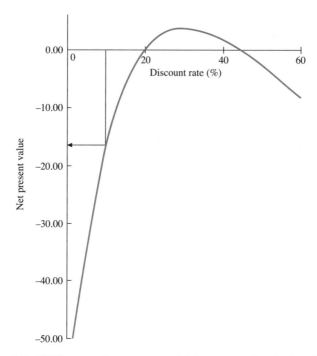

Figure 6.3 NPV versus discount rate with large, negative final cash flow.

Project	IRR (%)	NPV	Payback
1	20	37.9	5
2	20	26.8	3
3	19.9, 44.4	−16.4	1.2

The results in the table span a wide range of cash flow profiles with different paybacks and suggest the following generalizations:

1.   The IRRs of projects with different cash flow profiles are not comparable. Even projects with equal IRRs can have different NPVs when they have different payback periods.

2.   Relying on just one investment criterion can be dangerous.

FALLACIOUS DISCOUNT RATES

The reason for these results is the fallacious use of the discount rate in the IRR calculation. The calculation uses the IRR itself as the discount rate. In principle, a project's required rate of return depends upon the project's risk. Use of different discount rates than this results in biased IRRs. Unless a project's cash inflows have a bond-like profile, its IRR almost certainly does not reflect very accurately its actual rate of return.[3] So beware.

---

[3] Trivially, the IRR also gives the correct rate of return for a project when its IRR happens to equal its required rate of return.

What is the alternative? The NPV gives the most direct measure of net value for shareholders. Nevertheless, the boards of large companies usually also want to know the IRRs of proposed projects.[4] They must also consider other investment criteria if they wish to avoid the IRR pitfall.

DEFINITIONS

Annuity   Investment generating equal cash flows each period for a specified number of periods.

Discount rate   Required rate of return used in the calculation of a discount factor.

Internal rate of return (IRR)   Discount rate that would make the net present value for an investment equal to zero.

Net present value (NPV)   Difference between the present value of a project's expected after-tax operating cash flows and the present value of its expected after-tax investment expenditures.

Payback period   Time required for the project's expected after-tax incremental cash flow to repay the entire initial investment in the project.

Rate of return   After-tax cash income and capital gain divided by the investment.

Return   After-tax cash income and capital gain, if any.

6-3   THE PAYBACK PERIOD IS OFTEN AMBIGUOUS

LIQUIDITY

Liquidity is the ease with which cash is recoverable from an investment. The payback period measures the time required for a project's cash inflows to match its initial investment. So, payback represents an attempt by companies to measure the liquidity of proposed projects.

The use of the payback period is almost universal. Therefore, project liquidity appears to be a very important consideration for companies. Liquidity would be important because the majority of companies are relatively small and do not have ready access to the financial markets for funds. External financing is always more costly than internally generated funds, even for large companies. Accordingly, it suits many companies to operate as though they suffer from capital rationing.

PAYBACK DOES NOT MEASURE A PROJECT'S LIQUIDITY ACCURATELY

Recall that a project's payback period is the expected length of time taken for the project's after-tax incremental cash flows to repay the entire initial investment. Projects that are acceptable on this criterion must have paybacks that are shorter than a target level set by the board.

Payback's simplistic definition leaves room for ambiguity. Payback does not directly reflect the time value of money, although some companies discount the cash flows used in calculating payback. The

---

[4] The next chapter gives an alternative method of calculating the rate of return on a project.

standard definition of payback is unsuitable for projects requiring investment over a period of years. It ignores the often very significant cash flows expected beyond the immediate payback period. The method takes no account of the timing of the cash flows within the payback period. These deficiencies imply that the payback period is likely to be an inaccurate indicator of liquidity and potentially misleading.[5]

Nevertheless, for projects with conventional cash flow profiles, the payback method proves in practice to be a useful liquidity indicator.

DEFINITIONS

Capital rationing　Insufficient funds for investment in all acceptable capital projects.

Liquidity　Ease with which cash is recoverable from an investment.

Payback period　Time required for the project's expected after-tax incremental cash flow to repay the entire initial investment in the project.

Time value of money　Rate of return obtainable from comparable alternative investment in the financial market.

6-4　DISCOUNT RATES ARE FREQUENTLY WRONG

FALLACY OF THE SINGLE HURDLE RATE

Most European financial managers still believe that using the same discount rate or **hurdle rate** for all projects results in the correct investment decisions on average. Because projects have widely differing risks, however, it is easy to show that this approach leads on average to the wrong investment decisions.

HOW THE SINGLE-RATE APPROACH LEADS TO INCORRECT INVESTMENT DECISIONS

Figure 6.4 reveals why the single-hurdle-rate approach can be dangerous. The horizontal axis represents the **systematic risk** or **beta** of investments. The vertical axis represents the corresponding required rates of return for investments. The **Securities Market Line (SML)** begins at the risk-free rate at the left and slopes upward to reflect investors' requirements for higher return for higher risk. The broken horizontal line represents the company's hurdle rate for projects. This line does not require higher return for higher risk. On this criterion, a project is acceptable if its IRR exceeds the hurdle rate.

Risky Project B in the figure seems acceptable because it falls above the hurdle rate. This is wrong from the shareholders' point of view, however, because they can get a higher return at the same risk directly above on the SML. Low-risk Project A seems unacceptable because its IRR falls below

---

[5] The next chapter shows ways of correcting these deficiencies.

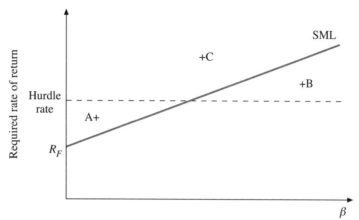

Figure 6.4   The hurdle rate and the Securities Market Line.

the hurdle rate. This is also wrong. Investing in Project A is better than investing below on the SML.

These two examples demonstrate a fact of crucial importance. Hurdle rates that are not risk-adjusted bias investment away from low-risk projects that create shareholder value toward high-risk projects that destroy shareholder value.[6]

SETTING THE HURDLE RATE TOO HIGH

Another common pitfall is to set the hurdle rate too high in the belief that this will "drive the firm to higher profitability." If management raises the broken line in Figure 6.4 higher, they would reject even more projects like Project A. They might reject Project C also. The result is increased bias in favor of higher risk and projects that reflect overly optimistic forecasts. The net result is that the firm will fail to achieve its potential for growth, and thus will not achieve maximum profitability. The result is loss of value for the shareholders.

COMPROMISING FOR ADMINISTRATIVE CONVENIENCE

One reason given for adopting a single hurdle rate for all projects is administrative convenience. Estimating the systematic risk of every individual project is not feasible. A better approach adopted by many companies is to assign risk-adjusted hurdle rates to risk classes rather than to individual projects. If a project falls into a particular risk class, then it is subject to the hurdle rate and the discount rate appropriate for that risk class.

Figure 6.5 illustrates such a system, where risk classes A, B, C, and D represent classes of projects with successively higher risks and correspondingly higher required rates of return. While the risk classification approach is inexact, it is superior to using just one hurdle rate and represents a system that is administratively feasible and efficient.[7]

---

[6] M. E. Rubinstein (1973) "A mean-variance synthesis of corporate financial theory," *Journal of Finance*, Vol. 28, No. 1, 167–181.

[7] A refinement of this system incorporating credit risk is in Chapter 13.

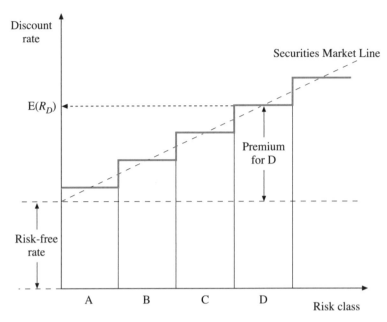

Figure 6.5 A risk classification system for hurdle rates.

6-5   RISING RATES OF INFLATION ARE DANGEROUS

RELEVANCE OF INFLATION TO INVESTMENT

Inflating prices, alternating with infrequent shorter periods of declining prices, beset modern economies. Both situations set traps for the unwary financial analyst. The expected general rate of inflation for an economy determines both interest rates and the expected cash flows of projects. Inflation and deflation do not just affect the required rate of return. They affect investment in working capital, the residual values of assets, sales revenues, costs of sales, and taxes. Because a project's discount rate reflects inflation, the analyst must ensure that all these elements of the cash flow reflect the same expected rate of inflation that has determined the project's discount rate.

REAL AND NOMINAL DISCOUNT RATES

When the expected rate of inflation is low, the nominal (money) rate of interest quoted in the financial market is equal approximately to the sum of the real (purchasing power) rate of interest and the rate of inflation. The real rate of interest is "real" in the sense that it reflects the real goods one can buy due to saving. For example, if the nominal rate of interest is just over 5% and the rate of inflation is 3%, then the real rate of interest is only $5 - 3 = 2\%$. By saving €1 we can buy only 2% more goods at the end of the year. More precisely, the relationship is:[8]

$$Nominal\ Rate\ of\ Interest = (1 + Real\ Rate) \times (1 + Inflation\ Rate) - 1$$

$$= (1 + 0.02) \times (1 + 0.03) - 1$$

$$= 0.0506\quad or\quad 5.06\%$$

For capital projects, the required rate of return found on the SML has a similar relationship to inflation:

$$Required\ Rate\ of\ Return = (1 + Real\ Required\ Rate) \times (1 + Inflation\ Rate) - 1$$

where

$$Real\ Required\ Rate\ of\ Return = Real\ Risk\text{-}free\ Rate + Real\ Risk\ Premium$$

These equations express the observed fact that a higher expected rate of inflation results in a higher nominal interest rate. Similarly, the higher rate of inflation implies a higher required rate of return for capital projects.

Inflation affects some, but not all a project's cash flows in the following way:

$$Inflated\ Cash\ Flow\ at\ Time\ t = Uninflated\ Cash\ Flow \times (1 + Inflation\ Rate)^t$$

If both the discount factor and the expected cash flow reflect inflation in this same way, the expected rate of inflation does not affect a project's NPV. In reality, inflation is not favorable for all the cash flows, and thus unexpected increases in the rate of inflation can reduce a project's NPV.

INCONSISTENCY BETWEEN REAL AND NOMINAL CASH FLOWS AND DISCOUNT RATES

A common pitfall is to use a nominal rate to discount cash flows that are not adjusted to reflect expected inflation. By definition, a nominal discount rate reflects expected inflation. This inconsistent practice can introduce a large negative bias against investment. The opposite pitfall is to discount inflated cash flows with a real discount rate. In this case, the discount rate is relatively too low, resulting in a positively biased NPV, wrongly favoring investment.

The third pitfall is to conclude that all we have to do is be consistent. While it is true that we should use a nominal discount rate to discount nominal (inflated) cash flows, discounting real cash flows with a real discount rate is not equally valid. The reason this apparent simplification fails is that not

---

[8] This relationship is the well-known Fisher effect published by Irving Fisher (1930) *The Theory of Interest* (New York: Macmillan [reprinted 1967]).

all cash flows change equally with the rate of inflation. Therefore, if we ignore the reality of inflation (or deflation), we do not have a correct project appraisal.

WHY INFLATION REDUCES NET PRESENT VALUE

Often we can assume that sales revenues and fixed and variable cash costs change proportionally with the rate of inflation. It would not be valid to do so for investment in a project's working capital or for its incremental taxes, however.

INFLATION INCREASES THE REQUIRED INVESTMENT IN NOMINAL WORKING CAPITAL

Inflation requires more investment each year in the cash account and in the net of debtors and creditors. (Residual values of physical assets such as land, buildings, and inventories will increase in value, but without additional inputs of cash.) Suppose the value of the investment in working capital (excluding inventory) required by the project is €1 million and the expected inflation rate is 5%. In this situation, the company can expect to have to invest an additional 5% of this or €50,000 in Year 1, and again each year (inflated) until the project ends. Analysis confined to uninflated cash flows causes this negative cash flow to go unnoticed.

INFLATION INCREASES CORPORATE TAXES

Corporate taxes usually increase faster than the rate of inflation, for two main reasons. First, most countries do not permit the depreciation allowable for tax purposes to be indexed for inflation. If revenues increase at the rate of inflation and allowable depreciation uses historic cost, then net taxable income must increase faster than the rate of inflation. As a result, the burden of taxes increases faster than the rate of inflation.

Second, if the cost of sales in taxable income uses FIFO (first-in-first-out) accounting, then "inventory appreciation" further inflates taxable income. In effect, the Government taxes the gain in value of the investment in inventory at the corporate tax rate. For example, suppose that inventory has a value of €1 million, that the rate of inflation is 5%, and that the corporate tax rate is 30%. Then the additional taxes are €1,000,000 × 0.05 × 0.30 = €1,500. A similar calculation applies to the inflated inventory value in each subsequent year of the project's life.

The combined working capital and tax effects discussed above can have a significant adverse effect on NPV, especially for long-lived projects. These effects become evident only when one is using nominal cash flow forecasts reflecting inflation.

DEFINITIONS

Nominal rate of interest Quoted rate of interest.

Real rate of interest Rate of interest adjusted for the expected rate of inflation for the same period.

Nominal working capital Net working capital excluding the value of inventory.

6-6 THE PRECISE TIMING OF CASH FLOWS IS IMPORTANT

TIMING MAKES A DIFFERENCE

Many examples in this book use end-of-year discounting for simplicity of presentation and ease of learning. Nonetheless, we would not want you to lose sight of the fact that precision can make the difference between a positive or negative NPV on an investment. It is as well for us to consider here what difference accuracy in the timing of cash flows can make to the NPV of a capital project.

TWO METHODS FOR PRECISION DISCOUNTING

We consider two ways of treating the timing of cash flows more accurately. One way is to discount monthly (weekly) using monthly (weekly) discount rates. The less cumbersome method, employed below, is to use the *annual* discount rate as usual and to define time in terms of decimal *fractions* of a year.

EXAMPLE 6.4

Consider the example in Table 6.1. An investment of €1,000 generates an expected net income of €300 per year for five years as shown in Column 1. The usual assumption is that the cash flows occur at the ends of the years indicated in column 2 of the same table. The calculation of the resulting NPV of €137.24 at 10% is in Columns 3 and 4 of the table.

Now suppose in reality that each cash flow comes at the middle of the year as in Column 5. (The result is quite close to assuming that cash flows spread evenly throughout the year.) In Column 6, we now have to compute the discount factors corresponding to 0.5 years, 1.5 years, and so on. For example, the 1.5-year discount factor in the table is:

$$1/(1.10)^{1.5} = 0.866\,78$$

The resulting NPV for the project found in the last column of the table is 192.76 for mid-year discounting compared with 137.24 obtained using end-of-year discounting. The difference $192.76 - 137.24 = 55.52$ is only about 5.5% of the sum invested. Nonetheless, it represents an increase of over 40% ($55.52/137.24 = 0.4046$ or 40.46%) for the NPV of this particular project. Clearly, the assumed timing of cash flows can make a significant difference. As a result, some companies use mid-year discounting as a better approximation, and banks use the exact dates of contractual payments when using discounted cash-flow (DCF) to evaluate deals with corporate customers.

DEFINITION

Discounted cash flow (DCF) Method of determining the present value of a cash flow expected to be received on a specific future date.

Table 6.1 Comparison between net present values for rounded and fractional times.

Net cash flow €	Year	Discount factor at 10%	Present value	Year at 10%	Discount factor value	Present
(1)	(2)	(3)	(4)	(5)	(6)	(7)
−1,000	0	1.000 00	−1,000.00	0.0	1.000 00	−1,000.00
300	1	0.909 09	272.73	0.5	0.953 46	286.04
300	2	0.826 45	247.93	1.5	0.866 78	260.04
300	3	0.751 31	225.39	2.5	0.787 99	236.40
300	4	0.683 01	204.90	3.5	0.716 35	214.91
300	5	0.620 92	186.28	4.5	0.651 23	196.37
		NPV = 137.24			NPV = 192.76	

6-7   FORECASTING IS OFTEN UNTRUTHFUL

THE INCENTIVE FOR PROJECT SPONSORS TO BE UNTRUTHFUL

Much of this chapter is about bias in project appraisal. Perhaps the greatest source of bias is due to project sponsors simply not telling the truth. They often are in competition with other sponsors for a share of the limited capital budget, and it is not in their interests to produce less optimistic forecasts than those of other sponsors.

COUNTERMEASURES

A crude defense against this bias is for the board to increase the hurdle rate by the amount of the expected average forecasting bias. Unfortunately, this arbitrary device can result in sponsors adjusting their biases to reflect the higher rate. It is not clear that the occasional practice of keeping the hurdle rate secret reduces the bias either.

A better procedure is to ask each sponsor for a subsidiary forecast. The subsidiary forecast details the most likely scenario of costs, prices, volumes and taxes that could result in an NPV of zero for the project. The sponsor must then justify why competition will permit costs, prices, or volumes to be sufficiently favorable to explain the positive NPV in the main forecast. Turning the spotlight onto the economic justification for a project's NPV makes forecasting bias more difficult to hide. It also helps focus the attention of the board on the strategic features of the project that make it valuable.

6-8   RISK ADDS VALUE TO REAL OPTIONS

MISUNDERSTANDING RISK LEADS TO WRONG DECISIONS

Often companies abandon research and development or fail to pursue commercial activities surrounded by uncertainty and hence considered too risky. The reasoning is that great uncertainty means high risk. High risk implies high discount rates, and high discount rates mean low or negative NPVs. This line of thought is not strictly correct and represents a major potential pitfall.

MANAGEMENT CONTROLS THE DOWNSIDE RISK

In many commercial activities, especially in R&D, management can control the "downside risk." That is, management can cut the losses when the activity is not succeeding and can increase the scale of the activity when it promises to do well. Management can make many such choices in the course of time as further information reveals itself and uncertainty is resolved. Nothing obliges managers to make unfavorable choices, and thus these real options have positive value.

The potential losses from R&D are limited to the R&D budget, but the potential gains are relatively unlimited, especially if the uncertainty is great. As a rule, greater uncertainty increases the value of R&D and thus justifies more spending on it.

RISK GIVES VALUE TO A PROJECT'S REAL OPTIONS

Most capital projects embody a number of real options, for example, the option to expand the project if it is going well or to abandon it if it goes badly. It is true that higher risk increases the discount rate, thus reducing the NPV, but the higher risk also increases the value of the project's real options, thus increasing the NPV. What is the net result of these conflicting forces on the NPV? We have no way of knowing without valuing the real options in the project. We return to these points in Chapters 8 and 9.

> **DEFINITION**
>
> **Real option** Right to make favorable future choices regarding real asset investments. More precisely, a real option is an opportunity for voluntary future investment in a nonfinancial asset when at least a part of the required investment expenditure is certain or, alternatively, when at least a part of the required investment expenditure is not perfectly positively correlated with the project's present value.

6-9   REAL OPTIONS AFFECT THE NPV RULE

EXCEPTIONS TO THE NET PRESENT VALUE RULE

The textbook net present value rule is to accept *all* projects that have NPV greater than zero, but few companies follow this rule strictly. For example, a firm often will invest in a project with a negative NPV because the project opens the way to subsequent projects with potentially large, positive NPVs. That is, the company regards the loss-making project as an investment in valuable real options on future investment. Much investment in loss-making Internet commerce attempted to implement such a strategy.

More often, a company will not invest in a project unless its NPV is substantially greater than zero. Why? Capital rationing is often the reason. Investment is being limited to the projects that create the most value for shareholders per unit of scarce funds.

The real option to delay investment provides another reason why the NPV rule can be an insufficient guide.

WAITING FOR THE MOST OPPORTUNE MOMENT

A company often does not want to invest in a project on the earliest feasible date that the NPV exceeds zero. "Wait and see" is the motive. The option to delay investment while improving the project and gathering more information from the business environment can have more value than the income that is lost as a result of waiting. Greater uncertainty increases the value of the option to wait and see. So, the NPV must be sufficiently greater than zero to justify investing now rather than waiting.

The modified NPV rule would be to accept projects for which the NPV of immediate investment is greater than the value of the option to delay. Without the ability to value these real options, management has to rely on judgment alone. Fortunately, valuing such options is not too difficult, as we shall see in Chapters 8 and 9.

DEFINITION

Net present value rule   Rule suggesting that investment in a project should take place if its net present value (NPV) is greater than zero because the project would contribute net positive value for shareholders.

6-10 CONCLUSIONS

Correctly specifying a project's incremental cash flow presents many snares for the unwary financial analyst. Incremental cash flow is the difference between the cash flows associated with two mutually exclusive scenarios. Under the first scenario, the project moves ahead. Under the second scenario, the project does not go forward. Examination of the second scenario enables the analyst to identify the opportunity costs of the project. A common error is to omit the after-tax opportunity costs from the project's incremental cash flow.

The boards of most companies want to know the expected rate of return on a project. The IRR is the most frequently used, although many companies also use the **accounting rate of return (ARR)**. The accounting rate of return does not incorporate the time value of money and, more seriously, omits the project's **opportunity costs**. Both these flawed measures can lead to wrong investment decisions.

The problem with the IRR is that it does not directly measure a project's rate of return: it measures instead the discount rate at which a project would break even. So, the IRR is a biased substitute for a project's true rate of return. Some projects can have more than one IRR, in which case the IRR becomes virtually meaningless. NPV is a more reliable investment criterion because it attempts to measure directly the value added for shareholders.

Most companies suffer from some degree of capital rationing for one or more of the following reasons. The companies are too small to have ready access to the securities market, or they feel that further borrowing is too risky, or they do not wish to incur the flotation costs of issuing securities. Therefore, it should not be surprising that the payback period, as a simple measure of a project's liquidity, is the single most popular investment criterion. Unfortunately, the measure is simplistic and occasionally can lead to a wrong investment decision.

Setting the correct discount rate for a project is essential because the project's NPV can be very sensitive to it. The discount rate represents the project's opportunity cost of capital. Consequently, the SML provides an estimate of the correct required rate of return at the point corresponding to the project's systematic risk. The SML implies a higher cost of capital for higher risk.

Most European companies still use only one hurdle rate for all projects regardless of their differing risks. This unfortunate practice biases investment away from safe projects that create shareholder value toward more risky projects that destroy value. A practical approach is to group projects into different risk classes and to assign one discount rate or hurdle rate to each risk class.

Some companies inadvertently use nominal discount rates with real cash flows or real discount rates with nominal (inflated) cash flows. This inconsistency generates mistaken investment decisions. Nominal rates should discount nominal cash flows. The suggestion in some textbooks that one can equally well discount real cash flows with real discount rates is unsatisfactory. The reason is that inflation does not just inflate the cash flows. It creates new cash flows and taxes that remain undetected when one values a project purely in real terms.

Textbooks commonly represent cash flows in examples as though they all occur at the end of the year. Unfortunately, this treatment is too imprecise. A more accurate approach is to treat daily cash flows as though they all occur mid-year and to discount them on this basis. A better practice, used to value financial contracts, specifies the timing of payments precisely to the day. One can use the relevant fraction of the year when discounting each such intra-year payment.

Project sponsors often produce excessively optimistic cash flow forecasts in order to improve chances of getting approval to spend a limited capital budget. Requiring them to justify in detail the favorable costs, prices and volumes necessary to justify a project's positive NPV can counteract this unfortunate tendency.

Perhaps the greatest source of error in project appraisal is failure to take into account the value of a project's real options. No one is to blame for this. A usable methodology simply has not been available until recently. Subsequent chapters show how to value the real options in capital projects.

DEFINITIONS

Accounting rate of return (ARR)   Rate of return as accounting income divided by the book value of all assets employed to generate the income.

Opportunity cost of capital   Rate of return forgone when investing in a project instead of the securities market.

FURTHER READING

J. Hirschleifer (1969) *Investment, Interest and Capital* (Englewood Cliffs, NJ: Prentice Hall).

M. E. Rubinstein (1973) "A mean-variance synthesis of corporate financial theory," *Journal of Finance*, Vol. 28, No. 1, 167–181.

QUESTIONS AND PROBLEMS

1   E-COMMERCE INTERNATIONAL has an opportunity to dispose of its existing warehouse near Paris at the very favorable price of €10 million. Taxes on the transaction would be €2 million. After five years, the expected after-tax residual value of the existing warehouse is only €4 million.

The plan would be to replace the warehouse with a new, purpose-built one closer to the airport and rail transport. Annual expenditures after tax (including costs of handling and transportation) associated with running the existing warehouse are €5 million annually. Expected annual cash income is €7 million after tax, which would be the same for the new warehouse.

The company expects to be able to build the new warehouse for only €8 million. New technology and better transport would save an expected €2 million per year after tax. The after-tax residual value of the new warehouse would be approximately €8 million at the end of Year 5.

(a)   Show the incremental cash flows for the new warehouse.
(b)   Show the incremental cash flows for the old warehouse.
(c)   If the discount rate is 10%, what is the NPV of investing in the new warehouse?
(d)   What is the NPV of continuing to operate the existing warehouse?
(e)   What is the NPV of the difference between the old and the new warehouses?
(f)   What is the payback on investing in the new warehouse instead of continuing to operate the old one?

2   Given below are the after-tax incremental cash flows for Projects A and B. Note the similarity between the two projects.

<table>
<tr><th colspan="4">End of year (€)</th></tr>
<tr><th></th><th>0</th><th>1</th><th>2</th></tr>
<tr><td>Project A</td><td>−10,000</td><td>−50,000</td><td>60,000</td></tr>
<tr><td>Project B</td><td>−10,000</td><td>50,000</td><td>−60,000</td></tr>
</table>

(a)   For each project plot NPV versus discount rate at the points where the discount rate equals 0, 50, 100, 150, and 200%.
(b)   Calculate the NPV at 20% for each project.
(c)   Calculate the IRR(s) for the two projects.
(d)   If you had to invest in one of the projects, which project would you prefer and why?

3   The expected rate of inflation is 3%, and the required nominal rate of return for a project is 12%. If the expected rate of inflation increases to 5%, what should be the corresponding new nominal required rate of return for the project?

4   The real (without inflation) required rate of return for a project is 10%. The corporate tax rate is 30%. Allowable depreciation in the third year of the project is €10,000. The tax effect of allowable depreciation on the cash flow of the project is favorable. It equals the allowable depreciation multiplied by the tax rate.

(a)   What is the effect of allowable depreciation in the third year on the present value (PV) of the project in the absence of inflation?

(b)   What is the effect of allowable depreciation in the third year on the PV of the project if the expected rate of inflation is 5%?

5   The working capital investment in a project initially is €2.5 million. Of this, inventory represents €1.5 million. Cash, debtors, and creditors represent the remaining €1 million.

(a)   If the expected rate of inflation is 10%, how much more investment in working capital is required in each of the next three years?

(b)   If the expected rate of inflation increases, will the effect of this working capital investment increase or reduce the NPV of the project?

6   In Problem 5, FIFO is the basis of the cost of goods sold in taxable income. The corporate tax rate is 30%.

(a)   If the rate of inflation is 10%, what is the tax effect in each of the next three years of the inventory investment?

(b)   Does this tax effect increase or reduce the NPV of the project?

7   A financial contract incorporates a continuously compounded annual rate of interest of 8%. The contract requires a first payment of €1 million in 30 days. The contract requires further payments of €1 million every 90 days thereafter until it expires. Base your calculations on a 365-day year.

(a)   What is the PV of the first payment?

(b)   What is the PV of the second payment?

(c)   If the interest rate is 8% compounded quarterly instead, what is the PV of the first payment?

8   A machine exploits a proprietary technology making costs per unit €10 less than for the next most efficient competitor. The machine produces 100,000 units per year. The expected life of this competitive advantage is five years. Management has decided not to change the price for the product unless forced to do so by the competition. Investment in the machine is the same as for competitors to make the equivalent product. The tax rate is 30%, and the discount rate is 10%.

(a)   Assuming a competitive market, what is the machine's NPV?

(b)   What would be the NPV of the machine if its cost becomes €200,000 more than the competitors must pay for their less efficient machines?

(c)   What is the minimum the NPV is likely to fall if a competitor can exploit an equally effective technology in two years instead of five years and seeks to increase market share by reducing its price?

9   The NPV for a project is €75,000. The "wait-and-see option" for the project is worth €100,000.

(a)   Should the project proceed immediately?

(b)   What is the minimum required NPV to justify immediate investment?

7 Further Project Appraisal Methods

We have discussed a number of pitfalls besetting those who make capital investment decisions. The best defense against mistaken investment decisions is good commercial judgment backed by sound financial analysis. Existing analytical methods incorporate many of the pitfalls, however. These methods are old and trusted but are somewhat simplistic. Methods embedded in company culture and procedures are hard to change. Better analytical methods can still help project sponsors design and select better projects for proposal, however, even if senior managers still require them to support each proposal using familiar criteria. This chapter takes a few steps beyond the more conventional procedures.

TOPICS

In particular, we consider:

O   *Adjusted Present Value method (APV);*

O   *multiperiod capital rationing: the Profitability Index Annuity (PIA);*

O   *multiperiod capital rationing: mathematical programming;*

O   *Project Yield (PY).*

7-1   ADJUSTED PRESENT VALUE METHOD

Myers's (1974) Adjusted Present Value method (APV) provides a means of obtaining the present value (PV) of a project involving special financing arrangements.[1] For example: How should we analyze the tax advantages of financing tied to a particular project? What discount rate should we use to discount the associated cash flow? The APV method resolves such questions.

DISCOUNTING THE OPERATING CASH FLOWS AND FINANCING BENEFITS SEPARATELY

Myers suggested separating the value of the project's operating cash flows from the benefits (or costs) of debt financing. If the tax benefits of debt financing are valued separately, the operating

---

[1] S. C. Myers (1977) "Determinants of corporate borrowing," *Journal of Financial Economics*, Vol. 5, No. 2 (November), 147–175.

cash flows of the project must be valued using a discount rate that does not already reflect the tax benefits.

EXAMPLE 7.1

Consider, for example, the following project:

	0	1	2	3	4
			End of year		
Investment	−1,000				
Operating cash flow after tax		500	500	500	500

The project requires investment of €1 million and generates an expected €500,000 per year. The company uses both debt and equity financing for such projects. Its Treasurer intends to borrow 40% of the company's total financing requirements during the next four years and to pay interest on this at 7%. The company can deduct all its interest payments from taxable income. It pays corporate taxes at 30%. How much do the resulting tax savings contribute to this project's net present value (NPV)?

We shall answer this question in two ways: the Weighted Average Cost of Capital (WACC) method and the APV method. Then we can then explain the advantages of the APV in answering questions that are more detailed concerning specific financing arrangements for particular projects.

THE WEIGHTED AVERAGE COST OF CAPITAL METHOD

If the project does not involve any special financing arrangements, we can use the WACC method to ascertain the PV of the tax savings resulting from deducting interest payments from taxable income. We can do so by first calculating the project's NPV using the usual after-tax WACC. Then, we calculate its NPV using the before-tax WACC. The NPV of the interest tax deductions equals the difference between these two results.

Table 7.1 gives the calculation of the after-tax and before-tax WACC. The table assumes that the project's cost of equity is 15%, the before-tax interest rate will be 7% and debt will represent 40% of total financing for the project. The company expects to pay taxes at 30%.

The formula used to obtain the 4.9% after-tax cost of debt used in the table is:

$$\text{Cost of Debt After Tax} = \text{Cost of Debt Before Tax} \times (1 - \text{Tax Rate})$$
$$= 7 \times (1 - 0.30) = 4.9\%$$

The tax deduction reduces the interest on the debt from 7% to 4.9% after tax. This beneficial tax effect accounts for the lower after-tax WACC of 10.96% compared with the before-tax WACC of 11.80% calculated in the table.

Table 7.1 Calculating the after-tax and the before-tax WACC.

	Cost (%)	Proportion	Weighted (%)
Cost of equity	15.00	0.60	9.00
Cost of debt after tax	4.90	0.40	1.96
		1.00	10.96
WACC after tax	10.96		

	Cost (%)	Proportion	Weighted
Cost of equity	15.00	0.60	9.00
Cost of debt before tax	7	0.40	2.80
		1.00	11.80
WACC before-tax tax	11.80		

We can now compare the project's NPV using the after-tax WACC with its NPV using the before-tax WACC as follows:

$$\text{NPV of project discounted at after-tax WACC} = €552.55$$

$$\textit{Less}: \quad \text{NPV of project discounted at before-tax WACC} = €525.09$$

$$\text{PV of tax benefits of debt} \qquad\qquad = €27.45$$

Therefore, the WACC method obtains the value of €27.45 for the PV of the tax benefits assuming 40% debt financing at the expected interest rate of 7%.

THE ADJUSTED PRESENT VALUE METHOD

The WACC method is quick but relies on a simplifying assumption. The assumption is that the debt repayment schedule keeps the amount borrowed equal to the assumed 40% of the PV of the project's remaining cash flows. We shall use the APV method to prove this. We can then see how to use the APV method with other assumptions about the debt retirement schedule.

Table 7.2 gives the APV calculation for a project. In the APV method, we simply discount a project's operating cash flow and its financing benefits separately at the appropriate discount rate:

$$APV \text{ of the Project} = \frac{NPV \text{ of Project's}}{\text{Operating Cash Flows}} + \frac{PV \text{ of Project's}}{\text{Financing Benefits}}$$

The table shows how to apply this principle. The third row of the table shows for each year the PV of the remaining operating cash flows in the row above. The discount rate used for this purpose is the before-tax WACC. If we had used the after-tax WACC instead, we would have double-counted the tax benefit in the APV calculation. The fourth row of the table shows the assumed borrowing equal to 40% of the PV in the row above. In Row 5, we see the annual interest payments calculated at 7% of the loan balance at the beginning of each year. For example, in Year I the interest paid is:

$$42.70 = 0.07 \times 610.04$$

Table 7.2 Applying the APV method.

		End of year			
	0	1	2	3	4
Investment	−1,000				
Operating cash flow after tax		500	500	500	500
PV of remaining cash flows at 11.8%	1,525.09	1,205.06	847.25	447.23	0.00
Borrowing at 40%	610.04	482.02	338.90	178.89	0.00
Interest at 7%		42.70	33.74	23.72	12.52
Tax benefits at 30%		12.81	10.12	7.12	3.76
PV of tax benefits at 11.8%	27.05				

The resulting tax benefit at the 30% tax rate for that year is:

$$12.81 = 0.30 \times 42.70$$

Discounting the tax benefits at the 11.8% before-tax WACC, we obtain €27,050 for the PV of the tax benefits.[2]

Notice that this value of €27,050 is slightly less than the value of €27,450 obtained earlier using the WACC method. The reason is that the WACC method assumes that borrowing is a fixed proportion of the total PV of the project's remaining cash flows. This PV includes the value attributable to the tax benefits from borrowing. In our Table 7.2 calculation, the borrowing is 40% of the remaining after-tax operating cash flows and thus excludes the PV of the tax benefits of borrowing. We had to omit this additional value from the calculation because it was unknown at that stage of the calculation. Now that we have an estimate of the PVs of the tax benefits each year at the bottom of Table 7.2, we could include them in a second stage of the APV calculation.

In the second stage, we just add the PV of the remaining tax benefits to the PV of the remaining upgrading cash flows each year. We then recalculate the loan balance each year as the assumed 40% of this total annual value. The resulting increased value of the loan balances implies correspondingly higher interest payments and tax benefits. This increases the calculated APV for the project to €552,540, which very nearly equals the PV that we obtained using the WACC method. We obtain an even closer result by adding a third stage to the calculation.

So, why do we bother with the APV method when we can get the same result more easily using the WACC method? We have the same result only because we used the same assumption that the loan balance always equals a fixed proportion of the PV of the project's remaining cash flows. In a number of situations encountered in practice, however, this assumption does not give a sufficiently accurate result. For example, loans usually relate to the accounting book values of assets rather than to their PVs. Instead of assuming in Table 7.2 that the borrowing is some fixed proportion of

---

[2] We use the same rate to discount the tax benefits of debt because they depend on risky taxable income. Another assumption is that the tax system is symmetrical. That is, when the firm has taxable income, it pays taxes; and when it makes taxable losses, some direct or indirect form of tax rebate is provided by the tax collector.

the PV of the remaining cash flows, we enter the actual loan balances implied in the loan contract. We then complete the calculation in Table 7.2. A second-stage calculation is not required because the loan balances no longer depend on the total PV.

DEFINITIONS

Adjusted Present Value method (APV)   Discounting the operating cash flows and financing benefits separately.

Debt   Sum of money or other assets owed by one party to another. Usually, a legally enforceable obligation to pay agreed interest and to repay the principal of a loan to the lender promptly on schedule.

Discount rate   Required rate of return used in the calculation of a discount factor.

Equity   Net worth or shareholder's capital represented by common stock (ordinary shares) and preferred stock.

Net present value (NPV)   Difference between the present value of a project's expected after-tax operating cash flows and the present value of its expected after-tax investment expenditures.

Present value (PV)   Value of an investment now as the cost of a comparable investment in the financial market (calculated by multiplying the investment's expected after-tax cash income by the appropriate discount factors).

Treasurer   Senior financial manager reporting directly to the Chief Financial Officer. Primarily responsible for funding and cash management.

Weighted Average Cost of Capital (WACC)   Value-weighted average of expected after-tax costs of debt and equity financing.

7-2   MULTIPERIOD CAPITAL RATIONING: THE PROFITABILITY INDEX ANNUITY

THE PROFITABILITY INDEX

When a company suffers capital rationing, its capital budget becomes too small to permit acceptance of all projects offering positive NPVs. Instead, management must set priorities and try to extract maximum PV from the capital budget. A widely recommended procedure starts with ranking projects in descending order of their Profitability Index (PI) values:

$$Profitability\ Index = Present\ Value\ /\ Investment$$

$$PI = \frac{PV}{I}$$

The projects with the highest values of the PI generate the largest present value per unit of investment.[3]

---

[3] The alternative definition $PI = NPV/I$ gives the same rankings.

The second step in the procedure is to select projects with the highest remaining ranks until the total investment in projects exhausts the capital budget.

This procedure is most appropriate for a company facing capital rationing for just the current year. Only large companies have constant, low-cost access to additional funds from the financial markets. Therefore, most companies encounter periods of capital rationing for more than one year. Such companies prefer projects with short payback periods because they need projects that return cash quickly for reinvestment. Consequently, the PI is not a sufficient selection criterion for companies expecting capital rationing beyond the current year. A better criterion for them would combine the advantages of rapid payback with high PV per unit of investment.

THE PROFITABILITY INDEX ANNUITY

The need for combining the advantages of rapid cash generation with high PV per unit of investment suggests ranking projects using the following annuity:

$$Profitability\ Index\ Annuity = Profitability\ Index / Annuity\ Factor$$

$$PIA = \left(\frac{PV}{I}\right) \Big/ A_{N,R_j}$$

in which N represents the project's life and R_j its required rate of return.

Rankings based on this Profitability Index Annuity (PIA) have some desirable properties. Projects with shorter lives tend to have higher ranking PIAs, and short life implies rapid cash generation. Consequently, choosing projects ranked by their PIA values can help managers to invest in projects combining three desirable characteristics: high PV, low capital requirement and rapid cash generation.

EXAMPLE 7.2

We can use a comparatively simple example to demonstrate why the annuity form of the PI is better for companies facing capital rationing beyond one year. Below are cash flows for four projects having different lives ranging from two to six years. We shall compare selection from these projects using the PI and the PIA.

Project	0	1	2	3	4	5	6
				End of year			
C	−100.00	31.60	31.60	31.60	31.60		
D	−112.00	73.76	73.76				
E	−85.00	43.91	43.91	43.91			
F	−98.00	28.46	28.46	28.46	28.46	28.46	28.46

Table 7.3 compares the project's rankings using the two criteria. The upper half of the table relates to the PI and the lower half to the PIA. In the first column, we see that descending values of the PI

Table 7.3 Comparison between project rankings using the PI and the PIA criteria.

Project	Cumulative capital required	Cumulative Period 1 cash flow	Cumulative NPV
PI			
D	0.219 112	73.76	24.6
F	0.111 210	102.22	35.4
C	0.061 310	133.82	41.5
E	0.046 395	177.73	45.5
PIA			
D	0.117 112	73.76	24.6
F	0.029 210	102.22	35.4
E	0.023 295	146.14	39.4
C	0.018 395	177.73	45.5

rank the four projects in the order D, F, C, and E. In contrast, the PIA ranks the projects in the order D, F, E, and C.

The difference between the two rankings reflects the difference in preference for Project E. Whereas the PI ranks Project E last at No. 4, the PIA ranks E at No. 3. Whether this makes any difference depends upon the size of the capital budget, as indicated in the third column of the table. The third column gives the cumulative capital required to invest in more of the projects.

For example, Projects D and F require a total investment of:

$$112 + 98 = 210$$

as indicated in the second row of the third column. There would be no difference in selection between the two criteria if the capital budget were to equal 210 because both criteria rank D and F highest, and this budget would be just sufficient for investment in both projects.

The comparison becomes more interesting when the capital budget equals 310. At this level, the PI criterion also includes Project C, whereas the PIA includes Project E instead. Comparison between the last two columns of the table indicates why the PIA selection of D, F, and E might be preferable compared with D, F, and C. It requires less initial investment, generates more cash flow in Period 1, and sacrifices very little NPV to achieve these benefits. This example demonstrates how PIA rankings tend to create more slack in the capital budget, making extra cash available for investment in more projects.

DEFINITIONS

Annuity Investment generating equal cash flows each period for a specified number of periods.

Capital budgeting Procedure for allocating funds to capital projects.

Capital rationing Insufficient funds for investment in all acceptable capital projects.

Payback period Time required for the project's expected after-tax incremental cash flow to repay the entire initial investment in the project.

Profitability index (PI)   Present value of a project divided by the required investment.

Profitability Index Annuity (PIA)   Project's Profitability Index divided by the annuity factor for its life and required rate of return.

Rate of return   After-tax cash income and capital gain divided by the investment.

7-3   MULTIPERIOD CAPITAL RATIONING: MATHEMATICAL PROGRAMMING

While the PIA offers a better criterion for choosing projects when management expects capital rationing beyond the current year, it will not usually suffice for selecting the best combination of projects. The PIA is just a single number and thus does not reflect the detail necessary to squeeze the best combination of projects into a sequence of annual capital budgets. When there are large sums of money at stake, it can be worthwhile using mathematical programming for a better solution to the project selection problem under capital rationing.

MANUAL SOLUTION OF A MATHEMATICAL PROGRAMMING PROBLEM

EXAMPLE 7.3

Table 7.4 illustrates four projects (G, H, I, and J), which start in different periods. Cash generated by the selected projects supplements the initial €1,000 capital budget. The company Treasurer invests unused funds in short-term money market securities until the funds are required for projects. The expected rate of interest from the money market investments is 7%. What combinations of these four projects would be feasible within the resulting future budgets? Which is the most profitable combination? Mathematical programming can provide the answers.

Table 7.4   Four prospective capital projects and the capital budget.

Period ending	Projects				Budget
	G	H	I	J	
0	−900				1,000
1	200	−500			
2	200	100	−550		
3	200	100	100	−660	
4	200	100	100	132	
⋮	⋮	⋮	⋮	⋮	

This capital investment-planning problem can most easily be solved by the method demonstrated in Table 7.5 (derived from Table 7.4). All the figures after the first row in Table 7.5 are cumulations of the corresponding figures in Table 7.4 compounded at the 7% money market rate. Take, for

Table 7.5 NPVs, cumulative requirements, and cumulative budget.

Period ending	Projects				Cumulative budget
	G	H	I	J	
NPVs	767	298	226	313	
Cumulative requirements					
0	−900				1,000
1	−763	−500			1,070
2	−616	−435	−550		1,145
3	−460	−365	−489	−660	1,225
4	−292	−291	−423	−574	1,311
⋮	⋮	⋮	⋮	⋮	⋮

example, the figures shown for Project G. The first figure is still −€900. The second figure is − €763 = − €900 × 1.07 + €200. The third figure is − €616 = − €763 × 1.07 + €200, and so on. The revised figures express the following constraint on the selection of projects:

> The cumulative total net cash requirements of selected projects must be less than or equal to the cumulative capital budget.[4]

Adhering to this constraint involves ensuring that sums from left to right in Table 7.5 are less than or equal to the cumulative budget in the final column. By this means, we can identify all feasible combinations of projects satisfying the budgetary constraint.

Let us find out which combinations of Projects G, H, I, and J are feasible. We could include Project G since the €900 required does not exceed the initial capital budget of €1,000. Can we include a second project within the cumulative budget? Consider Project H. Since the cumulative net requirements of €763 for G combined with the cumulative net requirements of €500 for H exceed the cumulative budget of €1,070, the combination of G and H is not feasible. Neither is a combination of G and I feasible within the cumulative budget.

Now consider G and J. The cumulative net requirement for G and J is €1,120 = €460 + €660. Since €1,120 does not exceed the cumulative budget of €1,225 at that stage, both G and J are feasible within the budget.

Now consider combinations of Project H with projects other than G (already considered). Project H can be combined with Project I since the cumulative net requirements for funds, €985 = €435 + €550, does not exceed the cumulative budget of €1,145. Similarly, Project H combines with Project J within the cumulative budget. In addition, Projects I and J combine within the cumulative budget.

---

[4] J. E. Broyles (1976) "Compact formulations of mathematical programs for financial planning problems," *Operational Research Quarterly*, Vol. 27, No. 4, 885–893.

Table 7.6 NPVs and feasibility of project combinations.

Projects	NPV	Cumulative total requirements	Cumulative budget
G + H	1,064	1,263	1,070
G + I	993	1,166	1,145
G + J	1,080	1,120	≤1,225
H + I	523	985	≤1,145
H + J	611	1,025	≤1,225
J + I	539	997	≤1,225

To summarize, projects are feasible in the following combinations within the cumulative budget:

$$G + J, \quad H + I, \quad H + J, \quad J + I$$

The immediate decision is whether to invest in Project G since investment in G preempts investment in any other project but J. If project combinations including H or I were more advantageous, we would not invest in G. To make the choice, we simply add the NPVs as of Period 0 for each feasible combination of projects. The combination with the largest total NPV is the optimum selection of projects within the cumulative budget.

Table 7.6 summarizes the results. The second column in the table shows that the project combination G and J has the highest combined NPV, and is feasible. Therefore, the optimum choice is investment first in Projects G and J. Combinations of H + I, H + J, and J + I are also feasible but have lower combined NPVs.

FORMAL STRUCTURE OF THE MATHEMATICAL PROGRAM

We have just demonstrated the manual solution of an **integer programming** problem. Table 7.7 gives a more formal presentation of the problem. Comparison with Table 7.6 clarifies the meaning of the terms in Table 7.7.

We now show the objective function that we want to maximize. The objective function is the total NPV for the selected combination of projects:

$$\text{Maximize} \quad P_1 X_1 + P_2 X_2 + P_3 X_3 + P_4 X_4$$

where P_j represents the NPV of Project j and X_j is a variable signifying selection of Project j. In the integer programming method, X_j can have only two values, 1 or 0, depending on, respectively, whether the project is or is not selected.

Also shown in Table 7.7 are the budget constraints. These constraints are that the cumulative investment in projects by the end of each year must be less than or equal to the cumulative cash available in the capital budget. Again, the values of the Xs signify selection within the budget. The signs of the cumulative compound net cash requirements are positive because they appear on the left-hand side of the constraints.

Table 7.7   The integer programming optimization problem.

Period ending		Projects			Cumulative budget
	G	H	I	J	
Objective function:					
Maximize	P_1X_1 +	P_2X_2 +	P_3X_3 +	P_4X_4	
Subject to constraints					
0	$900X_1$				$\leq$ 1,000
1	$763X_1$ +	$500X_2$			$\leq$ 1,070
2	$616X_1$ +	$435X_2$ +	$550X_3$		$\leq$ 1,145
3	$460X_1$ +	$365X_2$ +	$489X_3$ +	$660X_4$	$\leq$ 1,225
4	$292X_1$ +	$291X_2$ +	$423X_3$ +	$74.2X_4$	$\leq$ 1,311
and					
	$x_j = 0, 1$		$j = 1, 2, \ldots, N$		

The method can also include other types of constraint than capital rationing. For example, we could add rows to Table 7.7 containing constraints each year on the availability of experienced management or of qualified technical personnel to implement selected projects successfully. The coefficient P_j in such rows of Table 7:7 could represent the number of man-years required to implement Project j in each year; and in the final column of the same row, we would have the man-years available for the corresponding years. If two of the projects are mutually exclusive, we can include the constraint:

$$1X_j + 1X_k \leq 1$$

where Projects j and k are the mutually exclusive projects. So, if X_j takes the value 1 in the optimum solution, X_k would have to take the value 0 and vice versa.

If, instead, Project j were contingent on Project k (i.e. if Project j could not be undertaken unless Project k were undertaken first), we would include the constraint:

$$1X_j - 1X_k \leq 0$$

Note that this constraint is equivalent to:

$$X_j \leq X_k$$

Therefore, if the value of X_k is 0, the value of X_j must also be 0. Only if the value of X_k is equal to 1 can the value of X_j be 1. Accordingly, this constraint ensures that Project j will be contingent on Project k in the optimal solution.

The arrangements of the Xs in Table 7.7 are of the form usually required for input to mathematical programming software. Broadly speaking, there are two methods used to solve mathematical programming problems: integer programming and linear programming. If values of X are only 0 or 1, the problem is an integer programming problem. On the other hand, if X can have fractional values, we have a linear programming problem.

A linear programming solution allows fractional values of X, indicating that fractions of projects enter the optimal solution. Fractional projects often are not technically possible, and the expected costs and revenues might not scale proportionally to the fractional investments.

Unfortunately, simply rounding fractions to 0 or 1 usually does not give the optimum integer solution, even if the constraints are still satisfied. Nevertheless, linear programming solutions can provide a useful decision aid. Many linear programs allow sensitivity analysis, providing additional insights about the best choice of projects.

A problem with most mathematical programming analyses is that they require a high degree of certainty. In reality, one rarely has full information about future projects. Unknown investment opportunities can emerge unexpectedly. In addition, competitive developments often make anticipated projects obsolete. Furthermore, capital budgets can increase or reduce depending on cash generation elsewhere in the company and on financing in the capital market. Finally, the concept of a budget can be too simple in cases where leasing, joint ventures, and mergers provide alternative methods of financing particular projects.

Nevertheless, motivation for using mathematical programming arises from several real needs. Because of financing economies of scale, companies issue securities in large blocks. Short-term bank loans fill the gaps between security flotations. When the money supply tightens, bank borrowing becomes more difficult and even quite large companies can experience capital rationing. Mathematical programming promises to help management to make the most of its scarce resources. Even when capital is readily available to the Group, management may wish to allocate capital budgets to divisions as though financial capital were a scarce resource. This practice forces divisional managers to set priorities in their investment programs. Mathematical programming can play a useful role in helping to set the investment priorities.

DEFINITIONS

Capital market Market for long-term securities. Consists of the banks, insurance companies, and other financial intermediaries (including the stock market) competing to supply companies with financial capital.

Integer programming Mathematical programming method only permitting integer values of the variables.

Linear programming Mathematical programming method optimizing a linear objective function subject to linear constraints and permitting noninteger values of the variables.

Mathematical programming Quantitative procedure obtaining the optimum value of an objective function subject to defined constraints.

Sensitivity analysis Testing the effect of changes to individual variables on a project's net present value.

7-4 MEASURING PROJECT YIELD

The Accounting Rate of Return (ARR) and the internal rate of return (IRR) are the two most widely used rate-of-return measures used by companies. Most finance textbooks promote the IRR as the preferred alternative, however. They often assert that the IRR is less arbitrary because it uses discounted cash flow rather than accounting book values. Detractors of the IRR method argue that it uses discount rates that do not reflect project risk. As a result, the asset values implicit in the IRR usually are not correct. Consequently, the IRR would not ordinarily equal the rate actually earned by a project.

Resolving this debate requires returning to first principles.

BOND YIELD

We need to start with an unambiguous definition of the rate of return and build on that. For example, what is the yield to the investor who pays €100 for the following bond?

			End of year			
	0	1	2	3	4	5
Investment	−100					100
Interest		10	10	10	10	10
Cash flow	−100	10	10	10	10	110

The bondholder pays €100 and receives annual interest of €10 on the €100 face value of the bond. The borrower owes the bondholder €100 until the bond matures at the end of Year 5. So, the value of the bondholder's investment remains at €100 for the entire life of the bond. On this investment of €100, the bondholder earns €10 per year. Unquestionably, the bond provides a yield of $10/100 = 10\%$ to the investor.[5]

If the market rate of interest for other bonds of the same risk is 10%, we can discount the bond's payments at this rate. Unsurprisingly, the resulting PV of the bond equals its price when the bond pays the market rate of interest.

YIELD ON PROJECT A

The calculation of the yield on a capital project involves the same reasoning, with one major difference: we need to include the project's NPV in the calculation.

EXAMPLE 7.4

Consider, for example, the cash flow for Project A encountered in the last chapter:

			Year ending		
0	1	2	3	4	5
−100	33.44	33.44	33.44	33.44	33.44

---

[5] The simplicity of this depends on the price of the bond being equal to its face value. The standard method identifying a bond's yield with its IRR gives a better approximation for bonds than for projects.

The discount rate for Project A is 10%, and the resulting NPV equals €26.76.

The yield on this project is not immediately obvious. We can estimate the yield, however, by comparing the project with the alternative of investing in an equivalent bond having the same risk, the same life, and the same NPV. We can then identify the yield on the project with the yield on the equivalent bond. The market rate of interest on a bond with the same risk as the project would equal the project's 10% discount rate. The NPV for such bonds is zero, however. Consequently, we need a higher yield than the market rate of interest from the bond if it is to be equivalent. How much higher must the bond's yield be to generate the same NPV as the project? The additional interest must be such that:

$$PV \text{ of Additional Interest} = NPV \text{ of Project}$$

That is,

$$Additional\ Interest \times Annuity\ Factor = €26.76$$

Thus,

$$Additional\ Interest = €26.76 / Annuity\ Factor$$

In this formula the value of the five-year annuity factor at 10% is:

$$A_{5,0.10} = \frac{1}{0.10}\left[1 - \left(\frac{1}{1+0.10}\right)^{5}\right] = 3.7908$$

Accordingly,

$$Additional\ Interest = €26.76 / 3.7908 = €7.06$$

The necessary additional €7.06 interest on the hypothetical €100 bond is 7.06%. Accordingly, the yield on such a bond with the same risk and the same NPV as Project A would equal:

$$10 + 7.06 = 17.06\%$$

As we would be indifferent between investing in Project A and in a bond yielding 17.06%, we can consider that project's yield is equivalent to 17.06%.[6]

THE PROJECT YIELD FORMULA

The above calculations generalize to the following formula.[7] The yield on any N-year project with investment I in year 0 and required rate of return R is:[8]

---

[6] This procedure neglects a second-order effect. The additional coupon changes the bond's duration, increasing its risk.

[7] J. E. Broyles (1996) *The True Rate of Return on Long-lived Assets*, Research Bureau Paper No. 222 (Coventry, UK: Warwick Business School, University of Warwick).

[8] If the investment phase lasts beyond Period 0, the suggestion is to compound the investment cash flow forward to the final period of investment. The resulting total compound investment becomes the value for investment I in the formula. Consistent with this, we let the final period of the investment phase represent Period 0 for the calculation of the NPV and the annuity factor in the formula.

$$Project\ Yield = Required\ Rate\ of\ Return + \frac{Net\ Present\ Value}{Annuity\ Factor\ Investment}$$

$$PY = R_j + \frac{NPV/A_{N,R_j}}{I}$$

where R_j represents the required rate of return for projects in Risk Class j.

For Project A, the formula gives the same result as obtained earlier:

$$PY = 0.10 + \frac{26.76/3.7908}{100} = 0.1706 \quad or \quad 17.06\%$$

The Project Yield (PY) formula has three important features. First, it uses the project's required rate of return as the only discount rate. Second, the formula does not give spurious multiple rates of return for a project. Third, the formula reflects directly the value of the project's NPV, which appears in the second term on the right-hand side of the equation. For these reasons, the PY is always greater than the discount rate when the NPV is positive and always less the discount rate when the NPV is negative. So, accepting projects with yields greater than their required rates of return:

$$PY - R_j > 0$$

results in the same investment decisions as accepting projects that have NPVs greater than zero:

$$NPV > 0$$

EXAMPLE 7.5

We can now use our formula to estimate the yield on Project B from the last chapter:

		Year ending			
0	1	2	3	4	5
−100	85.22	85.22	85.22	85.22	−300.00

At the 10% discount rate, the NPV for this project is − €16.14. Accordingly, the yield on Project B is:

$$PY = R_j + \frac{NPV/A_{N,R_j}}{I}$$

$$= 0.10 + \frac{-16.14/3.7908}{100} = 0.0574 = 5.74\%$$

In the last chapter, we obtained two IRRs for this project, 19.94% and 44.42%. We knew that these two rates could not simultaneously equal the project's rate of return. Furthermore, the project's negative NPV implies that its rate of return would have to be less than the required rate of return. Consistent with this we find that the 5.74% yield on Project B is less than its 10% required rate of return.

DEFINITIONS

Accounting Rate of Return (ARR)   Rate of return as accounting income divided by the book value of all assets employed to generate the income.

Annuity factor   Present value of one unit of currency paid in each of a specified number of periods. Equals the sum of the corresponding discount factors.

Bond   An interest-bearing security with usually long-term maturity. Interest payments may be fixed or variable (floating).

Capital project   Investment in a non-financial asset.

Coupon   When detached from a bond, a coupon serves as evidence of entitlement to an interest payment. The word coupon more usually refers to the rate of interest on an interest-bearing security, however.

Face value (par value)   Redemption value printed on a bond or share certificate. The actual market price for the security need not equal its face value.

Internal rate of return (IRR)   Discount rate that would make the net present value for an investment equal to zero.

Project Yield (PY)   Rate of return on a project obtained by comparing the project with a hypothetical bond with the same investment, remaining life, and risk.

7-5   CONCLUSIONS

This chapter takes a few steps beyond the project selection criteria found in most company capital budgeting manuals. The chapter discusses three main topics: APV, capital rationing, and PY.

APV represents a refinement of straightforward discounted cash flow. The refinement provides the means of reflecting specific advantages of special financing arrangements in a project's NPV.

Most companies encounter periods of several years when they have to ration capital available for projects. The widely recommended PI selection criterion is most effective when the capital rationing does not extend beyond the current year. The PIA is a better project selection criterion when expected capital rationing extends beyond the current year. While the PIA offers a better criterion, it still does not reflect sufficient detail to permit obtaining the optimum combination of projects from a limited capital budget. Mathematical programming can aid in finding better combinations of projects under capital rationing. Particularly when large sums of money are at stake, it can be worthwhile making mathematical programming a part of the project selection procedure.

The final topic considered in the chapter is the PY. The PY equals the yield on a hypothetical bond having the same required rate of return, the same life, and the same NPV as the project. The PY formula given in the chapter has at least three advantages over the IRR. First, it uses the project's required rate of return as the only discount rate. Second, the formula never gives spurious multiple rates of return for a project. Third, accepting projects with yields greater than their required rates of return always results in the same investment decisions as accepting projects that have NPVs greater than zero.

FURTHER READING

A. A. Alchian (1955) "The rate of interest, Fisher's rate of return over cost and Keynes' internal rate of return," *American Economic Review*, Vol. 45 (December), 938–942.

T. A. Luehrman (1997) "Using APV: A better tool for valuing operations," *Harvard Business Review*, Vol. 75 (May–June), 145–154.

H. M. Weingartner (1963) *Mathematical Programming and the Analysis of Capital Budgeting Problems* (Englewood Cliffs, NJ: Prentice Hall).

QUESTIONS AND PROBLEMS

1   APVAL PLC is negotiating a bank loan to help fund the following project:

	End of year				
	0	1	2	3	4
Investment	−1,200				
Operating cash flow after tax		500	500	500	500

The company usually aims to borrow half the funds required for projects. The company's treasurer expects to pay 8% on all new borrowing during the next four years. She also expects the company to pay corporate taxes at 30%. Consistent with 50% debt financing, she expects the cost of equity for the project will be 12%.

Use the WACC method to estimate the PV of the tax benefit from borrowing to finance half the cost of this project. Assume the company will continue to pay corporate taxes during the next four years.

2   The bank proposes to lend the company €600,000 toward the €1.2 million required to invest in the project in Problem 1. The rate of interest would be 8%. The loan is repayable in three equal annual instalments, the first paid at the end of the first year.

Use the APV method to calculate the PV of the tax benefit of the loan if the company continues to pay taxes during the next four years.

3   Because of a possible merger with a company having accumulated losses, APVAL could find itself in a non-tax paying position for the next two years, however. The implication is that the company would not get the benefit of deducting interest payments from taxable income until Year 3. The company can carry forward its accumulated tax deductions to that year, however.

Using the APV method, estimate the PV of the tax benefit of the bank loan in Problem 2 if APVAL will not be paying taxes until Year 3.

4   In anticipation of the possible merger, APVAL PLC's finance director wants to strengthen the company's cash position. To facilitate this, he is rationing the funds available for investment in capital projects. Given below are the expected cash flows of four projects currently under consideration. Assume a 10% discount rate for all the projects.

Project	End of year					
	0	1	2	3	4	5
A	−63	25	25	25	25	25
B	−107	128				
C	−52	19	19	19	19	
D	−77	28	28	28	28	28

(a)   Use the PI to rank the four projects in descending preference order if the finance director imposes capital rationing only in the current year.

(b)   Use the PIA to rank the four projects in descending preference order if the finance director expects capital rationing to extend beyond the current year.

(c)   Explain why the two sets of ranks are different.

5   The finance director is also considering the following four projects but wants to limit the initial capital budget available for investment in them to €1.4 million over the next two years.

Period ending	Projects				Budget
	G	H	I	J	
0	−900	−500			1,400
1	200	100			
2	200	100	−550	−660	
3	200	100	100	132	
4	200	100	100	132	
⋮	⋮	⋮	⋮	⋮	

He is willing to invest cash generated by any of the projects in the following year's projects. Treating this decision as an integer programming problem, use the manual method shown in this chapter to find the best choice of this year's projects.

6   Calculate the PY for each of the projects in Problem 5. Assume that the discount rate equals 10% for all the projects.

8 Appraising Projects with Real Options

Contemporary corporate project appraisal procedures treat capital projects as though they were stocks or bonds. Can this be correct? Well, not entirely. The problem is that most stocks and bonds are quite rigidly specified financial instruments, whereas you can design flexibility into projects, creating options for change. Management is largely about making advantageous decisions in the light of new information, and the potential to adapt a project to the evolving business environment adds value to the project. Conventional discounted cash flow (DCF) analysis does not lend itself to estimating the correct value of flexible projects because it does not provide the methodology for measuring the value of real options.

Real options are features that make a project flexible. The word *real* signifies that the options concern real assets rather than financial securities. The value of a real option derives from the fact that managers have the right to make ongoing favorable decisions concerning a project's investment and about its subsequent operation.

The simplest example of a real option is the right to choose a project if its net present value (NPV) is positive and to reject it if the NPV is negative. The potential to abandon a project sooner than expected or to operate it for longer than originally intended are also real options. Real options enable management to make such decisions. Because nothing obliges managers to choose unfavorable alternatives, real options have value.[1] If this value exceeds the incremental cost of the option, it increases the NPV of the project. While this is just common sense, conventional project appraisal methodology does not include the value of real options.

Strategically minded managers understand the need for flexible responses to unexpected changes in a competitive business environment. Accordingly, they like incorporating appropriate real options into projects. Corporate analytical procedures that do not measure the value of real options make it difficult for managers to judge how much to invest in project flexibility.

TOPICS

In this chapter, we consider the nature of real options and outline how to value them. So, we discuss the following:

---

[1] The value is positive only for options held long. The option to limit production capacity in exchange for lower initial investment is an option held short. The value is negative because the value of the opportunity to fill demand beyond capacity is lost. An option to invest subsequently in increased capacity can only partially offset this negative value. Chapter 9 shows how to measure such interacting effects.

O   *ten real options in capital projects;*

O   *the impact of uncertainty on project profitability;*

O   *how uncertainty creates real option value;*

O   *how to estimate the expected payoff on a real option;*

O   *refining the valuation of a real option;*

O   *estimating the spread of the probability distribution;*

O   *applications.*

We show here how to value individual real options. The next chapter shows how to analyze the ways in which interrelationships between the many different real options in a project affect its NPV.

8-1   REAL OPTIONS IN CAPITAL PROJECTS

A real option gives management the right without obligation to make a future choice that has favorable economic consequences for a real asset. At least ten real options can be relevant to project appraisal.

INVEST IN A FUTURE CAPITAL PROJECT[2]

Feasibility studies, R&D, patents, prototypes, and pilot plants, for example, can create options to invest. The possibility of optional future investment opportunities can add value to a company now, even if their precise nature is as yet unknown. Biotechnology, media, telecommunications, and Internet companies are contemporary examples. Just having a market foothold, enhanced by the strength of a brand, also provides valuable future opportunities to invest.

DELAY INVESTMENT BEYOND THE FIRST FEASIBLE DATE OR TO STAGE THE INVESTMENT[3]

The right to delay investing in the project is an option. Although delay usually entails loss of income, it can create positive net value if the delay enables management to obtain further information that could prevent wrong decisions.

CHOOSE THE PROJECT'S INITIAL CAPACITY

A project with infinite capacity would meet all possible demand, but greater capacity requires increased investment. The initial capacity decision is the option to choose a level of capacity that

---

[2] See J. E. Broyles and I. A. Cooper (1981) "Real asset options and capital budgeting," in *Nijenrode Studies in Business* (Boston: Martinus Nijhoff) and M. Brennan and E. Schwartz (1985) "A new way of evaluating natural resource investments," *Midland Journal of Corporate Finance*, Vol. 3, 78–88.

[3] See J. E. Broyles and I. A. Cooper (1981) "Real asset options and capital budgeting," in *Nijenrode Studies in Business* (Boston: Martinus Nijhoff) and R. McDonald and D. Siegel (1986) "The value of waiting to invest," *Quarterly Journal of Economics*, Vol. 101, November 707–727.

reduces the initial investment but does not sacrifice too much of the opportunity to meet unexpected increases in demand.

EXPAND THE CAPACITY OF THE PROJECT SUBSEQUENT TO THE ORIGINAL INVESTMENT

If demand can increase unexpectedly, features that permit increasing the project's capacity can be valuable.

CHANGE THE PROJECT'S TECHNOLOGY

Increasingly, commercial activities depend upon technology for greater efficiency and quality. The potential to adopt new technology and to improve the cost structure and quality of output adds value.

CHANGE THE USE OF THE PROJECT DURING ITS LIFE

Investing in features giving the asset the potential for alternative uses that are more profitable can be worthwhile.

SHUT DOWN THE PROJECT WITH THE INTENTION OF RESTARTING IT LATER

If business conditions are likely to turn favorable again, keeping the project ready for future operation can be more profitable than simply scrapping it or selling it.

ABANDON OR SELL THE PROJECT DURING ITS INTENDED LIFE[4]

The potential to abandon or to sell a project that has gone wrong releases the owner from further fixed expenditures and can realize cash from its residual value.

EXTEND THE LIFE OF THE PROJECT

The potential to extend the project's economic life, for example, by overhaul and modernization, has value that can exceed the expected additional cost.

INVEST IN FURTHER PROJECTS CONTINGENT ON INVESTMENT IN THE INITIAL PROJECT

The expected NPVs of resulting subsequent investment opportunities motivate much commercial activity and investment.

Clearly, capital projects can incorporate many real options, and we need to know how to include their values in a project's NPV.[5]

---

[4] S. C. Myers and S. Majd (1990) "Abandonment value and project life," *Advances in Futures and Options Research*, Vol. 4, 1–21.

[5] A. G. Z. Kemna (1993) "Case studies on real options," *Financial Management*, Autumn, 259–270.

DEFINITIONS

Bond   An interest-bearing security with usually long-term maturity. Interest payments may be fixed or variable (floating).

Capital project   Investment in a non-financial asset.

Net present value (NPV)   Difference between the present value of a project's expected after-tax operating cash flows and the present value of its expected after-tax investment expenditures.

Net value   Expected net present value measured as at some specified future date.

Real option   Right to make favorable future choices regarding real asset investments. More precisely, a real option is an opportunity for voluntary future investment in a nonfinancial asset when at least a part of the required investment expenditure is certain or, alternatively, when at least a part of the required investment expenditure is not perfectly positively correlated with the project's present value.

8-2   THE IMPACT OF UNCERTAINTY ON PROJECT PROFITABILITY

The fundamental issue in this chapter is how uncertainty affects the NPV of an investment decision. Simply adjusting the discount rate for risk does not account for the full impact of uncertainty. Adjusting the discount rate is not adequate because uncertainty also changes the expected cash flow when the project has a limited capacity and when management has real options. It is important to identify whether the combined impact of uncertainty on the discount rate and on the expected cash flows and options is favorable or unfavorable.

Uncertainty affects real investment in two ways. First, management can be uncertain about the investment I required. Second, management virtually always is uncertain about the present value (PV) that the future investment might generate. The real option is management's right at some future point in time to exchange funds I for a project with present value PV. When the time comes to invest, management need not exercise the option unless PV is greater than I.[6]

Since the future values (FVs) of variables I and PV may both be uncertain, we need to simplify by combining them into just one familiar variable. The obvious such variable is the Profitability Index (PI):

$$Profitability\ Index = Present\ Value / Investment$$

$$PI = PV / I$$

This permits managers to focus on the spread of possible values for the investment's PI.

We can easily define a real option in terms of its PI. That is, we exercise the real option only if PI

---

[6] In general, real options are exchange options. See W. Margrabe (1978) "The value of an option to exchange one asset for another," *Journal of Finance*, Vol. 33 (March), 177–186.

turns out to be greater than or equal to 1.00. Otherwise, we keep the funds *I* invested in the financial market where the value of the PI virtually always equals 1.00.

DEFINITIONS

Discount rate   Required rate of return used in the calculation of a discount factor.

Future value (FV)   Value obtainable from investing a given sum of money for a specified number of years at the required compound rate of return.

Uncertainty   Risk not measurable with historical data.

Profitability index (PI)   Present value of a project divided by the required investment.

8-3   HOW UNCERTAINTY CREATES REAL OPTION VALUE

Real options concern the way management will operate a project and thus affect its value to the company's shareholders. Uncertainty is what gives value to a capital project's real options. In the following example of an investment option, we show how to calculate the value of a real investment option under uncertainty.

EXAMPLE 8.1

In the year 2000, GROWTHCO PLC had a prospective project under development. The decision whether actually to invest in the project was not to be made until three years later in 2003. The company expected to have completed by that time the required research and development and to know more about potential competition. Investment in the project was to be contingent upon the project's PI being greater than 1.00 in 2003. So, in 2000 the potential to invest in the project in 2003 was a real option for GROWTHCO.

Management needed to know right away the PV of the investment option in order to ascertain whether to continue the required R&D. That is, the PV of the option needed to be greater than the PV of the required R&D budget.

Based on analysis and experience with a number of similar projects, GROWTHCO's management had views concerning the distribution of possible values of the investment's PI. Management expected to invest €25 million in the actual project if its PI proved to be greater than 1.00. The actual scale of this investment, however, was uncertain. It depended upon market information not fully available until 2003.

GROWTHCO assumed initially that the market for the product would be semiperfect.[7] This conservative assumption implies that the project's expected NPV would be due entirely to its real

---

[7] The standard definition of a perfect market assumes certainty together with other assumptions assuring perfect competition. An implication of a perfect market is that all NPVs equal zero due to perfect competition. We adopt the phrase "Semiperfect market" to denote a market under uncertainty in which real options are the only imperfections generating positive NPVs.

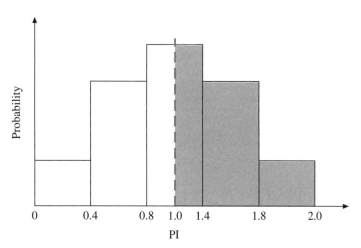

Figure 8.1 Real option payoff histogram.

options. Given this assumption, the expected NPV excluding the real options equals 0, and the corresponding expected value of *PI* equals 1.00.

$$E(PI) = 1.00$$

With the passage of time, management would receive new information relating to the value of the PI, causing it to deviate above or below its initially expected value of 1.00. Because management could not predict the actual effect of this unknown future information, it had to quantify the different possible deviations of the PI in terms of a probability histogram.

Figure 8.1 shows the histogram used by management in a preliminary analysis of the investment option. The figure represents what management feels is a realistic expectation for the spread of possible values for the investment's PI. The horizontal axis represents different possible PI values divided into discreet intervals, while the vertical axis represents the probability assigned to each interval.

Management associated each interval with a different cash flow scenario. Each scenario reflected a different combination of factors concerning, for example, market size, market share, and the resulting effects on price, variable cost, investment, fixed expenditure, and cash flow.[8]

Management intended to exercise the option for outcomes only in the part of the histogram shaded blue where the value of the PI is greater than or equal to 1.00. In the unshaded portion to the left where the PI is less than 1.00, management will not invest in the project because the alternative of investing in the financial market where the PI equals 1.00 is more attractive.

The expected value of the investment option's PI is just the sum of the probability-weighted PIs, which are all either greater than or equal to 1.00. As a result, the expected value E(*PI*) for the PI of payoffs is greater than 1.00, and the investment option has positive value.

---

[8] In general, the intervals would not necessarily be evenly spaced when based on different scenarios.

DEFINITIONS

Histogram   Bar chart depicting a frequency distribution, or a probability distribution associated with interval values for a random variable.

Payoff   Net positive difference between the price of the underlying asset and the exercise price on an option being exercised.

Scenario   Plausible sequence of events.

8-4   ESTIMATING THE PI OF THE EXPECTED PAYOFF ON A REAL OPTION

GROWTHCO's management needed to know whether the PV of the required R&D expenditure during the three years to 2003 would be less than the PV of the expected payoff on the investment option. If not, it would be better to drop the project and let the R&D people work on something more promising. That is:

$$PV(Required\ R\&D\ ) < PV(Expected\ Option\ Payoff)$$

The PV of the required R&D represents the "price" of the investment option. If the required price is more than the value of the option, it is not worth "buying" the option.

Obtaining the PV of the option first requires calculating the expected value of the PI including the expected value of the option's payoff. An option's payoff is the net positive benefit from exercising the option. Table 8.1 calculates the expected value of the PI with payoff. The method is to multiply each value of the PI by its probability. Each such PI value reflects management's right to choose only those alternatives for which the PI is greater than or equal to 1.00. The resulting expected PI for the option is the sum of these probability-weighted PIs.

The first column of Table 8.1 shows the selected intervals of the PI used in the histogram. The second column contains the average value of the PI for each interval. The third column gives the probability management assigned to each interval. The fourth column gives the value of the PI of the payoff depending on whether or not management would exercise the investment option. The final column gives the product of the PI and its probability for each interval. The sum at the bottom of the column gives the expected value of the expected PI of the payoff.

Table 8.1   Calculation of the expected PI of payoff (€ millions).

Interval	Interval value	Probability	PI of payoff	Expected PI of payoff
$0 < x \leq 0.4$	0.2	0.16	1.00	0.160
$0.4 < x \leq 0.8$	0.6	0.21	1.00	0.210
$0.8 < x \leq 1.2$	1	0.26	1.05	0.273
$1.2 < x \leq 1.6$	1.4	0.21	1.40	0.294
$1.6 < x \leq 2$	1.8	0.16	1.80	0.288
		1.00		1.225

For example, consider the data in the fourth row of the table. In this row, the PI falls between 1.2 and 1.6. The average value for this interval is therefore 1.4 as indicated in the second column. The probability assigned to this interval is 0.21 found in the third column. Because the average interval value of 1.4 is greater than 1.0, management would intend to invest in this interval, gaining an average PI value of 1.4 with probability 0.21. Therefore, the expected PI for this interval equals $0.21 \times 1.4 = 0.294$ as shown in the final column. The PIs in the final three rows of the table are similarly greater than 1.00.

In the first two rows, however, the corresponding calculation would indicate PI values less than 1.00, but the fourth column shows 1.00s instead. The reason is that management does not intend to invest in the project if the PI is less than 1.00. Instead, they could invest in the financial market where the PI equals 1.00. Therefore, we substitute the value 1.00 in place of each value of the PI less than 1.00.

The third row of the table requires further explanation. In this particular row, the interval spans the breakeven value 1.0 of the PI. So, we must split the interval into two parts. The part below 1.0 reflects investment of the funds in the financial market with PI equal to 1.0. The part between breakeven 1.0 and the top of the interval at 1.2 implies investment at a PI between 1.0 and 1.2. The average value for this subinterval is $(1.2 + 1.0)/2 = 1.1$. So, PI for this subinterval is 1.1. The value of 1.05 in the fourth column is a weighted average of 1.1 from the project and 1.0 from the financial market. The first weight is the fraction of the interval $[(1.2 - 1.0)/(1.2 - 0.8)] = 0.50$. The second weight is just the remainder $1.0 - 0.50 = 0.50$. Consequently, the weighted average PI is:

$$0.50 \times 1.1 + (1 - 0.50) \times 1.0 = 1.05$$

as indicated in the third row of the fourth column.

The investment's expected PI with the option payoff equals the sum of the individual probability-weighted PIs in the final column. The expected value of the the the investment's PI with option payoff is thus 1.225 as shown in the bottom row.

This expected value of the PI occurs at a point three years in the future. So, obtaining its PV requires discounting. Unfortunately, we do not know what discount rate to use. To resolve this problem we turn to the risk-neutral valuation approach.

DEFINITIONS

Discounting   Multiplying each of an investment's expected cash flow by its present value per unit (discount factor) to obtain the total net present value for the investment.

Payoff   Net positive difference between the price of the underlying asset and the exercise price on an option being exercised.

8-5   RISK-NEUTRAL VALUATION OF REAL OPTIONS

As we have seen, management's option to reject unfavorable payoffs alters the distribution of the PIs because alternative investment in the financial market has a PI equal to 1.00. For this reason, we no longer know the risk and thus have no direct method of using a risk-adjusted discount rate to

Table 8.2   Risk-neutral valuation of the PI with payoff (€ millions).

Interval	Risk-neutral interval	Interval value	Probability	Risk-neutral PI of payoff	Risk-neutral expected PI of payoff
$0.0 < x \leq 0.4$	$0.00 < x \leq 0.37$	0.18	0.16	1.00	0.160
$0.4 < x \leq 0.8$	$0.37 < x \leq 0.74$	0.55	0.21	1.00	0.210
$0.8 < x \leq 1.2$	$0.74 < x \leq 1.10$	0.92	0.26	1.01	0.264
$1.2 < x \leq 1.6$	$1.10 < x \leq 1.47$	1.29	0.21	1.29	0.271
$1.6 < x \leq 2.0$	$1.47 < x \leq 1.84$	1.66	0.16	1.66	0.265
			1.00		1.169

obtain the PV of the PI. Fortunately, we can use an indirect method borrowed from the financial option valuation literature.[9] This is the risk-neutral valuation approach. In this example, risk-neutral valuation merely requires changing the intervals in Table 8.1 before doing the rest of the calculation.

In the risk-neutral valuation method, we translate the data to the corresponding numbers for a risk-neutral world in which we do not need to adjust discount rates for risk. Table 8.2 demonstrates the altered procedure. The first step is to transform the values of the intervals in the first column to their risk-neutral equivalents in the second column. Then, the calculations for the succeeding columns proceed exactly as in Table 8.1.

RISK-ADJUSTMENT FACTOR

We obtain the transformed intervals in the second column of Table 8.2 simply by multiplying all the intervals in the first column by a risk-adjustment factor F. Because the PI is a ratio, the risk-adjustment factor F is also a ratio of two such factors:

$$F = \frac{\text{Risk-adjustment Factor for PV}}{\text{Risk-adjustment Factor for } I}$$

in which

$$\text{Risk-adjustment Factor for PV} = \frac{(1 + R_F)^T}{(1 + R_{PV})^T}$$

and

$$\text{Risk-adjustment Factor for } I = \frac{(1 + R_F)^T}{(1 + R_I)^T}$$

where R_I represents the discount rate for the future investment expenditure, R_{PV} is the project's discount rate, and T is the time left before exercise of the option. Dividing the two factors we obtain:

$$F = \frac{(1 + R_I)^T}{(1 + R_{PV})^T}$$

[9] See J. C. Cox and S. A. Ross (1976) "The valuation of options for alternative stochastic processes," *Journal of Financial Economics*, Vol. 3, 145–166.

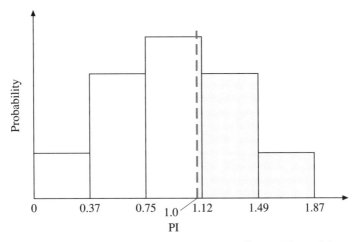

Figure 8.2   Risk-adjusted histogram corresponding to Figure 8.1.

Thus, the risk-adjustment factor in this case is:

$$F = \frac{(1 + R_I)^T}{(1 + R_{PV})^T} = \frac{(1 + 0.05)^3}{(1 + 0.10)^3} = 0.870$$

As a result of these risk adjustments to the PIs, the picture in Figure 8.1 changes to the one in Figure 8.2. The histogram shifts to the left relative to break-even at 1.00, leaving the smaller blue-shaded area on the right. The result is a smaller expected payoff, but one that does not require discounting.[10]

PRESENT VALUE OF THE OPTION

By multiplying the intervals in the first column of Table 8.2 by F, we obtain the risk-adjusted intervals in the second column. The rest of the calculation proceeds exactly as before in Table 8.1. Accordingly, we now obtain the lower value of 1.169 for the expected PI of the payoff compared with 1.225 obtained earlier. The advantage is that we do not have to discount this smaller number.

Now that we have the value of 1.169 for the PV of the expected PI of the payoff, we can use it to calculate the PV of the investment option:

Present Value of Option = Present Value of Expected Investment Expenditure

$$\times \ (\textit{Present Value of PI} - 1)$$

$$= \frac{25}{(1 + 0.07)^3} \times (1.169 - 1) = €3.449 \text{ million}$$

Management compared the required R&D expenditure with the €3.449 million value of the option. The R&D budget regarded as necessary to make the project ready by 2003 was €1 million per year. The PV of this three-year annuity discounted at 5% is €2.723 million. Therefore, continuing

---

[10] In the risk-neutral approach one might have expected to discount at the risk-free rate. In the case of exchange options, however, the risk-free discount factors cancel.

the R&D expenditure required to keep this investment option alive appears worthwhile. The PV in 2000 of the option to invest in 2003 exceeds the PV of the required investment expenditure by:

$$3.449 - 2.723 = €0.726 \text{ million}$$

Therefore, this analysis indicated that continuing with the R&D would be worthwhile because it added an estimated €726,000 to shareholder value.

Some questions remained, however. Was this preliminary analysis sufficiently accurate? Could management put the limited R&D resources to better use?

DEFINITIONS

Annuity   Investment generating equal cash flows each period for a specified number of periods.

Discounting   Multiplying each of an investment's expected cash flow by its present value per unit (discount factor) to obtain the total net present value for the investment.

Risk-neutral valuation   Option valuation method translating risky cash flows into their equivalents in a risk-neutral world and then discounting them at the risk-free rate.

Risk-adjustment factor   Factor translating risky cash flows into their equivalents in a risk-neutral world.

8-6   REFINING THE VALUATION

An important area for refinement concerns the probability distribution, particularly its mean and its spread (standard deviation). We consider the spread first.

SPREAD

If the estimated spread is too great, we overvalue the option. If it is too small, we undervalue it. Historical data virtually always are insufficient to estimate the relevant spread. Furthermore, few managers have experience quantifying their subjective uncertainty. For this reason, GROWTHCO adapted a technique commonly employed in the financial options market. The company's procedure determines the spread that would be required to achieve an acceptable value for the option.[11] If the spread of the resulting distribution is implausibly large, they reject the project. The procedure is as follows:

1.   *Estimate the shape of the histogram.* For example, the upper tail of the probability distribution will be limited by competition in a finite market.

---

[11] Traders know the current price (PV) of an actively traded financial option. Thus, the trader can assume a value for the standard deviation in the option valuation formula that gives this price. The trader can then use this value of the standard deviation (implied volatility) to value similar options. See H. Latané and R. J. Rendleman (1976) "Standard deviation of stock price ratios applied by option premia," *Journal of Finance*, Vol. 31 (May), 369–382.

Table 8.3 Implied spread method (€ millions).

Interval	Risk-neutral interval	Interval value	Probability	Risk-neutral PI of payoff	Risk-neutral expected PI of payoff
$0.17 < x \leq 0.50$	$0.16 < x \leq 0.46$	0.31	0.16	1.00	0.160
$0.50 < x \leq 0.83$	$0.46 < x \leq 0.77$	0.62	0.21	1.00	0.210
$0.83 < x \leq 1.17$	$0.77 < x \leq 1.07$	0.92	0.26	1.01	0.262
$1.17 < x \leq 1.50$	$1.07 < x \leq 1.38$	1.22	0.21	1.22	0.257
$1.50 < x \leq 1.83$	$1.38 < x \leq 1.68$	1.53	0.16	1.53	0.245
			1.00		1.133

Option value $= 2.723$

2. *Obtain the spread for the histogram that is consistent with the minimum acceptable value for the option. In practice, this means adjusting the interval values in a consistent manner to achieve the required option value.*

Table 8.3 illustrates the second step of this procedure applied to the investment option in Tables 8.1 and 8.2. The calculations in the table are exactly as employed previously in Table 8.2 but use different starting values for the intervals in the first column.

We want to know the spread of the distribution that results in the minimum acceptable option value, which in this case is €2.723 million. The resulting spread in the first column (using the spreadsheet Solver function) is actually narrower than the spread assumed earlier in the first column of Table 8.2. Therefore, Table 8.3 implies that the investment option is attractive because the spread required to make the option value acceptable is narrower than the spread that management was prepared to accept as a realistic expectation in Table 8.1.

The interval adjustment procedure used in Table 8.3 involves changing the interval adjustment factor K until the PV of the option reaches its minimum acceptable value. Consider, for example, the adjustment of the intervals in the first column of Table 8.1 to those in the first column of Table 8.3. The interval in the fifth row of Table 8.1 is:

$$1.6 < x \leq 2.0$$

The factor $K = 0.826$ adjusted this interval in the following way:

$$1.0 + K \times (1.6 - 1.0) = 1.50$$

and

$$1.0 + K \times (2.0 - 1.0) = 1.83$$

The adjusted interval in Table 8.3 therefore is:

$$1.50 < x \leq 1.83$$

to two decimal places.

The factor K adjusted all the intervals and interval values in this way. The chosen value of 0.826 for K made the PV of the option in Table 8.3 equal to the minimum acceptable value of €2.723 million. The spreadsheet Solver function obtained this value for K using a fast trial-and-error algorithm.

EXPECTED VALUE OF THE PROFITABILITY INDEX

In their preliminary analysis, management employed a conservative assumption that caused them to underestimate the value of the investment option. They assumed a semiperfect market, in which the expected value of the NPV, excluding the option value, would equal zero. Relaxing this assumption increases the PV of the investment option.

Assuming an expected value equal to zero for the investment option was conservative because a part of the intended R&D expenditure covered a comprehensive set of patents. Effective patent protection would raise the expected PI above 1.00 and thus would increase the expected payoff on the investment option. Consequently, their analysis in Table 8.2 undervalued the expected PI for the payoff. The undervaluation did not concern management in this instance because the resulting conservative PV for the option exceeded the PV of the required R&D expenditure. So, their existing course of action still appeared to be the right one.

If the value of the option net of the required R&D expenditure had been negative, however, they would have refined the analysis before deciding whether to abandon the R&D. In addition, if there were attractive alternative uses for the same R&D resources, they would need a more refined analysis of this option and of competing options.

For example, when including the value added to the expected NPV by patents, they use the following procedure specified in their Project Appraisal Manual:

1.   Estimate the expected total industry market volume achievable for the product in each future period.

2.   Estimate the company's proportionate share of this market volume in each period, given its expected competitive advantage including the expected effectiveness of the patent protection.

3.   Estimate the company's expected pricing and costs of the product in each future period given expected changes in the relative strength of its competitive position in the market.

The resulting expected product volume, prices, costs, and investment generate the expected future PI used in the more refined analyses. That is, the histogram centers on a mean value greater than the value of 1.00 used in the earlier figures and tables.

DEFINITIONS

Option   Contract granting the right without obligation to engage in a future transaction on terms specified in the contract.

Standard deviation   Square root of the variance.

Volatility   Standard deviation of percentage changes in the asset price. More precisely, standard deviation of changes in the natural logarithm of the asset price.

8-7 APPLICATIONS

The beginning of the chapter lists 10 different real options that can be relevant to a project. We outline below adaptations of the above procedure for these applications.

INVEST IN A FUTURE CAPITAL PROJECT

The procedure above shows how to value the option to invest in a future capital project. The option increases shareholder value if the PV of the option to invest in the future exceeds the PV of the R&D or other expenditure required to make the future investment feasible.

The value of this option is significant for companies having growth opportunities.

DELAY INVESTMENT BEYOND THE FIRST FEASIBLE DATE OR TO STAGE THE INVESTMENT

The same procedure applies to the option to delay investments beyond the first feasible date or to stage the investment. In place of R&D expenditure, we have the opportunity cost of lost income during the delay period. The option increases shareholder value if the PV of the option to invest in the project on a future date net of the PV of the opportunity cost is greater than the NPV from investing in the project immediately.

Whether delay is a valuable option depends upon the immediacy of competition and the potential effect of emerging new information during the delay.

CHOOSE THE INITIAL CAPACITY OF A PROJECT

Most real options are options "bought" by increased investment. The initial capacity option, however, is "sold" in exchange for reduced investment. The payoffs are negative. Limited capacity sacrifices value requiring capacity above its chosen limit. All the probability associated with the sacrificed value attaches to PIs at the capacity limit. Reflecting this change in the histogram permits quantifying the effect of limited capacity on the NPV of the project.

Conventional appraisal procedures include the benefit of the lower investment but fail to reflect the value sacrificed due to limited capacity. Because managers design most projects to run close to capacity, this failure to reflect the expectation of lost contributions beyond the capacity limit significantly overvalues the NPV of a project.

EXPAND THE CAPACITY OF THE PROJECT SUBSEQUENT TO THE ORIGINAL INVESTMENT

When valuing the option to expand the capacity of the project subsequent to the original investment, first examine the effect of a future increase of capacity on the probability histogram for the PIs and then calculate the resulting effect on the PV of the project. The option increases the NPV of the project if the option's PV exceeds the additional initial investment required to make future capacity expansion feasible.

This option is unlikely to have great value if management makes a wise choice of initial capacity.

CHANGE TECHNOLOGY

The histogram for the option to change technology concerns the spread of the probabilities of the PIs reflecting the new technology. The investment includes the lost PV of continuing operations with the old technology.

An intelligent choice of technology and cost structure for the project tends to limit the value of the option to change.

CHANGE THE USE OF THE PROJECT DURING ITS LIFE

The procedure for the option to change the use of the project during its life is the same as for the option to change technology. This option is most valuable in industries where products have short lives.

SHUT DOWN A PROJECT WITH THE INTENTION OF RESTARTING IT LATER

The histogram for the option to shut down a project with the intention of restarting it later concerns the probabilities of the PIs for operating the restarted project. The investment includes the PV of the cost of shutting the project down, the opportunity cost of not operating during the shutdown, and of the costs of restarting it.

This option is most valuable in natural resource industries subject to widely varying commodity prices.

ABANDON OR SELL THE PROJECT DURING ITS INTENDED LIFE

The histogram represents the spread of the probabilities of the PIs for abandonment or sale of the project. The numerator of the PI includes the net proceeds of the sale. The investment in the denominator is the PV from continuing to operate the project.[12] The option increases the NPV of the project if the PV of the option exceeds any additional initial investment required to make sale of the project a feasible option.

The value of this option is not large if the probability of sale is small and if the selling price would be low in the circumstances that would force management to sell the project.

EXTEND THE LIFE OF THE PROJECT

The procedure for valuing the option to extend the life of the project is identical to the procedure for the investment option discussed earlier in the chapter. The histogram concerns the spread of probabilities of the PIs for continuing operation of the project for a specified number of periods beyond its assumed economic life. The investment includes the expected cost of overhauling the project. The option increases the NPV of the project if the PV of the option exceeds the additional initial investment required to make extending the life of the project feasible.

The long delay before exercise of this option reduces its PV, usually to a relatively small value.

---

[12] This assumes that the PV of continued operation is greater than 0. If it is negative, we simply choose the least negative alternative, including abandonment.

INVEST IN FURTHER PROJECTS CONTINGENT ON INVESTMENT IN THE INITIAL PROJECT

Valuing the option to invest in further projects contingent on investment in the initial project is a straightforward application of the investment option procedure described earlier in the chapter. The histogram concerns the spread of the probabilities for the PIs of further projects. The option increases the NPV of the initial project to the extent that it creates valuable options on future investment in related projects.

This option is most valuable in a growth environment characterized by great uncertainty.

The problems at the end of the chapter provide an opportunity to try your hand applying the suggested valuation procedure to many of these options.

DEFINITIONS

Opportunity cost of capital Return forgone when investing in a project instead of the securities market.

Shareholder value Economic value of the shareholders' financial claim on the business.

8-8 CONCLUSIONS

At least 10 real options can be associated with a capital project. All have the potential to change the project's NPV. Therefore, traditional project appraisal methods that omit the value of a project's real options values are unlikely to estimate correctly its NPV.

Many real options have relatively low values, however. For example, positive payoffs for the option to sell a project usually have low probability, making the PV of the expected payoff relatively small.

In contrast, the initial capacity option is associated with relatively large probabilities. Because managers try to run operations at full capacity, the probability of losing contributions due to limited capacity approaches 50%. Traditional appraisal procedures fail to reflect the negative effect of the lost contributions. For this reason, they often give too high a value to a project's NPV.[13]

We have shown how to estimate the NPV of individual real options. The procedure has four steps. First, estimate the probability distribution of the PI at the exercise date. Second, obtain the corresponding risk-adjusted probability distribution. Third, calculate the PV of the expected payoff for the real option based on the risk-adjusted probabilities. Fourth, compare the PV of the option with the initial incremental investment required to create the option. This gives the NPV of the real option.

---

[13] Earlier literature claiming that traditional project appraisal methods undervalue project NPVs failed to recognize that traditional methods generally do not reflect the relatively large negative effect of limited capacity under uncertainty.

Unfortunately, we cannot simply add up the NPVs of all a project's individual real options. The reason is that the existence of one option can affect the values of the project's other options.[14] The whole value is not equal to the sum of the parts.

In the next chapter, we demonstrate the use of the binomial tree method. This method facilitates the analysis of complex interactions between the many real options in a capital project. Accordingly, the binomial tree enables us to ascertain the joint effect of many real options on a project's NPV.

FURTHER READING

M. Amram and N. Kulatilaka (1999) *Real Options: Managing Strategic Investment in an Uncertain World* (Boston: Harvard Business School Press).

T. Copeland and V. Antikarov (2001) *Real Options, A Practitioner's Guide* (London: Texere).

K. Leslie and M. Michaels (1998) "The real power of real options," *Corporate Finance*, Vol. 158, January, 13–20.

L. Trigeorgis (1997) *Real Options, Managerial Flexibility and Strategy in Resource Allocation* (London: MIT Press).

QUESTIONS AND PROBLEMS

I   BIOTEK SA is developing a genetically engineered drug. Tests indicate that the drug can almost certainly arrest particular types of cancer. Before the drug can become a marketable product, however, it must go through a long process of clinical testing and government approval. The time expected to complete this process is 10 years.

Ten years from now the NPV might turn out to be very much greater than zero, however, or it could be less. If the NPV should be negative at that time, nothing obliges the company to launch the product. If the NPV should be positive instead, BIOTEK will invest in the product. An expected total investment of €2 billion (€2,000 million) in manufacturing capacity, advertizing, and distribution will be required.

The spread of possible PI values will be quite wide. After contemplating a number of market scenarios, management estimated the following table for the PI.

Interval	Average value	Probability
$0.00 < x \leq 0.20$	0.10	0.07
$0.20 < x \leq 0.58$	0.39	0.24
$0.58 < x \leq 1.71$	1.15	0.38
$1.71 < x \leq 5.00$	3.35	0.24
$5.00 < x \leq 14.60$	9.80	0.07
		1.00

[14] An exception is options exercised independently on the same date. If their payoff values are independent, their PVs are additive.

BIOTEK's discount rate for the project's PV is 15%. Its discount rate for the expected €2,000 million investment is 10%.

(a)   What is the PV now of the real option to launch this new drug?

(b)   How much money (in PV) can the company plan to spend on clinical testing and approval without losing value for shareholders?

2   If HARDWARE PLC invests now in the Alpha Project, the NPV would be €45,000. If the company delays investing in the project for one year instead, the expected NPV at that time would be €50,000. The expected required investment one year from now is €300,000. Therefore, the expected PV at that time is €350,000. The discount rate for the PV is 12%. Unfortunately, the PV of the after-tax income lost during the one-year delay would be €85,000.

Management's estimated histogram for the PI reflects a significant spread, however, as seen in the table below.

Interval	Average value	Probability
$0.00 < x \leq 0.36$	0.18	0.07
$0.36 < x \leq 0.71$	0.54	0.24
$0.71 < x \leq 1.40$	1.06	0.38
$1.40 < x \leq 2.75$	2.08	0.24
$2.75 < x \leq 5.40$	4.08	0.07
		1.00

Management intends to use a discount rate equal to only 9% for the expected investment.

(a)   What is the NPV now of the real option to invest in the Alpha Project next year?

(b)   What would be the minimum required NPV from the Alpha Project to justify investment right away? Should the company delay investing in the project?

3   HARDWARE PLC is considering how much to charge for the extra benefit customers would derive from incorporation of reconfigurable microprocessor chips in the company's Gamma Product. Reconfiguration permits a customer to change the design of an existing chip for new requirements. Therefore, the chips give customers a valuable real option to change technology. The customer benefits by saving the cost of replacing chips and of installing them.

HARDWARE's financial analyst estimates that customers will need to reconfigure about once a year. The analyst expects that the cost of a replacement chip and installing it would be €80 on average, but the spread of possible replacement costs is not small. One of HARDWARE's analysts produced the following table of rough estimates for the PI for replacement. The discount rate for the cost of a replacement is 15%.

Interval	Average value	Probability
$0.00 < x \leq 0.47$	0.24	0.07
$0.47 < x \leq 0.78$	0.63	0.24
$0.78 < x \leq 1.28$	1.03	0.38
$1.28 < x \leq 2.12$	1.70	0.24
$2.12 < x \leq 3.49$	2.80	0.07
		1.00

The cost to the customer of each reconfiguration is €60. The discount rate for the cost of reconfiguring the microprocessor is 8%.

(a)   What is the PV now of the real option to reconfigure the microprocessor after one year?

(b)   Assuming that customers will have just one opportunity to reconfigure, what is the most that HARDWARE PLC can justify charging for the reconfigurable chips if reconfiguration occurs just once after one year?

(c)   Say how you would solve the problem in (b) if customers will have three annual opportunities to reconfigure the chip instead of just one.

4   The industrial engineers at HARDWARE PLC are designing a new factory building. By altering the design, they can make it feasible to sell the building in the future. The design change would increase its initial cost. The company will require the building for at least five years, however. The question is what is the justifiable upper limit on the cost of the building if it is to be attractive to potential buyers.

The industrial engineers expect that the value of the altered building in five years' time should be worth around €10 million to the company. The discount rate for this would be only 6%. The expected market price for the altered building is also €10 million, but the actual price could deviate widely from this figure. The following table represents the estimated distribution of probabilities for the PI for selling the building in five years' time. The discount rate for the market price is 14%.

Interval	Average value	Probability
$0.00 < x \leq 0.76$	0.38	0.07
$0.76 < x \leq 0.91$	0.84	0.24
$0.91 < x \leq 1.10$	1.00	0.38
$1.10 < x \leq 1.32$	1.21	0.24
$1.32 < x \leq 1.59$	1.45	0.07
		1.00

(a)   What is the PV now of the real option to sell the building in five years' time?

(b)   How much more can HARDWARE afford to spend on the building now to make it attractive to potential buyers in five years' time?

5   HARDWARE's industrial engineers are also contemplating the option to expand the size of the factory building five years from now. The limited space on the site means that increasing the size of the building requires adding a second story. This would require

spending now on stronger foundations and a stronger structure costing €1 million. The question is whether it is worth spending this sum now to create the expansion option.

The expected cost of adding the second story to the building is €6.5 million, and the discount rate for this is 6%. The assumed expected value to the company of building the extra story is the same as the cost of doing so. The following table summarizes the analyst's views concerning the different possible outcomes for the expansion's PI five years from now.

Interval	Average value	Probability
$0.00 < x \le 0.76$	0.38	0.07
$0.76 < x \le 0.91$	0.84	0.24
$0.91 < x \le 1.10$	1.00	0.38
$1.10 < x \le 1.32$	1.21	0.24
$1.32 < x \le 1.59$	1.45	0.07
		1.00

The discount rate for these possible values is 14%.

(a)   Recompute the spread of the intervals in the table such that the value of the expansion option equals the cost of strengthening the foundations and structure.

(b)   What does the recomputed spread tell us about the desirability of investing in the stronger structure?

6   HARDWARE's industrial engineers want to know the value of the option to use the new building longer than expected. The company expects to use the building for 10 years. The expected residual value of the building is approximately €5 million. The engineers expect that keeping the building will be worth €4 million at that time. The discount rate is 10% for both values.

The spread of probabilities for the PI for keeping the building 10 years from now is summarized in the table below.

Interval	Average value	Probability
$0.00 < x \le 0.44$	0.22	0.07
$0.44 < x \le 0.76$	0.60	0.24
$0.76 < x \le 1.31$	1.04	0.38
$1.31 < x \le 2.27$	1.79	0.24
$2.27 < x \le 3.91$	3.09	0.07
		1.00

What is the PV of the real option to continue using the building in 10 years' time?

7   INTERNATIONAL MACHINERY PLC is interested in establishing a small manufacturing operation in China. The expected NPV for this operation is −€6 million. The justification for this loss-making operation is that it could lead to a more profitable investment opportunity when the company has more experience of doing business in China. The issue is whether the company should move forward with this €10 million preliminary investment.

After five years, the company might shut down the operation, depending on economic and political developments in China. Alternatively, the company might commit €100 million to further investment at that time.

If the NPV should turn out to be negative, the company expects to shut down its operations in China. The expected value for the PV of the contributions in five years' time equals €116 million. But the expected spread around this value is quite large, however, as indicated in the following table for the PI prepared by the company's analysts.

Interval	Average value	Probability
$0.00 < x \leq 0.47$	0.24	0.07
$0.47 < x \leq 0.78$	0.63	0.24
$0.78 < x \leq 1.28$	1.03	0.38
$1.28 < x \leq 2.12$	1.70	0.24
$2.12 < x \leq 3.49$	2.80	0.07
		1.00

The discount rate used for the PV of these investments is 25%.

(a)   What is the PV of the real option to make the further investment in China?

(b)   Should the company make the initial negative NPV investment in China?

9 Valuing Interrelated Real Options

Chapter 8 showed a way to value the effect of individual real options on a project's net present value (NPV). We did not consider, however, how the values of real options in a capital project depend on one another. In this chapter, we explain a method employing the binomial tree to incorporate the interdependent values of a project's real options in its NPV. First, we indicate how we can get a better perspective on the ways in which real options relate to the boundaries of a project's possibilities. We then show how to use the binomial tree to incorporate the effects of real options under uncertainty in a project's NPV. Finally, we show how to use sensitivity analysis to explore a project's possibilities and to reveal the corresponding, interrelated benefits of its real options.

TOPICS

Therefore, we discuss the following aspects:

○ *the project frame;*

○ *the one-step binomial tree: two branches;*

○ *multistep binomial trees: more branches;*

○ *incorporating the values of real options;*

○ *obtaining the NPV of the project;*

○ *real options sensitivity analysis.*

9-1 THE PROJECT FRAME

We need to know how to include the values of combinations of real options in a project's NPV. Because option values depend in part on their relationship with other options, ascertaining their net effect on the NPV is not trivial. So, it is necessary to understand how the values of different options in a project can depend on one another.

STRUCTURE OF INTERRELATED OPTIONS

There are many possible interdependencies, and it is necessary to get the right perspective to avoid confusion. The majority of capital projects encountered in industry can be characterized in terms of what we shall call the "project frame." The project frame has four "sides," that is, front, top, bottom, and back. The options most closely identified with the four sides are:

FRONT (BEGINNING)

The following two options determine if or when a project begins:

○   Invest. *The option to invest in a future capital project.*

○   Delay. *The option to delay investment in the project beyond the first feasible date or to invest in it in stages.*

TOP (CAP)

The following options concern the project's capacity:

○   Cap. *The option to limit the project's capacity in order to reduce the initial investment.*

○   Expand. *Options to expand the capacity of the project subsequent to the initial investment.*

BOTTOM (FLOOR)

The following options provide alternatives that put a floor under the project's value:

○   Change technology. *Options to change technology or the cost structure of the project during its life.*

○   Change use. *Options to change the use of the project during its life.*

○   Shut down. *The option to cease operating the project.*

○   Restart. *The option to restart the project.*

○   Sell. *Options to sell the asset to other firms or to abandon it.*

BACK (ENDING)

The following option affects when a project ends:

○   Extend. *The option to extend the life of the project.*

OUTSIDE

Often, contingent real options lie outside the frame. They are expected investment opportunities resulting from investment in the current project:

○   Collaborate. *Options to engage in joint ventures or strategic partnerships related to the project.*

○   Invest subsequently. *Options to invest in further projects contingent on investment in the initial project.*

The boundaries of the frame are not rigid. Real options capture value by providing opportunities to move the sides of the frame. Doing so can be expensive, and moving one side can affect the values obtainable from moving the other sides. We need an analytical method that reflects these value interrelationships. This will help us to devise ways to obtain the full value of a project's potential. The binomial tree is one of the most favored methods for this type of problem.

DEFINITIONS

Binomial tree   Tree with two branches from each node.

Capital project   Investment in a non-financial asset.

Net present value (NPV)   Difference between the present value of a project's expected after-tax operating cash flows and the present value of its expected after-tax investment expenditures.

Real option   Right to make favorable future choices regarding real asset investments. More precisely, a real option is an opportunity for voluntary future investment in a nonfinancial asset when at least a part of the required investment expenditure is certain or, alternatively, when at least a part of the required investment expenditure is not perfectly positively correlated with the project's present value.

Sensitivity analysis   Testing the effect of changes to individual variables on a project's net present value.

Uncertainty   Risk not measurable with historical data.

9-2   THE ONE-STEP BINOMIAL TREE: TWO BRANCHES

The binomial tree is one of the best means of valuing interrelated real options. A tree diagram sets out the answers to three questions that recur throughout the life of a project:

O   *Where are we in the decision process?*

O   *Which options should we exercise?*

O   *Where might chance lead us next?*

Real options permit altering the cash flow in real time by exercising the options. For simplicity, we first describe a one-step binomial tree. Afterwards we can consider how to construct multistep trees out of one-step trees.

RISK-NEUTRAL VALUATION

As in Chapter 8, we will need to do our calculations within the **risk-neutral valuation** framework.

EXAMPLE 9.1

Consider a one-period project involving an expected cash flow of 100 at the end of the period. Using the discounted cash flow (DCF) method, assuming the appropriate discount rate is 10%, the present value (PV) of the project is:

$$PV_0 = \frac{100}{(1+0.10)^1} = 90.91$$

The risk-neutral valuation procedure gives the same result. First, obtain the risk-neutral cash flow multiplying by the risk-adjustment factor F:

$$c = F \times 100$$

If the risk-free rate is 6%,

$$F = \frac{(1+0.06)^1}{(1+0.10)^1} = 0.9636$$

So, the risk-neutral value of the cash flow is 96.36. Next, discount the risk-neutral cash flow using the risk-free rate:

$$PV_0 = \frac{96.36}{(1+0.06)^1} = 90.91$$

This gives the same PV of 90.91 obtained earlier in the conventional manner.

Uncertainty, however, means that the expected cash flow of 100 and its corresponding risk-neutral value of 96.36 could end up being different from their originally expected values. Figure 9.1 illustrates just two of the many alternative ways the risk-neutral value could change with the passage of time before the cash flow actually occurs.

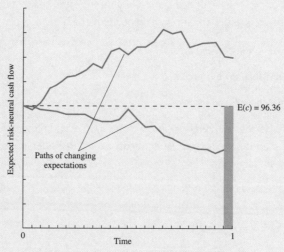

Figure 9.1 Paths of changing expected risk-neutral values.

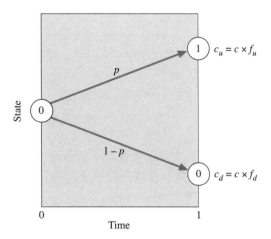

Figure 9.2 A one-step binomial tree.

BINOMIAL REPRESENTATION

As time passes, we learn more about the likely outcome, and the risk-neutral value changes accordingly. We assume that the path of such changing expectations follows a random walk as illustrated in Figure 9.1.[1] The figure illustrates just two of the virtually infinite number of different paths the expected risk-neutral value might take until we know the actual outcome. We can represent a sample of these paths as branches in a binomial tree.

The simplest binomial tree is the one-step tree with only two branches as illustrated in Figure 9.2. In the binomial framework, we suppose that the risk-neutral value of the cash flow can only deviate two ways. It can deviate up by a factor f_u to State 1 with probability p or down to State 0 by a factor f_d with probability $(1 - p)$ as illustrated in Figure 9.2. The corresponding risk-neutral values are:

$$c_u = 96.36 \times f_u$$
$$c_d = 96.36 \times f_d$$

We assume initially that these outcomes are unaltered by any real options.

ONE-STEP DEVIATION FACTORS

Assuming our expectation for the cash flow follows a random walk,[2] the formulas for the appropriate values of the deviation factors f_u and f_d are:

$$f_u = e^{\sigma\sqrt{\Delta t}}$$
$$f_d = \frac{1}{f_u} = e^{-\sigma\sqrt{\Delta t}}$$

---

[1] The obvious alternative is to assume that the PV follows a random walk. We do not follow this approach because it does not facilitate incorporating the effect of a project's limited capacity.

[2] Actually, we assume that the natural logarithms of the expected values follow a random walk.

This implies that changing the time gap Δt (a fraction or a multiple of a year) represented by one step in the tree would change the deviation represented by the branches of the tree. In addition, changing the uncertainty (represented by the annualized standard deviation σ) changes the deviation represented by the branches of the tree.

EXAMPLE 9.2

Suppose that the annualized standard deviation of the cash flow equals 0.2. The corresponding values of the deviation factors for a step of one year are:

$$f_u = e^{0.2\sqrt{1}} = 1.2214$$

$$f_d = \frac{1}{1.2214} = 0.8187$$

Accordingly, in our example the two branches of the tree represent the up and down values:

$$c_u = 96.36 \times f_u = 96.36 \times 1.2214 = 117.69$$

$$c_d = 96.36 \times f_d = 96.36 \times 0.8187 = 78.89$$

both of which are risk-neutral values for discounting at the risk-free rate.

DEVIATION PROBABILITIES

We need to know how to get values for the probabilities p and $1 - p$ so that we can calculate the probability-weighted expected value of the cash flows and options. By definition, the Period 1 expected risk-neutral cash flow is the probability-weighted average of the two branches:

$$96.36 = p \times c_u + (1 - p) \times c_d$$

By substitution we have:

$$96.36 = p \times (96.36 \times f_u) + (1 - p) \times (96.36 \times f_d)$$

Note that the cash flow 96.36 cancels, and thus we can solve for the probability p in terms of f_u and f_d only:[3]

$$p = \frac{1 - f_d}{f_u - f_d}$$

The probabilities p and $1 - p$ defined in this way are the risk-adjusted probabilities, because they are probabilities that relate only to the risk-neutral cash flow rather than to the original unadjusted cash flow.

---

[3] This expression for p does not incorporate the risk-free rate because we are using the tree to represent uncertainty rather than to represent directly the value of the underlying asset.

In our example:

$$p = \frac{1 - 08187}{1.2214 - 0.8187} = 0.4502$$

This probability together with $1 - p$ calculates the probability-weighted expectations of the risk-neutral cash flows and options in the binomial tree.

EXPECTED CASH FLOW

In our example the upper branch leads to a value of $c_u = 117.69$. The lower branch leads to the value $c_d = 78.89$. Therefore, the expected value for these risk-neutral values is:

$$c_1 = p \times c_u + (1 - p) \times c_d$$
$$= 0.4502 \times 117.69 + (1 - 0.4502) \times 78.89$$
$$= 96.36$$

which equals the result obtained earlier.

PRESENT VALUE

To get the resulting PV at the root of the tree, we can discount this expected risk-neutral value at the risk-free rate:

$$V_{0,0} = \frac{E(c_1)}{1 + R_f} = \frac{96.36}{1 + 0.06} = 90.91$$

So, we can see that the result from discounting the branch values in the one-step tree is consistent with our previous result for this example. We obtain the same PV of 90.91.

DEFINITIONS

Binomial tree   Tree with two branches from each node.

Discount rate   Required rate of return used in the calculation of a discount factor.

Discounted cash flow (DCF)   Method of determining the present value of a cash flow expected to be received on a specific future date.

Discounting   Multiplying each of an investment's expected cash flow by its present value per unit (discount factor) to obtain the total net present value for the investment.

Present value (PV)   Value of an investment now as the cost of a comparable investment in the financial market (calculated by multiplying the investment's expected after-tax cash income by the appropriate discount factors).

Risk-neutral valuation   Option valuation method translating risky cash flows into their equivalents in a risk-neutral world and then discounting them at the risk-free rate.

Random walk   Process in which successive changes to the value of a random variable are identically normally distributed, are uncorrelated, and have an expected value equal to zero.

Risk-adjustment factor   Factor translating risky cash flows into their equivalents in a risk-neutral world.

Standard deviation   Square root of the variance.

9-3   MULTISTEP BINOMIAL TREES: MORE BRANCHES

OBTAINING ACCURACY

Getting closer to reality requires more branches because an uncertain cash flow can have very many possible outcomes. We can have as many branches as we like by dividing time into smaller intervals Δt. For example, if we divide a year into two steps, then $\Delta t = 0.5$. Each such shortened interval corresponds to one step in a multistep tree. A two-step tree would then span $2\Delta t = 1$ year. We construct the two-step tree by chaining identical one-step trees together as in Figure 9.3. The combined two-step tree now has three branches as seen in the figure. Similarly, an N-step tree would have $N + 1$ branches. We can make N as large as necessary to obtain the required accuracy.

CONSTRUCTING A MULTISTEP TREE

Unlike the simple one-period project in the last section, a capital investment normally generates a sequence of cash flows over several years. Therefore, we need to expand the multistep tree across time to embrace all the cash flows in subsequent periods. Construction of a large multistep tree is not difficult to program when constructed of identical one-step trees as in Figure 9.3.

Construction of the binomial tree as multiples of the elementary one-step tree means that the resulting deviation factors and probabilities associated with the branches represent multiples of the deviation factors for the one-step tree.

DEVIATION FACTORS AND CORRESPONDING PROBABILITIES

In Figure 9.3, we see that there are many possible paths through a multistep tree. After just two steps, paths lead to three different states, numbered 0, 1, and 2 in the figure.

Only one path leads to State 2 on the uppermost branch. Getting there requires two steps up. Therefore, the combined deviation factor is:

$$f_{2,0} = f_u \times f_u = f_u^2$$

Each step up toward State 2 has the probability p. Thus the probability of getting to State 2 is:

$$P_{2,2} = p \times p = p^2$$

The bottommost State 0 is similar but requires two steps down. Thus:

$$f_{2,0} = f_d \times f_d = f_d^2$$
$$P_{2,0} = (1 - p) \times (1 - p) = (1 - p)^2$$

In contrast, there are two paths leading to the middle State 1. The first is one step up followed by one step down. The second path is one step down followed by one step up. The combined deviation factor is the same for State 1 regardless of the path taken to reach that state:

$$f_{2,1} = f_u \times f_d = f_d \times f_u$$

The probabilities behave differently, however. We must *add* the combined probabilities for each of

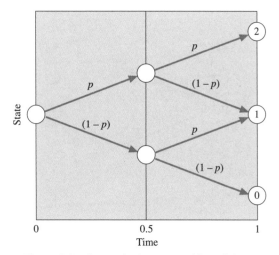

Figure 9.3 A standard two-step binomial tree.

the separate paths leading to the same state:

$$P_{2,1} = p \times (1-p) + (1-p) \times p = 2p(1-p)$$

It is easy to appreciate that as the number of steps in a tree increases, the number of possible paths to any given state increases rapidly.

For step n in a binomial tree the formula for the combined deviation factor is:

$$f_{ij} = f_u^j f_d^{i-j}$$

where j identifies the relevant state at Step i. Using this formula in the two-step tree example considered earlier, the deviation factor for State 1 after two steps is:

$$f_{2,1} = f_u^1 f_d^{2-1} = f_u f_d$$

as we found earlier without using this formula.

We do not actually need the corresponding formula for the state probabilities because we use the probabilities p and $(1-p)$ one step at a time in the tree-based calculations demonstrated below.

9-4 INCORPORATING THE VALUES OF REAL OPTIONS

Our objective is to incorporate the interdependent values of real options into a project's NPV. To do this we must calculate the value of the choices that management can make in each state and stage in the life of a project. The multistep binomial tree provides a framework within which we can incorporate the values of these choices or options.

We perform the calculations from right to left in the tree. That is, we start with the outermost branches of the tree and discount cash flows one step at a time backward toward the root. The result at the root gives the project's PV. At each such step, we have an opportunity to include the values of real options.

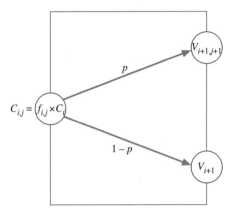

Figure 9.4 Node i, j and branches.

A node is a point at which the tree divides into two further branches. Figure 9.4 illustrates node i, j in the tree. This node represents State j at Step i. The risk-neutral expected value for the cash flow for Step i is c_i. Therefore, if there is no limit on the project's capacity, the node represents the outcome:

$$c_{ij} = f_{i,j} c_i$$

$$= f_u^j f_d^{i-j} \times c_i$$

We cannot always use this value, however, because the project's capacity might restrict the cash flow to a smaller value. So, we must incorporate the cap on the cash flow imposed by the project's limited capacity.

CAPACITY FORMULA

Because of limited capacity, the project cannot meet all the demand that the market might require. We must incorporate this limit in the calculation.

Let cap_i represent the risk-neutral value of the capacity limit for the contribution cash flow. The before-tax **contribution cash flow** equals unit volume multiplied by the difference between the price per unit and the direct (variable) cost per unit. The value attached to the cash flow at this node is the smallest of the contribution cash flow or the capacity:

$$c_{i,j} = \text{Min}[f_{i,j} c_i, cap_i]$$

The cap obviously is important because it limits the upside possibilities for the cash flow.

The cap is the product of three factors. The first factor is the mean contribution per unit.[4] The second factor is the maximum physical capacity of the project to produce units. The third factor is the risk-adjustment factor. The Capacity Formula simply reflects that if demand exceeds the capacity of the project, the project can supply only what it can produce.

The physical capacity of the project thus caps the contributions used in the calculation.

---

[4] If the project produces a basket of different products, then the first factor is the volume-weighted mean difference between the price per unit and the variable cost per unit of the products in the basket.

FLOOR FORMULA

To this value, we also need to include any further value from the better of two possible sources. The first source is the PV expected from continuing to operate the existing project as it is. The second source is the value from the option to change the project in a favorable way (or to abandon or sell it). This second source of value places a floor under the value of the project.

At each step, the PV from continuing to operate the existing project is an expected risk-neutral value discounted at the risk-free rate. This expected value is just the probability-weighted average of the two values associated with the next two branches of the tree. Thus the expected value is:

$$E(V_{i+1}) = p \times V_u + (1 - p) \times V_d$$
$$= p \times V_{i+1,j+1} + (1 - p) \times V_{i+1,j-1}$$

This value, discounted at the risk-free rate, needs comparison with the value from changing the project, for example, selling it. Let $alt_{i,j}$ represent the risk-neutral value of the best such alternative. At each node, we exercise the option to choose between continuing to operate the existing project or the best alternative. We then add this best value to the risk-neutral cash flow to obtain the Floor Formula:

$$V_{i,j} = c_{i,j} + \text{Max} \left[\frac{E(V_{j+1})}{1 + R_f}, alt_{i,j} \right]$$

OPTION EXERCISE FORMULA

Combining the Capacity Formula and the Floor Formula, we have the Option Exercise Formula, which occupies every node in the binomial tree:

$$V_{i,j} = \text{Min}[F_{i,j}c_i, cap_i] + \text{Max} \left[\frac{E(V_{j+1})}{1 + R_f}, alt_{i,j} \right]$$

The Option Exercise Formula gives the PV $V_{i,j}$ of the project contingent on finding market demand at the level represented by State j at the point in time represented by Step i. It incorporates both the capacity constraint and the expectation that management will exercise the most favorable option at every point in the tree. We use the value from the formula in the similar calculations for preceding nodes linked directly to the current one.[5]

Suppose that the alternative is to abandon the project and not sell it. Does $alt_{i,j}$ then have any value? The answer is yes because the financial advantage of abandonment is the resulting reduction in overhead expenditures. Accordingly, if abandonment is the only alternative to continuing to operate the project, the value of $alt_{i,j}$ is equal to the PV of the resulting saving of fixed expenditure (after tax). If the project is sellable, then $alt_{i,j}$ equals the sum of two parts. The first part is the PV

---

[5] The value of $alt_{i,j}$ in the Option Exercise Formula presents a temptation to add much complexity to the analysis, but we shall refrain from doing so. The complexity arises if each alternative is the root of yet another multistep tree. This would represent a reasonable task for a competent computer programmer but an impossible task for the user trying to understand the workings of the program. In most cases, the additional complexity is not justifiable because usually the floor options have relatively low probabilities and thus do not require great accuracy.

of this saving of fixed expenditure. The second part is the estimated resale value net of transaction costs and taxes that would pertain in State j at Step i. Even so, this alternative does not add much expected value if its probability is small.

DEFINITIONS

Contribution cash flow   Unit volume multiplied by the difference between the price per unit and the direct (variable) cost per unit.

9-5   OBTAINING THE NET PRESENT VALUE OF THE PROJECT

Using the Option Exercise Formula, the method begins by calculating the values of each branch at the end of the final period. Let the final period be Period T. There are $n + 1$ possible states (branches) in the final period where $n = T/\Delta t$. We use the equation to roll back the values of the states to the preceding periods. Each proceeding period has one less possible state. At Period 0, there is only one possible state. The value of this state is the rolled-back PV of the contributions and options. The NPV of the project is then:

$$Net\ Present\ Value = Present\ Value\ of\ Contributions\ and\ Options$$

$$- Present\ Value\ of\ Fixed\ Expenditure$$

$$- Present\ Value\ of\ Investment\ Expenditures$$

This provides the minimum framework that we require to incorporate the value of the principal real options in a capital project.[6] This model enables us to use sensitivity analysis to ascertain which of the real options most significantly affect the NPV of the capital project.

9-6   REAL OPTIONS SENSITIVITY ANALYSIS

The model described in the previous section is programmable in a spreadsheet macro. A macro is a computer program written in a language designed for operation in conjunction with spreadsheet input and output. We use a macro written in the Visual Basic for Applications (VBA) language for the Excel spreadsheet in the sensitivity analysis below. This macro can be downloaded from our website.

We first consider the value of a project's capacity option. Then we examine the effects of the option to abandon the project and to extend its life. Finally, we consider the option to delay investing in the project.

---

[6] It is the minimum framework because we could compound the number of branches in the tree by representing each alternative at every node as the root of another tree.

THE BASE CASE

To appreciate the effect of real options, we must compare with a base case. The base case is the equivalent project that has no cap, no floor, nor any other real options. Table 9.1 provides the details of our base case, a simple five-year annuity of €100 per year.

The required investment is €300. At 10%, the NPV of the annuity is €79. The Profitability Index (PI) equals $(300 + 79)/300 = 1.26$. As the PI is somewhat greater than 1.00, investment in this project would not seem controversial. This could be an illusion, however, because this calculation of the PI does not reflect the value of the project's real options.

In our binomial model, we discount the fixed expenditures separately. Discounting the fixed expenditures at 6%, we have:

	Base case
PV of investment	−300
PV of fixed expenditure	−421
	−721

In Table 9.1, we obtain the value of €79 for the project's NPV. This implies that the PV of the contributions must be equal to €800. This must be the case because:

$$800 - 721 = €79$$

Therefore, the discount rate for the contributions must be the rate that makes their PV equal to €800. We find this rate to be 7.916%, and we shall use this rate in the calculation of the risk-neutral values of the contributions. There is a fundamental reason why the discount rate for the contributions is less than the 10% used in Table 9.1 for the *net* cash flows. The reason is that the contributions have no operational gearing (by definition, they are stripped of fixed costs). So, the contribution cash flows are less risky than the net cash flows and require a lower discount rate.

Table 9.1 The base case, a simple annuity (€).

	End of year					
	0	1	2	3	4	5
Investment	−300					
Contribution cash flow		200	200	200	200	200
Fixed expenditure		−100	−100	−100	−100	−100
Net cash flow		100	100	100	100	100
NPV at 10%		79				

LIMITED CAPACITY

As a rule, real options add value to a project. An exception is the capacity option. Finite capacity is a negative factor because it reduces flexibility by limiting the upside potential of a project. In order to contain the investment expenditure, management must choose a limit for a project's capacity. In other words, management "sells" this particular real option in exchange for a reduction in the initial investment expenditure. Management can pay the cost of increasing a project's capacity, but this just reduces a self-imposed limitation.

The question is, what is it worth to increase the capacity? To answer this question we need to calculate the degree to which the existing capacity limitation reduces the PV of a project. The model described in the sections above enables us to see how much the capacity restriction in conjunction with other options affects a project's NPV. Sensitivity analysis can then show whether paying to remove a part of this constraint adds value to the project.

Therefore, our first step in the sensitivity analysis is to see how the capacity limitation affects the project's value. Let the standard deviation of demand be 30% per year initially and assume that the standard deviation increases with the square root of time. Suppose, however, that limited capacity restricts contributions to no more than the expected €200 per year. Rolling back the Option Exercise Formula (but excluding all options other than the capacity restriction), we obtain the following result, listed next to the base case for comparison:

	Base case	Capacity limited
PV of investment	−300	−300
PV of contributions and options	800	652
PV of fixed expenditure	−421	−421
NPV	79	−69

Making the capacity limit equal to the expected contribution cash flow has reduced the PV of contributions from 800 to only 652, and the NPV falls to −€69 from +€79.

How can this be? The reason is that the project has just sufficient capacity to generate the expected contributions of €200 per year. It cannot cope with more. If demand rises, there is no benefit.[7] If it falls, the contributions fall. On balance, we can expect a net loss in the PV of the contributions. Indeed, we find a significant loss of PV. This illustrates how dangerous it can be to ignore the impact of limited capacity. Obviously, there could be some advantage in changing the initial capacity. We examine this possibility later.

THE FLOOR

Fortunately, we have not reached the end of the story. The cap has an obvious negative effect, but can the floor help to restore the NPV? If market conditions deteriorate too far, management can abandon the project. The next step in our sensitivity analysis is to include this floor along with the cap in the Option Exercise Formula. We show the result below together with our previous results:

---

[7] This assumes that we do not increase the price of the product.

	Base case	Capped	Abandonment option
PV of investment	−300	−300	−300
PV of contributions and options	800	652	678
PV of fixed expenditure	−421	−421	−421
NPV	79	−69	−43

Introducing the possibility to abandon the project cuts the negative PV only slightly, from −€69 to −€43. This is a small step in the right direction but is insufficient. The benefit of abandonment came from the elimination of any further fixed expenditure in states where the project becomes a losing proposition. Fortunately, the probability of having to abandon the project is small. The small probability means that the expected benefit from the option to abandon is also small, however.

Additional value might be obtainable from selling the project rather than just abandoning it. Predicting the expected selling price is difficult, however. The reason is that management will not be in a strong negotiating position to sell a project expected to lose money. Scrap value might be all the project is worth in such circumstances. Let us suppose nevertheless that the project will be sellable at its written-down value (depreciated at 25% per year on a reducing balance basis). Obviously, the possibility to sell will raise the project's floor. We show the result below next to our previous results. The possibility to sell the project at its written-down value would lift the NPV to +€27.

	Base case	Capped	Abandonment option	Sell option
PV of investment	−300	−300	−300	−300
PV of contributions and options	800	652	678	748
PV of fixed expenditure	−421	−421	−421	−421
NPV	79	−69	−43	27

The option to sell the project at such favorable prices takes us further toward offsetting the adverse effect of the limit on capacity. At least the NPV is now positive.

THE CAPACITY OPTION

As mentioned earlier, there could be scope for increasing the capacity. Then, if demand should rise above the former capacity, the project will be able to cope with some of the additional demand. Unfortunately, the additional capacity requires more investment, and adding more capacity could cost more than the resulting additional PV is worth.

If additional capacity were sufficiently cheap, increasing it would increase the NPV. If adding capacity is too expensive, it could even be better to reduce the investment and operate at lower capacity. Suppose that additional capacity is expensive. For example, suppose that to double the capacity we would have to double the level of investment (and the resulting fixed expenditure). In this example, we find that it is better to *reduce* the investment in capacity quite substantially, as indicated below:

	Sell option	Capacity option
PV of investment	−300	−174
PV of contributions and options	748	467
PV of fixed expenditure	−421	−244
NPV	27	49

Several things are happening here simultaneously. By reducing the capacity we have reduced the investment by $300 − 174 = €126$. The lower capacity means lower fixed expenditure, and the PV of this is reduced by $421 − 244 = €177$. The total gain from these two effects is €303.

Mostly offsetting this gain, however, is the loss in the PV of contributions and options. The loss in the PV of contributions and options comes from two sources. The first is obvious: there is less capacity to meet the possible demand. The second is that lower capacity would imply lower resale values. These negative effects do not quite offset the positive advantage from reduced investment expenditure and the resulting lower fixed operating expenditure after tax. On balance, we have a modest net increase in NPV for a large reduction in capacity.

Would you invest at the lower level? The net benefit from reducing the capacity is not great. Therefore, strategic considerations are likely to be the deciding factor. Not being able to satisfy demand causes customer dissatisfaction and invites competition. Unless the company cannot fund all its projects, management might justify investing at the higher level of €300, or possibly even more as long as the NPV remains sufficiently above zero.

An implication is that additional capacity has to be relatively cheap if increasing it is to increase the NPV of this project.

Although we have assumed that the resale value falls proportionally with reduced investment, it does not follow that the resale value would increase much with increased investment. Exercise of the resale option usually takes place in adverse market conditions when the seller's negotiating position is relatively weak. The resale value would also depend on the strength of market demand for the buyer's intended use of the asset.

On balance, we shall assume for the remainder of this analysis that the initial investment will be €300 and that any additional real options improve the figures in the next-to-last column above. So, our new base case is capped capacity with the real option to sell the project.

We can now investigate how introducing further options changes this new base case.

THE LIFE OPTION

We have already introduced the effects of the capacity limitation and of the resale option on the NPV of the project. We can now investigate what it would be worth to change the life of the project. Exercising the life option would require some additional investment at the end of Year 5. If we can determine what it would be worth extending the project's life, we can compare this value with the PV now of the future additional investment expenditure.

For example, sensitivity analysis indicates that extending the project's life by an additional five years would be worth investing no more than €100 at the end of Year 5. This future investment expenditure increases the total PV of investment expenditure from €300 to €375. At this level of investment expenditure, there is no net increase in the NPV of €27 for the project.

	Sell option	Life option
PV of investment	−300	−375
PV of contributions and options	748	1243
PV of fixed expenditure	−421	−841
NPV	27	27

This result is attributable to two factors. The first is obvious. Increasing the life of the project provides additional contributions that add to the project's NPV. On top of this, the additional investment at the end of Year 5 increases the resale value of the project subsequently. Weighing against this is the additional fixed expenditure. If doubling the project's life is going to cost more than €100 then the life option is unlikely to add any net value to the project.

THE DELAY OPTION

Delaying the starting date for this project reduces the NPV to just + €4. There are two reasons. Delaying the starting date means a loss of income in the first year. In addition, the delay pushes the project farther into the future where uncertainty is greater. This makes greater the negative impact of the risk-adjustment factor. Increased uncertainty also gives the capacity limit a greater negative effect on the NPV of the project.[8] The floor does not entirely compensate for this. Therefore, we would not contemplate delaying the start of this project unless the delay would enable us to capture additional information that could significantly affect the investment decision.

DEFINITION

Annuity   Investment generating equal cash flows each period for a specified number of periods.

9-7   CONCLUSIONS

This chapter provides a model permitting us to incorporate the values of interdependent real options in a project's NPV. Using the familiar example of a five-year annuity cash flow, we used the model to show how uncertainty can affect the NPV of a capital project. We find that the conventional approach of simply increasing the discount rate to reflect risk is grossly inadequate.

In reality, most projects have limited capacity. Unit volume can rise only to the extent permitted by the project's capacity, but it can fall to zero. The conventional DCF methodology ignores this asymmetry imposed by limited capacity. To this extent at least, the conventional approach is biased in favor of investment. Other real options can partly offset the negative effect of limited capacity. These additional options serve to put a floor under the PV of a project. For example,

---

[8] We cannot mitigate this by increasing the project's capacity in this instance, as additional capacity is too costly.

management can terminate further losses by abandoning an unprofitable project. Better still, management can perhaps sell the project. Improved technology or uses that are more profitable might also lift the floor. Because the probabilities of the circumstances in which these options might be exercised are often small, their values can be relatively small.

The option to extend the life of a project is of limited value when uncertainty is great. The value is limited for at least two reasons. First, the exercise of the option is distant in time and therefore discounted to a smaller value. Second, uncertainty is greater for the more distant cash flows thus reinforcing the negative impact of limited capacity.

The option to delay starting a project is likely to be attractive only in unusual circumstances. In our example, delay implies a loss of some early cash income. Furthermore, pushing the project farther into the future can surround it with greater uncertainty. The greater uncertainty increases the negative impact of limited capacity. This also increases the negative impact of the risk-adjustment factor. An exception is waiting for the revelation of new information that could make or break the project.

We have shown how to incorporate the interdependent values of a number of real options in the NPV of a project. Sensitivity analysis based on this procedure demonstrated the large negative impact under uncertainty of limited capacity. As a rule, the other real options only partially offset the negative effect of limited capacity.

FURTHER READING

M. Amram and N. Kulatilaka (1999) *Real Options: Managing Strategic Investment in an Uncertain World* (Boston: Harvard Business School Press).

L. Trigeorgis (1996) "Interactions among multiple real options," chapter 7 in *Real Options: Managerial Flexibility and Strategy in Resource Allocation* (Cambridge, MA: MIT Press).

QUESTIONS AND PROBLEMS

1   The expected value of an uncertain cash flow in the fifth year of a project's life is €100,000. The following data are relevant to the cash flow. The risk-free rate is equal to 6%. The risk premium is 4%. What is the risk-neutral value of the cash flow?

2   The data below are the risk-neutral values of a project's cash flows. The risk-free rate equals 6%. Calculate the rolled-back PV of the remaining risk-neutral cash flows in each year of the project's life.

	Year ending				
	1	2	3	4	5
Risk-neutral value	94	90	85	80	76

3 The expected price per unit of a product is €100 each. The variable cost is €33 per unit and the project's expected annual fixed expenditure is €100,000. The project can produce 2,000 units per year. Management expects to operate at full capacity.

(a) What is the value of the project's contribution cash flow?
(b) What is the value of its net cash flow before tax?

4 A project's contribution cash flow can be €2 million or €500,000 per year with equal probability. If there is no limit on capacity, what is the expected contribution cash flow? If capacity limits the contribution cash flow to only €1 million per year, what is the resulting expected cash flow?

5 Expected demand implies that the risk-neutral value of the unrestricted contribution cash flow in Year t is €1.4 million. There is a 0.40 probability of more demand in the following period and a 0.60 probability that it will be less. If demand increases, the PV in Year $t + 1$ of contributions and options is €5 million. If the demand falls instead, the PV of the contributions and options is only €2.5 million. A noncompetitor might buy the project in Year t for an expected €4 million. The project's capacity limits contributions to a maximum of €1 million per year. The cash flow data and capacity limit are risk-neutral values. Use the Option Exercise Formula to determine the PV of the project in Year t. Would selling the project be worth considering at that time?

6 In Period $t = 2$, the risk-neutral value of the expected unrestricted contribution $E(c)$ would be €2 million. Of course, the risk-neutral contribution could have any number of different values around this value of €2 million. In the binomial tree representation, however, there can only be $t + 1 = 3$ possible values, one for each State j if each step in the tree is one year. If the annual standard deviation σ is equal to 0.40, what are the three possible values of the unrestricted contributions in period 3? *Hint:* The formula is:

$$f_u^j f_d^{i-j} \times E(c)$$

where

$$f_u = e^{\sigma \sqrt{\Delta t}} \qquad f_d = \frac{1}{f_u}$$

In this case, the time increment Δt equals 1.00.

7 In the binomial tree the unrestricted contributions can move up in the next period to the next higher state with the risk-adjusted probability p or down with probability $1 - p$. In Problem 7 what are the probabilities p and $1 - p$? *Hint:* The required formula for p is:

$$p = \frac{1 - f_d}{f_u - f_d}$$

10 Valuation of Companies with Real Options

Conventional applications of the discounted cash flow (DCF) method are too simplistic for accurate company valuations. For example, one assumption often used is that the company being valued has homogeneous cash flows that grow for ever. An alternative assumption is that the company has some very significant terminal value reflecting subsequent free cash flows. The truth is that a company consists of a collection of existing assets and products, virtually all of which have finite lives. Will the company continue to operate beyond the lives of its existing products? The answer depends on management's ability to generate suitable new products in the uncertain future business environment. Put another way, whether the value of the company is greater than the value of its already existing operations depends upon whether one can expect financially worthwhile opportunities for further investment. The purpose of this chapter is to outline a useful procedure for the valuation of companies with such real options.

TOPICS

Accordingly, we consider the following:

○ *whether financial ratios are sufficient to value a company;*

○ *the Investment Opportunities Approach;*

○ *formulation of the Investment Opportunities Approach;*

○ *valuation of Amazon.com;*

○ *inputs to the Investment Opportunities Approach;*

○ *investment opportunities as* **expected payoffs** *on real options.*

The material in this chapter provides the tools to value the equity of virtually any company, including start-ups with zero or negative earnings.

10-1 ARE FINANCIAL RATIOS SUFFICIENT TO VALUE A COMPANY?

PRICE-TO-EARNINGS RATIO METHOD

The most popular method of valuing the equity of a company is the price-to-earnings (P/E) ratio method. Simply multiply the earnings of the "target" company by its expected PE ratio.

Estimate the expected PE ratio using the P/Es of similar companies quoted in the stock market.

The method is simple, and its strength is that it reflects prevailing market P/Es. In this way the method is sensitive to the current values of similar assets in the stock market. Problems with the method have to do with inconsistency between comparison companies regarding accounting conventions, nonperforming assets, low or negative earnings, investment opportunities and risk.[1] The method also ignores other vital information specific to the target company. In short, the PE's of comparison companies are not strictly comparable.

PRICE-TO-SALES RATIO OF METHOD

Some of these problems can be resolved by using the price-to-sales (P/S) ratio method. Multiply the target company's sales by its expected P/S ratio. The numerator of the P/S ratio is the sum of a company's market capitalization of its equity and the present value of its liabilities. The denominator is its annual sales. Multiplying a company's sales by its expected P/S ratio gives an estimate of the total value of the company. The company's equity is then the difference between the value of the company and the value of its liabilities.[2] Estimate the expected P/S ratio using the P/S ratios of similar companies quoted in the stock market.

The method is simple, and its strength is that it reflects prevailing P/S ratios in the stock market. Problems with the method have to do with inconsistency relating to nonperforming assets, investment opportunities, and risk. The method also ignores other vital information specific to the target company. For example, the company could be achieving large sales while making losses.

LIMITATIONS OF RATIO METHODS

Specific information that both ratio methods ignore includes the following:

1.   Nonperforming or unwanted assets that can be sold.

2.   Remaining lives of existing products.

3.   Expected scale of investment in new products.

4.   Expected lives of new products.

5.   Expected profitability of new products.

6.   Risk.

The framework of the Investment Opportunities Approach facilitates incorporation of this additional information in a company valuation.

---

[1] Nonperforming assets are assets that have significant resale value but which are not expected to generate earnings.
[2] If the target company's sales are low relative to its debt, low values of the expected P/S ratio can still give a negative estimate for the value for the target's equity.

DEFINITIONS

Debt   Sum of money or other assets owed by one party to another. Usually, a legally enforceable obligation to pay agreed interest and to repay the principal of a loan to the lender promptly on schedule.

Discounted cash flow (DCF) method   Comparison of the value of an investment with the cost of a comparable investment in the financial market. Also, comparison of the internal rate of return on a project with its cost of capital.

Equity   Net worth or shareholder's capital represented by common stock (ordinary shares) and preferred stock.

Expected (mean)   Probability-weighted average of all possible outcomes for a random variable.

Free cash flow   After-tax cash flow from operations net of capital investment and increases in net working capital.

Investment Opportunities Approach   Valuation method characterising the value of a firm as the sum of the present value of its existing business and the net present value of its future investment opportunities.

Market capitalization   The stock market value of a company's equity. The market price per share multiplied by the number of shares issued.

Nonperforming assets   Asset holdings currently reporting little or no earnings, often held as long-term investments or as real options on further future investments.

Payoff   Net positive difference between the price of the underlying asset and the exercise price on an option being exercised.

Price-to-earnings (P/E)   Price per share divided by reported earnings per share.

Price-to-sales (P/S) ratio   Ratio of the sum of a company's market equity capitalization and its liabilities to its annual sales.

10-2   THE INVESTMENT OPPORTUNITIES APPROACH

MILLER AND MODIGLIANI

The Miller and Modigliani (1961) Investment Opportunities Approach characterizes the value of an ongoing firm as the sum of the present value (PV) of its existing business and the net present value (NPV) of its future investment opportunities.[3]

Value of Unlevered Company = Value of the Existing Business

+ Value of Investment Opportunities

---

[3] M. Miller and F. Modigliani (1961) "Dividend policy, growth and the valuation of shares," *Journal of Business*, Vol. 34, No. 4 (October), 411–433.

An unlevered (ungeared) company is a company that has no debt. So, the value of the equity of a levered (geared) company is:

Value of Equity = Value of Unlevered Company − Value of Company's Debt

Segmenting the sources of value in this way facilitates incorporation of the six items of specific information listed above in Section 10-1. In the following, we use a straightforward adaptation of the Miller–Modigliani Investment Opportunities Approach to show how to do this.

The essence of the approach is to analyze the values of a company's existing investments and future investment opportunities separately. The Miller and Modigliani Investment Opportunities Approach does not recognize explicitly that the investment opportunities are best characterized as the expected exercise of real options, however. We will examine the financial significance of this later when we introduce real options into the Investment Opportunities framework.

DEFINITIONS

Investment Opportunities Approach   Valuation method characterising the value of a firm as the sum of the present value of its existing business and the net present value of its future investment opportunities.

Levered (geared) company   Company partially financed by debt.

Real option   Right to make favorable future choices regarding real asset investments. More precisely, a real option is an opportunity for voluntary future investment in a nonfinancial asset when at least a part of the required investment expenditure is certain or, alternatively, when at least a part of the required investment expenditure is not perfectly positively correlated with the project's present value.

Unlevered (ungeared) company   Company that has no debt.

10-3 FORMULATION OF THE INVESTMENT OPPORTUNITIES APPROACH

Practical application of the Investment Opportunities Approach requires the introduction of some detail not explicitly identified in Miller and Modigliani's theoretical treatment. For example, the authors made no explicit distinction between the disposable asset value and the value due to product cash flows (product value). Furthermore, they used the same discount rate for both the existing business and for the investment opportunities.

VALUE OF THE COMPANY

Introducing this additional detail, we have:

Value of the Company = Disposable Asset Value + Product Value

+ Investment Opportunity Value

$$V = A + P + O$$

in which

$$P = \sum_{t=1}^{N} \frac{C_t}{(1+R_P)^t} \quad \text{and} \quad O = \sum_{t=0}^{\infty} \frac{I_t(PI_t - 1)}{(1+R_O)^t}$$

N represents the life of the existing investments, C_t the cash flow from existing products at time t, R_P the appropriate discount rate for product cash flows, I_t represents the capital expenditure for period t, PI_t the profitability index (PI) for investment opportunities in period t, and R_O the discount rate for the expected net values of the investment opportunities (investment opportunity value). Note that the difference $PI_t - 1$ between the expected PI and 1 equals the net value per unit of investment at time t.

VALUE OF THE EQUITY

Having obtained the value of the company using these equations, we can calculate the corresponding PV of the firm's equity capital from:

Value of the Company's Equity = Value of the Company − Value of the Company's Debt

$$E = V - D$$

In this form, the Investment Opportunities Approach provides a framework permitting incorporation of important information omitted in the various ratio methods for company valuation.

Application of the Investment Opportunities Approach requires skills best demonstrated in the context of an example.

DEFINITIONS

Discount rate   Required rate of return used in the calculation of a discount factor.

Disposable asset value   Market value of existing disposable assets and present value of expected residual values of assets disposable in the future.

Investment opportunity value   Present value of expected net values of future investment opportunities.

Net value   Expected net present value measured as at some specified future date.

Product value   Present value of expected cash flow from a company's existing products during their remaining lives.

Profitability index (PI)   Present value of a project divided by the required investment.

EXAMPLE 10.1   AMAZON.COM

From the day of its founding Amazon.com was the first and foremost Internet retailer. It pioneered electronic retailing in 1995 with the launch of online bookselling. By 2000, it was selling CDs, toys, electronics, videos, DVDs, computer games, software, home improvement tools, and patio furniture. Additionally, it provided an auction site and hosted thousands of other online shops. The company had expanded its operations outside the USA to the UK and Germany.

In the previous 12 months, Amazon's revenues had increased by 169%. Nevertheless, the company's losses were increasing faster than its sales. In 1999 losses were an astounding $720 million on sales revenues of $1.6 billion. Despite these large and mounting losses, the company's stock market capitalization had reached nearly $40 billion in 1999. Its market capitalization fluctuated widely around half that level during most of the year. The annualized standard deviation of the log share price was nearly 100%.

In the first half of 2000 investors' increasing concern about competition, profit potential, and the sustainability of the company's growth led in June to a precipitous decline in market value to around $13 billion. Some attributed even this value to investors' "irrational exuberance." Others, however, continued to buy the company's shares with the expectation that the company's growing investment opportunities would bring future profits and dividends.

A financial analyst produced the following data thought to be relevant to the valuation of the company:

○	Equity beta (from market data)	$\beta_E = 1.85$
○	Asset beta (subjective)	$\beta_A = 1.50$
○	Risk-free rate (market data)	$R_F = 6.5\%$
○	Risk premium on the market portfolio (subjective)	$R_{MF} = 4\%$
○	Free cash flow (estimate)	$C_0 = -\$380$ million
○	Current annual rate of product investment by the company (estimate)	$I_0 = \$0.5$ billion
○	Disposable assets (estimate)	$A = \$0.5$ billion
○	Long-term debt (balance sheet)	$D = \$1.93$ billion

SHORTCUT FORMULA FOR PRODUCT VALUE

The data provided for Amazon.com is typical in that details of the existing product cash flows and of investment opportunities were unknown. Usually we can use shortcut formulas that require less of such detail.[4]

For example, due to product obsolescence, cash flows from existing products experience long-term decline. Often we can assume that the cash flows from the existing products continue to decline at a constant compound rate G_C where $G_C < 0$. Because such negative growth rates are almost certainly less than the growth rate G_E for the economy, we can use the familiar Gordon–Williams

---

[4] Miller and Modigliani also used shortcut formulas. They assumed that all cash flows are perpetuities, and they employed only one discount rate. These simplifications helped to clarify the theory. They acknowledged that they could have used more realistic formulas, however.

model as the shortcut:

$$P = \frac{C_0(1 + G_C)}{(R_P - G_C)} \qquad (G_C < G_E)$$

Amazon.com's cash flow from existing products appeared to be negative. Therefore, the rate G_C in this case represents the expected rate at which the cash flow will become less negative. Suppose we feel that the company can reduce this by 20% per year compounded. Then:

$$P = \frac{C_0(1 + G_C)}{(R_P - G_C)}$$

$$= \frac{-380 \times [1 + (-0.20)]}{[0.125 - (-0.20)]} = -\$935 \text{ million}$$

Clearly, this negative value for the existing products cannot account for the $13 billion market capitalization at that time. We need to look for other sources of value, for example, the value of the investment opportunities.

SHORTCUT FORMULAS FOR INVESTMENT OPPORTUNITY VALUE

We have two shortcut formulas for the value O of the investment opportunities. The choice between the two depends upon the expected long-term rate of growth of the company.

COMPOUND GROWTH SHORTCUT

If the expected growth rate G_O for the company is no greater than the expected nominal growth rate G_E for the economy, we can use the Gordon–Williams formula. If the expected long-term compound rate of growth in new investment opportunities equals G_O, the formula gives:

$$O = \left[\frac{I_0(1 + G_O)}{R_O - G_O} \right] \times (PI - 1) \qquad (G_O \leq G_E)$$

If the expected growth rate of the company is greater than that of the economy, the Gordon–Williams model is biased if not invalid. Amazon.com's expected rate of growth was very much greater than average, so we have to use a different shortcut formula that can accommodate high initial rates of growth.

LINEAR GROWTH SHORTCUT

The analyst's estimate of Amazon's initial annual investment in new opportunities was $I_0 = \$500$ million. Let us suppose that annual investment will grow by an additional $500 million annually. Therefore, the annual pattern of investment in new opportunities would be:

0	1	2	3	4
500	1,000	1,500	2,000	2,500 ...

million dollars. The formula for this pattern is:

$$I_t = I_0 + t\Delta I$$

So, the investment in the third year is:

$$I_3 = 500 + 3 \times 500 = \$2,000 \text{ million}$$

This is an example of linear growth, which is growth without compounding. Linear growth implies decline in the corresponding *rates* of growth. For example, the rate for the first year is:

$$\frac{1,000}{500} - 1 = 1 \quad \text{or} \quad 100\%$$

Three years later, the rate is only:

$$\frac{2,500}{2,000} - 1 = 0.125 \quad \text{or} \quad 12.5\%$$

After 17 years, the annual rate of growth falls below 6%.

A declining rate of growth is consistent with an increasingly competitive market. The assumption of pure linear growth implies that rates of growth eventually approach zero. We can expect such a pattern because if new firms experience above-average growth, then the remaining, mostly older firms must experience below-average growth.[5]

We can substitute this formula into the equation for the PV of the investment opportunities. Letting the PI for the investment opportunities have the same value PI in every period, and after some algebra,[6] we obtain the following for the PV of the investment opportunities:

$$O = \left[(1 + R_O) \left(\frac{I_0}{R_O} + \frac{\Delta I}{R_O^2} \right) \right] \times (PI - 1) \qquad (\Delta I \geq 0)$$

This formula is only suitable for companies with initial growth greater than or equal to zero.

IMPLICATIONS FOR AMAZON.COM

For Amazon.com and using a 12.9% discount rate, this formula gives:

$$O = \left[(1 + R_O) \left(\frac{I_0}{R_O} + \frac{\Delta I}{R_O^2} \right) \right] \times (PI - 1)$$

$$= \left[(1 + 0.129) \left(\frac{500}{0.129} + \frac{500}{0.129^2} \right) \right] \times (PI - 1)$$

$$= 38.298 \times (PI - 1) \quad \text{billion dollars}$$

---

[5] Our linear growth shortcut formula rules out negative growth, however.
[6] We sum infinite geometric series implicit in the discounting of the cash flow. The derivation assumes that the first option is exercised at time $t = 0$.

This valuation obviously depends on the expected value PI of the investment opportunities and on the assumed growth in investment. If the expected PI were to be as high as 1.40, for example, the PV of the investment opportunities would be:

$$O = 38.298 \times (PI - 1)$$
$$= 38.298 \times (1.40 - 1) = \$15.319 \text{ billion}$$

Using this result, we can estimate a value for Amazon.com and its equity:

$$\text{Value of the Company} = \text{Disposable Asset Value} - \text{Product Value}$$
$$+ \text{Investment Opportunity Value}$$
$$V = A - P + O$$
$$= 0.5 - 0.935 + 15.319 = \$14.884 \text{ billion}$$
$$\text{Value of the Company's Equity} = \text{Value of the Company} - \text{Value of the Company's Debt}$$
$$E = V - D$$
$$= 14.884 - 1.930 = \$12.954 \text{ billion}$$

This value is very close to Amazon.com's market capitalization of $13 billion at the time of the case.

This result is sensitive to the values of particular variables, however. Figure 10.1 illustrates the effect of changes in two of the most important variables. Each of the three curves represents a value of Amazon's equity for different combinations of values for growth ΔI and profitability index PI.

The relative positions of the three curves illustrate that higher equity values require higher growth and profitability. The shapes of all three curves show that without very high growth, maintaining any of the indicated equity values requires much higher profitability than Amazon appeared capable of achieving.

For example, Amazon.com's equity market capitalization at the time of the case was $13 billion. The corresponding curve for $13 billion in the figure shows that if Amazon's expected increases in annual investment were to be $500 million per year, it would have to achieve a PI equal to 1.4. Even if the increases in annual investment were as high as $1 billion annually, the PI would still have to equal 1.21. The corresponding figures even for the $4 billion valuation appear optimistic in relation to past and likely future performance.

The Miller and Modigliani Investment Opportunities Approach did not recognize expected costs of bankruptcy. Neither have we included the negative effect of dilution due to the eventual exercise of management stock options. If we included these, we would find that Amazon must achieve even higher levels of profitability than indicated in Figure 10.1. So, our application of the Investment Opportunities Approach suggests that investors were being overly optimistic about the amount and profitability of Amazon's future investment opportunities.

Other variables also affect the positions of the curves. The curves shift upward and to the right if we increase the discount rate R_O for the investment opportunities, for example. The reason is that if the discount rate is higher, we require a greater growth of investment and higher profitability to achieve the same PV for the investment opportunities. The sensitivity of the valuation to the

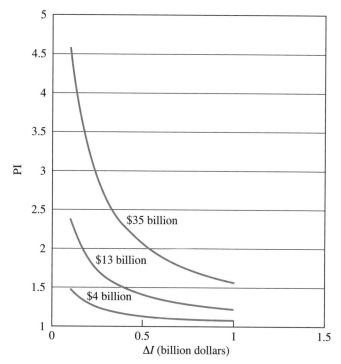

Figure 10.1 Combinations of growth and profitability necessary for three levels of equity value (Investment Opportunities Approach).

variables demonstrates why we must understand the inputs to the Investment Opportunities Approach.

DEFINITIONS

Beta factor A measure of the market risk of an asset. The factor by which mean returns on the asset reflect returns on the market portfolio.

Dilution Increase in the number of a company's shares without a proportionate increase in the company's assets and earnings (more precisely, an increase in the number of shares that reduces shareholder value per share).

Discounting Multiplying each of an investment's expected cash flow by its present value per unit (discount factor) to obtain the total net present value for the investment.

Option Contract granting the right without obligation to engage in a future transaction on terms specified in the contract.

Perpetuity Equal sum of money paid in each period for ever.

Risk premium on the market portfolio Extra return necessary to persuade investors to invest in the market portfolio.

Standard deviation Square root of the variance.

10-4 INPUTS TO THE INVESTMENT OPPORTUNITIES APPROACH

Successful application of this approach to company valuation requires understanding of the variables affecting company value. Therefore, we need to discuss the variables that we have used.

DISPOSABLE ASSET VALUE

A change of ownership is an opportune time to dispose of nonperforming assets. If another organization can put an asset to better use, then it might be willing to pay enough for the asset to make immediate sale worthwhile. Value in this situation represents the anticipated outcome of negotiations with potential buyers. In addition, discount the expected residual values for future disposals of assets and include them in the *Disposable Asset Value*.

PRODUCT VALUE

Product Value P represents the PV of the existing products and services. Competition, technical obsolescence, and product replacement erode the free cash flows from the existing products and services. Accordingly, the free cash flows will usually taper away to a low value or zero within perhaps 5–10 years or less, depending on the distribution of the remaining product lives and their respective cash flows.

As the volume of sales of existing products and services declines, less of the expenditure on replacement and on research and development will be attributable to them. In addition, less working capital will be required as remaining product lives diminish. Therefore, the definition of free cash flow from the existing products and services is:

> After-tax earnings from existing products and services
>
> *Plus*   Depreciation and other noncash charges
>
> *Plus*   R&D expenditure after tax for new products
>
> *Plus*   Interest after tax
>
> *Plus*   Working capital released by the decline of the existing products
>
> *Less*   Replacement investment apportioned to existing products

Discounting the free cash flow defined in this way enables us to value the existing goods and services during their remaining lives without double-counting the cash flows generating the Investment Opportunity Value O considered below.

After the free cash flow from existing products dies away, the usually small residual values of the redundant assets are the only terminal values that need consideration. The PVs of these residual values were already included in the *Disposable Asset Value* above.

INVESTMENT OPPORTUNITY VALUE

Investment Opportunity Value O represents the value of the company's opportunities to invest in future new products and services.

Suppose we believe that the average investment opportunity at time t will have a life N_t and that the cash flow profile will not be significantly different from an annuity. In this case, the investment opportunity value at time t is:

$$O_t = I_t(PI_t - 1)$$

where the following equation provides an estimate of the profitability index PI_t:

$$PI_t = \frac{A_{N_t,R_A}}{A_{N_t,R_t^*}}$$

and A_{N_t,R_A} and A_{N_t,R_t^*} are annuity factors, I_t represents the capital budget, R_t^* represents the expected internal rate of return (IRR) on the investments at time t, and R_A is the discount rate for the cash flows.[7]

In the case of Amazon.com, let the life $N_t = 10$ be the same for all investment opportunities in every period. Then if the typical investment opportunity could earn as much as, say, 21.8% and the discount rate is 12.5%, the value of the PI would be:

$$PI = \frac{A_{10,0.125}}{A_{10,0.218}} = \frac{5.5364}{3.9488} = 1.40$$

Of course, the financial analyst must draw upon knowledge of the industry, its products, and competition to judge expected product lives and their rates of return. Without such knowledge, forecasting the expected pattern of the cash flows from the company's portfolio of existing and future products and services becomes problematic. Due diligence requires such information. If the information is unavailable or not capable of estimation, then buying the company's equity becomes more of a gamble.

EXPECTED CAPITAL BUDGETS

When there are many expected investment opportunities, we need to simplify the calculation. A useful method for valuing the opportunities is to multiply the net investment opportunity value per unit of investment for time t by the corresponding expected future capital budget I_t as done in the previous section. One reason the method is useful is that projected capital budgets do not double-count contingent projects. In addition, expected capital budgets subsume the probabilities of actual investments taking place. This method is much simpler than trying to sum the values of mostly unknown individual future investment opportunities.

In principle, one can forecast capital budgets using a spreadsheet cash flow model of the firm, but this is difficult to implement for distant future years. We suggested some shortcut formulas to use instead. Virtually all methods, however, begin with an estimate of the current annual rate I_0 of investment in new opportunities. If the current capital budget I_0 is unknown, one can try to estimate it as follows:

---

[7] Miller and Modigliani used the perpetuity version of this formula but acknowledged the existence of alternatives.

Retained Earnings × (1 + Target Debt Equity Ratio)

Plus Depreciation and other noncash charges apportioned to new products

Plus R&D expenditure after tax for new products

Plus Net Working Capital released by decline of existing products.

For companies such as Amazon.com with negative earnings this approach is not applicable, however.

DISCOUNTING INVESTMENT OPPORTUNITY VALUES

Capital asset pricing theory provides a means of obtaining discount rates. First, however, we need to have the values of the beta factors reflecting the systematic risks of the relevant assets.

The starting point is the value of the company's equity beta β_E estimated in the usual way, regressing share returns on market index returns. The value of the equity beta is our starting point for estimating the beta of the investment opportunities. The procedure is:

1.   Unlever the equity beta.

2.   Use the unlevered equity beta to determine the investment opportunities beta.

The details are as follows.

1 UNLEVER THE EQUITY BETA

In this step, we remove the effect of the company's debt on its equity beta. If the company is a net borrower, this will reduce the beta value.[8] The following equation can estimate the unlevered beta value:

$$\beta_U = \beta_E \left(\frac{E}{E + D} \right)$$

where equity E and debt D should be average market values during the period of the data used to estimate β_E.[9]

In the case of Amazon:

$$\beta_U = 1.85 \times \left(\frac{13}{13 + 1.95} \right) = 1.61$$

There was no difficulty in obtaining the data to calculate the value of Amazon.com's equity beta for use in the equation above. The reason is that the shares actively trade in the stock market.

If a company's shares trade infrequently, one must estimate its equity beta value indirectly. Often one can use the "method of similars." The method is to select a sample of companies listed on the

---

[8] Some companies such as banks are net lenders. For net lenders unlevering beta increases its value instead of reducing it. The reason is that if a company is a net lender, the term D in the formula is negative.

[9] This formula assumes the equilibrium of Miller (1977) rather than Modigliani and Miller (1969) and therefore requires no tax adjustment. The formula also assumes that the beta value for the debt is equal to zero. The asset beta is really a value-weighted average of the equity and debt betas.

stock exchange similar to the firm being valued. Obtain their equity beta values from a reputable risk measurement service. Then unlever the betas with the above equation using the respective values of the equity and debt of each company. Use an average of the resulting unlevered beta values as an estimate of the unlevered beta for the company being valued.

2 USE THE UNLEVERED EQUITY BETA TO ESTIMATE THE INVESTMENT OPPORTUNITIES BETA

As discussed earlier, the unlevered value of the firm is just the sum of the PVs of the residual assets, the existing products, and the investment opportunities:

$$V = A + P + O$$

Dividing by V, we obtain the respective proportions of these PVs, which must add up to 1.00:

$$1.00 = \frac{A}{V} + \frac{P}{V} + \frac{O}{V}$$

Capital asset pricing theory tells us that the beta factor for this portfolio of assets is the weighted average of the betas of the constituent assets:[10]

$$\beta_U = \frac{A}{V}\beta_A + \frac{P}{V}\beta_A + \frac{O}{V}\beta_O$$

We can now solve this equation for the investment opportunities beta:

$$\beta_O = \frac{\beta_U - \left(\dfrac{A}{V} + \dfrac{P}{V}\right)\beta_A}{1 - \left(\dfrac{A}{V} + \dfrac{P}{V}\right)}$$

where the unlevered value V of the firm equals the total value of the firm's equity and of its debt.

For Amazon.com the value of the beta of the investment opportunities would be:

$$\beta_O = \frac{1.61 - \left(\dfrac{0.5}{14.884} + \dfrac{(-0.395)}{14.884}\right) \times 1.5}{1 - \left(\dfrac{0.5}{14.884} + \dfrac{(-0.395)}{14.884}\right)}$$

$$= 1.611$$

Therefore, the beta of Amazon's investment opportunities is very nearly equal to the value of its unlevered equity beta. The reason is that Amazon's value was almost entirely attributable to its perceived investment opportunities.

[10] J. E. Broyles and I. A. Cooper (1981) "Real asset options and capital budgeting," *Nijenrode Studies in Business* (Boston: Martinus Nijhoff).

Using the **Capital Asset Pricing Model (CAPM)**, we can now obtain the corresponding value of the discount rate for the investment opportunities:

$$R_O = R_f + \beta_O R_{MF}$$

This formula provides the discount rate we used earlier to obtain the PV of Amazon's investment opportunities:

$$R_O = 0.065 + 1.606 \times 0.04 = 0.129 \quad \text{or} \quad 12.9\%$$

In this section, we have shown how to obtain the values used for the variables in the equations that generated the curves in Figure 10.1.

The Investment Opportunities Approach requires the assumption of an imperfect market for the investment opportunities if they are to have positive NPVs. The Investment Opportunities Approach does not recognize that investment opportunities are best characterized as payoffs on real options, however. Nevertheless, the approach provides a natural framework for incorporating the values of investment opportunities as real options.

DEFINITIONS

Annuity   Investment generating equal cash flows each period for a specified number of periods.

Beta factor   A measure of the market risk of an asset. The factor by which mean returns on the asset reflect returns on the market portfolio.

Capital Asset Pricing Model (CAPM)   Linear model attempting to explain the expected return on a risky asset in terms of the risk-free rate, its beta factor (systematic risk), and the risk premium on the market portfolio.

Capital budgeting   Procedure for allocating funds to capital projects.

Internal rate of return (IRR)   Discount rate that would make the net present value for an investment equal to zero.

Rate of return   After-tax cash income and capital gain divided by the investment.

Share (stock)   Security legally certifying that its registered holder is a part-owner of the corporation.

10-5 INVESTMENT OPPORTUNITIES AS EXPECTED PAYOFFS ON REAL OPTIONS

Above, we used the following shortcut formula to estimate the PV of a company's investment opportunities:

$$O = \left[(1 + R_O) \left(\frac{I_0}{R_O} + \frac{\Delta I}{R_O^2} \right) \right] \times (PI - 1) \qquad (\Delta I \geq 0)$$

In this section, we take a similar approach. We recognize, however, that the value of the factor $(PI - 1)$ for the investment opportunities really should reflect expected conditional values of real option payoffs per unit of investment. Therefore, the value of an investment opportunity in the shortcut formula becomes:

$$PI - 1 = \frac{o}{pr}(1 + R_O)^T$$

in which o represents the present value per unit of investment of payoffs on investment options assumed to be exercised T periods after they are created, and pr is the probability that the options will be exercised.[11] The value o of the individual investment options reflects their probability of exercise. The capital budgets I also subsume this probability. For this reason we divide by pr in the above equation to avoid double-counting it. We can obtain the value of the probability of exercise from a histogram such as the one used in Figure 8.1. We can also obtain a value for o using the method in Table 8.2.[12]

For example, suppose Amazon's expected investment option value per unit of investment was 0.12, the probability of exercise equals 0.5, and each option matures four years after its creation. Then:

$$\frac{o}{pr}(1 + R_O)^T = \frac{0.12}{0.5}(1 + 0.129)^4 = 0.4$$

Using the same data we first used in the shortcut formula for Amazon, we have:

$$O = \left[(1 + R_O)\left(\frac{I_0}{R_O} + \frac{\Delta I}{R_O^2}\right)\right] \times \left(\frac{o}{pr}(1 + R_O)^T\right)$$

$$= 38.298 \times 0.4 = \$15.319 \text{ billion}$$

By chance, this value for the PV of the investment opportunities is the same as obtained earlier using $PI = 1.40$. The difference is that we can now use what we learned in Chapter 8 about the valuation of investment options to obtain the option value o. In many cases the real options treatment can provide a better estimate of the value of the investment opportunities.

SUMMARY

Pulling some strands together, we have:

Value of Unlevered Company = Disposable Asset Value + Product Value

+ Real Investment Options Value

$$V = A + P + O$$

If we can assume that the cash flows from the existing products decline at a constant compound rate G_C where $G_C < 0$, we can use the following formula to calculate a value P for the existing products:[13]

---

[11] Note that pr is the true probability, not the risk-adjusted probability.

[12] Note that the maturity T of each investment option is the length of its existence between its creation and its expected exercise. Most options begin their existence in the future, although some exist already.

[13] In this equation, we have ignored the value of real options associated with the existing products. Including these would increase greatly the complexity of the model for relatively little difference in value for growth companies. Including the capacity limit would reduce the value as demonstrated in Chapter 9.

$$P = \frac{C_0(1 + G_C)}{(R_A - G_C)} \qquad (G_C < 0)$$

If we can assume that expected investment will grow by the constant amount ΔI and that the expected PI will be the same for all the investment opportunities, we can use the following shortcut equation for the value of the investment opportunities:

$$O = \left[(1 + R_O)\left(\frac{I_0}{R_O} + \frac{\Delta I}{R_O^2}\right)\right] \times (PI - 1) \qquad (\Delta I \geq 0)$$

Finally, if we want to value the investment opportunities as real options, we let:

$$PI - 1 = \frac{o}{pr}(1 + R_O)^T$$

for which methods, such as those in Chapter 8, give the value o of the investment options and the probability pr of exercise.

From the resulting value V, we subtract the PV of the company's debt to obtain the value of its equity.

10-6   CONCLUSIONS

The Miller and Modigliani Investment Opportunities Approach offers a number of advantages over other discounted cash flow company valuation models. The approach incorporates more of the essential detail required for a full company valuation. For example, it enables one to disentangle expected cash flows from existing assets and products from the values of future investment opportunities. This permits bringing strategic information more directly to bear on the valuation. The relevant strategic information includes product life cycle data of both existing and new products, and the expected profitability of new product investment opportunities. It also permits incorporating explicitly the scale of expected capital budgets and of growth and risk. The Investment Opportunities Approach also provides a framework for incorporating the treatment of the investment opportunities as real options.

FURTHER READING

T. Copeland, T. Koller, and J. Murrin (2000) *Valuation, Measuring and Managing the Value of Companies*, 3rd edn (Chichester, UK: John Wiley & Sons).

Aswath Damodoran (2001) *Investment Valuation*, 2nd edn (Chichester, UK: John Wiley & Sons).

QUESTIONS AND PROBLEMS

1   A financial analyst at INVESTMENTBANK INTERNATIONAL is attempting to value the equity of IPCO. This growing company approached the bank about the possibility of an Initial Public Offering (IPO) of the company's shares. The company is looking to sell a substantial proportion of its equity to finance expected growth.

The analyst collected the following IPCO data for the preceding year:

Sales	100
Earnings	6.93
Free cash flow	36.93

In addition, she compiled the following range of estimates for the coming year:

	Low	Mid	High
Sales	103	122	140
Earnings	1.39	10.62	19.85
Free cash flow	31.39	40.62	49.85

She intends to use a number of valuation methods and then compare the results. The first is the P/E ratio method using prospective earnings. The prospective P/E ratio that she uses for a company is its current price per share divided by the analysts' consensus for its earnings in the following year.

She needs to have a range of suitable P/E values for the valuation. So, her first step was to collect a sample of prospective P/Es for similar companies already trading in the stock market. She found that most of the prospective P/Es fell in the following range:

	Low	Mid	High
Prospective P/E	13	18	23

Show how the analyst can obtain nine values for IPCO's equity using data selected from the two tables above.

2   The financial analyst at INTERNATIONAL wants to continue her valuation of IPCO using some additional valuation methods. The second is the prospective P/S method. The prospective P/S ratio she uses for a company is its total market value divided by the analysts' consensus for its sales in the following year. The total market value in the numerator of the ratio is the market value of the company's equity plus the value of its debt.

She needs to have a range of suitable P/S values for the valuation. So, her first step was to collect a sample of prospective P/Ss for companies already trading in the stock market. She found that most of the prospective P/Ss fell in the following range:

	Low	Mid	High
Prospective P/S	2.31	2.44	2.57

The company's debt is 100. Show how the analyst can obtain nine values for IPCO's equity using the above information and data selected from Problem 1.

3   The third method INTERNATIONAL's analyst wants to use for valuing IPCO is discounted free cash flow. Her range of estimates for the coming year's free cash flow and for the corresponding initial growth rates are:

	Low	Mid	High
Prospective free cash flow	31.39	40.62	49.85
Growth rate (%)	−15.00	10.00	35.00

The value of IPCO's debt is 100. The analyst considers 20% to be the appropriate discount rate in this calculation for IPCO.

(a)   Use this data in the Gordon–Williams compound growth model to obtain values for the company and for its equity.

(b)   Explain why you were unable to obtain more than two values for the company using these data.

(c)   What reservations have you about using initial growth rate data in a compound-growth valuation model?

4   INTERNATIONAL's analyst believes that compound growth models overvalue companies. She prefers linear growth models, which give more conservative valuations. IPCO's free cash flow for the current year is 39.63. Her range of estimates for the absolute amounts of additional cash flow in each year is:

	Low	Mid	High
Absolute growth	−5.54	3.69	12.93

The value of IPCO's debt is 100. The analyst considers 20% to be the appropriate discount rate in this calculation for IPCO.

(a)   Use these data in the linear growth model to obtain values for the company and for its equity if its debt equals 100. The equation for the linear growth model in this application is:

$$V = \frac{FCF}{R} + \frac{\Delta FCF}{R^2} \qquad (\Delta FCF > 0)$$

(b)   Explain why you were unable to obtain more than two values for the company using these data.

(c)   Is there justification for feeling more confident about using initial absolute increments of growth in the linear model rather than using the corresponding initial percentage growth rates in the compound growth model (Problem 3)?

5   INTERNATIONAL's analyst thinks it would be worthwhile valuing IPCO in two parts: the company's existing business and its investment opportunities. This would facilitate incorporating additional relevant information in the analysis. She would like to start with a valuation of its existing business. She needs to seek more precise information about the company's products but wants to move ahead in the meantime with the following rough estimates.

The company's existing cash flow comes almost equally from three products A, B, and C. The expected remaining lives of the three products are two, three, and four years, respectively. The cash flow from each product during its life is roughly one-third of the company's existing 36.93 annual free cash flow. The analyst thinks that 12% would be the appropriate discount rate for cash flows from existing products.

(a)   Calculate the value of the appropriate annuity factor for each of the three products and obtain the resulting total PV of IPCO's existing products.

(b)   What (negative) growth rate in the Gordon–Williams model would give the same value for the existing products?

6   After obtaining the PV of the cash flows from IPCO's existing products, the next step is to calculate the PV of the company's investment of opportunities. The analyst favors using the value 1.77 for the PI of the new investments. She suggests discounting the net future values $I_t \times (PV - 1)$ using a discount rate R_O equal to 23%. The initial annual investment expenditure I_0 is 40. This annual investment is expected to grow by $\Delta I = 4$ per year. Use this information in the following equation given in the chapter to obtain the PV of the investment opportunities:

$$O = \left[(1 + R_O) \left(\frac{I_0}{R_O} + \frac{\Delta I}{R_O^2} \right) \right] \times (PI - 1) \qquad (\Delta I \geq 0)$$

7   The analyst used the following equation to obtain the value $PI - 1 = 1.77$ supplied in Problem 6:

$$PI - 1 = \frac{o}{pr} (1 + R_O)^T$$

For example, suppose the PV o of each real investment option equals 0.314 per unit of investment and the probability pr of investing is 0.50. The value of R_O given in Problem 6 is 23%. The expected time T for each real investment option to mature is five years. Calculate the future net value $PI - 1$ of an investment opportunity having these characteristics.

DEFINITION

Initial Public Offering (IPO)   A limited company's first public issue of common stock (ordinary shares).

Mergers and Acquisitions

Imagine a rigid Soviet-style command economy in which unsuitable people manage obsolete assets that no longer are required. The result would be colossal waste. Now imagine instead a market economy that facilitates the reemployment of managers and rapid redeployment of assets in response to changing consumer requirements. This latter market exists in an increasing number of countries. It is the market for corporate control, more commonly known as the mergers and acquisitions (M&A) market. Clearly, an M&A market is one of the requirements of a healthy economy.

Companies can combine their operations and create efficiencies by means of a friendly merger. In addition, a strong company can acquire a weaker one and create similar efficiencies, often by removing much of the top management of the weaker company. The corporate control market can operate in any economy with legal frameworks that permit a corporation to purchase the majority of the voting shares from willing shareholders in another. The new majority shareholder then has control and thus the right to take whatever actions permitted by law that are necessary to satisfy actual market demand and to do so efficiently.

In this chapter, we examine the types of mergers and acquisitions, causes of merger waves, motivations for mergers, sources of merger gains, valuation, and financing. We also consider the bidding process and defences against hostile takeovers. Finally, we consider who gains and loses from mergers and acquisitions.

TOPICS

Issues covered are:

- distinctions between mergers and acquisitions;

- types of merger and acquisition;

- merger waves in the economy;

- motives for mergers and acquisitions;

- how much to pay for an acquisition;

- sources of synergy;

- financing mergers and acquisitions;

- bidding for an acquisition;

○   *defending against a bid; and*

○   *beneficiaries of acquisitions and mergers.*

11-1 WHAT ARE MERGERS AND ACQUISITIONS?

A merger is a business transaction with the purpose of forming one business organization from two or more preexisting ones. A consolidation is a merger that results in the creation of an entirely new entity. An acquisition is the transfer of the control of a company from one group of shareholders to another. An exchange of either cash or shares in the acquiring company for shares in the acquired company implements the transfer of control. A takeover is the hostile acquisition of another firm. If it opposes the acquisition, the board of the acquired company attempts to block the bid by various actions. A leveraged buyout is buying shares in an acquisition using a large proportion of debt financing. A management buyout is a leveraged buyout in which the acquirer is the acquired firm's existing management.

DEFINITIONS

Acquisition Transfer of control of a company from one group of shareholders to another.

Consolidation Merger resulting in an entirely new entity.

Debt Sum of money or other assets owed by one party to another. Usually, a legally enforceable obligation to pay agreed interest and to repay the principal of a loan to the lender promptly on shedule.

Leveraged buyout Buying shares in an acquisition financed with a large proportion of debt financing.

Management buyout Leveraged buyout in which the acquirer is the acquired firm's existing management.

Merger Transaction forming one business organization from two or more preexisting ones.

Share (stock) Security legally certifying that its registered holder is a part-owner of the corporation

Takeover Hostile acquisition.

11-2 TYPES OF MERGER

Mergers and acquisitions fall into three broad categories, commonly called horizontal, vertical, and conglomerate mergers.

A horizontal merger involves combining companies operating in the same industry. The products of both firms are often close substitutes. In a vertical merger, the firms engage in related activities but at different stages of production. For example, an oil refining company might merge forward by combining with another company that markets petroleum products directly to consumers.

Similarly, the firm could merge backward by combining with a company engaged in exploring for oil. Conglomerate mergers involve combining companies in unrelated lines of business. The motive for a conglomerate merger can be mere diversification to reduce risk, or it can be to produce administrative efficiencies. A product extension merger is a conglomerate combination intended to create marketing efficiencies. For example, complementary products market more efficiently through merged channels of distribution.

DEFINITIONS

Conglomerate merger Combination of companies in unrelated lines of business.

Horizontal merger Combination of companies operating in the same industry.

Merging forward Combining with customers or potential customers.

Merging backward Combining with suppliers or potential suppliers.

Product extension merger Combination of companies intended to create marketing efficiencies.

Vertical merger Combination of firms engaged in related activities but at different stages of production.

11-3 MERGER WAVES

A curious feature of the market for corporate control is that mergers and acquisitions tend to occur in waves. Waves of mergers and acquisitions occurred early in the last century, in the 1920s, the late 1980s, and in the second half of the 1990s. A buoyant stock market accompanied each such episode.

Why do such waves occur? A number of possible factors could help to trigger waves of acquisitions and mergers:

1. **Real options.** An expanding economy creates real options often best exercised by combinations of companies.

2. The *"hubris* hypothesis".[1] When times are good, managers become overconfident.

3. *Technology.* Rapid changes in technology and changes in the costs of the factors of production oblige managers to find ways such as acquisitions to make economies.

4. *Chaos theory.* If an acquisition or merger upsets the balance of power in a product market, competitors feel forced to combine in order to restore the balance.

5. *Strong financial markets.* In a bull market, it is easier to raise the necessary finance for acquisitions.

---

[1] Richard Roll (1986) "The hubris hypothesis of corporate takeovers," *Journal of Business*, Vol. 59 (April), 198–216.

Inflation, interest rate volatility, privatization, and deregulation can also characterize merger waves.

Many of these factors suggest that mergers and acquisitions are more likely to occur when economic prospects are favorable.

DEFINITIONS

Hubris   Acquirer's excessive optimism concerning the benefits from acquisitions and mergers.

Real option   Right to make favorable future choices regarding real asset investments. More precisely, a real option is an opportunity for voluntary future investment in a nonfinancial asset when at least a part of the required investment expenditure is certain or, alternatively, when at least a part of the required investment expenditure is not perfectly positively correlated with the project's present value.

11-4   MOTIVATIONS FOR MERGERS AND ACQUISITIONS

SYNERGY

The principal economic motive for corporate combinations is to increase **shareholder value** by means of **synergy**. Synergy literally means working together. Merging permits companies to work more closely together, thereby creating efficiencies and increasing power in the marketplace. It also permits them to create real options that might not otherwise exist. For example, it was necessary to create the Airbus Consortium to compete with Boeing in the large airframe business.

DIVISION OF THE SPOILS

Even if there are overall net gains from a merger or acquisition, the shareholders of the two combining companies generally do not split the benefit evenly. Normally one of the two companies is the aggressor and the other is the target. In order to make the acquisition happen, the aggressor must acquire sufficient of the shares in the target to gain control. Doing so drives up the market price of the target's shares. The increase in the market value of the shares reflects the expected **bid premium**. The bid premium is the additional value the acquirer must pay to induce the target's shareholders to sell their shares.

Consequently, the gains from an acquisition tend to transfer to the target's shareholders by means of the higher share price. So, the target's shareholders are the main beneficiaries of the acquisition because they are the recipients of the bid premium.

That the target company's shareholders are the natural financial beneficiaries of an acquisition is a consequence of an efficient stock market. The **Perfectly Competitive Acquisitions Market Hypothesis (PCAMH)** suggests that the bid premium transfers the entire value of the synergy expected from an acquisition to the acquired company's shareholders. This hypothesis applies most strictly to the case of one unique seller (the target company's shareholders) and many potential acquirers. The seller can hold out for the highest price. Perfectly competing buyers end up paying full value, which includes all the expected gains from the synergy.

Although the strict conditions of the PCAMH are unlikely to hold, many empirical studies have been unable to reject the hypothesis. On average, the premium paid for the acquired company's shares appears to have equalled virtually all the gains from merging.[2]

The winner's curse is one reason that the PCAMH appears to hold. The winner is the buyer most likely to have misjudged the value of the acquisition and thus pays too much for it.[3] An example of the winner's curse was the acquisition of the US clothing retailer Brooks Brothers by the UK retailer Marks & Spencer, paying a very large premium that exceeded any likely gains from synergy.

HUBRIS

Why might the winner's curse ensnare the management of an aggressor company? Hubris is a behavioral explanation. Managers frequently are too optimistic when forecasting the synergistic benefits of an acquisition. Backing out of an acquisition can involve the acknowledgement of earlier misjudgments. Once publicly and financially committed to the chase, a company chairman frequently sees it through to eventual capture rather than enduring the public humiliation of giving up beforehand.

DEFINITIONS

Bid premium   Additional payment by the acquirer necessary to induce the acquired company's shareholders to sell their shares.

Expected (mean)   Probability-weighted average of all possible outcomes for a random variable.

Hubris   Acquirer's excessive optimism concerning the benefits from acquisitions and mergers.

Perfectly Competitive Acquisitions Market Hypothesis (PCAMH)   Proposition that the bid premium transfers the entire value of the synergy expected from an acquisition to the acquired company's shareholders.

Shareholder value   Economic value of the shareholders' financial claim on the business.

Synergy   Efficiencies and market power resulting from organizations working more closely together.

Winner's curse   Proposition that the winning buyer is the one most likely to have overvalued the asset and thus paid too much for it.

---

[2] J. R. Franks, R. S. Harris, and S. Titman (1991) "The postmerger share-price performance of acquiring firms," *Journal of Financial Economics*, Vol. 29 (March), 81–96.
[3] R. H. Thaler (1992) *The Winner's Curse, Paradoxes and Anomalies of Economic Life* (New York: Free Press).

11-5 HOW MUCH TO PAY FOR AN ACQUISITION

After identifying an acquisition target, the would-be acquirer must answer three essential questions. The first is, What are the identifiable sources of synergy? Second, What is the synergy worth? Third, What price should one bid for the target's equity?

VALUE OF THE SYNERGY

Synergy can generate overall gains for shareholders if the value of the synergy exceeds the costs of creating it. Appraisal of the present value (PV) of expected synergy is much the same as for any other capital project. That is, for both merging companies A and B:

1. Identify the relevant after-tax cash flows changed by the merger and the real options created by it.

2. Forecast the expected relevant after-tax cash flows and real options of the combined firm if the merger takes place. Let V_{AB} represent their PV.

3. Forecast the expected relevant after-tax cash flows and real options for the two companies if the merger does not take place. Let $V_A + V_B$ represent their PV.

Thus

$$Synergy = V_{AB} - (V_A + V_B)$$

The relevant discount rates used should reflect the nondiversifiable risk of each of the three sets of cash flows.[4]

NET GAIN FOR SHAREHOLDERS

The above steps enable one to determine whether the gain for the shareholders from merging Companies A and B is positive, net of opportunity costs and transaction costs:

$$Gain = Synergy - OC - TC$$

where OC represents opportunity costs and TC represents transaction costs. The opportunity costs OC equal the PV of the best alternative capital investment preempted by the merger or acquisition. The chief opportunity cost is management time. The time required for the acquisition process and managing the postmerger synergy is substantial. This time could otherwise have been devoted to other profitable activity. For example, management could pursue an alternative investment that serves the same strategic purpose as the proposed acquisition. The transaction costs TC include fees paid to investment banking advisors, underwriters, lawyers, and accountants and to the relevant stock exchange.

---

[4] The alternative approach is to identify directly the incremental cash flows for the synergy. The relevant discount rate for these cash flows must then reflect the nondiversifiable risk of the synergy itself. So, appraising the value of the synergy is no different in principle from appraising the PV of any other capital project.

THE BID

How much can the acquirer afford to bid for the target company's shares? The answer is straightforward. The acquirer should bid no more than the value of the target's equity plus the net gain from merging. The value of the target's equity for this purpose equals the total stock market value of all its shares adjusted for any effect due to market anticipation of a bid.[5] This adjusted value is the **ex-bid prospects market capitalization.**

Let XMC_B represent the ex-bid prospects market capitalization of target firm B. Then XMC_B is equal to the ex-bid prospects share price multiplied by the number of B's shares outstanding in the market. The maximum value that A could justify paying for B's equity would be:

$$Bid < Ex\text{-}bid\ Prospects\ Market\ Capitalization\ of\ B + Gain\ from\ Merging$$

$$= XMC_B + Gain$$

Thus

$$Bid < XMC_B + Synergy - OC - TC$$

That is, the bid must be less than the right-hand side of this equation if it is to be financially worthwhile for the acquiring company.

One of the key variables in this formula is the ex-bid prospects share price XP_B determining the ex-bid prospects market capitalization:

$$XMC_B = XP_B \times N_B$$

where N_B is the number of shares of Company B outstanding in the market.

The ex-bid share price XP_B is always less than or equal to the current share price P_B. The reason is that the current share price equals the ex-bid share price increased by any abnormal return attributable to bid prospects. That is:

$$Current\ Share\ Price = Ex\text{-}bid\ Prospects\ Share\ Price \times (1 + Bid\ Prospects\ Abnormal\ Return)$$

$$P_B = XP_B \times (1 + R_{BP})$$

Solving for the ex-bid prospects share price we have:

$$XP_B = \frac{P_B}{(1 + R_{BP})}$$

Multiplying by the number of shares N_B we obtain the target's ex-bid prospects market capitalization to which we referred earlier:

$$XMC_B = \frac{P_B \times N_B}{(1 + R_{BP})}$$

The bid prospects abnormal return R_{BP} is the part of the return R_B on B's shares attributable to expectations of a bid. This part of the target's return is merely the remainder after removal of all other influences on the return. Broadly, two main influences other than expectations of a bid

---

[5] If the target company's shares do not trade in the stock market, one must estimate the total value of its equity by other means. Chapter 10 shows how to value the equity of unlisted companies for acquisition.

require removing. The first is the influence $E(R_B)$ of market-wide movement. The company's **beta factor** governs this influence in the **Capital Asset Pricing Model (CAPM)**. The second influence R_O results from news of specific company developments other than bid prospects:

Bid Prospects Abnormal Return = Return on B − Expected Return on B − Other Return

$$R_{BP} = R_B - E(R_B) - R_O$$

DEFINITIONS

Beta factor   A measure of the market risk of an asset. The factor by which mean returns on the asset reflect returns on the market portfolio.

Capital Asset Pricing Model (CAPM)   Linear model attempting to explain the expected return on a risky asset in terms of the risk-free rate, its beta factor (systematic risk), and the risk premium on the market portfolio.

Discount rate   Required rate of return used in the calculation of a discount factor.

Ex-bid prospects market capitalization   Market capitalization of the company being acquired, adjusted for any effect due to market anticipation of a bid.

Incremental cash flow   Difference between the relevant expected after-tax cash flows of the firm if the project goes forward and if it does not go forward.

Nondiversifiable risk   Systematic risk. Market risk. Risk that portfolio diversification cannot eliminate.

Opportunity cost of capital   Rate of return forgone when investing in a project instead of the securities market.

Present value (PV)   Value of an investment now as the cost of a comparable investment in the financial market (calculated by multiplying the investment's expected after-tax cash income by the appropriate discount factors).

Underwriter   Investment bank or stockbroker undertaking to manage the issuance of securities for a corporate client, often buying the entire issue and reselling it to institutional clients and other investors.

EXAMPLE 11.1

GREEN PAGES plc publishes local telephone directories listing the numbers of retailers who advertize in the directories. It is a large national business with annual sales averaging more than €500 million. The company also operates web pages containing similar information about retailers. Competing with GREEN PAGES is BLUE.com. BLUE.com's web pages employ a more sophisticated technology providing a better service to users. For example, they permit users to find the nearest retailer currently stocking any desired product or brand. GREEN PAGES would like to exploit BLUE's technology to enhance services to their clientele. They would also like to remove BLUE as a competitive threat. Thus, GREEN PAGES contemplates a bid for BLUE.com, which is a stock exchange listed company.

Accountants advised GREEN's Finance Director that the expected potential synergy from the acquisition is €150 million. She also assembled the following summary information relating to the bid. Investment banking advisers conducting the usual due-diligence investigation of the target company will refine all these data later. The investigation will reveal details of BLUE's financial circumstances, contractual obligations, stock options, patents, copyrights, etc. In the meantime, she wants an overview of the likely scale of the bid before approaching the advisers.

The table below provides data denominated in millions of euros:

V_A	1,000
V_B	100
V_{AB}	1,150
OC	50
TC	10

With these data, she could easily estimate the implied synergy and the expected gain from merging the two companies:

$$Synergy = V_{AB} - (V_A + V_B)$$

$$= 1,150,000,000 - (1,000,000,000 + 100,000,000) = 150,000,000$$

$$Gain = Synergy - OC - TC$$

$$= 150,000,000 - 50,000,000 - 10,000,000 = 90,000,000$$

BLUE's current share price is €10 per share, and there are 10 million shares outstanding. During the preceding three months, BLUE's share price rose 12% despite a decline in the market index of 5.5%. BLUE's equity beta was equal to 2.00. During the three months, only one significant piece of news emerged about the company. This news implied an additional 10% on the share price. The following summarizes the relevant data:

P_B	€10
N_B	10,000,000 shares
R_B	12%
R_F	5%
R_M	−5.5%
β_B	2.00
R_O	10%

With these data, she can calculate the value of the bid in the context of the current market. The expected rate of return R_B on B's shares estimated in the CAPM is:

$$E(R_B) = R_F + \beta_B \times (R_M - R_F)$$

$$= 5 + 2.00 \times (-5.5 - 5) = -16.0\%$$

Therefore, the ex-bid prospects return on BLUE's shares during the preceding three months was:

$$R_{BP} = R_B - E(R_B) - R_O$$
$$= 12 - (-16.0) - 10 = 18\%$$

Consequently, BLUE's ex-bid prospects market capitalization currently is:

$$XMC_B = \frac{P_B \times N_B}{(1 + R_{BP})}$$
$$= \frac{10 \times 10,000,000}{(1 + 0.18)} = 84,745,000$$

To be worthwhile for GREEN, its bid for BLUE's equity would have to be less than:

Maximum bid $< XMC_B + Synergy - OC - TC$

$$< 84,745,000 + 150,000,000 - 50,000,000 - 10,000,000 = 174,745,000$$

The bid premium on the ex-bid prospects market capitalization would have to be less than:

$$174,745,000/84,745,000 - 1 = 106.2\%$$

This represents a premium on the current market capitalization of no more than:

$$174,745,000/(10 \times 10,000,000) - 1 = 74.7\%$$

Most successful bids require premia somewhat less than these figures. Thus, BLUE should take the prospective bid a step further with its advisers.

In the subsequent month or two required to prepare a formally announced bid, relevant new information will emerge and stock market prices will have changed. The actual bid premium at that time will need adjustment accordingly.

We have outlined a procedure for obtaining the PV of the merger gain resulting from synergy and the resulting maximum value of the bid. More fundamentally, the acquirer must be able to identify the obtainable synergies from the particular acquisition. Let us now consider the different types of synergy claimed to result from mergers and acquisitions.

DEFINITIONS

Expected rate of return (mean)   Probability-weighted average of all possible outcomes for the rate of return.

Market capitalization   The stock market value of a company's equity. The market price per share multiplied by the number of shares issued.

11-6 SYNERGY

Many potential sources of synergy can result when two or more companies combine. Listed below are 10 claimed sources of synergy. Obviously, it is best if the acquirer can identify and exploit as many such synergies as possible.

REAL OPTIONS

New combinations of economic and commercial factors generate real options to do new things and to conduct existing activities differently. Mergers and acquisitions create such new combinations and might do so in areas that existing management could be uniquely qualified to exploit. Therefore, acquisitions and mergers can create valuable real options that benefit shareholders. Unfortunately, real options have no value until management perceives that they exist. If management is not sensitive to the new opportunities and not sufficiently agile to exercise the perceived new options, much of the value is needlessly lost. Many of the synergies listed below are real options.

ECONOMIES OF SCALE

Companies often merge to create economies of scale. A horizontal merger often permits combined manufacturing concentrated at fewer sites. Other economies of scale from merging include reduced administrative overheads, combined planning and logistics, common channels of distribution, and joint advertizing.

When the market for a product is growing, firms with the largest market share benefit more rapidly from the economies of scale that come from additional new plant. Companies with a smaller share of the market could find it necessary to combine their market shares in order to justify the new plant that would provide comparable economies of scale.

MARKET POWER

Small companies with outstanding products often do not have the marketing skills to sell their products effectively. Acquisition by a company with strong marketing and channels of distribution can increase a product's potential sales manyfold.

A merger can increase power in the marketplace. The resulting larger company can negotiate better prices from suppliers, for example. In addition, upstream mergers can limit supplies to competitors.

By acquiring competitors, a company could seek to gain greater control over pricing by creating an oligopoly, if not an actual monopoly. Furthermore, downstream mergers can help assure the market for some of the acquirer's products and perhaps shut out some competition. Referral of such mergers and acquisitions to regulatory authorities frequently results, however. A legal objection to a bid thus can prevent or at least delay an acquisition or merger.

In addition, high profits resulting from such corporate combinations can attract new entrants and encourage the development of close substitutes. Therefore, the market power benefits from mergers can be temporary.

MARKET ENTRY

Purchasing an existing player can permit an acquirer to gain a foothold in a new geographical area or in a different product market.

Acquirers often target small firms that have desired technical knowledge but lack the scale necessary to manufacture and market their products effectively. Acquisition can permit deployment of the technical knowledge on a wider scale. It could also improve the acquiring company's existing and future products.

A friendly acquisition can provide a rapid means of recruiting an intact management and technical team. In a contested takeover, hostile managers and key personnel may resign and take their talents elsewhere, however.

NEW PRODUCTS

If a new product requires new production or distribution facilities that require a long time to put in place, there will be less time for the company to exploit competitive advantage. Competitors will have more time to adapt their existing products or to produce new ones if they already have the required facilities. Acquisition of another company's existing facilities can permit a more rapid exploitation of a new product's competitive advantage. This can make it possible to capture net present value (NPV) from the new product before the competition can seek its share.

In addition, the costs of establishing a brand name and the resulting delay in exploiting a new product can make it worthwhile to acquire another company's brand by means of a merger or acquisition.

UNDERVALUED ASSETS

Markets for products, materials, and labor are imperfect. Given imperfect information, share prices do not always fully reflect the value of assets in more profitable alternative uses. Because there are costs and impediments to obtaining such information, both the stock market and the incumbent management can be unaware of the specific alternative uses available to an acquiring company. Therefore, the acquirer might succeed in acquiring a pre-bid stake in the target company before its stock price fully reflects the value of the intended alternative use.

In the depths of a bear market one can sometimes discover companies whose stock market capitalization represents less than the net replacement value of their assets. An acquirer having a specific use for such assets might choose to acquire the assets through acquisition rather than to purchase equivalent assets from primary producers.

TAXES

An incentive to acquire companies with accumulated tax losses exists in a number of countries. The losses reduce the taxable income of the merged company thereby reducing taxes on current profits. For example, UK companies can use accumulated losses of acquired companies in this way if the profits arise from the same line of business.

RISK DIVERSIFICATION

Conglomerate mergers can reduce risk through diversification. A wide variety of products in diverse markets makes the combined cash flow of conglomerates less volatile. While no one doubts that properly controlled corporate diversification reduces corporate risk, it is not clear that much of the benefit reaches the shareholders.

Shareholders can reduce risk for themselves by constructing portfolios of quoted firms operating in diverse markets. They can do so without paying the bid premiums that conglomerate companies must pay to acquire entire companies. Shareholders do not appear to need corporate managers to reduce risk on their behalf.

A different argument would be that conglomerates can reduce risks in ways not accessible to shareholders. Shareholders can only diversify holdings of financial assets. In contrast, corporate managers can combine real assets and exploit confidential information to reduce risks before shareholders are aware of them. Furthermore, reducing risks for management and employees can have indirect benefits for shareholders if it engenders greater loyalty and reduces the loss of talented personnel.

It seems unlikely that the benefits of conglomerate diversification alone are sufficient to justify the high bid premiums necessary to achieve it, however.

COINSURANCE

Reduced risk through corporate diversification can reduce borrowing costs. The coinsurance effect explains why mergers can reduce the cost of borrowing. Imperfect correlation of earnings implies that the two partners in a merger effectively insure one another's obligations to creditors. Coinsurance reduces the risk of default. While obtaining a better credit rating in this way can indeed reduce the rates of interest paid by the combined firm, it is not clear that its shareholders benefit.

Consider first any new borrowing subsequent to the merger. The debt market is very competitive. In an efficient debt market, lenders do not give away NPV to borrowers and thus they leave no net gain from new borrowing for the shareholders. The lower interest rates merely reflect that the borrower's option to default has become less valuable. Accordingly, lenders require the payment of less interest for the option.

Now consider the effect on existing loans. Lower default risk on the existing debt increases the market value of the existing debt. The value of the borrower's equity equals the market value of its assets minus the market value of its debt. Therefore, the increase in the market value of existing debt reduces the value of the equity. This is a zero-sum game: what the debt holders gain the shareholders lose.

In summary, shareholders do not gain from new borrowing after a merger and they can lose because of the increased market value of existing debt. Therefore, any direct financial benefit for shareholders from the coinsurance effect of mergers is unlikely.

UNUSED DEBT CAPACITY

A number of authors have suggested that companies that have not exhausted their borrowing capacity are attractive targets for acquisition. An acquirer can borrow against the target's assets and enjoy two advantages. The first is liquidity: borrowing against the target's assets makes the acquisition at least partially self-financing. The second concerns value: there may be tax benefits from the additional borrowing.

The liquidity argument is difficult to dismiss on theoretical grounds. The reason is that current finance theory does not attach value to liquidity. The theory is incomplete in this respect. Everyone knows that liquidity is important. We just do not know how much it is worth.

The second argument is that the acquirer can capture tax advantages from the additional borrowing. The validity of this argument hinges on the existence of an optimum capital structure. As will be shown in Chapter 16, recent theoretical developments support the existence of optimum capital structures. So, increasing the debt of an underborrowed firm to its optimum level captures value.

Consequently, it seems possible that increased borrowing can be one of the sources of synergy in a merger. On its own, however, a value gain from additional borrowing would not justify the relatively high bid premium usually required to effect an acquisition.

As we have seen, many potential sources of synergy can result from a merger or acquisition. Indeed, a combination of several sources of synergy can be necessary to justify paying the bid premium.

DEFINITIONS

Competitive advantage   Comparative advantage permitting a firm to earn economic rents in an imperfect product market.

Default   Failure to make a payment of interest or a repayment of principal on the due date.

Diversification   Reduction of a portfolio's risk by holding a collection of assets having returns that are not perfectly positively correlated.

Equity   Net worth or shareholders' capital represented by common stock (ordinary shares) and preferred stock.

Liquidity   Ease with which cash is recoverable from an investment.

Net present value (NPV)   Difference between the present value of a project's expected after-tax operating cash flows and the present value of its expected after-tax investment expenditures.

11-7 OTHER MOTIVES FOR MERGERS AND ACQUISITIONS

MANAGERIAL MOTIVES

Roll's (1986) "hubris hypothesis" suggests that managers frequently have excessive faith in their abilities to manage other companies. This overoptimism leads them to overvalue the benefits of merging.

Managers who believe themselves vulnerable to takeover often try to preempt this by expansion. Accordingly, one of the motives for many mergers and acquisitions is job protection rather than shareholder value maximization.

Expanding a firm has additional advantages for the incumbent managers. Managing a larger firm can help to justify higher salaries and bonuses, and other benefits such as the use of executive aircraft.

FREE CASH FLOW

Free cash flow is cash flow not required for investment in the available projects having positive NPVs. Jensen (1986) suggested that managers often prefer to use free cash flow for acquisitions rather than paying higher dividends or buying back shares from the shareholders. Buying other firms instead confers more power.

DEFINITIONS

Buyback   Buying the company's shares from its shareholders instead of using the cash to pay them dividends.

Free cash flow   After-tax cash flow from operations net of capital investment and increases in net working capital.

11-8 FINANCING MERGERS AND ACQUISITIONS

Exchange of cash or shares for the shares in the acquired company pays for the merger or acquisition. The payment package can also include corporate bonds, preference shares, or convertibles.

EXCHANGE FOR CASH

A target's shareholders can most easily understand an exchange for cash, helping to get their agreement to the bid. Another advantage of the cash bid is that proportionate holdings and control remain unaltered for the acquirer's shareholders. A disadvantage of a cash bid, however, is that it results in an immediate capital gain for many of the target's shareholders, creating a tax liability for them.

EXCHANGE FOR SHARES

Exchange of the target's shares for the acquirer's shares has the advantage that the acquirer does not need to find cash to finance the acquisition. In addition, the target's shareholders retain an interest in the combined entity by means of the resulting new share holding. An additional advantage of this is that the target's shareholders can continue to defer capital gains tax liability.

THE PREFERRED METHOD

Franks et al. (1991) examined the effects of cash and stock-financed bids on the acquirer's share price. They used a very large sample of bids during the period 1975 to 1984. They found that the acquirer's share price rose on average by 0.8% (relative to the market) following announcements of cash-financed bids. In contrast, the acquirer's share price fell by 3.2% on average following announcement of a stock-financed bid.[6] So, this evidence suggests that the acquirers' shareholders favored cash-financed bids.

---

[6] J. R. Franks, R. S. Harris, and S. Titman (1991) "The postmerger share-price performance of acquiring firms," *Journal of Financial Economics*, Vol. 29 (March), 81–96.

DEFINITIONS

Bond   An interest-bearing security with usually long-term maturity. Interest payments may be fixed or variable (floating).

Convertibles   Bonds or preferred stocks that give the holder the option (effectively a warrant) to convert the security into the issuing company's ordinary shares (common stock) according to specified terms during some stated period of years.

Preference shares (preferred stock)   Equity security that pays a (normally fixed) dividend. The issuer must pay the preference dividend before paying any dividends on common stock (ordinary shares). Cumulative preference shares carry forward entitlement to unpaid preference dividends. Participating preference shares also entitle holders to a share of profit.

11-9 THE BIDDING PROCESS

The most active mergers and acquisitions market in Europe has been in the UK. Therefore, it would be appropriate to use the UK example to illustrate the bidding process.

PRE-BID PHASE

The obvious first step is for the bidding firm and its investment banking advisers to identify and to value suitable targets for mergers or acquisitions.

The bidder then approaches the target's board with an informal offer. To have any hope of acceptance the bid must include a substantial premium above the target's existing market value. Ordinarily the premium must be 20% to 50% above the pre-bid share price. The initial bid is more likely to be toward the lower end of this range. If the board rebuffs the informal approach, the bid is a hostile bid.

If the acquirer wishes to proceed, it must communicate a formal notice of the bid to the target's board and to its advisers. The board in turn must immediately inform the shareholders of the bid and advise them of the board's view regarding the bid's acceptability.

Even before the informal approach, a hostile bidder can begin accumulating the target firm's shares by purchasing them secretly in the stock market. Upon accumulating 3% of the outstanding shares, however, the acquirer must publicly announce the holding. The announcement is likely to stimulate speculation that the target is "in play," and the share price begins to rise in anticipation of an eventual bid premium.

In the meantime, the potential acquirer is free to continue accumulating the target's shares in the stock market. When the acquirer's holding reaches 30% of the target's outstanding ordinary share capital, the acquirer is obliged to launch a formal bid for all the remaining outstanding shares. By this time, the market price of the target's shares will normally have risen quite dramatically, reflecting the market's expectation of the size of the eventual bid premium.

BID PHASE

Within 28 days of the formal notice of the bid, the acquirer must post the offer document to the target firm's shareholders. The offer document formally specifies the terms of the bid. The acquirer must notify its shareholders if the acquisition would increase the total value of the acquirer's assets by more than 15%. Indeed, if the acquirer's assets would increase by more than 25%, acquirer shareholder approval is required.

The offer remains open for 21 days, during which time the target's individual shareholders must decide whether to accept the offer for their shares. During this period the target's share price will have risen substantially; and the shareholders need to consider whether the bid is attractive relative to the resulting price in the open market. If the acquirer increases the offer, the revised offer must remain open for a further 14 days, permitting the target's shareholders additional time to consider the revision. In response to the increased bid, the share price is likely to rise further in the stock market.

The maximum overall period allowed for the offer and for any subsequent revisions to remain open is 60 days. If the acquirer fails to gain control within the 60 days, the acquirer cannot try again until a further year has elapsed.

POST-BID PHASE

If the acquirer succeeds in acquiring 50% of the target's voting shares during the offer period, the bid becomes unconditional. That is, the bid is recognized to have been successful. The target's remaining shareholders usually accept the offer quite rapidly once the bid is unconditional.

After acquisition of 90% of the target's voting shares, the remaining shareholders have four months to sell their shares at the final offer price. Those who fail to sell their shares remain as one of a relatively small proportion of minority shareholders.

11-10 DEFENDING AGAINST A BID

A hostile bid is usually less acceptable to the incumbent management than to the shareholders. Boards generally like to have the option to prevent bids that their shareholders might accept.

PRE-BID PHASE

Companies that feel vulnerable to a bid monitor the names in their shareholder register for signs that particular companies or individuals might be accumulating a significant stake in the company.

A threatened company often accumulates a defensive cross-holding in a friendly firm with whom it might merge as a means of preempting a hostile takeover.

In addition, the company may take measures that make hostile bids more difficult to succeed. The following is a list of such measures, not all of which are legal in every country:

O   Restricted voting rights. *The company's Articles of Association stipulate a large majority of voting shares for approval of an acquisition.*

○ Dual-class shares. *The company issues and controls a class of shares with superior voting rights, thus preempting control of voting by a hostile bidder.*

○ Executive share option plans. *The company repurchases a substantial proportion of its voting shares on the open market. Existing management receive options to buy and vote these shares.*

○ Leveraged recapitalization. *The company borrows a large sum of money, increasing gearing to the maximum feasible level. It then distributes the money to existing shareholders as a special dividend. This maneuver helps to preempt a bidder using borrowings to fund the acquisition.*

○ Crown jewels. *Management sells those parts of the company that it considers would be most attractive to a potential bidder.*

○ Golden parachute. *Management awards itself huge severance payments conditional on the company falling prey to a hostile bid.*

○ Poison pill. *The existing shareholders have the right to buy a large number of shares at a deep discount in any combined entity resulting from a hostile bid.*

○ Poison put. *Debt holders have the right to require immediate repayment in the event of a hostile acquisition.*

BID PHASE

The following two well-known measures refer to the bid phase:

○ Greenmail. *The company offers to buy back the bidder's share holding at a premium.*

○ PacMan. *The target company launches a counter-bid for the would-be acquirer.*

The board of a company that is subject to a hostile bid needs to present a convincing case to shareholders why they should not accept the bid for their shares. For example, the board may attack the commercial logic of the bid. They might also attempt to impugn the quality of the managers of the bidding firm.

At the same time, the board can take steps to improve the public image of the target by, for example, revising earnings projections and by increasing the dividend.

Especially in the case of an attempted horizontal takeover, the board may attempt to get the bid referred to the relevant regulatory authority. If successful, the referral would add considerably to the acquirer's costs and delay the acquisition for a significant period representing a deterrent for the acquirer.

Furthermore, the board might find it possible to enlist the firm's other stakeholders in opposition to the merger. These might include relevant unions, customers, suppliers, politicians, and the local community.

Finally, the board could invite a rival bid from a friendly company, a so-called "white knight" acquirer.

The existing management of an acquisition target can hardly pretend to be disinterested in the outcome of a bid. One might easily question whether any of the measures listed above serve anyone's interests other than those of the incumbent management.

11-11 WHO GAINS FROM MERGERS AND ACQUISITIONS?

As indicated earlier, the market for corporate control is a prerequisite for a healthy, modern economy. Mergers and acquisitions activity helps to put corporate assets to their most productive uses and to ensure that the right people manage them. Synergies from merging benefit society when they make the economy more productive. Mere increases in monopoly power, however, benefit only one group of managers and shareholders at the expense of consumers. So, enlightened governments encourage the market for corporate control but use regulation to prevent the creation of monopolies.

THE PERFECTLY COMPETITIVE ACQUISITIONS MARKET HYPOTHESIS

Evidence from the stock market is mostly consistent with the Perfectly Competitive Acquisitions Market Hypothesis. That is, most of the value of the gains from merging end up in the hands of the target company's shareholders. That is, the bid premium equals on average the PV of the merger benefits. A value-weighted average of market returns of the acquirer and the acquired company for large samples reveals overall market gains attributable to announcements of bids, however. This evidence suggests that investors expect net gains from merging, even if the gains are not equally distributed between the target company's and acquirer's shareholders.

GAINS TO THE SHAREHOLDERS OF ACQUIRED COMPANIES

Bid premiums have been increasing during the last several decades. Does this mean that the gains from merging are increasing? Perhaps it really implies an increasingly competitive mergers and acquisitions market, forcing acquirers to pay excessively high bid premiums. If bid premiums are excessive, who gains and who loses? Although some shareholders might object to their companies paying high bid premiums, well-diversified shareholders have little incentive to object. This is because they receive the high premiums for target companies already in their portfolios. They win more than they lose when the net gains from mergers are positive. Therefore, high bid premiums appear to function as a market lubricant facilitating the net gains from merging. The economy benefits and so do the shareholders in aggregate and in the long run.

A number of studies, nevertheless, have suggested that the postmerger performance of acquisitions disappointed the managers of the acquiring companies. This evidence supports the management hubris hypothesis and the winner's curse. In a competitive acquisitions market the winning bids come from the managers who are the most optimistic. Overoptimism leads to disappointment. As indicated earlier, the economy still benefits even if the gains from merging are less than expected and bid premiums are excessive.

POWER AND STATUS FOR ACQUIRING MANAGERS

Acquiring firms' senior managers can gain status, power, and improved remuneration packages because of growth through acquisition. Senior managers of target firms often receive generous compensation payments. Although not all individuals can benefit in every merger or acquisition, it is likely that senior managers as a group enjoy rewards from causing the economic gains from acquisitions and mergers.

LOSERS

Many employees including middle managers can expect to lose their jobs because of economies of scale and redeployment of assets. The resulting upheaval is costly for the individuals and their families. When accountants add up the gains from a merger they do not include such personal costs. The personal costs have no obvious direct effect on the resulting stock market prices either. Perhaps it is not entirely coincidence, however, that those countries with the most active mergers and acquisitions markets have the strongest job markets. A strong job market helps to mitigate some of the personal costs due to mergers and acquisitions.

THIRD-PARTY WINNERS

Obviously, the investment bankers and other professionals who advise acquirers and their targets benefit from substantial fees. They receive their fees regardless of the outcome of a bid. The issue would be whether the market for these services is competitive and whether the service providers deliver full value for money. As indicated earlier, however, there are still net gains from merging when the value of the synergy resulting from mergers and acquisitions exceeds both the opportunity costs and the transaction costs, which include the fees of professional advisers.

11-12   CONCLUSIONS

The market for corporate control plays an important role in advanced economies. It helps to put corporate assets to their best uses and to ensure that the right people manage them. Waves of mergers and acquisitions have occurred during particular periods of economic history. Strong economic growth and rising stock markets have characterized such periods when merger and acquisition activity was greatest.

The principal motive for mergers and acquisitions is to obtain economic benefits that result when companies combine their commercial and managerial resources. The resulting synergy derives from factors such as economies of scale, increased market power, access to new markets, real options, and possible tax advantages. Although conglomerate mergers can reduce risk, the fact that shareholders can diversify much of the risk more cheaply within their own portfolios diminishes this benefit from merging.

Exchange of cash or securities for the voting stock of the acquired company pays for mergers and acquisitions. Securities used in an exchange can include one or more of: shares in the acquiring company, corporate bonds, preference shares, and convertibles. Share price reactions to acquisitions suggest that target company shareholders prefer being paid cash for their shares.

The PCAMH suggests that the target company shareholders can hold out for a high price that leaves little net value for the acquiring company. Indeed, empirical work shows that on average target company shareholders receive virtually all the merger gains in the bid premium. Weighted averages combining the abnormal returns for both the acquirer's and the target company's shareholders, however, indicate overall positive abnormal returns from mergers and acquisitions. This evidence supports the theory that the stock market expects net gains from merging.

It seems that there are net gains from merging that benefit at least the stockholders of acquired companies. Who else can benefit? Senior managers who are the architects of these gains also benefit. They can acquire increased status, power, and remuneration from managing a larger combined firm. Even the acquired firm's senior managers often receive substantial payoffs. Economies of scale from merging usually entail loss of employment for many employees and middle managers. Mitigating this is the strong jobs market that accompanies the economic growth associated with merger waves. Finally, yet importantly, the investment bankers and other professionals who conduct the market for corporate control and advise the protagonists receive substantial fees regardless of the outcome of a bid.

DEFINITION

Portfolio   Collection of investments in financial securities and other assets.

FURTHER READING

P. A. Gaughan (2002) *Mergers, Acquisitions, and Corporate Restructurings*, 3rd edn (Chichester, UK: John Wiley & Sons).

L. Herzel and R. Shepro (1990) *Bidders and Targets: Mergers and Acquisitions in the U.S.* (Cambridge, MA: Basil Blackwell).

M. C. Jensen (1986) "Agency costs of free cash flow, corporate finance and takeovers," *American Economic Review*, Vol. 26 (May), 323–329.

J. F. Weston, K. S. Chung, and J. A. Siu (1998) *Takeovers, Restructuring and Corporate Finance*, 2nd edn (Upper Saddle River, NJ: Prentice Hall).

QUESTIONS AND PROBLEMS

I   Two companies operate factories having virtually the same capacity and efficiency. They each have an equal share of the market for product X. New manufacturing technology would permit increased efficiency but would require twice the volume being produced by either company. The two companies contemplate a merger that would allow them to exploit the new technology. The operating costs would be reduced from an equivalent annual cost of €12.0 per unit to €9.6 per unit after tax, assuming combined total production remains the same at 2 million units.[7]

---

[7] Equivalent annual cost allows for differences in the lives of assets. To obtain the equivalent annual cost divide the PV of the costs by the corresponding annuity factor reflecting the life of the cash flow and its discount rate.

(a)   Estimate the potential merger benefits.

(b)   How should the benefits be distributed between the companies?

2   AEROFOAM TECHNOLOGY 's board believes that acquiring the production facilities of LIGHT PLASTICS, instead of building and equipping their own, would save the company €50 million in capital costs and would enable it to meet the increased demand for its products. The PV of the merger benefits from increased production and sales is estimated to be €15 million. An expected €3.5 million could be realized from unneeded assets but expenditure of €18 million would be required to close some operations. All figures are after tax.

(a)   Ignoring opportunity costs and transaction costs, what is the maximum premium that can be paid on LIGHT PLASTICS share price, given that there are 5 million shares outstanding, and the current price is €50 per share?

(b)   What would be the effect on the premium if opportunity costs and transaction costs total €30 million after tax?

3   SAILMAKER operates at full capacity but needs to meet increased demand for windsurfer sails. One of its main competitors has spare operating capacity and has approached SAILMAKER for a merger. The remaining competitors operate at full capacity and cannot meet the increased demand.

The deal would cost SAILMAKER €6 million, however. Given projected revenues and costs, the expected NPV resulting from the resulting synergy would be €22 million. This NPV would be divided between the two companies on the basis of their market values. The stock market value of the competitor s equity is €10 million. SAILMAKER 's equity market value is €30 million.

The alternative to the merger would be buying for €5 million the manufacturing facilities of a bankrupt company. This purchase would increase the PV of transportation costs by €1.5 million after tax, however. Assuming both options offer the same operating capacity and the same delay to start-up, which should SAILMAKER accept?

4   LEISURE has identified a new product and is considering whether to buy new facilities from another company for €2 million or to build the facilities to manufacture it. Building would cost the company €850,000 in the first year, and €420,000 and €350,000, respectively, in the second and third years. The incremental cash flows from the new product are expected to decline with time because of increasing competition. In the first three years the expected incremental income would be €480,000, €360,000, and €240,000, respectively, after tax.

If the company's cost of capital is 15%, should it buy or build? Assume that the facilities can be purchased immediately but the building would require three years to complete.

5   LOSSMAKER has accumulated tax losses over the last five years amounting to €4.8 million. As the company anticipates profits in the future, it expects to absorb the accumulated losses over the next four years. Taxable profits are given below (in millions of euros):

End of year	0	1	2	3	4
Taxable profits		0.86	1.18	1.32	1.44

The CONGLO conglomerate approached LOSSMAKER's board, proposing a merger. CONGLO can use the accumulated tax losses immediately to offset its taxable income, thereby reducing its taxes. LOSSMAKER's operations would remain unchanged. The company uses a discount rate of 10%.

(a)   If the only reason for merging is to exploit the tax losses, what is the most that CONGLO could justify paying for LOSSMAKER? (Corporate tax rate is 30%.)

(b)   What other ways than merging are there to obtain tax benefits?

6   QUANTUM is about to announce a takeover bid for ELECTRODYNAMICS at a price of €100 per share. The current share price is €90. Over the past six months the share price rose from €50 to its current level. The market index rose from 1,000, six months ago to its current level of 1,250. Assuming that the beta coefficient for ELECTRODYNAMICS equals 1.25, estimate the bid premium being paid by the acquiring firm. The risk-free rate is 5%. What qualifications, if any, would you put on your conclusions?

7   SLY purchased 10% of a potential acquisition three months prior to the launch of a bid. These shares were purchased at a price of €90 when the market index was 1,000. At the time of the bid three months later the share price was €110, and the market index was at 1,100. The target company's beta coefficient equaled 1.00. The bid price was €115 and there were 900,000 shares to be acquired. The risk-free rate was 5%.

(a)   What was the value of the expected bid premium?

(b)   Compute the profit on the pre-merger equity interest.

8   GASTRONOMICS has made a takeover bid for DELECTIBLE, a small company engaged in food manufacturing. The offer price is €100 in cash for every share in DELECTIBLE. Prior to the bid announcement the market price of DELECTIBLE's shares was €90. DELECTIBLE's board strongly recommends that its shareholders reject this offer on the grounds that the company's shares are worth more than €100. In particular, they argue that, as DELECTIBLE's earnings per share for the past year were €25, GASTRONOMICS' offer values DELECTIBLE on a price-to-earnings (PE) ratio of only 4.0. Because the average PE ratio for companies engaged in food manufacturing is currently 7.0, DELECTIBLE's board argues that the company shares must be worth at least €175 and that an offer of €200 would be more realistic considering the company's growth opportunities. DELECTIBLE's shareholders seem convinced, and, as DELECTIBLE's shares currently stand at €115 in the market, GASTRONOMICS' bid appears to have little chance of succeeding. GASTRONOMICS is considering whether to make an increased offer, and, if so, at what price. As an adviser to GASTRONOMICS, you are asked to write a brief report explaining the principles of acquisition valuation and how GASTRONOMICS should establish the maximum bid price.

9   Two companies, KAPPA and PI consider merging in order to undertake a new project. Both companies are totally equity financed, and the new project will also be equity

financed. What will be the market value of the combined company, KAPPA–PI, and its new beta value, given the following information?

	Kappa	Pi	Project
Market value (€ millions)	6.54	14.23	
Beta (without project)	1.1	0.90	
Beta of project			1.30
NPV of project			3.60

DEFINITIONS

Annuity factor   Present value of one unit of currency paid in each of a specified number of periods. Equals the sum of the corresponding discount factors.

Price-to-earnings (PE)   Price per share divided by reported earnings per share.

PART 3

Financial Structure

12 Portfolio Theory and Asset Pricing[1]

Earlier chapters suggested that the opportunity cost of investment in a capital project is the rate of return available to shareholders from securities having the same risk. We used the Capital Asset Pricing Model (CAPM) to represent this financial market benchmark for required rates of return. This model assumes that shareholders diversify their assets efficiently. Imperfect correlation between security returns implies that when the prices of some assets in the portfolio fall, others in the portfolio can be rising. The net effect is reduction of risk for the portfolio as a whole. Portfolio theory helps an investor to use efficient diversification to obtain an optimum balance between the expected return on a portfolio and its risk.

If all investors diversified efficiently in this way, an equilibrium relationship between expected returns and risk in the financial market would result. The CAPM portrays this equilibrium. Arbitrage is another method that investors can use to reduce the risk of investments. Arbitrage Pricing Theory (APT) represents an alternative and more robust model of market equilibrium. The APT equilibrium includes the single-factor CAPM as a special case, but permits the use of additional factors to explain expected rates of return in the financial market.

Portfolio management underpins much of the activity in the financial services industry, and thus portfolio theory is an important subject in its own right. In addition, portfolio theory is the foundation of much of what we know about asset pricing.

TOPICS

Consequently, this chapter concerns the following:

- *expected returns;*
- *risk;*
- *risk reduction through portfolio diversification;*
- *portfolios of two securities;*
- *portfolios of more than two securities;*
- *efficient portfolio diversification;*

---

[1] Adapted with permission from J. R. Franks, J. E. Broyles, and W. T. Carleton (1985) *Corporate Finance Concepts and Applications* (Boston: Kent).

○   *optimum diversification;*

○   *the Capital Asset Pricing Model;*

○   *using the Capital Asset Pricing Model;*

○   *limitations of the Capital Asset Pricing Model; and*

○   *the Arbitrage Pricing Theory.*

12-1 RETURNS TO EQUITY INVESTORS

The definition of returns to investors plays a fundamental role in financial policy. If managers wish to increase the value of the firm, they need to understand how the financial market values the firm. There are two obvious variables that market participants must consider when attempting to value a firm. The first is the expected (mean) rate of return from investing in its securities. The second is the risk of such investment. There are various measures of the rate of return and of risk. Portfolio theory adopts particular definitions of these two variables.

HOLDING PERIOD RATE OF RETURN

With few exceptions, equity investors in public companies realize returns in just two forms—dividends and capital gains. Accordingly, portfolio theory defines returns to shareholders in terms of dividends received and capital gains enjoyed during the period an investor holds the shares. Expressed as a rate, the holding period rate of return for the equity investor is:[2]

$$Holding\ Period\ Rate\ of\ Return = \frac{Dividends + Change\ in\ Market\ Value}{Initial\ Market\ Value}$$

Portfolio theory assumes that investors prefer more wealth to less and therefore prefer larger holding period returns to smaller ones. This is not the whole story, however. The theory also assumes that investors are risk-averse. That is, for any given level of expected return, they prefer less risk to greater.

DEFINITIONS

Arbitage Pricing Theory (APT)   Multi-factor linear model of expected asset returns assuming a market equilibrium resulting from arbitrage.

Capital Asset Pricing Model (CAPM)   Linear model attempting to explain the expected return on a risky asset in terms of the risk-free rate, its beta factor (systematic risk), and the risk premium on the market portfolio.

Capital project   Investment in a non-financial asset.

---

[2] This definition assumes that each dividend when paid comes at the end of a holding period. Portfolio theory applications usually employ a series of monthly holding periods. The precise timing of the dividend is not material within a period as short as a month.

Diversification   Reduction of a portfolio's risk by holding a collection of assets having returns that are not perfectly positively correlated.

Dividend yield   Annual dividends per share divided by the current price per share.

Equity   Net worth or shareholders' capital represented by common stock (ordinary shares) and preferred stock.

Expected (mean)   Probability-weighted average of all possible outcomes for a random variable.

Expected (mean) rate of return   Probability-weighted average of all possible outcomes for the rate of return.

Holding period rate of return   Dividends and capital gain for the period divided by the required investment at the beginning of the period.

Opportunity cost of capital   Rate of return forgone when investing in a project instead of the securities market.

Portfolio   Collection of investments in financial securities and other assets.

Rate of return   After-tax cash income and capital gain divided by the investment.

Risk-averse   Describes an investor who prefers less risk to greater risk associated with an expected return. Implies that the investor requires higher expected return as a reward for taking greater risk.

Risk   Probability of an unacceptable loss. In portfolio theory, the standard deviation of holding period returns.

Security   Bond or share certifying legal ownership of a financial asset or a claim on the assets or cash flow of a company. Also denotes collateral for a loan.

12-2 RISK TO EQUITY INVESTORS

Every investor knows that expected dividends and capital gains are not the only factors to consider: risk threatens the outcome of every investment decision. Virtually all decisions involve a large element of uncertainty about the future. Investors know that realized returns could turn out to be lower than expected.

WHAT IS RISK?

Investors think of risk as the probability of having to suffer an unacceptable loss. Mathematicians and statisticians, however, measure risk in terms of variation from the mean or expected return. That is, "How wrong might the estimate be?" These two representations of risk are related. Portfolio theory assumes that the normal distribution describes returns on financial assets, which implies that the standard deviation is a sufficient measure of risk. That is, controlling the standard deviation also controls the probability of loss.[3]

---

[3] For a number of utility functions commonly employed in economic theory, the standard deviation of returns provides an adequate measure of risk for portfolio-building purposes when returns reflect a normal distribution.

DISTRIBUTION OF THE RATE OF RETURN

The histogram in Figure 12.1 reflects a distribution of monthly returns on a share. Table 12.1 contains the corresponding data. The first column in Table 12.1 shows various ranges for the rates of return, and the second contains the frequency distribution, or the number of times returns in each range were observed to occur. The third column expresses these frequencies in terms of probabilities. Dividing the frequency in a range by the total number of trials (in this case 100) gives its estimated probability.

The most likely return on the investment in the table falls in the range of −5% to +5%. The observed frequency of returns in this range is 26 chances out of 100, corresponding to an estimated probability of 0.26. As the −5% to +5% range includes the most probable returns, the likelihood of other returns below −5% and above +5% tapers away to smaller probabilities.

THE NORMAL DISTRIBUTION

For the normal distribution, more than two-thirds of the frequency (68.3%) is contained within ±1 standard deviation. That is, for a mean of 0% and a standard deviation of 15%, the probability is 68.3% that the realized return will fall in the range 0 ± 15%.

THE STANDARD DEVIATION

The standard deviation is the square root of the variance of the distribution. Table 12.2 shows a calculation estimating the variance of the frequency distribution in Table 12.1 (a formula for calculating the variance is given in Appendix 12.1). The first column of Table 12.2 lists the midpoint for each of the ranges given in the first column in Table 12.1. The second column of Table 12.2 calculates the amount by which the returns in the first column deviate from the mean rate of return for the investment. As the mean of the distribution in this case is 0%, Column 2 obtains the deviations by subtracting 0 from each of the figures in Column 1.[4] Column 3 squares all the deviations in the preceding column. Column 5 multiplies the squared deviations by the probabilities in Column 4 to obtain the results in Column 6. Finally, the sum of Column 6 gives the estimated variance as 170.

This calculation reflects that the variance is the probability-weighted average of the squared deviations from the mean.[5] We obtain the standard deviation by taking the square root of the variance. The square root of 170 is just over 13, and therefore the estimated standard deviation of the distribution of returns in Table 12.2 equals approximately 13%.

We might have guessed from Table 12.1 that the standard deviation would be 15% because the mean ±15% includes 68% of the probability. The reason we calculate a standard deviation of only 13% is that the distribution of observed returns in Figure 12.1 does not quite represent a normal

---

[4] The mean of the monthly returns on a company share typically is nearer 1% rather than 0 as in our simplified example.

[5] When one estimates the mean and the variance simultaneously from the same data, a degree of freedom is lost. So, one should reduce the sample size by 1 in the calculation of the variance. See Appendix 12.2.

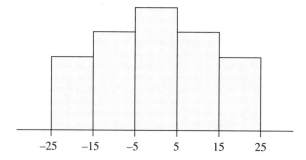

Figure 12.1   Histogram of monthly holding period rates of return (%).

Table 12.1   Frequency distribution of returns.

Rate of return x (%)	Frequency (observations)	Probability
$-25 \leq x < -15$	16	0.16
$-15 \leq x < -5$	21	0.21
$-5 \leq x < 5$	26	0.26
$5 \leq x < 15$	21	0.21
$15 \leq x < 25$	16	0.16
	100	1.00

distribution. If the histogram in the figure more accurately patterned a normal distribution, we would observe a few of the returns below −25% and above +25%.

It is important for us to be able to obtain the standard deviations of monthly returns on securities in a portfolio. We need these to calculate the portfolio's standard deviation of returns. The standard deviation of returns on the whole portfolio is not just an average of the standard deviations for the individual assets, however, The reason is that the risk of a portfolio virtually always is less than the weighted average of the risks of its constituent parts.

DEFINITIONS

Histogram   Bar chart depicting a frequency distribution, or a probability distribution associated with interval values for a random variable.

Normal probability distribution   Symmetric bell-shaped probability distribution completely defined by its mean and standard deviation.

Share (stock)   Security legally certifying that its registered holder is a part-owner of the corporation.

Standard deviation   Square root of the variance.

Uncertainty   Risk not measurable with historical data.

Variance   Mean squared deviation.

Table 12.2   Calculation of the variance of returns.

Rate of return x (%)	Probability	Deviation	Squared deviation	Probability × squared deviation
−20	0.16	−20	400	64
−10	0.21	−10	100	21
0	0.26	0	0	0
10	0.21	10	100	21
20	0.16	20	400	64
	1.00			170

12-3   RISK REDUCTION THROUGH PORTFOLIO DIVERSIFICATION

Reducing risk is the purpose of portfolio diversification. Therefore, the standard deviation of returns for a single investment overstates its risk when it is part of a diversified portfolio. To the extent that the returns on securities move independently of one another, diversification reduces the amount of risk that each security contributes to the portfolio. If the deviations of returns are not perfectly correlated, then positive deviations for some securities in the portfolio offset negative deviations for others. The key issue therefore concerns the extent to which returns on individual securities correlate with the returns on other securities in the portfolio. Therefore, we need to be able to measure the tendency of the holding period returns on pairs of securities to deviate in the same direction.

THE CORRELATION COEFFICIENT

A convenient measure of the degree to which returns on pairs of securities deviate together is the correlation coefficient. In principle, the correlation coefficient can have any value from $r = -1.00$ to $+1.00$.[6]

The scatter diagrams in Figure 12.2 illustrate four different degrees of correlation. Figure 12.2(a) illustrates virtually perfect positive correlation. The horizontal axis measures the returns on Security 1 while the vertical axis measures the corresponding returns on Security 2. Each point in the diagram represents the simultaneous returns on two securities for a different month. The pattern of the points shows almost perfect positive correlation because they fall on an upwardly sloping straight line, implying that $r_{1,2} = +1.00$. Portfolios composed of such securities with perfectly positively correlated returns cannot diversify risk because deviations of returns on one security have a perfectly predictable positive linear relationship to deviations of the other. In other words, when one deviates negatively, so will the other. Accordingly, they cannot reduce each other's risk in a portfolio.

---

[6] See Appendix 12.2 for the method of calculating the correlation coefficient.

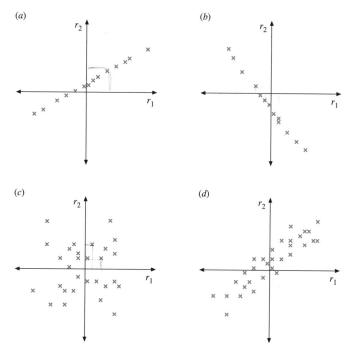

Figure 12.2 Correlations between pairs of securities.

Figure 12.2(b) illustrates the opposite situation. The points fall on a straight line, but now the slope of the line is negative, implying that $r_{1,2} = -1.00$. A deviation in the return on one security always accompanies a perfectly predictable linearly related deviation of the return on the other but in the opposite direction. Ideally, if we could find securities with perfectly negatively correlated returns, we could eliminate all the risk by combining them into an appropriately balanced portfolio.

Figure 12.2(c) illustrates an example of zero correlation ($r_{1,2} = 0$) between the returns on two shares. The points are scattered at random, and, therefore, it is not possible to find a line that would describe a significant relationship between their returns. Combining a sufficient number of such securities with uncorrelated returns achieves a significant reduction of risk, though not as great as could be achieved with negative correlation. Diversification reduces risk for zero-correlated returns, because nonnegative deviations of returns on some securities in the portfolio help to counterbalance negative deviations on others, thus reducing the combined risk.

Figure 12.2(d) illustrates the very much more usual case of imperfectly positive correlation. Corresponding returns display an upward-sloping pattern but do not fall precisely on a straight line. So, the value of the correlation coefficient is between zero and one ($0 < r_{1,2} < 1.00$). As the positive correlation is less than perfect, portfolio diversification still reduces risk, although by a smaller amount than when the value of the correlation coefficient is zero or negative.

These four examples illustrate why the degree of correlation between the holding-period rates of return on pairs of securities in a portfolio provides the key to the effectiveness of diversification for reducing risk. We need now to examine the effect of two other variables on the risk of a portfolio. These additional variables are the number of different securities in the portfolio and the variances of their returns.

12-4 THE TWO-SECURITY PORTFOLIO

First, let us consider the simplest case, a portfolio composed of only two securities. We need to be able to calculate the portfolio's expected return and its risk.

PORTFOLIO EXPECTED RETURN

The expected return on the portfolio is just the value-weighted average of the expected returns on its assets, Securities 1 and 2:

Portfolio Expected Return = Proportion in Security 1 × Expected Return on Security 1

+ Proportion in Security 2 × Expected Return on Security 2

$$E(R_p) = x_1 E(R_1) + x_2 E(R_2)$$

in which $x_1 + x_2 = 1$ and where

$E(R_p)$ = Expected return on Portfolio p

x_1 = Proportion of the value of the portfolio invested in Security 1

$E(R_1)$ = Expected return on Security 1

x_2 = Proportion of the value of the portfolio invested in Security 2

$E(R_2)$ = Expected return on Security 2

The standard deviation of the returns on the portfolio is equal to the square root of the variance of the portfolio's returns.

PORTFOLIO OF VARIANCE

The following formula gives the variance of the returns on this two-security portfolio:

Portfolio Variance = Variance Due to Security 1 + Variance Due to Security 2

+ Covariance of Security 1 with 2 + Covariance of Security 2 with 1

= Variance Due to Security 1 + Variance Due to Security 2

+ 2 × Covariance of Security 1 with 2

$$s_p^2 = (x_1 s_1)^2 + (x_2 s_2)^2 + 2r_{1,2}(x_1 s_1)(x_2 s_2)$$

in which $x_1 + x_2 = 1$ and where

s_p^2 = Variance of the returns on Portfolio p

x_1 = Proportion of the value of the portfolio invested in Security 1

s_1 = Standard deviation of the returns on Security 1

x_2 = Proportion of the value of the portfolio invested in Security 2

s_2 = Standard deviation of the returns on Security 2

$r_{1,2}$ = Correlation coefficient for the co-movement between the returns on Securities 1 and 2

This equation gives the variance of a two-security portfolio as the sum of three parts represented by the three terms on the right-hand side of the equation. The first part $(x_1 s_1)^2$ represents the contribution that Security 1 makes independently to the total variance of the portfolio. Similarly, the second part $(x_2 s_2)^2$ represents the contribution that Security 2 makes independently to the total variance of the portfolio. The third part represents the contributions to the total variance due to the covariance of each security with the other.

EXAMPLE 12.1

Suppose, for example, that we divide investment equally between shares in two companies. If the expected annual returns are 15% and 25%, respectively, the expected annual return on this portfolio is:

$$E(R_p) = x_1 E(R_1) + x_2 E(R_2)$$
$$= 0.5 \times 0.15 + 0.5 \times 0.25 = 0.20 \quad \text{or} \quad 20\%$$

Suppose also that the annualized standard deviations of the returns on the shares are 30% and 50%, respectively, and their correlation is equal to +1.00. The variance of the portfolio is:

$$s_p^2 = (x_1 s_1)^2 + (x_2 s_2)^2 + 2r_{1,2}(x_1 s_1)(x_2 s_2)$$
$$= (0.5 \times 0.30)^2 + (0.5 \times 0.50)^2 + 2 \times 1.00 \times (0.5 \times 0.30)(0.5 \times 0.50)$$
$$= 0.16$$

The standard deviation equals the square root of the variance. Therefore, the standard deviation of the returns on the portfolio is:

$$s_p = 0.16^{0.5} = 0.40 \quad \text{or} \quad 40\%$$

Note that this result falls midway between the standard deviations of 30% and 50%, respectively, for the two individual securities. So, we have gained nothing from diversification. The reason, of course, is that the correlation coefficient equals 1.00, signifying that the returns on the two securities are perfectly positively correlated making diversification useless.

If instead the correlation between the returns equals zero, diversification becomes effective:

$$s_p^2 = (x_1 s_1)^2 + (x_2 s_2)^2 + 2r_{1,2}(x_1 s_1)(x_2 s_2)$$
$$= (0.5 \times 0.30)^2 + (0.5 \times 0.50)^2 + 0$$
$$= 0.085$$

The square root of this is only 0.2915 and thus the portfolio standard deviation is now only 29.15%. This value is somewhat less than the 40.0% obtained with perfectly positive correlation.

Any correlation that is less than +1.00 like this reduces portfolio risk depending on the value of the correlation coefficient. A smaller value of the correlation coefficient results in a smaller standard deviation for the returns on the portfolio.

IMPLICATIONS OF CORRELATION

The above example demonstrates that portfolio diversification reduces risk when the returns on the constituent assets are less than perfectly positively correlated. The correlations between the returns on company shares normally are very much less than 1.00 but rarely as low as zero. So, share portfolios reduce risk but cannot do so completely.[7]

Points A and B in Figure 12.3 plot the above results for perfectly positive correlation and for zero correlation, respectively, for the above two-security portfolio. Portfolio standard deviations measure along the horizontal axis and corresponding expected returns on the vertical axis. Therefore, Point A represents the portfolio standard deviation of 40% and expected return of 20% obtained earlier for the case of perfect positive correlation and equal investment in both securities. Point A falls on a straight line. This line reflects all possible combinations of positive investments in Securities 1 and 2 with perfectly positively correlated returns. The line is straight because diversification cannot reduce the standard deviation of perfectly positively correlated returns.

Point B represents the case of zero correlation and equal investment in the two securities. Point B lies to the left of Point A because zero correlation implies the lower standard deviation of 29.15%, although the portfolio's expected return remains the same at 20%. Point B falls on a curve. This curve reflects all possible combinations of positive investments in Securities 1 and 2. The curve

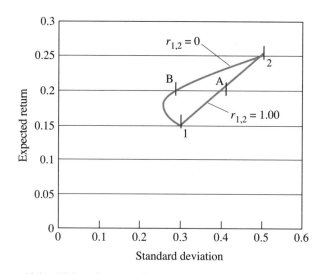

Figure 12.3 Risk and expected return on portfolios of two securities.

---

[7] Negative correlations are obtainable by short selling and by buying put options, for example. In practice, portfolio strategies employing these devices cannot quite eliminate all the risk.

bends to the left toward lower standard deviation because diversification can reduce the combined standard deviation of a portfolio's returns when the correlation between the constituent security returns is less than 1.00.

The example demonstrates that a portfolio can reduce risk if the securities' returns do not correlate perfectly. Further diversification using three or more securities can reduce risk even further.

DEFINITIONS

Put option   Opton giving the holder the right without obligation to sell the option's underlying asset at a specified price on or before a specified date.

Short selling   Selling of borrowed securities that later must be repurchased to repay the lender.

12-5 PORTFOLIOS OF MORE THAN TWO SECURITIES

THREE SECURITIES

The portfolio formula for portfolios that contain three or more securities requires more terms. The additional terms are necessary to reflect the variances of the extra securities and for the many additional covariances. For example, the formula for the variance of a portfolio of three securities now is:

$$s_p^2 = (x_1 s_1)^2 + (x_2 s_2)^2 + (x_3 s_3)^2 + 2r_{1,2}(x_1 s_1)(x_2 s_2) + 2r_{1,3}(x_1 s_1)(x_3 s_3) + 2r_{2,3}(x_2 s_2)(x_3 s_3)$$

The formula has six terms. The first three terms on the right-hand side of the equation are the contributions that each of the three securities makes independently to the total variance of the portfolio. The remaining three terms represent the covariances between the returns of all possible pairs of the three securities.

N SECURITIES

In a portfolio of four securities, there are six possible pairs of correlated securities. In a portfolio of N securities, there are $N(N-1)/2$ different possible correlations between pairs of securities. For example, in a portfolio of only 50 securities there are 1,225 such pairs, and thus 1,225 covariance terms in the equation.

EXAMPLE 12.2

A simple example shows the effect of increasing the number of securities in a portfolio on its risk. For simplicity, we assume that all N securities in the portfolio have the same standard deviation s and that all correlations equal r. With these simplifications, the portfolio formula becomes:

$$s_p^2 = N(xs)^2 + [N(N-1)]r(xs)^2$$

The first term on the right-hand side represents the sum of the independent contributions of the N securities to the portfolio's total variance, and the second term represents the sum of all the covariances. To simplify further, we invest an equal amount in each of the N securities. Therefore, the proportion invested in each security is $x = 1/N$. Substituting for x in the equation, we obtain:

$$s_p^2 = \frac{s^2}{N} + \frac{(N-1)rs^2}{N}$$

Now we can see how the risk of the portfolio changes as we increase the number N of securities in the portfolio. For example, if we let N get very large, the first term s^2/N approaches zero. The second term approaches rs^2 for large N as the ratio $(N-1)/N$ approaches 1.00. As N goes to infinity, the first term disappears and all we have left is the second term, which becomes rs^2. This last term represents the portfolio's nondiversifiable risk and remains above rs^2 no matter how much we increase the number N of securities in the portfolio.

The degree to which portfolio diversification can reduce the variance of holding period returns thus depends upon the number N of securities in the portfolio and the average correlation r between them. We illustrate this relationship in Figure 12.4, in which we assume that $s = 0.40$ for all the securities and $r = 0.30$ for all pairs of securities. The curve in the figure illustrates the way in which the variance of the portfolio declines with increasing numbers N of securities in the portfolio.

It is clear in Figure 12.4 that increasing the number of securities in the portfolio from 1 to 10 sharply reduces the variance of the portfolio. Beyond 10 securities, the risk reduction is very much less steep.

In this simplified example, we invest equal sums in each security, and all the securities have the same variance. Also all correlations between pairs of securities are equal. If we relax these assumptions and permit different investments in the different securities, different variances, and different correlation coefficients for different pairs of securities, we must use the earlier

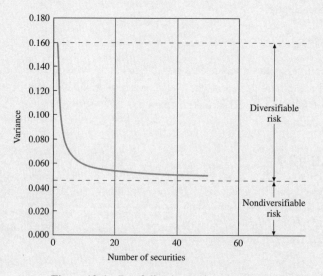

Figure 12.4 Portfolio size and variance.

portfolio variance formula to obtain the variance of the portfolio. For large numbers of securities, the computation becomes much more tedious than in our simplified example, but the general principles remain the same. The first 10 or 15 securities (in roughly equal proportions) eliminate most of the diversifiable risk. Nevertheless, nondiversifiable risk remains no matter how many different company shares we include in the portfolio.

We now need to consider how to determine the optimum proportions to invest in each security when the standard deviations of the holding period returns for the securities and the correlations between them are not necessarily the same.

DEFINITIONS

Diversifiable risk   Risk eliminated in a well-diversified portfolio.

Nondiversifiable risk   Systematic risk. Market risk. Risk that portfolio diversification cannot eliminate.

12-6 EFFICIENT PORTFOLIO DIVERSIFICATION

We can select securities for a portfolio in a virtually infinite number of combinations of proportions. How should we choose the best combination? We have a very interesting problem: How do we obtain the maximum expected return from these proportions while controlling the resulting risk? To solve this problem, we need to know how to choose efficient portfolios.

EFFICIENT PORTFOLIOS

An efficient portfolio maximizes the expected return given its level of risk and minimizes the risk given its expected return. The complete set of such portfolios is the efficient set. The efficient set represents a relatively small proportion of all the possible portfolios that one could choose from a given set of securities. For a risk-averse investor, the optimum portfolio of risky securities must be one of the portfolios in the efficient set.

THE EFFICIENT SET OF PORTFOLIOS

The upper side of the curved boundary in Figure 12.5 represents the set of portfolios that maximize the expected return for each level of risk. The left-hand side of this boundary represents the set of portfolios that minimize the risk for each level of expected return. The point of tangency between the vertical line and the left end of the boundary identifies the minimum variance portfolio.

Although each portfolio on the boundary below the minimum variance portfolio minimizes risk for its level of expected return, all of them have other portfolios directly above with higher expected return. On the boundary above the minimum variance portfolio, we have a better story. Each of these portfolios maximizes the expected return for its risk as well as minimizing the risk for its expected return. So, all the portfolios on this part of the frontier belong to the efficient set. The efficient frontier consists of the entire set of efficient portfolios on the upper part of the boundary to the right of the minimum variance portfolio.

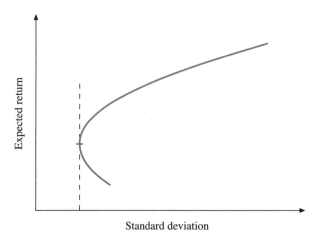

Figure 12.5   Identifying the efficient frontier.

In his Nobel prize-winning exposition of portfolio theory, Markowitz (1952) developed a mathematical method that, with the aid of a computer, finds the portfolios in the efficient set.[8] This efficient set still represents a large number of possible portfolio combinations, however. Which of the many portfolios in the efficient set should a rational investor choose? This question has a remarkable answer: the optimum choice of risky portfolio does not depend on the investor's degree of risk aversion as one might expect. It only depends on whether the investor is a net borrower or a net lender.

> **DEFINITIONS**
>
> **Efficient portfolio**   Portfolio maximizing expected return given its level of risk and minimizes risk given its expected return.
>
> **Efficient set**   Set of all efficient portfolios.
>
> **Minimum variance portfolio**   Efficient portfolio with the least variance of returns.

12-7   THE OPTIMUM PORTFOLIO OF RISKY SECURITIES

The efficient set presents a large choice of portfolios from which to choose. Fortunately, the optimum choice only depends upon the portfolio investor's opportunities to lend or to borrow.

LENDING PORTFOLIOS

The investor who holds some short-term Government bonds (Treasury bills) is lending to the Government. She holds a lending portfolio. Lending short-term to the Government is virtually

---

[8] H. M. Markowitz (1952) "Portfolio selection," *Journal of Finance*, Vol. 7 (March), 77–91.

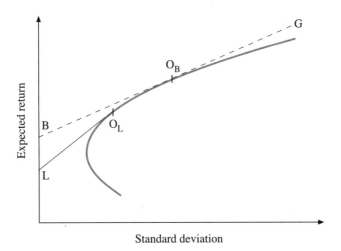

Figure 12.6   Lending portfolios.

risk-free. The possibility to invest in a risk-free security has crucial implications for the choice of the optimum portfolio of risky securities.

Figure 12.6 illustrates this fact. Point L in the figure represents the risk (zero) and the expected return (rate of interest) for risk-free lending. The tangent line LO_L between Point L and the efficient set of risky securities at Point O_L represents all possible combinations of lending and the risky portfolio at Point O_L.[9]

The line LO_L has an important property. Because it is tangent to the efficient set, we cannot obtain a steeper line that would combine risky securities with lending. Therefore, we now have a new efficient set represented by the line LO_L. Except at Point O_L, all points on the line offer expected returns that are greater than obtainable from any portfolios of the same risk below the line.

A quite risk-averse investor will hold some Government securities and correspondingly less of Portfolio O_L. One who is less averse to risk will move up the line toward O_L by reducing the proportion invested in Government securities and increasing the proportion in Portfolio O_L. Therefore, the investor's attitude toward risk determines what proportion of her assets she should lend to the Government, but Portfolio O_L remains her optimum portfolio of risky assets. She might choose to hold more or less of this optimum portfolio, but the relative proportions of risky assets within the optimum portfolio remain unchanged. This distinction between the optimum choice of risky assets at O_L and optimum lending is called the separation property.[10]

---

[9] The two-security portfolio formulas show algebraically that these combinations fall on the straight line LO_L. The first security in the portfolio is the risk-free asset F and the second "security" is Portfolio O_L. Substitute the value zero for the standard deviation of the risk-free asset and zero for its correlation with the returns on Portfolio O_L. The resulting expression is just a straight-line function of the proportion invested in Portfolio O_L.
[10] J. Tobin (1958) "Liquidity preference as behavior toward risk," *Review of Economic Studies*, Vol. 25 (February), 65–86.

BORROWING PORTFOLIOS

Now let us suppose that the investor borrows at the rate indicated by Point B. She holds a borrowing portfolio. Borrowing is the opposite of lending. For this reason borrowing can be represented by the line from O_B through G in the figure. The line from O_B through G represents all levered (geared) portfolios formed by using borrowed funds to buy more of Portfolio O_B. Now the efficient set has become the line from O_B through G. Except at the initial Point O_B, all investment strategies in this new efficient set have one thing in common: holding Portfolio O_B. Therefore, Portfolio O_B is the optimum portfolio of risky securities for the borrower.

With an understanding of the principles of rational portfolio management, we can try to understand the implications for financial market prices if investors manage their portfolios rationally.

DEFINITIONS

Borrowing portfolio   Levered portfolio. Portfolio financed partly by borrowing.

Lending portfolio   Portfolio including virtually risk-free assets such as short-term government securities.

Levered (geared) portfolio   Portfolio partially financed by debt.

Separation property   Independence of an investor's optimum portfolio from the investor's risk aversion.

Treasury bill   Short-term security sold by a central bank to meet a government's short-term financial requirements. Also used as an instrument of monetary policy, influencing credit and the money supply. The bills sell at a discount because the central bank pays no cash interest on Treasury bills.

12-8 THE CAPITAL ASSET PRICING MODEL (CAPM)

THE MARKET PORTFOLIO

We have already seen that the interest rate on risk-free lending determines the lending investor's choice of the optimal portfolio from those in the efficient set. To derive a useful theory of asset pricing, one needs to make some simplifying assumptions. Let us assume that all investors have identical expectations regarding all financial assets. Then all investors would perceive the same efficient set of portfolio investment opportunities. Because they can all lend to the Government at the same risk-free rate, they would all choose the same optimum portfolio from this efficient set. This implies that the optimum portfolio includes all risky assets if all investors have the same expectations. The portfolio of all risky assets is the market portfolio.

DIVERSIFIABLE AND NONDIVERSIFIABLE RISK

With these assumptions Portfolio O_L in Figure 12.6 becomes the market portfolio M. As the market portfolio offers maximum diversification, all diversifiable risk virtually disappears. So, only the nondiversifiable part of the risk would be of any concern to investors. Figure 12.7 illustrates the

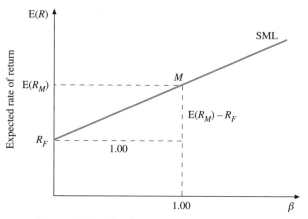

Figure 12.7 The Capital Asset Pricing Model.

resulting relationship between expected rates of return and nondiversifiable risk. The horizontal axis in Figure 12.7 represents the nondiversifiable risk β_i (beta) contributed by asset i to the market portfolio M. The beta value for a security equals the covariance of its returns with the returns on the market portfolio M as a proportion of the variance of the returns on portfolio M:

$$Beta = \frac{Covariance\ between\ the\ Asset\ Returns\ and\ Market\ Returns}{Variance\ of\ the\ Market\ Returns}$$

By definition, the mean value of beta is equal to 1.00. The observed beta values of most risky securities fall in the range 0.5 to 1.5, though many fall outside this range.

THE SECURITIES MARKET LINE

Figure 12.7 shows the market equilibrium famously known as the Capital Asset Pricing Model (CAPM). The line extending from the risk-free rate at R_F through Point M is the Securities Market Line (SML). The SML gives the equilibrium relationship between risk and expected return in the CAPM for all financial assets. If a security were to be overpriced in relation to its risk, its expected return would fall below the line. Investors would not want to own the security because they could do better on the line by investing in the appropriate combination of the risk-free asset and Portfolio M. So, the price of the security would fall thereby raising its expected return back to the SML. Similar reasoning applies to underpriced securities. Accordingly, in the market equilibrium described by the CAPM, all securities fall on the SML.

The CAPM is the equation for the SML. The equation therefore represents a straight line relating expected return to the variable beta for any Security i. The risk-free rate is the line's intercept, and its slope is the risk premium on the market portfolio. The risk premium on the market portfolio is the extra return $[E(R_M) - R_F]$ that investors require to persuade them to invest in the market portfolio of risky assets as well as in the risk-free asset. The expected return $E(R_i)$ on Security i therefore is:

Expected Return = Risk-free Rate + Beta × Risk Premium on the Market Portfolio

$$E(R_i) = R_F + \beta_i \times [E(R_M) - R_F]$$

Professor William Sharpe of Stanford University earned the Nobel Prize in Economics for the CAPM.[11] A reason for the Nobel Prize was that implications of the CAPM provide some of the foundations for Modern Finance taught throughout the world.

DEFINITIONS

Beta factor   A measure of the market risk of an asset. The factor by which mean returns on the asset reflect returns on the market portfolio.

Market portfolio   Portfolio of all risky assets.

Risk premium on the market portfolio   Extra expected return necessary to persuade investors to invest in the market portfolio rather than in risk-free assets.

Securities Market Line (SML)   Hypothesized linear relationship in the Capital Asset Pricing Model between the expected return on a security and its systematic risk.

12-9   USING THE CAPITAL ASSET PRICING MODEL

Before we use the CAPM, we must decide what set of assets can represent the market portfolio. Strictly speaking, the market portfolio includes all assets including real property, works of art, and human capital. In practice, however, we cannot measure reliably the returns on many of these assets.

The usual practice is to use a broadly representative stock market index as a substitute for the market portfolio. Assuming this works well enough for the purpose at hand, we can use the returns on the index in the estimation of the betas of individual securities. The procedure uses Ordinary Least Squares Regression. The dependent (explained) variable is the difference between the monthly return on the security and the monthly risk-free rate. The independent (explanatory) variable is the difference between the monthly holding period return on the market index and the monthly risk-free rate of return. Therefore, we regress a sample of monthly excess returns for a security on the corresponding excess returns for the market index. Usual practice calls for a sample of 60 consecutive monthly excess returns. The purpose of the regression is to estimate the value of the coefficient of the independent variable because the security's beta equals this value. If all this sounds troublesome, take heart: certain organizations regularly publish updated beta values for thousands of listed companies on the World Wide Web. For example, select Stock Screener on Smartmoney.com for beta values of over 7000 US companies.

An important feature of the CAPM is the degree to which it simplifies portfolio management. In order to calculate the variance of a portfolio containing N securities, portfolio theory requires us to obtain the standard deviations of all N securities plus $N(N-1)/2$ correlations between the

---

[11] William F. Sharpe (1964) "Capital asset prices: A theory of market equilibrium under conditions of risk," *Journal of Finance*, Vol. 19 (September), 425–442. Two other seminal publications also deriving the CAPM are: John Lintner (1965) "The valuation of risk assets and the selection of risky investments in stock portfolios and capital budgets," *Review of Economics and Statistics*, Vol. 47 (February), 13–37 and Jan Mossin (1966) "Equilibrium in a capital asset market," *Econometrica*, Vol. 34 (October), 768–783.

returns of all possible pairings of the N securities. For a modest portfolio of 50 different securities, portfolio theory thus requires 1,225 correlations. Compare this with the relatively modest data requirements of the CAPM. The model requires just N security betas to calculate the portfolio beta:

$$\text{Portfolio Beta} = \text{Value Weighted Average of Security Betas}$$

$$\beta_p = x_1\beta_1 + x_2\beta_2 + \cdots + x_N\beta_N$$

where the value proportions $x_1, x_2, \ldots, x_N$ must sum to 1.00. The expected return on the portfolio is still the weighted average:

$$E(R_P) = x_1 E(R_1) + x_2 E(R_2) + \cdots + x_N E(R_N)$$

but now we have the CAPM to give us objective estimates of the expected rates of return in this equation.

The CAPM is very easy to use, and it virtually always provides reasonable expected returns, explaining its popularity. The precision of the model depends ultimately on how accurately it describes the expected asset pricing behavior of the financial market, however.

12-10 LIMITATIONS OF THE CAPITAL ASSET PRICING MODEL

An important issue is whether the financial market behaves as if investors were evaluating securities in the manner assumed by the CAPM. This issue is not yet completely resolved.

AN EMPIRICAL TEST

Black *et al.* (1972) measured beta values each year for each of 1,200 shares traded on the New York Stock Exchange.[12] They then created 10 portfolios. The first portfolio contained the 10% of securities with the highest beta values. The second portfolio contained the 10% with the next largest beta values, and so on. They plotted the excess returns over the risk-free rate against the beta value for each of the 10 portfolios for the period 1935–1965. A straight-line relationship appears to exist between excess returns and portfolio betas. This evidence suggests that shareholders obtained proportionately higher excess returns on portfolios with higher betas during the 30-year period.

LIMITATIONS OF EXISTING TESTS

Roll (1977), however, drew attention to deficiencies in such tests.[13] He showed that beta value estimates are sensitive to the choice of market index to represent the market portfolio. Obviously, finding an index that truly reflects the values of all risky assets such as land, antiques, and, above all, human capital is problematic. Roll argued that testing the model requires showing that the

---

[12] Fischer Black, Michael C. Jensen, and Myron Scholes (1972) "The capital asset pricing model: Some empirical tests," in M. C. Jensen (ed.), *Studies in the Theory of Capital Markets* (New York: Praeger).
[13] Richard Roll (1977) "A critique of the asset pricing theory's tests," *Journal of Financial Economics*, Vol. 4, 129–176.

market portfolio itself is efficient. Such a test is beyond reach since many important assets trade very infrequently. Roll gave mathematical reasons why Black et al. could have found the linear relationship between risk and return even if they had used an incorrect market index. As a result, Roll concluded that existing methods are not sufficiently powerful to test the CAPM.

STRENGTHS AND LIMITATIONS OF THE CAPM

The strength of the CAPM is that it emphasizes the likely impact of nondiversifiable risk on investors' required rates of return. It assumes that market returns on securities relate only to the market index and that the other determinants of returns are unique to the individual company and thus diversifiable.

This model could be too simple, however. Additional indices might help to explain security returns. An obvious choice would be the industry index (an average of the returns on stocks of companies in the industry in which the company operates). Some other candidates might be company size, industrial production, the term structure of interest rates, unanticipated inflation, oil prices, exports, and foreign exchange rates.

12-11 ARBITRAGE PRICING THEORY (APT)

ATTRACTIVE FEATURES OF THE APT

Ross (1976) offered the Arbitrage Pricing Theory (APT) as a potential successor to the CAPM.[14] Arbitrage is another way of attempting to minimize risk and involves simultaneously buying and selling different assets that have highly correlated returns. Accordingly, the derivation of the APT does not require the existence of an efficiently diversified market portfolio. As a result, it can make use of more than one index to explain returns. The form of the APT is similar to the CAPM but includes more explanatory variables with a different beta for each:

$$E(R_i) = R_F + \beta_{i,1}\lambda_1 + \beta_{i,2}\lambda_2 + \cdots + \beta_{i,n}\lambda_n$$

where

R_F = Risk-free rate

$\beta_{i,j}$ = Security i's "beta" for risk factor j ($j = 1, 2, \ldots, n$)

λ_j = Premium for risk factor j.

Note that if $\lambda_1 = [E(R_M) - R_F]$ and all the other $\lambda_j = 0$, then the APT reduces to the CAPM. In this way, the CAPM becomes a special case of the APT. APT is more robust than the CAPM because it requires fewer assumptions. For example, the APT makes no assumptions regarding the empirical distribution of asset returns and no strong assumptions about individuals' utility functions other than greed and risk aversion. The APT applies to any subset of assets and does not require a market portfolio embracing the entire universe of assets. In this way, the APT avoids Roll's most

---

[14] Stephen A. Ross (1976) "The arbitage theory of capital asset pricing," *Journal of Economic Theory*, 13 (December), 341–360.

important criticism of the CAPM since it does not depend upon the existence of an efficiently diversified market portfolio.

AN EMPIRICAL TEST

Chen *et al.* (1986) tested the APT for the years 1958–1984 for a number of economic factors.[15] The factors were two versions of the New York Stock Exchange Index, monthly growth and annual growth in industrial production, change in expected inflation, unanticipated inflation, unanticipated change in the risk premium on bonds, and unanticipated change in the term structure of interest rates. Of these factors, only industrial production, the risk premium on bonds, and unanticipated inflation appeared to have significant explanatory power. The explanatory power of both versions of the stock market index became insignificant when tested alongside these more significant factors.

This test was preliminary in nature, but suggested that a multifactor CAPM or the APT model will one day replace the widely used single-factor CAPM. Current research is working toward developing valid tests of the APT and identifying more precisely the risk factors that explain security returns.

WILL THE APT REPLACE THE CAPM?

After more than two decades, however, use of the CAPM appears to be more frequent than the APT for estimating expected rates of return for individual assets such as individual company shares or capital projects. Development of a more generally accepted methodology for using the APT for these purposes seems not yet to have arrived.[16] In the meantime, the CAPM continues to provide a simple and useful way to estimate expected returns.

DEFINITIONS

Arbitrage Pricing Theory (APT)   Multifactor linear model of expected asset returns assuming a market equilibrium resulting from arbitrage.

Risk premium   Extra return expected from a risky asset compared with the return from an alternative risk-free asset.

Term structure of interest rates   Observed relationship between yields on bonds and their maturities.

12-12   SUMMARY

Portfolio theory shows how to minimize the risk for a given expected return and maximize the expected return for a given level of risk. It shows how increasing the numbers of different risky

---

[15] N. Chen, R. Roll, and S. Ross (1986) "Economic Forces and the Stock Market," *Journal of Business*, Vol. 59, 383–403.

[16] A significant application of the APT is E. J. Elton, M. J. Gruber, and J. Mei (1994) "Cost of capital using arbitration pricing theory: A case study of nine New York utilities," *Financial Markets, Institutions, and Instruments*, Vol. 43 (February), 46–73.

securities in a portfolio reduces risk. The theory also explains why the degree of correlation between returns on the different securities limits the potential for risk reduction. So, even a large and efficiently diversified portfolio cannot eliminate all the risk. Although investors can safely ignore the risk already eliminated by portfolio diversification, they cannot ignore the remaining nondiversifiable risk. A security's nondiversifiable risk is attributable to the covariance of its returns with the returns on the other risky securities in the portfolio.

Efficient portfolios have the lowest risk for a given expected return or the highest expected return for a given level of risk. Accordingly, only a subset of all possible portfolios of risky securities is efficient. An investor's optimum choice must be one of the portfolios in this efficient set.

The typical investor holds some Government securities that are virtually risk-free. Portfolio theory shows that the risk-free rate determines which of the efficient portfolios is optimum for the investor who lends to the Government in this way. Some less risk-averse individuals do not lend, however. Instead, they use borrowed funds to increase their investment in their chosen portfolio of risky securities. The theory shows that the rate of interest paid determines which of the efficient portfolios is optimum for a borrower.

Portfolio theory has implications for the equilibrium trade off between risk and expected return in a competitive financial market. The first is that a security's nondiversifiable risk is a function of the covariance of its returns with the returns on the market portfolio. The second is that there is a simple, straight-line relationship between expected returns on a security and its nondiversifiable risk. The CAPM captures this equilibrium relationship in a precise formula.

Another approach is to assume that investors eliminate risk through arbitrage transactions. The resulting APT includes the CAPM as a special case of a more general model that can include more risk factors.

FURTHER READING

Z. Bodie, A. Cane, and A. Marcus (2001) *Investments*, 5th edn (London: Irwin).

E. J. Elton and M. J. Gruber (1995) *Modern Portfolio Theory and Investment Analysis*, 5th edn (New York: John Wiley & Sons).

Bruno H. Solnik (1999) *International Investments*, 4th edn (London: Addison Wesley).

Stephen Lofthouse (2001) *Investment Management*, 2nd edn (Chichester, UK: John Wiley & Sons).

Stephen A. Ross (1976) "The arbitrage theory of capital asset pricing," *Journal of Economic Theory*, 13 (December), 341–360.

W. F. Sharpe (1964) "A theory of the market equilibrium under conditions of risk," *Journal of Finance*, Vol. 19 (September), 425–442.

QUESTIONS AND PROBLEMS

1   In what form do shareholders of a publicly quoted company receive their returns? How is this different from returns to the owners of a privately held company?

2   How does the Net Present Value Rule improve shareholders' returns?

3   Why is diversification in the shareholders' interest? Should the company diversify? If so, under what circumstances should it do so?

4   Describe how you would measure the beta coefficient of a company traded on the Stock Exchange. How would you convert this into a required rate of return on an investment in the company's shares?

5   How might an increasing level of debt affect the beta coefficient of a company?

6   If an investor held a diversified portfolio of shares valued at €100,000, with a beta coefficient equal to 1.00, how could she most effectively change the beta value of the portfolio to:

(a)   0.5?
(b)   2.0?

7   What is the expected rate of return and risk for the two-security portfolio composed equally of Securities A and B? The correlation coefficient $r_{A,B}$ between the returns on the two securities equals 0.2. Other relevant data for the two securities follow:

	Expected return (%)	Standard deviation (%)
Security A	10	30
Security B	12	40

8   What would be the expected return and standard deviation of returns on the portfolio if we invest equally in a third security in addition to the two in Question 3? The relevant data are below.

	Expected return (%)	Standard deviation (%)	Correlation	
			(C, A)	(C, B)
Security C	15	50	0.15	0.30

9   What is the required rate of return on the shares in Company X? The relevant data are:

Beta = 1.50
Return on the market index = 10%
Risk-free rate = 6%

What use is this rate of return for appraising a capital investment within the company?

10   Three securities have beta coefficients of 1.00, 0.50, and 0.80, respectively. An investor puts his money into each of the securities in equal amounts. What is the value of the beta coefficient for his portfolio?

11   Estimate the beta coefficient of an interesting company quoted on the Stock Exchange. Use monthly data for a period of at least two years.

DEFINITIONS

Debt Sum of money or other assets owed by one party to another. Usually, a legally enforceable obligation to pay agreed interest and to repay the principal of a loan to the lender promptly on schedule.

Net present value rule Rule suggesting that investment in a project should take place if its net present value (NPV) is greater than zero because the project would contribute net positive value for shareholders.

APPENDIX 12.1   CALCULATION OF THE STANDARD DEVIATION

The standard deviation is a measure of the degree to which a random variable, such as a monthly holding period return on a security, deviates from its expected value. For practical implementation of portfolio analysis it is necessary to assume that standard deviations measured from historic series of stock returns provide valid estimates of the standard deviations for the next period. Samples of five or more years of monthly data usually are adequate. The following formula gives the holding period returns:

$$R_{i,t} = \frac{D_{i,t} + (P_{i,t} - P_{i,t-1})}{P_{i,t-1}} = \frac{D_{i,t} + P_{i,t}}{P_{i,t-1}} - 1$$

where

$P_{i,t}$ = Price of Security i in holding period t

$D_{i,t}$ = Value of any dividends paid by Security i during holding period t

The resulting value of $R_{i,t}$ represents dividends and capital gains for the holding period as a proportion of the price at the beginning of the period.

The square root of the variance gives the standard deviation s_i of returns on a security. The following equation gives the value of the variance s_i^2 of the returns on security i:

$$s_i^2 = \frac{1}{n-1} \sum_{t=1}^{n} (R_{i,t} - \bar{R}_i)^2$$

where

n = Number of observations

$R_{i,t}$ = Holding period return on Security i for period t

$\bar{R}_i$ = Mean of the return $R_{i,t}$

The first step is to compute the mean $\bar{R}_i$ by adding up $R_{i,t}$ for all periods t and dividing by n. The second step is to calculate all the deviations $(R_{i,t} - \bar{R}_i)$ by subtracting the mean from each of the holding period returns $R_{i,t}$. The third step is to square all the deviations, add them up, and divide by $n-1$. This gives the variance of the observations from the mean. The square root of the variance gives the standard deviation s_i of returns on Security i.

APPENDIX 12.2 CALCULATION OF THE CORRELATION COEFFICIENT

The correlation coefficient $r_{i,j}$ can be used to measure the degree of linear relationship between the holding period returns (see Appendix 12.2) on investment in Securities i and j. The correlation coefficient can have any value from -1.00 to $+1.00$. The value for the correlation between the holding period returns on two securities is usually somewhat less than 1.00 but greater than 0.

The value of the correlation coefficient $r_{i,j}$ for returns on Security i and Security j can be obtained using the following formula:

$$r_{i,j} = \frac{\dfrac{1}{n-1}\displaystyle\sum_{j=1}^{n}(R_{i,t} - \bar{R}_i)(R_{j,t} - \bar{R}_j)}{s_i s_j}$$

where

$n = $ Number of observations

$R_{i,t} = $ Holding period returns on Security i for period t

$\bar{R}_i = $ Mean of the returns $R_{i,t}$

$s_i = $ Standard deviation of the holding period returns on Security i

Appendix 12.1 gives the method for obtaining the values of the standard deviations s_i and s_j of the two correlated securities i and j in the denominator.

13

Calculating the Cost of Capital

The cost of capital is the single most important financial decision-making criterion. For example, the cost of capital determines the economic value of fixed assets, acquisitions, divestments, and new products. Additionally, product-pricing decisions, rate setting for regulated public utilities and financial control all require the cost of capital. Moreover, the pricing of new issues of securities requires estimating the relevant costs of capital. If the rate of return on a strategic investment does not cover its cost of capital, it cannot add value for shareholders. Clearly, accurate estimation of the cost of capital is essential for effective management.

All modern finance textbooks include cost of capital theory. More difficult to find, however, are detailed procedures a company can use to calculate the cost of capital for capital investments with differing risks. Without correct implementation, the theory is of relatively little relevance. This chapter provides pragmatic methods a company can use to calculate the cost of capital for virtually any capital investment.[1]

TOPICS

We consider the following:

- *adjusting the Weighted Average Cost of Capital (WACC) for risk;*

- *estimating a company's WACC;*

- *costs of debt and equity;*

- *extracting the company's risk premium from its WACC;*

- *adjusting the company's risk premium for project risk;*

- *adjusting the WACC for a project's risk premium; and*

- *the differing costs of capital for project risk classes.*

---

[1] Adapted from J. E. Broyles (1999) "The cost of capital," *Management Quarterly*, Part 5 (October) and J. E. Broyles (2000) "The cost of capital," Malcolm Warner ed. *International Encyclopaedia of Business and Management*, 2nd edn (London: Thompson Learning).

13-1 ADJUSTING THE WEIGHTED AVERAGE COST OF CAPITAL FOR RISK

The Weighted Average Cost of Capital (WACC) is a weighted average of the expected after-tax costs of debt and equity capital, in which the weights are the expected proportions of debt and equity financing. Because different capital investments have different systematic risks, we need to adjust the company's WACC for risk. The procedure for doing this follows:

1.   Estimate the company's expected WACC during the life of the project.

2.   Extract the company's risk premium from its WACC.

3.   Scale the company's risk premium to reflect the relative risk of the project (or of its risk class).

4.   Adjust the WACC for the difference between the project's risk premium and the company's risk premium.

In the next section, we begin the detail of this procedure.

DEFINITIONS

Acquisition   Transfer of control of a company from one group of shareholders to another.

Cost of capital   Cost of funds used by a company for investment.

Debt   Sum of money or other assets owed by one party to another. Usually, a legally enforceable obligation to pay agreed interest and to repay the principal of a loan to the lender promptly on schedule.

Equity   Net worth or shareholders' capital represented by common stock (ordinary shares) and preferred stock.

Expected (mean)   Probability-weighted average of all possible outcomes for a random variable.

Rate of return   After-tax cash income and capital gain divided by the investment.

Risk premium   Extra return expected from a risky asset compared with the return from an alternative risk-free asset.

Risk   Probability of an unacceptable loss. In portfolio theory, the standard deviation of holding period returns.

Security   Bond or a share certifying legal ownership of a financial asset or a claim on the assets or cash flow of a company. Also denotes collateral for a loan.

Systematic risk   Risk that portfolio diversification cannot eliminate.

Weighted Average Cost of Capital (WACC)   Value-weighted average of expected after-tax costs of debt and equity financing.

13-2 ESTIMATING THE COMPANY'S WEIGHTED AVERAGE COST OF CAPITAL

WEIGHTED AVERAGE COST OF CAPITAL

The formula for the WACC is the weighted average of the after-tax costs of debt and equity:

$WACC = W \times \textit{Expected Cost of Debt After Tax} + (1 - W) \times \textit{Expected Cost of Equity}$

In this formula, W is the expected market value proportion of debt in the company's financing during the life of the project.

Let B represent the market value of expected debt financing and S be the market value of expected equity financing during the life of the project. The weight W is the Treasurer's intended target ratio between debt financing and total financing:

$$W = \frac{B}{S + B}$$

and the remaining weight for the equity financing is:

$$1 - W = \frac{S}{S + B}$$

For example, if the plan is to borrow €1 for every €2 of new equity including reinvested earnings, then:

$$W = \frac{B}{S + B} = \frac{1}{2 + 1} = 0.3333$$

and

$$1 - W = 0.6667$$

The cost of debt is also a weighted average. It is the market value weighted average of the expected after-tax interest rates on the various intended forms of debt financing.

If the company does not expect to pay taxes for several years and the effect of the expected time lag before tax deductions is significant, discounting the tax rate in the after-tax cost of debt calculation can be necessary.[2] Thus:

$\textit{Expected Cost of Debt After Tax} = \textit{Expected Cost of Debt} \times (1 - \textit{Present Value of Tax Rate})$

If the company does not expect to pay any taxes for two years, for example, it must carry forward its tax deductions on interest payments until then. Consequently, we discount the tax rate in the above expression for the intervening period using the after-tax cost of debt as the discount rate. This discount rate changes each year, however. The reason is that the lag in tax payment shortens as the time approaches when the company will again pay taxes. Consequently, the discount rates closer to the date when the company expects to resume paying taxes are lower. Calculating the resulting effect on the after-tax interest rates and corresponding WACCs for each future year requires the procedure given in Appendix 13.1.

---

[2] This adjustment becomes significant if the company uses a large proportion of debt financing in countries where interest rates and corporate tax rates are high.

COST OF EQUITY

Two approaches are available for calculating the cost of equity. The first approach is the discounted dividends method. The second is the Capital Asset Pricing Model (CAPM).

DISCOUNTED DIVIDENDS APPROACH

Financial analysts frequently use the discounted dividends approach to estimate a company's equity cost of capital. The present value (PV) per share equals the expected stream of dividends per share discounted at the company's equity cost of capital. Therefore, a company's equity cost of capital equals the internal rate of return (IRR) on its per-share dividend stream.

If you are reasonably confident of the company's dividend payments over, say, the next five years, you can discount both them and the Year 5 expected share price:

$$P_0 = \frac{D_1}{(1+R_E)^1} + \frac{D_2}{(1+R_E)^2} + \cdots + \frac{D_5}{(1+R_E)^5} + \frac{D_5 + P_5}{(1+R_E)^5}$$

In this formula, D_t and P_t represent the expected dividends per share and the price per share, respectively, for Year t. The cost of equity R_E equals the IRR for this cash flow.

Obviously, this formula requires the expected share price in Year 5. You can estimate this future price by assuming that dividends after Year 5 will grow for ever at an annual compound rate of growth G less than or equal to the expected growth rate for the economy. You can then solve for the final price P_5 using the Gordon–Williams growth formula:

$$P_5 = \frac{D_5 \times (1+G)}{R_E - G}$$

Unfortunately, this formula is valid only within a narrow range of growth rates. When the rate G is less than the difference between the risk-free rate and the prospective dividend yield on the share, the formula implies a cost of equity less than the risk-free rate. Clearly, this is not correct. On the other hand, if the growth rate G is greater than the expected growth rate G_{Ec} for the economy, the resulting estimate of the cost of equity capital is too large. Accordingly, it is important to keep the value of G used in the formula within the range:

$$\left(R_F - \frac{D_6}{P_5}\right) < G \leq G_{Ec}$$

Equivalently

$$\left(\frac{R_F - Y_5}{1 + Y_5}\right) < G \leq G_{Ec}$$

in which Y_5 represents the expected dividend yield in Year 5.

This formula can be a good means of estimating the equity cost of capital for listed companies with modest growth beyond Year 5 and paying generous dividends.[3] Appendix 13.2 gives an alternative

[3] Williams, and subsequently Gordon, derived the formula starting from time $t = 0$. Thus, $P_0 = D_0(1+G)/(R_E - G)$. The derivation restricts growth to $G < R_E$ throughout, however. Some authors suggest deriving the cost of equity from the formula, giving $R_E = D_0(1+G)/P_0 + G$. This algebraic result has little validity, however, unless G falls in the range given above. See J. B. Williams (1938) *The Theory of Investment Value* (Cambridge, MA: Harvard University Press) and M. J. Gordon (1959) "Dividends, earnings and stock prices," *Review of Economics and Statistics*, Vol. 41, 99–105.

formula more suitable for high-growth companies. The formula assumes that the stockmarket is informed and the share price efficiently reflects relevant information such as the effect of dilution by executive stock option schemes.

Dividend-discount formulas are less useful when dividends are abnormally low. Dividends can be low because of, for example, reinvestment of earnings, cash accumulation, temporarily low earnings, or because the company is distributing significant cash to shareholders by buying back their shares. In this situation, it is perfectly valid to replace dividends per share in the formula with free cash flow per share (net of debt payments).

THE CAPITAL ASSET PRICING MODEL

The Capital Asset Pricing Model (CAPM) suggests that the expected rate of return on a company's equity equals the sum of the expected risk-free rate and a premium for the nondiversifiable risk of the equity. The risk premium in turn equals the risk premium on the market portfolio multiplied by the company's equity beta factor. Thus:

$$
\begin{aligned}
\textit{Expected Required Rate of Return on Equity} = {} & \textit{Expected Risk-free Rate} \\
& + \textit{Equity Premium for Nondiversifiable Risk} \\
= {} & \textit{Expected Risk-free Rate} + \textit{Equity Beta} \\
& \times \textit{Premium on Market Portfolio}
\end{aligned}
$$

The usual recommendation is to use the expected rate on 90-day Treasury bills as a surrogate for the risk-free rate on equities. This expected rate should relate to the periods falling within the life of the capital project. The yield on a Government bond with longer maturity would not be appropriate as an estimate of the risk-free rate, even if the maturity coincides with the life of the project. Unfortunately, bond yields reflect premiums due to liquidity preference and reflect price risk attributable to unexpected changes in interest rates.[4] Accordingly, bond yields usually exceed the risk-free rate.

The realized risk premium on the stock market index averaged around 8% over the latter half of the 20th century. At the end of the sustained equity bull market in the 1990s, however, the premium appeared to have fallen to around 4–5%.

The beta factor scales the risk premium on the market portfolio up or down proportionally to the particular stock's relative volatility. Beta factors tend to be lowest for businesses that are less sensitive to the relevant country's economic cycle. The London Business School's Risk Measurement Service publishes quarterly updated equity beta values for UK companies and DataStream publishes equity betas for companies listed in the UK and other countries.

Unlisted companies have to estimate their equity betas using comparisons with the beta values of similar companies having published betas. Appendix 13.3 gives the leverage adjustments required for these comparisons.

---

[4] For example, when market rates of interest rise, medium- and long-term Government bond prices fall, thereby reducing the market value of the bondholder's wealth.

Having determined the costs of the company's debt and equity, one can easily calculate its expected WACC using the WACC formula given earlier. The WACC includes the company's weighted average risk premium. This premium provides a starting point for estimating risk premia for individual capital projects with differing risks.

DEFINITIONS

Beta factor A measure of the market risk of an asset. The factor by which mean returns on the asset reflect returns on the market portfolio.

Capital Asset Pricing Model (CAPM) Linear model attempting to explain the expected return on a risky asset in terms of the risk-free rate, its beta factor (systematic risk), and the risk premium on the market portfolio.

Capital project Investment in a nonfinancial asset.

Cost of debt Weighted average of the rates of interest on the company's borrowings and debt insecurities.

Dilution Increase in the number of a company's shares without a proportionate increase in the company's assets and earnings (more precisely, an increase in the number of shares that reduces shareholder value per share).

Discount rate Required rate of return used in the calculation of a discount factor.

Discounting Multiplying each of an investment's expected cash flow by its present value per unit (discount factor) to obtain the total net present value for the investment.

Dividend yield Annual dividends per share divided by the current price per share.

Free cash flow After-tax cash flow from operations net of capital investment and increases in net working capital.

Internal rate of return (IRR) Discount rate that would make the net present value for an investment equal to zero.

Liquidity Ease with which cash is recoverable from an investment.

Market portfolio Portfolio of all risky assets.

Nondiversifiable risk Systematic risk. Market risk. Risk that portfolio diversification cannot eliminate.

Present value (PV) Value of an investment now as the cost of a comparable investment in the financial market (calculated by multiplying the investment's expected after-tax cash income by the appropriate discount factors).

Risk premium Extra return expected from a risky asset compared with the return from an alternative risk-free asset.

Treasurer Senior financial manager reporting directly to the Chief Financial Officer. Primarily responsible for funding and cash management.

Treasury bill   Short-term security sold by a central bank to meet a government's short-term financial requirements. Also used as an instrument of monetary policy, influencing credit and the money supply. The bills sell at a discount because the central bank pays no cash interest on Treasury bills.

13-3   EXTRACTION OF THE COMPANY'S RISK PREMIUM FROM ITS WACC

A company's WACC already reflects its weighted average risk premium. In theory, we could extract the value of the weighted average risk premium simply by subtracting the risk-free rate from the WACC. In practice, it is better to follow a slightly different procedure because the company cannot actually borrow at the risk-free rate. Instead of subtracting the risk-free rate, we subtract the company's expected after-tax borrowing rate:

Weighted Average Risk Premium = WACC − Cost of Debt After Tax

For consistency, we use the same after-tax cost of debt as used in the WACC. This prevents double-counting the company's credit risk premium in the subsequent calculations.[5] The credit risk premium is the additional interest above the risk-free rate that the company must pay to compensate lenders for the possibility that the company might default on its payments to lenders.

DEFINITION

Default   Failure to make a payment of interest or a repayment of principal on the due date.

13-4   ADJUSTING THE COMPANY'S RISK PREMIUM FOR PROJECT RISK

The next step is to adjust the company's risk premium by the relative risk factor of the project or of its risk class.

THE RELATIVE RISK FACTOR

We can do so by multiplying the company's risk premium by a scaling factor F_j adjusting the company premium for the relative risk of Project j:

Risk Premium for Project $j = F_j \times$ Company Risk Premium

For example, if the PV of Project j is twice as volatile as for the company's average project, then $F_j = 2.00$. We can estimate the relative risk factor by comparing the project with a benchmark

---

[5] We follow Miller (1977) and use the company's expected after-tax cost of borrowing in place of the risk-free rate on equity. By doing so in this equation we ensure that the resulting company risk premium does not include the credit premium on its debt, which should not be included in the risk adjustments we employ in this chapter. See M. H. Miller (1977) "Debt and taxes, presidential address at the Annual Meeting of the American Finance Association," *Journal of Finance*, Vol. 32, No. 2 (May), 261–275.

project typifying company risk. The indicator of volatility for this purpose is the sensitivity of the project's PV to an unfavorable change in the economy.

ESTIMATING THE RELATIVE RISK FACTOR

The procedure for estimating the value of the relative risk factor is as follows:

1.   Estimate the volatility of the project in question.

2.   Estimate the volatility of the benchmark project.

3.   Obtain the value of the project's relative risk factor F_j by dividing the volatility in Step 1 by the volatility in Step 2.

In this way, we obtain the value of the relative risk factor F_j for project j:

$$F_j = \frac{Volatility\ of\ Project\ j}{Volatility\ of\ Benchmark}$$

PROJECT VOLATILITY

A project's volatility measures the change of its PV due to a change of scenarios relative to its PV under the most likely scenario. In the numerator of the ratio is the difference between the PVs of its cash flow (other than investment cash flow) under Scenario A and Scenario B. In the denominator is its PV under Scenario A. Scenario A simply reflects the assumed most likely future economic environment whereas Scenario B is the most plausible pessimistic economic scenario.

ESTIMATING PROJECT VOLATILITY

EXAMPLE 13.1

Figure 13.1 illustrates the sensitivity of a project's PV to the discount rate (horizontal axis) and its volatility with respect to the two scenarios. The upper curve plots the PV of the cash flow predicated on the most likely scenario (A). The lower curve plots the PV of the cash flow expected in the pessimistic scenario (B). The discount rate for the project in the most likely scenario happens to be 10% as indicated in the figure, and the corresponding PV at point A is $PV_A = 379.08$. The discount rate for this project under the pessimistic scenario is somewhat larger (indicated as 17% in the figure) because the pessimistic scenario reduces the project's contribution cash flow relative to its fixed expenditure, making the net cash flow more risky. At 17% the project's PV in the pessimistic scenario is $PV_B = 159.97$. Therefore, the volatility of this project is equal to:

$$Project\ Volatility = \frac{PV_A - PV_B}{PV_A}$$
$$= \frac{379.08 - 159.97}{379.08} = 0.578$$

We shall obtain the value of the relative risk factor as the ratio of the project's volatility divided by the benchmark project's volatility.

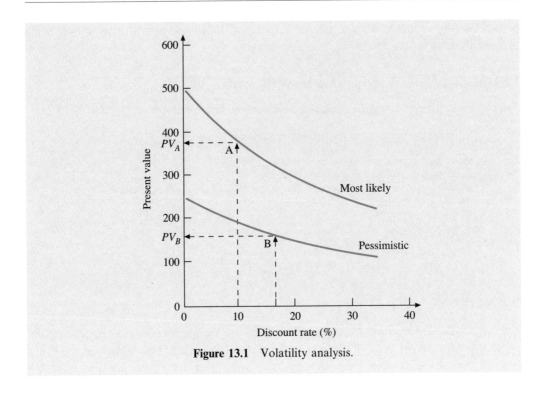

Figure 13.1 Volatility analysis.

ESTIMATING THE VOLATILITY OF THE BENCHMARK

We estimate the volatility of the benchmark in the same way as above for the volatility of other projects. At each point in time, we need to use the same two (updated) scenarios (A and B) in the analysis of all projects.

Choosing the right benchmark is central to the system. The ideal benchmark project displays the average volatility for the company. Consistent use of the chosen benchmark is necessary for the calculation of all relative risk factors, at least until superseded by a better benchmark.[6]

CALCULATION OF THE RELATIVE RISK FACTOR FOR THE PROJECT

The relative risk factor for Project j is the ratio of Project j's volatility to the volatility of the benchmark:

$$F_j = \frac{Volatility\ of\ Project\ j}{Volatility\ of\ Benchmark}$$

In our example, if the volatility of the benchmark project is 0.40, then the value of the relative risk factor for Project j is:

$$F_j = \frac{0.578}{0.40} = 1.45$$

[6] For example, use a weighted combination of projects as the benchmark, each typifying a different risk class.

We use the resulting value of the project's relative risk factor to scale the risk premium in its risk-adjusted WACC.

DEFINITIONS

Relative risk factor   Ratio of the volatility of PV of the project to the volatility of the PV of the benchmark asset.

Scenario   Plausible sequence of events.

Sensitivity analysis   Testing the effect of changes to individual variables on a project's net present value.

Volatility   Standard deviation of percentage changes in the asset price. More precisely, standard deviation of changes in the natural logarithm of the asset price.

13-5 ADJUSTING THE WACC FOR THE PROJECT'S RISK PREMIUM

We obtain the risk-adjusted WACC for a project or for its risk class simply by adding to the company's expected WACC the difference between the project's risk premium and the company's risk premium:

Adjusted WACC = WACC + (Project Risk Premium − Company Risk Premium)

The resulting risk-adjusted WACC provides discount rates reflecting the differing risks of the company's projects.[7]

13-6 THE COST OF CAPITAL FOR A RISK CLASS

Risk adjustment would be cumbersome if used for every individual project, and most companies using risk-adjusted discount rates divide projects into risk classes. They can use the procedure given above to estimate the cost of capital for projects typifying each risk class. The cost of capital for the risk class equals the cost of capital for the project typifying the risk class. They then use the discount rate assigned to a particular class for all projects falling within that class. Consequently, just one discount rate is used for all projects in a given risk class.

STRUCTURE OF THE COST OF CAPITAL FOR RISK CLASSES

Figure 13.2 illustrates how to relate discount rates to risk in the risk class method. Classes A, B, C, and D on the horizontal axis represent the systematic risk of each project risk class. The vertical

---

[7] It is worth noting that many companies fail to alter discount rates frequently enough to reflect changes in market rates of interest and for corresponding changes in the cost of equity capital.

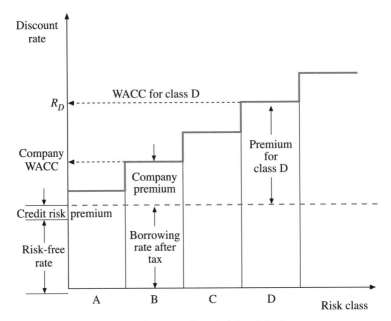

Figure 13.2   The cost of capital for risk classes.

axis represents corresponding levels of the cost of capital. The stepped graph in the figure shows how the risk-adjusted WACC moves to a higher level for each succeeding risk class.

Class B in the figure represents the class of projects deemed to be of average risk for the company. The cost of capital for all projects in Class B therefore equals the company WACC as indicated in the figure. The costs of capital for Class A and for Classes B, C, D, ... scale higher or lower according to their respective average relative risk factors.

Each cost of capital level in the figure is the sum of the company's expected after-tax borrowing rate and the risk premium for a risk class. The risk premium for a class is equal to the risk premium for the company multiplied by the relative risk factor for the class, as discussed earlier. The relative risk factor for the risk class is equal to the relative risk factor of the project or average of projects typifying the risk class.

Once installed, this procedure facilitates assignment of discount rates to preclassified projects.

EXAMPLE 13.2

Healthcare International is an Internet business enabling traveling executives to stay in contact with their doctors worldwide and permitting medical practice via email, medical data transfer, and teleconferencing links on the Internet. The company requires a discount rate to help it to evaluate one of its proposed networking systems. The following data are potentially relevant:

○   *Growth rate*   *100%*

○   *Dividend yield*   *0*

○	*Equity beta*	*1.60*
○	*Expected risk premium on the market*	4%
○	*Expected risk-free rate on equity*	5%
○	*Expected borrowing rate*	7%
○	*Target proportion of debt financing*	60%
○	*Corporate tax rate*	30%
○	*Relative risk factor for project*	*1.20*

ANALYSIS

1. **Estimate the company's WACC for the life of the project.** First, we estimate the costs of debt and equity for the WACC.

   Cost of debt

$$Cost \ of \ Debt \ After \ Tax = 7\left(1 - \frac{0.30}{1.07^{0.25}}\right) = 4.94\%$$

   This calculation assumes a three-month delay in the payment of Corporation Tax at 30%, thus discounted at 7% for 0.25 years.

   Cost of equity. The IRR on the dividend stream would give a nonsense answer for the cost of equity for two reasons. First, the company pays no dividends currently. Second, even if the company were to be paying dividends, its 100% growth rate is much too large relative to the growth rate of the economy.

   Thus, we use the CAPM instead:

$$Cost \ of \ Equity = Risk\text{-}free \ Rate + Equity \ Beta \times Market \ Risk \ Premium$$
$$= 5 + 1.6 \times 4 = 11.4\%$$

   We can now calculate the expected WACC for the company:

$$WACC = W \times Expected \ Cost \ of \ Debt \ After \ Tax + (1 - W)$$
$$\times Expected \ Cost \ of \ Equity$$
$$= 0.60 \times 4.94 + (1 - 0.60) \times 11.4 = 7.52\%$$

   The discount rate for the typical or benchmark project would be 7.52% for the period. However, the project under consideration is 1.20 times as volatile as the benchmark.

2. **Obtain the company's risk premium**

$$Company \ Risk \ Premium = WACC - Cost \ of \ Debt \ After \ Tax$$
$$= 7.52 - 4.94 = 2.58\%$$

3.   Adjust the company's risk premium to obtain the risk premium for the project or for its risk class

$$Risk\ Premium\ for\ Project\ j = Fj \times Company\ Risk\ Premium$$
$$= 1.20 \times 2.58\% = 3.10\%$$

4.   Adjust the WACC for the difference between the project's risk premium and the company's risk premium

$$Adjusted\ WACC = WACC + (Project\ Risk\ Premium - Company\ Risk\ Premium)$$
$$= 7.52 + (3.10 - 2.58) = 8.04\%$$

Result: The estimated risk-adjusted discount rate for the new system is 8.04%.

13-7 CONCLUSIONS

This chapter shows how to estimate the risk-adjusted cost of capital for any project or project risk class. Many companies do not calculate their cost of capital correctly and most use the same hurdle rate for all projects. A company that uses the same discount rate or hurdle rate for all projects is prone to rejecting low-risk projects that add shareholder value and accepting high-risk projects that actually reduce value. High-risk projects add value only if the extra return expected from them is commensurate with the extra risk for shareholders. The fact that so many companies have not yet learned how to adjust their hurdle rates for risk suggests that misallocation of capital budgets is widespread, representing an unnecessary burden on the economy.

DEFINITIONS

Hurdle rate   Minimum acceptable rate of return for proposed capital projects.

Shareholder value   Economic value of the shareholders' financial claim on the business.

FURTHER READING

M. C. Jensen (ed.) (1972) *Studies in the Theory of Capital Markets* (New York: Frederick A. Praeger).

S. C. Myers and L. S. Borucki (1994) "Discounted cash flow estimates of the cost of equity capital—A case study," *Financial Markets, Institutions and Instruments*, Vol. 3 (August), 9–45.

QUESTIONS AND PROBLEMS

1   QUERON PLC expects to borrow at an average rate of 12% during the next five years. Interest payments will be tax-deductible and tax payments are quarterly with an average time lag of nine weeks. QUERON expects the Corporation Tax rate to remain at 30%. What is QUERON's expected after-tax cost of borrowing?

2   QUERON has just paid a dividend, and its share price is now exactly €1. The company pays dividends of 2.5 cents every six months. Management expects to increase the

dividend at a compound rate of 7% per year indefinitely. What does this share price imply for the cost of equity capital?

3   QUERON's corporate treasurer would like to compare the company's cost of equity capital as implied by the CAPM with other methods of estimating this cost. The Treasury bill rate is 6%, and she expects that the risk premium on the market will be 4%. A popular risk measurement service has published an estimated beta factor for the company equal to 1.20. What rate do the data imply for QUERON's cost of equity capital?

4   Suppose, on another occasion, the company's treasurer ascertained that the expected cost of debt after tax was equal to 6%. Suppose also that the expected cost of equity was equal to 20%. The treasurer's target debt-to-equity ratio for the company was equal to 0.8. What is the company's WACC?

5   What is the implied weighted average risk premium for the company in Question 4?

6   Queron simplifies its investment appraisal procedure by classifying each project according to its estimated systematic risk. The company uses four risk classes A, B, C, and D. Calculate the cost of capital for each risk class using the data given in the table below.

After-tax Borrowing Rate = 6%

Weighted Average Risk Premium = 7%

Risk class	Relative risk factor
A	0.33
B	1.00
C	1.67
D	2.33

7   One of the companies in the QUERON group is CUBEON Ltd. No stock exchange quotes CUBEON's shares, and thus direct estimation of its equity beta factor from share price data is impossible. QUERON's treasurer would like to estimate an equity beta factor for the CUBEON subsidiary. She needs this value to calculate CUBEON's cost of equity for use in its WACC. She has gathered relevant data in the table below for three companies listed on the stock exchange that specialize in products perceived to be of much the same risk as CUBEON's products. These companies, however, have different amounts of debt in their capital structures and require adjustments to eliminate the effect of these differences. Having used these adjustments to obtain the corresponding asset betas, she then needed to take account of QUERON's own level of leverage. Using the method of similars (see Appendix 13.3), help her to calculate the value of CUBEON's equity beta.

Company	Equity beta	Debt/equity ratio
A	1.50	1.7
B	1.30	1.2
C	1.00	1.0
QUERON		0.8

APPENDIX 13.1 AFTER-TAX INTEREST RATES FOR TEMPORARILY NON-TAXPAYING COMPANIES

The calculation of after-tax interest rates for a temporarily non-taxpaying company requires a number of steps. Consider the example in which the firm is non-taxpaying for two years: the first tax deduction for interest payment, therefore, is in Year 3.

In this example, we have three different tax years. The interest payments at the end of Years 3 and 4 are not subject to delay in tax deduction because they fall within taxpaying years. The tax deduction for interest paid at the end of Year 2, however, is subject to a one-year tax lag. That is, the first tax benefits come in Year 3 on Year 2's interest payment. Finally, the tax for the interest payment at the end of Year 1 is deducted in Year 3.

We shall now calculate the after-tax interest rate for each year. It is quite easy to determine the rate for Year 4 in which there is no tax lag. The after-tax interest rate r_4 for Year 4 if the firm expects to pay interest at 10% and taxes at 30% is simply 7%:

$$10 \times (1 - 0.30) = 7\%$$

Similarly, rate r_3 for Year 3 is also 7%, because interest paid at the end of Year 3 is deductible immediately. The single-year discount factor for both these years is $1/1.07$.

Interest paid at the end of Year 2 is subject to a tax lag of one year, however. That is, for interest payments made in Year 2, the tax deduction is in Year 3. Accordingly, we obtain the after-tax interest r_2 for Year 2 using the following procedure. For interest payments occurring in Year 2, the tax benefits accrue to Year 3 as outlined below.

	Year 2	Year 3
Interest	10	
Tax		−3

We can calculate the after-tax interest rate for Year 2 by discounting the tax benefits for one year using Year 3's discount factor (calculated previously as 1.07):

$$r_2 = 10 - \frac{3}{1.07}$$
$$= 7.1963\%$$

The discount factor for Year 2, therefore, will be $1/1.071\,963$. We use exactly the same procedure to calculate the after-tax interest rate r_1 for Year 1, except that we recognize that the tax benefit occurs with a lag of *two* years.

	Year 1	Year 2	Year 3
Interest	10		
Tax			−3

We discount the tax benefits in Year 3 to Year 1 using the discount factor calculated for Year 2, which was $1/1.071963$, and for Year 3 was $1/1.07$. That is:

$$r_1 = 10 - 3 \times \frac{1}{1.071963} \times \frac{1}{1.07}$$

$$= 7.384\,482\%$$

The discount factor for Year 1 is therefore $1/1.073\,844\,82$.

Suppose that a company's cost of equity equals 15% and that it expects that 50% of its future financing will be debt. The after-tax interest rates and the corresponding WACC each year would be as follows.

Year t	Cost of debt after tax r_t	Cost of equity after tax r_e	WACC$_t$
1	7.3845	15	11.192 25
2	7.1963	15	11.098 15
3	7	15	11
4	7	15	11

Consequently, the discount factor for a cash flow in Year 4 would be:

$$\frac{1}{(1+WACC_1)} \times \frac{1}{(1+WACC_2)} \times \frac{1}{(1+WACC_3)} \times \frac{1}{(1+WACC_4)} = \frac{1}{(1.111\,922\,5)}$$

$$\times \frac{1}{(1.110\,981\,5)} \times \frac{1}{(1.11)} \times \frac{1}{(1.11)}$$

$$= 0.657\,01$$

APPENDIX 13.2   LINEAR GROWTH AND THE COST OF EQUITY

As discussed in this chapter, the validity of the Gordon–Williams formula is restricted to a relatively narrow band of compound growth rates. An alternative to the compound growth assumption is linear growth.

Let D_t represent dividends per share paid at time t ($t = 0, 1, 2, \ldots$). Then for linear growth:

$$D_t = D_0 + \Delta D \times t$$

Let the price P_0 per share equal the PV of the dividend payments. Then:

$$P_0 = \sum_{t=0}^{\infty} \frac{D_0 + \Delta D \times t}{(1 + R_E)^t}$$

$$= D_0 \sum_{t=0}^{\infty} \frac{1}{(1 + R_E)^t} + \Delta D \sum_{t=0}^{\infty} \frac{t}{(1 + R_E)^t}$$

The first term on the right-hand side of the equation is a perpetuity with value D_0/R_E. The second term on the right-hand side is a perpetuity of perpetuities, each having the value $\Delta D/R_E$. Restricting expected dividends to nonnegative values, we have:

$$P_0 = \frac{D_0}{R_E} + \frac{\Delta D}{R_E^2} \qquad (\Delta D \geq 0)$$

This equation is the linear equivalent of the Gordon–Williams model. The linear model remains valid for any nonnegative level of linear growth.

Because we know the values of P_0 and D_0, we can solve this quadratic equation for the cost R_E of equity as a function of ΔD. The solution is:

$$R_E = \frac{D_0 \pm \sqrt{D_0^2 + 4P_0\Delta D}}{2P_0} \qquad (R_E > R_F)$$

Acceptable solutions require that the cost R_E of equity must be greater than the risk-free rate R_F, as indicated.

> **DEFINITION**
>
> **Perpetuity**   Equal sum of money paid in each period for ever.

APPENDIX 13.3   THE METHOD OF SIMILARS

Unlisted companies do not have share price data suitable for estimating beta values. In this situation, we can try estimating an unlisted company's beta using the measured betas of similar companies that have actively traded stocks. The following steps are required:

1.   Obtain equity beta values for similar companies from a reputable beta measurement service.

2.   These similar companies normally will have borrowed. This borrowing has levered up each of their beta values to a differing degree making them not directly comparable with the unlisted company. Unlever these equity beta values to their corresponding asset beta values using:[8]

$$\beta_{ASSET_i} = \beta_{EQUITY_i} \times \left(\frac{S_i}{S_i + B_i} \right)$$

where S_i represents in this case the average equity capitalization of listed firm i during the period (usually five years) of the sample used to estimate its published equity beta. $S_i + B_i$

---

[8] This formula is an approximation that assumes that the beta value of the debt equals zero. The exact formula is:

$$\beta_{ASSET_i} = \beta_{EQUITY_i} \times \left[\frac{S_i}{S_i + B_i} \right] + \beta_{DEBT_i} \times \left[\frac{B_i}{S_i + B_i} \right]$$

The beta value of variable interest rate debt is quite close to zero. The beta value of fixed interest debt is small and likely to be less than 0.25 depending on the maturity of the debt.

represents the average of the sum of the equity capitalization and the debt of listed firm *i* during the period of the sample used to estimate its published equity beta.

3.   Obtain a suitable average of these asset betas. Use this average to inform one's estimate of the unlisted company's asset beta.

4.   Obtain the unlisted company's equity beta by levering up its estimated asset beta (Step 3) to reflect the unlisted company's expected level of debt financing.

$$\beta_{EQUITY} = \beta_{ASSET} \times \left[1 + \left(\frac{DEBT}{EQUITY} \right) \right]$$

where *DEBT/EQUITY* represents the company's intended ratio of debt to equity financing during the relevant future period.

This value in the CAPM gives the expected cost of equity in the WACC of the unlisted company.

# Long-term Financing

Virtually all enterprises require start-up capital, and subsequently they require additional capital to finance growth. Company financing falls into the two broad categories, equity and debt. Equity is the owners' initial and subsequent investment in the company. For the majority of companies most of the additional equity comes from retained earnings. Retained earnings are after-tax profits remaining in the company after payment of dividends to shareholders. Issuing new shares in the company provides a further possible source of new equity when needed.

The remaining source of external financing, loosely termed debt, consists mainly of various short-term and long-term borrowings including the issuance of corporate bonds. Borrowing is the most accessible external funding, and the interest on the debt is tax-deductible. Unfortunately, borrowing burdens the company with legally enforceable obligations to pay interest and to repay the debt on a contractually agreed schedule. If unable to pay on time, the company is insolvent and technically bankrupt. Potentially, the company's lenders could then begin taking legal steps that could force the company into liquidation.

Banks provide the major short-term source of borrowed funds. Bank term loans are also available for terms of up to around 10 years and sometimes longer. The focus of this chapter is on long-term corporate financing.

TOPICS

In this chapter we discuss:

○ *financial policy;*

○ *the sources of long-term external financing;*

○ *primary and secondary financial markets;*

○ *corporate securities;*

○ *government debt;*

○ *corporate debt;*

○ *corporate equity;*

○ *how securities are issued;*

○ *rights issues; and*

○ *new issues.*

14-1 FINANCIAL POLICY

BALANCING DEBT AND EQUITY FINANCING

Experienced Chief Financial Officers (CFOs) and their corporate Treasurers borrow sparingly, and aim to keep equity and debt in balance; that is, they have a target debt-to-equity ratio. Therefore, when the company retains earnings, it uses additional borrowing to maintain the target debt-to-equity ratio. Risky firms that are well managed aim for a relatively low debt-to-equity ratio. They also aim for the optimum mix of short-term and long-term borrowing, and of fixed versus floating rate debt. In addition, they try to balance foreign exchange income with foreign currency-denominated debt obligations. These efforts help the company to avoid financial distress (danger of default due to insolvency). Insolvency is the inability of a firm to find the cash needed to pay its bills.

FINANCIAL OBLIGATIONS AND CLAIMS

The providers of capital have claims on the company. The debt holders have a contractual claim on interest payments and prompt repayments of principal on schedule. Interest and repayments are the part of the company's cash flow belonging to the debt holders. In the event of company liquidation, the debt holders have a senior claim on a part of the value of assets sold off (although some debts are subordinated in this respect to others). The tax collector also has a claim as do employees (for unpaid wages) and trade creditors. The equity shareholders can claim only the remainder after the legitimate claims of all others have been satisfied.

CONSTRAINED OBJECTIVES

The objective of the CFO must be to try to maximize the market value of the firm. This objective is constrained by the legitimate interests of stakeholders in the company other than the shareholders, however. Stakeholders include debt holders and employees. The company must also honor its obligations to suppliers and customers if it is to continue to trade.

DEFINITIONS

Borrowing portfolio   Levered portfolio. Portfolio financed partly by borrowing.

Claims   Refers to financial claims on the company by governments and by other creditors including lenders, bondholders, trade creditors, employees, and the company's shareholders.

Chief Financial Officer (CFO)   A company's most senior financial manager, often a member of the company's board of directors.

Debt   Sum of money or other assets owed by one party to another. Usually, a legally enforceable obligation to pay agreed interest and to repay the principal of a loan to the lender promptly on schedule.

Default   Failure to make a payment of interest or repayment of principal on the due date.

Equity   Net worth or shareholders' capital represented by common stock (ordinary shares) and preferred stock.

Floating rate   Variable interest rate changing in response to changes in a specified index of market rates of interest.

Financial distress   Condition in which a company might not be able to meet its obligations to creditors, that is, in danger of becoming insolvent or technically bankrupt.

Insolvency   Condition in which a company is unable to meet its obligations to creditors when due; that is, being technically bankrupt.

Share (stock)   Security legally certifying that its registered holder is a part-owner of the corporation.

Subordinated loan   A loan ranked below another loan in order of priority for payment.

Treasurer   Senior financial manager reporting directly to the Chief Financial Officer. Primarily responsible for funding and cash management.

14-2   PRIMARY AND SECONDARY FINANCIAL MARKETS

The financial market is the source of external financing for companies. The financial market divides into two distinct phases of activity: the primary market and the secondary market.

PRIMARY MARKET

The purpose of the primary market is to raise new long-term capital for companies. The primary market consists of the services of financial institutions such as commercial banks, investment banks, and stockbrokers. These financial institutions generate external financing for companies by arranging for the sale of and investing in new issues of companies' securities.

SECONDARY MARKET

The purpose of the secondary market is to provide the means for investors to buy and sell securities previously issued in the primary market. One or more stock exchanges in each country and stockbrokers who act on behalf of investors on the exchanges provide this service.

Although established companies must turn to the primary market for new equity and debt funds, the secondary market is the key to the whole process. The secondary market provides a rapid and cheap means of exchanging ownership in a company, allowing shareholders to exchange and to diversify the risk associated with investment. The secondary market provides objective pricing that serves as a guide both to management and to providers of funds in the primary market. Without this objective pricing mechanism and without this means of easily diversifying risk, investors would expect a much higher return on the funds that they provide to companies. The resulting increase in the cost of capital would discourage capital investment by companies and restrict the growth of the economy.

DEFINITION

Cost of capital   Cost of funds used by a company for investment.

Diversification   Reduction of a portfolio's risk by holding a collection of assets having returns that are not perfectly positively correlated.

Primary market   New issue market. The services of financial institutions such as commercial banks, investment banks, and stockbrokers arranging for the sale of and investing in new issues of companies' securities.

Risk   Probability of an unacceptable loss. In portfolio theory, the standard deviation of holding period returns.

Secondary market   Market providing the means for investors to buy and sell securities previously issued in the primary market. One or more stock exchanges in each country and stockbrokers who act on behalf of investors on the exchanges operate the market.

Security   Bond or a share certifying legal ownership of a financial asset or a claim on the assets or cash flow of a company. Also denotes collateral for a loan.

14-3   CORPORATE SECURITIES

Securities represent most debt claims and all equity claims on listed companies.

EQUITIES

Ordinary share (common stock) certificates and preference shares (preferred stock) represent the equity claims on the company.

Preferred stock is equity granting the preferred stockholders claims on dividends that are senior to the ordinary shareholders' claims. When issuing preference shares, companies stipulate beforehand the schedule of future preference dividends. If a company fails to pay a preference dividend, it cannot pay a dividend to the ordinary shareholders in that financial year. With cumulative preferred stock, however, the company must have paid all preference dividends to date before paying any further dividends to the ordinary shareholders.

BONDS

Debt holders' claims mainly are bank loans, loan stock (corporate bonds), and debentures (secured by specific assets).

WARRANTS

Warrants are securities representing the right of the warrant holder to buy additional shares from the company at prices and at times that are specified when the warrants are issued.

CONVERTIBLES

Convertible securities combine the features of both loan stock and warrants, or of preferred stock and warrants. That is, they are exchangeable for ordinary shares on terms and at times specified on the security.

DEFINITIONS

Bank loans Overdrafts and secured loans negotiated with the company's bankers. Normally for a fixed maturity and a specific purpose. Repaid in regular installments. Interest charged at rates varying with the bank's base rate.

Bond An interest-bearing security with usually long-term maturity. Interest payments may be fixed or variable (floating).

Convertibles Bonds or preferred stocks that give the holder the option (effectively a warrant) to convert the security into the issuing company's ordinary shares (common stock) according to specified terms during some stated period of years.

Debentures Bonds. In London, debentures are usually secured against specific assets of the firm (mortgage debentures) or by a floating charge on the firm's assets. In New York, debentures are unsecured bonds, however.

Loan stock (corporate bonds) A fixed-interest security (bond) not secured on a specific asset.

Ordinary shares (common stock) UK term for common stock, a security certifying the shareholder's proportionate ownership in a public company (corporation) and the shareholder's proportionate claim on declared dividends.

Preference shares (preferred stock) Equity security that pays a (normally fixed) dividend. The issuer must pay the preference dividend before paying any dividends on common stock (ordinary shares). Cumulative preference shares carry forward entitlement to unpaid preference dividends. Participating preference shares also entitle holders to a share of profit.

Warrants Securities giving the holder the right to buy shares directly from a company at potentially advantageous prices. Warrant terms specify the number of shares, prices, and dates when the warrant may be exercised.

14-4 GOVERNMENT DEBT

Corporations have to compete with governments in the bond market. Governments tend to be very big borrowers dominating the market. So, one must understand the characteristics of government debt in order to understand the market for corporate bonds.

GOVERNMENT DEBT

Governments and their various departments borrow by issuing a variety of fixed and variable interest rate bonds to finance public expenditure and to influence the supply of credit in the

Table 14.1 Selected UK Government fixed interest gross yields to redemption.

		16 April 2002 (%)
Treasury bills	3 months	4.08
Low coupons	2 years	4.93
	10 years	5.22
	30 years	4.97
Medium coupons	2 years	5.03
	13 years	5.43
	19 years	5.17
High coupons	4 years	4.80
	9 years	5.24
	15 years	5.25
Irredeemables (undated)		5.87
Index-linked	1 year	1.77
	14 years	2.37
	28 years	2.19

Source: Financial Times, 17 April 2002.

economy. Table 14.1 classifies some UK Government bonds according to their maturities and to the relative size of their coupons.

COUPON

The coupon is the interest rate paid per £100 of debt. Therefore, bonds issued when interest rates were higher now sell in the bond market at a higher price than when first issued. Similarly, bonds issued when interest rates were lower now sell in the bond market at a lower price. This is just the consequence of the bond price being the present value (PV) of the remaining cash flows to the bondholder, discounted at the currently prevailing interest rates.

EXAMPLE 14.1

Consider Treasury 12 pc (2013–2017) priced at £158.25. Each year the bond pays interest of £12.00 on the £100 face value of the bond. The annual interest is payable in two semiannual install-ments of £6 each.

MATURITY

The bond matures in 2013–2017. Therefore, at some time during those years, the UK Government pays the investors a final £6 plus the face value of £100. The payment of £100 repays the loan and thus redeems the bond. Interest rates in the year 2002 had fallen since the original issue date.

NOMINAL VALUE

So, on 17 April 2002, the bond's market price of £158.25 was well above its par value (nominal value) of £100. The fact that the market price of each £100 of the debt was worth £158.25 on 17 pril 2002, implied that the current annual running yield on the bond was only 7.58% at that point in time. The running yield is the annual interest (£12) divided by the current market price (£158.25).

YIELD TO REDEMPTION

The running yield does not reflect the capital loss that the bondholder will suffer when the UK Government redeems the bond for £100 in 2013–2017. Therefore, a capital loss of £158.25 − 100.00 = £58.25 will be suffered by the bondholders on redemption. The *Financial Times* calculates the bond's gross yield to redemption. This is the internal rate of return (IRR) on the bond reflecting its current market price, future interest payments and the capital loss (or gain), all before tax. For this bond, the yield to redemption is only 5.25% compared with the running yield of 7.58%. The difference is due to the capital loss, which is not included in the running yield.

TERM STRUCTURE OF INTEREST RATES

Why do we bother to differentiate in Table 14.1 between bonds of different maturity (the number of years to run before redemption)? As the table indicates, in April 2002 the bonds with medium and long maturities exhibited slightly higher yields to redemption than the short securities. This is an example of a rising term structure of interest rates. The term structure normally rises. A reason for a rising term structure is that prices of the longer term bonds are more volatile, and therefore investors demand a risk premium in the form of a higher yield to redemption. This premium can fall to a discount, however, if investors expect future market rates of interest rates to be lower. This expectation can at times result in a declining term structure of interest rates.

TAXES

Taxes can have interesting effects on Government bond prices and gross redemption yields. For example, in the UK capital gains on UK Government bonds (gilts) are tax-free if held for more than one year. This provision is important to those investors who pay high marginal rates of tax. They prefer tax-free capital gains to interest payments taxable at the investor's marginal rate. Because low coupon bonds offer greater capital gains than do high coupon bonds, they tend to be relatively more attractive to high-tax payers.

SHORTS, MEDIUMS, AND LONGS

Treasury bills are Government bonds of very short maturity (three months and six months issued weekly using the auction method. Bonds with a maturity of less than 5 years are known as shorts, 5–15 years are known as mediums, and over 15 years (but dated) are known as longs. Undated bonds or irredeemables (i.e. Consols) are in a category of their own.

INDEX-LINKED

Index-linked bonds are bonds that have their face value and coupons adjusted for the annual rate of inflation. Therefore, the gross redemption yields on the UK index-linked bonds in Table 14.1 are correspondingly lower than the gross redemption yields of other bonds in the table with similar maturities. The market prices and therefore the yields on the index-linked bonds reflect two additional factors. First, they reflect adjustment to the coupon for inflation. Second, they reflect investors' expectations for the effect of future inflation and the bond's face value at maturity.

RISK

Most Government bonds are relatively free from the risk of default. National governments in developed countries virtually always honor their obligations to pay coupons and redeem their bonds on schedule. Market prices of such default-free obligations are still subject to change, however. So, Government bonds are still risky in this sense. Bonds issued with fixed interest payments are subject to subsequent price changes reflecting changes in market rates of interest. When interest rates rise, fixed interest bonds must sell at lower prices to compete with newer bond issues paying higher coupons. Longer maturity fixed interest bonds are more sensitive to changes in market rates of interest.[1] Consequently, the bondholder is subject to price risk if she has to sell the bond before it matures.

By holding the bond to maturity, the bondholder assures receiving the face value of the bond from the Government. In this case, the only risk comes from uncertainty about future rates of inflation. Because inflation is subject to unexpected deviations from forecast, the bondholder cannot be completely certain how much goods the coupons and the redemption value from a fixed interest bond will buy.

DEFINITIONS

Coupon   When detached from a bond, a coupon serves as evidence of entitlement to an interest payment. The word coupon more usually refers to the rate of interest on an interest-bearing security, however.

Default   Failure to make a payment of interest or a repayment of principal on the due date.

Face value (par value)   Redemption value printed on a bond or share certificate. The actual market price for the security need not equal its face value.

Gilts   UK government securities (other than Treasury bills) traded in London.

Index-linked bond   Bond for which the values of interest and principal are linked to a retail price index.

---

[1] More precisely, the sensitivity of a bond's price to changes in interest rates is a function of its duration. A security's duration is the weighted average timing of its payments to the security holder. The formula for duration is:

$$D = \frac{1}{P}\sum_{t=1}^{N} t \times [C_t/(1 + R)^t]$$

Internal rate of return (IRR)   Discount rate that would make the net present value for an investment equal to zero.

Irredeemables   Government bonds with no fixed maturity.

Longs   Bonds with dated maturities greater than 15 years.

Maturity   Period between the creation of a financial claim and the date on which it is to be paid. The final date when a bond is due for repayment.

Mediums   Bonds with maturities of 5–15 years.

Par value (nominal value)   The face value printed on a bond or share certificate. The actual market price for the security need not equal its par value.

Present value (PV)   Value of an investment now as the cost of a comparable investment in the financial market (calculated by multiplying the investment's expected after-tax cash income by the appropriate discount factors).

Redeem   Repay the face value of a bond.

Redemption yield   Internal rate of return on a bond's interest and redemption payments.

Risk premium   Extra return expected from a risky asset compared with the return from an alternative risk-free asset.

Running yield (interest yield or flat yield)   Interest as a percentage at the price paid. Excludes expected capital gain or loss on a redeemable security.

Shorts   Bonds with maturities less than five years.

Term structure of interest rates   Observed relationship between yields on bonds and their maturities.

Treasury bill   Short-term security sold by a central bank to meet a government's short-term financial requirements. Also used as an instrument of monetary policy, influencing credit and the money supply. The bills sell at a discount because the central bank pays no cash interest on Treasury bills.

Uncertainty   Risk not measurable with historical data.

Volatility   Standard deviation of percentage changes in the asset price. More precisely, standard deviation of changes in the natural logarithm of the asset price.

14-5 CORPORATE DEBT

Companies as well as governments issue debt securities. One of the attractions of debt for companies is deductibility of interest payments from taxable income, saving tax. The possibility that the issuer of a corporate bond might default on obligations to bondholders is a risk for the bondholders. Accordingly, bondholders require higher yields on corporate bonds than on Government bonds.

DEFAULT RISK

Default is the borrower's failure to honor one or more agreements in a loan contract. The principal agreements are to pay interest and make repayments promptly on schedule. The borrower may also have agreed to covenants specifying the maintenance of favorable working capital ratios and limitations on dividend payments and on the disposal of the company's assets.

A company's default risk depends on a number of factors. These factors include the variability of the company's cash flow, the quality of its assets and the extent to which the company has borrowed already. Greater risk associated with these factors increases the probability that at some time in the future the company will be unable to pay interest charges and repayments out of its current revenues and reserves.

A company is likely to default if the value of the company's assets falls below the value of its liabilities. At this point, the company becomes legally bankrupt. Default often occurs before this point, however. It occurs if the company runs out of cash and is unable to sell assets sufficiently quickly to meet its obligations to creditors. This is a liquidity crisis. A company in a liquidity crisis suffers from financial distress. A company that is in financial distress and unable to pay its creditors is technically bankrupt. The option to default is of value to a limited liability company's shareholders because they are not personally liable for the debt. The shareholders must pay for the value of this option with higher interest rates than the Government would have to pay.

SINKING FUND

Corporate borrowers usually must repay a public bond issue into a sinking fund administered by independent trustees. A bond contract (indenture) frequently permits additional payments beyond those specified in the sinking fund schedule. Payments to the sinking fund can be in cash or with the bonds repurchased by the company in the open market. Alternatively, the company may redeem the bonds directly from the bondholders at call prices specified in the bond indenture if doing so would be less costly to the borrower. In addition, the trustee can use cash paid into the sinking fund to repurchase the bonds in the market or to redeem them directly (at preset prices) from the bondholders. The trustee selects the bond certificates for redemption using bond serial numbers identified by means of a lottery.

TRUSTEE

A company issuing a bond appoints the trustee department of a bank to act as the trustee for the bond. The duty of the trustee is to represent the bondholders and protect their interests. Therefore, the holders of corporate bonds enjoy a degree of protection by the trustees and the debt contract.

RECOURSE

Clauses in the contract state conditions when the trustees can require early repayment of the debt or to liquidate the company if necessary to obtain repayment. In a liquidation, the debt holders must share the proceeds with other creditors, employees, lawyers, accountants, and the tax collector before any remainder can be paid to equity shareholders.[2] Accordingly, the debt holders often prefer not to liquidate the company. Instead, they can agree to changes in the debt contract, for example, a postponement or reduction in interest payments.

SUBORDINATION

Companies often secure some of their debt with specific assets. Other debt is unsecured. If the secured debt is preference ranked, the company must pay the obligations on the debt before paying the obligations on lower ranked debt. A subordinated loan is one that ranks behind another loan. Clearly, the debt contract should state how the bond stands in relation to other loans in case of liquidation. The degree of subordination of a bond or of a loan influences the interest rate charged by the lender.

MARKETABILITY

A further reason for the interest rate differential between corporate and Government bonds is the lack of marketability of many of the corporate bonds. One can find it difficult to find an immediate buyer for a corporate bond. Fisher (1959) found that lack of marketability was an important explanatory variable for the size of the risk premiums and therefore the prices of US corporate bonds.[3]

BOND RATINGS

The two leading bond rating agencies, Moody's and Standard&Poor's, assign corporate bonds to comparable credit quality classes on the basis of their assessment of the borrowing company's risk. The rating agencies judge risk in part on an analysis of financial ratios. Appendix 14.1 gives Moody's rating definitions. The four highest bond ratings (Aaa, Aa, A, and Baa) make a bond eligible to be included in particular investment portfolios. For example, bonds rated at least Baa by Moody's are considered eligible for purchase by financial institutions (e.g., a pension fund portfolio managed by a commercial bank's trust department), which are legally bound not to hold speculative securities.

The rating agencies assess industry risk, the firm's business risk, and the quality of its accounting records. In addition, the agencies thoroughly analyze the firm's accounting statements and evaluate key financial statement ratios relative to industry norms.

DEFINITIONS

Bond rating Rating by an agency of the credit risk of the issuer of the bond.

Call option Option giving the holder the right without obligation to buy the option's underlying asset at a specified price on or before a specified date.

Indenture Formal agreement. Formally agreed terms of a bond issue.

---

[2] See J. R. Franks, K. Nyborg, and W. N. Torous (1996) "A comparison of US, UK and German insolvency codes," *Financial Management*, Vol. 25 (Autumn), 86–101.
[3] L. Fisher (1959) "Determinants of Risk Premium on Corporate Bonds," *Journal of Political Economy*, LXVII (3) June.

Legal bankruptcy   Condition in which a company's liabilities exceed the assets on its balance sheet.

Liquidity   Ease with which cash is recoverable from an investment.

Recourse   Means available to the lender to force repayment of the debt.

Secured debt   Loan contract giving the lender recourse to a specified asset or assets in case of default by the borrower.

Sinking fund   An account administered by independent trustees through which the borrower repays outstanding bonds.

Subordinated loan   A loan ranked below another loan in order of priority for payment.

Technical bankruptcy   Condition in which a company is unable to pay an invoice or other financial obligation such as interest or a repayment on a loan.

Trustee (for a bond)   Trustee department of a bank, acting on behalf of the bondholders, for example, by administering the bond's sinking fund.

14-6 CORPORATE EQUITY

SHARES

Ordinary shares or common stock certifies the owners' equity stake in a limited liability company or corporation. Cash dividends paid out of the company's earnings reward the shareholders for their investment in the company's equity. A disadvantage of equity relative to corporate debt is that dividend payments to shareholders are not deductible from taxable income. The principle advantages of equity for the company are that the issuer has no legal obligation to pay dividends or to make repayments to shareholders.

Retained earnings not paid out as dividends and reinvested in the company increase the value of the shareholders' existing equity. Retained earnings typically represent the largest source of equity funding for a company. Rapidly growing companies reinvest more of their earnings and raise more equity capital by selling further issues of shares to equity investors.

SHAREHOLDERS' CLAIM

Suppose that you own 100,000 shares in a corporation that has issued a million shares. This means that you are entitled to 10% of any dividends paid by the company to its equity shareholders. Usually, you also control 10% of the votes at meetings of the corporation's shareholders.

DIVIDENDS

Dividend payments on shares are like coupon payments on bonds but there are important differences. The company is not legally obliged to pay dividends or to redeem its equity. This added flexibility means that a company with uncertain income is less likely to find itself in financial distress than when financing with bonds or other debt involving obligatory payments.

Investors do not necessarily expect new growth companies to pay dividends. They understand that such companies need all available cash to finance the growth. The shareholders are content to forgo dividends in the present in favor of the large expected future dividends resulting from the growth.

Most mature corporations pay dividends even though they are not obliged to do so. One reason is that mature companies generate more cash from the business than they need for reinvestment. Understandably, shareholders expect to receive dividend payments from such companies. Shareholder dissatisfaction due to nonpayment of dividends can make them troublesome at the company's Annual General Meeting. Worse still, they could accept a takeover bid by another company, forcing many of the existing top managers to seek other employment.

EQUITY BUYBACK

Corporations generating surplus cash often buy back small proportions of their equity instead of paying correspondingly larger dividends. This has the effect of increasing the share price. The reason the share price increases is that when the company has fewer shares outstanding, the remaining shareholders are entitled to a greater proportion of the total dividends paid subsequently.

EXAMPLE 14.2

In Table 14.2, we have financial statistics for the Vodafone Group from the *Financial Times* newspaper. The newspaper provides such information for over 1,000 companies each day subsequent to trading on the London, international, and other stock exchanges. The table shows that the price of Vodafone shares closed on 16 April at $122\frac{3}{4}$p, 7p higher than on the previous trading day. This compares with prices ranging between a high of $231\frac{1}{2}$ and a low of only $109\frac{1}{2}$ during the year 2002 to date. Over 423 million shares traded on the day.

DIVIDEND YIELD

The dividend yield is simply the dividends paid per share (in pence) during the previous 12 months as a percentage of the share price. The dividend yield of 1.2% is net after shareholders' taxes at the basic rate of 10%.

PRICE-TO-EARNINGS RATIO

The final column tells us the value of Vodafone's price-to-earnings ratio (P/E). The value of Vodafone's P/E ratio is its market price per share divided by its earnings per share (after taxes). Vodafone's P/E ratio implies that it would take 28.6 years for the current earnings per share to accumulate to the price of the share. This suggests that the market expects future earnings per share to grow rapidly because 28.6 years would be an excessively long time before fully recovering the price of a share.

Table 14.2 Share prices and financial statistics.

	Price	+ or −	2002 High	2002 Low	Volume ('000s)	Yield	P/E
Vodafone Group	$122\frac{3}{4}$	+7	$231\frac{1}{2}$	$109\frac{1}{2}$	423,598	1.2	28.6

Source: Financial Times, 17 April 2002.

EARNINGS YIELD

The reciprocal of the P/E ratio is the earnings yield. Vodafone's earnings yield was only 3.50% ($1/28.6 = 0.0359$). Why would a shareholder pay $122\frac{3}{4}$p to obtain an earnings yield of only 3.50% and a dividend yield of only a little more than 1%? Clearly, Vodafone was investing much of the earnings in new projects. Consequently, investors expected dividends to grow, resulting in an IRR on Vodafone shares higher than was obtainable on bonds.

DIVIDEND COVER

Dividend cover is the ratio of earnings per share to dividends per share. Dividend cover helps investors to judge whether the company can afford to continue paying the same annual dividends or to increase them. A high dividend cover is essential when a firm's earnings per share are highly volatile.

DEFINITIONS

Annual General Meeting   Annual meeting of the company's shareholders.

Common stock   The US term (ordinary shares in the UK) for a security certifying the stockholder's proportionate ownership in a limited liability company or corporation and his or her proportionate claim on declared dividends.

Dividend cover   Earnings per share divided by dividends per share.

Dividend yield   Annual dividends per share divided by the current price per share.

Earnings yield   Annual earnings per share divided by the current price per share.

Price-to-earnings (PE)   Price per share divided by reported earnings per share.

14-7 HOW SECURITIES ARE ISSUED IN THE PRIMARY MARKET

RIGHTS ISSUE

In the EU the rights issue method is the prevalent method of issuing additional equity by established companies. Each shareholder receives the right to buy shares at a discount. The number of new shares offered to an individual shareholder is proportional to the number of shares held already.

UNDERWRITING

The company employs an investment banker or large stockbroker as the main underwriter or issuing house who makes the legal and administrative arrangements for the rights issue. In turn, the main underwriter recruits subunderwriters. The subunderwriters mainly are large pension funds, insurance companies, and unit trusts that are willing to buy all shares not taken or subscribed for by the shareholders. These arrangements ensure the success of the issue. The sub-underwriters charge a fee usually between 1% and 2% for this service. In the UK, virtually all issues of equity, warrants, and convertibles use the rights issue method. In the USA, the more frequent method is to *sell* the entire issue at a small discount to the underwriters (a bought deal) who then place (resell) the issue with institutional clients at a small discount.

PLACEMENT

In the UK, the majority of preference stock and corporate bonds use the placement method. Placement means selling the issue directly to institutional clients (mainly large pension funds, insurance companies, and unit trusts) of the issuing house.

EUROBOND MARKET

Highly creditworthy companies also sell their corporate bonds and occasionally equities in the Eurobond market, usually on relatively favorable terms. The market is for long-term securities denominated in any currency except the currency of the country conducting the market (usually the UK). Participants in the market are banks, firms, wealthy individuals, and government agencies. This market is largely unregulated. Participants rely on the reputations of the other participants rather than on regulation for protection.

DEFINITIONS

Bought deal   Issue of securities subscribed (bought) entirely by the underwriters and then placed (sold) by them to institutional clients.

Issuing house   Financial institution, usually an investment bank or stockbroker, organizing a new issue of securities.

Main underwriter   Issuing house undertaking to organize an issue of securities.

Placement   Procedure whereby the issuing house sells a new issue of securities to its institutional clients.

Rights issue   An offer of new shares by a public company to each of its existing shareholders in proportion to the number the shareholder already holds.

Subscribe   To subscribe for an issue is to undertake to buy the offered securities.

Subunderwriters   Financial institutions such as pension funds and insurance companies agreeing with the main underwriter (issuing house) to purchase a proportion of the remainder of a rights issue left unsubscribed by the issuer's shareholders.

14-8 THE RIGHTS ISSUE PROCEDURE

The rights issue procedure can take several months. Approval of the issue, if necessary, at an Extraordinary General Meeting of the shareholders can delay the process. The company must agree with the issuing house the timetable and the drafting of the circular sent to shareholders giving the terms of the issue. Decisions regarding the price and terms of the issue and completion of the underwriting and subunderwriting arrangements require completion one or two weeks before the ex-rights date. The ex-rights date is the first day on which trading of shares not entitled to the rights takes place. After completion of the underwriting arrangements, the next step is announcement of the issue and mailing of the circular letter and provisional allotment letter (PAL) to those who were shareholders on the registered date. The PAL tells each shareholder the number of shares she has a right to buy. The registered date is the last date on which newly registered shareholders can be entitled to the rights. After two days allowing for the provisional allotment letters to have been received, the shares not eligible for the rights are marked ex-rights and are traded at an ex-rights price. Shares eligible for the rights are traded at a cum-rights (rights-on) price, which is higher. Shareholders usually have three weeks to accept and make the full or part payment as required.

DEFINITIONS

Cum-rights Indicates that the buyer of the cum-rights stock is entitled to a previously announced rights distribution.

Ex-rights date Date on which shares not entitled to rights begin to trade in the stock market.

Extraordinary General Meeting General meeting of the shareholders convened for a special purpose; for example, to approve a rights issue.

Provisional allotment letter (PAL) Letter to each shareholder stating the number of shares provisionally reserved (allotted) to the shareholder for purchase in a rights offering. The allotment is proportional to the number of shares already held by the shareholder.

Registered date Investors registered as shareholders in the company's records on or before the registered date are entitled to subscribe to the rights issue.

Subunderwriting Undertaking by a financial institution to buy shares offered in a rights issue remaining unsubscribed by the existing shareholders.

14-9 RIGHTS ISSUES AND MARKET PRICES

EFFICIENT PRICING

Market supply and demand determine the ex-rights price. In an efficient market, the ex-rights price leaves existing shareholders no worse off if they either exercise or sell their rights.

EXAMPLE 14.3

Suppose, for example, the terms of the issue are 2 new shares offered for each 3 that a shareholder already holds. Suppose also that the current cum-rights price on the share is 100p and that the offer price for the new shares is only 75p. Thus, for every 3 shares held, the shareholder will end up with 5 shares. The ex-rights price that would leave the shareholder no worse off is $(3 \times 100p + 2 \times 75p) / 5 = 90p$. Therefore, if the cum rights price does not change, we expect the rights to be worth at least $90p - 75p = 15p$ each. If the shareholder does not wish to exercise her rights, she can sell them in the financial market for at least 15p. The market price should be a little higher than 15p because the right is essentially a call option (more precisely, a warrant). If the market price should fall below the 75p offer price during the three weeks, the rights holder need not exercise the right (it is a bad deal). On the other hand, if the price rises, the shareholder can exercise the right advantageously. So, the outcomes are unsymmetrical, and a higher market price for the right reflects the resulting net advantage. In principle, the shareholder finds herself no worse off whether she exercises the right or chooses to sell it instead.

ISSUE DISCOUNT

Similarly, the deal between the issuing company and the subunderwriters is a put option. The company has the right to sell (put) any of the unissued shares to the subunderwriters at the offer price. This would happen in the above example if the market price fell below the 75p offer price, and most of the shareholders declined to exercise their rights to buy at 75p.

This situation is good for the company and bad for the subunderwriters. The reason is that the issuing company has the potential to sell its issue of shares for more than the current market price to the subunderwriters. Naturally, the subunderwriters will charge for this valuable form of insurance. A typical fee in London, for example, is 1.25% of the value of the issue. As the fee is relatively fixed, the main underwriters will try to negotiate with the company for a deep discount on the issue. After all, if the issue price were only 50p rather than 75p, the subunderwriters are much less likely to have to do anything to justify the fee. Option valuation models have indicated that subunderwriting has been very profitable. This suggests that the main underwriters have been successful at negotiating sufficiently deep discounts to make it quite unusual for sub underwriters to have to buy any unsubscribed shares.

DEFINITIONS

Efficient financial market   A securities market in which prices rapidly reflect in an unbiased way all price-sensitive information available to market participants.

Deep discount   Exercise price on an equity rights issue set very much below the prevailing market price per share for the stock.

Put option   Option giving the holder the right without obligation to sell the option's underlying asset at a specified price on or before a specified date.

14-10   RIGHTS ISSUE SIGNALING EFFECTS

Early evidence suggested that large rights issues did not significantly depress the share price. More recent evidence suggests that there may be an adverse information effect. Companies often use equity issues to strengthen their balance sheets (reduce the debt-to-equity ratio). Accordingly, in many cases investors see a rights issue as an admission by management that it forsees some increased risks on the horizon. The resulting worry for investors would adversely affect the price of all the shares, not just those in the rights issue, and, consequently, the overall loss in value can be significant. Information signaling effects, however, are not unique to the rights issue method.

> **DEFINITION**
>
> **Information effect**   Refers to the interpretation given by investors to a company's financing decisions; for example, the motive for a rights issue, a change in the level of borrowing, or a change in the usual rate of dividend payment.

14-11   NEW ISSUES FOR UNQUOTED COMPANIES

INITIAL PUBLIC OFFERING

Before a private company can issue shares for trading on a stock exchange—Initial Public Offering (IPO)—it must obtain a quotation on the exchange. In order to obtain a quotation, the company's directors must satisfy the management of the exchange that the company is suitable for quotation. Suitability involves assurances about the way accounts are prepared and a sufficiently long history of profit. The costs of "going public" are substantial and they are difficult to justify for a small company. In addition, it could take more than a year to fulfill the legal requirements permitting a quotation.

OVER-THE-COUNTER MARKET

Other, cheaper methods are available for obtaining a market in a company's shares. Some stock-brokers will make an over-the-counter market (OTC) for a company's shares. In addition, it might be possible for permission for trading on a stock exchange under special rules without going through all the costs and formalities of a new issue. Although in this case exchange regulations govern the quality of the transactions, there is no monitoring of the quality of these securities. There is no formal relationship between an exchange and an unlisted company. It is up to the stockbroker to ensure that the company whose shares the broker promotes provides sufficient and accurate information about itself for reasonably sound investment decisions.

> **DEFINITIONS**
>
> **Initial Public Offering (IPO)**   A limited company's first public issue of common stock (ordinary shares).
>
> **Over-the-counter market (OTC)**   Market in specific securities or currencies conducted by a financial institution in its own offices.

14-12 CONCLUSIONS

The financial market provides numerous ways in which companies can obtain long-term financing. Companies can borrow by means of term loans up to around 10 years from banks or they can sell bonds or convertibles in the primary market for a longer term. Debt instruments require the payment of interest and repayment of principal according to a preset schedule, but the interest payments are tax-deductible. Default can be very serious, leading potentially to bankruptcy. Debt contracts usually involve various covenants that limit the company's freedom of action in order to protect the debt holder in case of default.

Most of the remaining capital is equity, consisting largely of earnings retained for reinvestment in the firm. The equity belongs to the equity shareholders whose individual claims on assets are proportional to the number of shares held. As with bonds, the primary market provides the means of selling new equity securities. If retained earnings are insufficient, then the sale of equity might be necessary to the existing shareholders via a rights issue or in some cases to institutions via a placing.

The stock market provides the means of trading equity and debt securities. Most trading in the market represents exchanges between investors of securities already issued. Although this activity does not provide funds directly to companies, secondary market activity is quite essential. If investors were unable to obtain current quotations in an active market, they would be very much more uncertain about the value of equity capital. They would also find it difficult to construct well-diversified portfolios or to change the composition of existing portfolios without the means of an active stock exchange. The resulting risks for shareholders would increase the cost of equity capital because investors would require additional financial inducement to invest in risky securities under such unfavorable circumstances.

DEFINITION

Portfolio   Collection of investments in financial securities and other assets.

FURTHER READING

I. Lee, S. Lochhead, J. Ritter, and Q. Zhao (1996) "The costs of raising capital," *Journal of Financial Research*, Vol. 19 (Spring), 59–74.

S. C. Myers and N. S. Majluf (1984) "Corporate financing and when firms have information that investors do not have," *Journal of Financial Economics*, Vol. 13 (June), 187–222.

R. G. Rajan and L. Zingales (1995) "What do we know about capital structure? Some evidence from international data," *Journal of Finance*, Vol. 50 (December), 1421–1460.

K. Rock (1986) "Why new issues are underpriced," *Journal of Financial Economics*, Vol. 15 (January–February), 187–212.

C. W. Smith (1986) "Investment banking and the capital acquisition process," *Journal of Financial Economics*, Vol. 15 (January–February), 3–29.

QUESTIONS AND PROBLEMS

1   List six types of security issued by companies to finance their activities.

2   How do the characteristics of preferred stock differ from those of ordinary shares?

3   Discuss the tax implications of a company issuing preferred stock.

4   What are the implications of limited liability of the corporation for its ordinary share-holders?

5   How might changes in the level of dividends cause conflicts of interest between holders of different kinds of the company's securities?

6   What are the important differences between rights issues and public offerings of ordinary shares?

7   How do existing shareholders benefit from the services of the underwriters in a rights issue?

8   How does the discount on the price of shares sold via a rights offering affect the wealth of existing shareholders?

9   What is a warrant, and why do companies issue them?

10   What is a convertible? Compare two examples of convertibles.

11   What is the net present value of a bond traded in a competitive market?

12   The ordinary shares in XYZ plc currently sell for 100 cents per share and there are 10,000,000 shares outstanding. The company announces a one-for-two rights issue. The issue grants existing shareholders the right to buy one share at a price of 85 cents for every two shares already held. The offer expires in 21 days. What are the cum-rights and the ex-rights prices of the shares, and for what minimum price would each right sell?

13   A company announces a two-for-one rights issue giving the shareholders the right to buy new shares for 200 cents. A shareholder who owns 2,000 of the shares is convinced that the company is selling the new shares too far below the current market price of €6. He thinks that the exercise price on the rights should have been more than €4 per new share. Explain to him why the terms of the offer do not directly affect his wealth. Illustrate with a numerical example. What indirect effect might there be on his wealth?

14   FOGLEY plc plans a private placement of 500,000 new shares to a new investor. The company offers new shares at a 10% discount on the present market price of €4. There are 200,000 shares outstanding. If the book value of shareholders' equity is €4,828,000, calculate the book value per share and the market value per share after the private placement. Can you say whether existing shareholders are better off because of the placement?

15   An investor has €10,000 of CLIPPER BOARD plc's bond paying 10% and redeemable in the year 2010. Each €1,000 bond carries 100 warrants. The conditions provide that the holder of four warrants can buy a share for €2.50. What is the minimum value of the 100

warrants if the current market price of one share is €2.70? Why would you expect the market price of the warrants to be higher?

16   MEGAZONE MANUFACTURING plc has issued €10,000,000 worth of convertible bonds with a 7% coupon (interest payable on the face or par value of the bond), which mature in three years. The €100 par value bonds are trading currently at €112. An investor has asked you whether she should convert the bonds to ordinary shares, as this is the last day of the conversion period. The terms specify a conversion price of €2.50, and the share sells currently for €2.85. Explain what the investor should do and why. State any necessary assumptions.

APPENDIX 14.1   MOODY'S CORPORATE BOND RATINGS[4]

LONG-TERM RATINGS

Debt ratings—taxable debt and deposits globally

Aaa   Bonds which are rated Aaa are judged to be of the best quality. They carry the smallest degree of investment risk and are generally referred to as "gilt edged." Interest payments are protected by a large or by an exceptionally stable margin and principal is secure. While the various protective elements are likely to change, such changes as can be visualized are most unlikely to impair the fundamentally strong position of such issues.

Aa   Bonds which are rated Aa are judged to be of high quality by all standards. Together with the Aaa group they comprise what are generally known as high-grade bonds. They are rated lower than the best bonds because margins of protection may not be as large as in Aaa securities or fluctuation of protective elements may be of greater amplitude or there may be other elements present which make the long-term risk appear somewhat larger than the Aaa securities.

A   Bonds which are rated A possess many favorable investment attributes and are to be considered as upper-medium-grade obligations. Factors giving security to principal and interest are considered adequate, but elements may be present which suggest a susceptibility to impairment some time in the future.

Baa   Bonds which are rated Baa are considered as medium-grade obligations (i.e., they are neither highly protected nor poorly secured). Interest payments and principal security appear adequate for the present but certain protective elements may be lacking or may be characteristically unreliable over any great length of time. Such bonds lack outstanding investment characteristics and in fact have speculative characteristics as well.

Ba   Bonds which are rated Ba are judged to have speculative elements; their future cannot be considered as well assured. Often the protection of interest and principal payments may

---

[4] *Source:* Moody's, Inc.

be very moderate, and thereby not well safeguarded during both good and bad times over the future. Uncertainty of position characterizes bonds in this class.

B   Bonds which are rated B generally lack characteristics of the desirable investment. Assurance of interest and principal payments or of maintenance of other terms of the contract over any long period of time may be small.

Caa   Bonds which are rated Caa are of poor standing. Such issues may be in default or there may be present elements of danger with respect to principal or interest.

Ca   Bonds which are rated Ca represent obligations which are speculative in a high degree. Such issues are often in default or have other marked shortcomings.

C   Bonds which are rated C are the lowest rated class of bonds, and issues so rated can be regarded as having extremely poor prospects of ever attaining any real investment standing.

15 Dividend Policy

Cash dividends are payments by a corporation to its equity shareholders. Corporate boards of directors like to pay dividends at a sustainable level, and most believe that shareholders favor steady growth in dividend income. So, companies with highly variable earnings tend to pay out a lower proportion of earnings to shareholders. This reduces the likelihood of having to reverse previous increases in annual dividends. Shareholders have come to expect stable dividends, and thus they interpret any significant deviation from the established pattern of dividend growth as information about the company's financial health. While this behavior is evident, some finance theorists have had difficulty explaining it when taxes do not favor dividends. The issues therefore require a closer look before the rationale for dividend policy becomes clear.

TOPICS

Therefore, this chapter covers the following issues:

○ *relationships between dividends and earnings;*

○ *dividends as signals;*

○ *dividend policy and taxes;*

○ *dividend policy and shareholder tax clienteles;*

○ *dividend policy and portfolio diversification;*

○ *alternatives to paying cash dividends;*

○ *macroeconomic considerations.*

15-1 DIVIDENDS AND EARNINGS

Lintner (1956) discovered a preference for sustainable dividends when interviewing American financial managers.[1]

---

[1] J. Lintner (1956) "Distribution of incomes of corporations among dividends, retained earnings, and taxes," *American Economic Review*, Vol. 46 (May) 97–113.

LINTNER'S PARTIAL ADJUSTMENT MODEL

Observed dividend behavior verifies Lintner's partial adjustment model.[2] The model suggests a typical company adopts a target payout ratio for dividends. Then it moves gradually away from the existing level of dividends toward this target as earnings change.

EXAMPLE 15.1

Table 15.1 gives an example of a typical dividend payment pattern as described by Lintner. The company in the example currently is preparing to announce earnings that have increased sharply to €6 per share. Its target payout ratio is 50% of after-tax earnings. Therefore, its target dividend payment is $0.50 \times 6 = €3$. The previous dividend was only €2, however. How large should be the next dividend?

Table 15.1 Example of the partial adjustment of dividends to a change of earnings.

Earnings per share	6.00
Target payment (0.50×6.00)	3.00
Less: Existing dividend per share	2.00
Potential change in dividend	1.00
Actual change in dividend (0.33×1.00)	0.33
Plus: Existing dividend	2.00
New dividend per share	2.33

The board of directors does not want to raise the €2 dividend all the way to €3 because the directors fear that the earnings increase might be temporary. They would not want to have to reduce the dividend if earnings fell back again. Instead, the directors decide to increase the dividend only one-third of the way toward the target. Therefore, the announced increase is only $0.33 \times 1 = €0.33$ for a total dividend of only $2 + 0.33 = €2.33$ per share.

Highly variable earnings call for a low-target payout ratio and a slow rate of dividend adjustment to corresponding changes in earnings. Lintner's partial adjustment model appears to describe average dividend payment behavior, although individual companies adopt particular payment patterns of their own.

Figure 15.1 shows average dividends paid by the 30 large UK companies in the Financial Times FTSE30 Stock Index compared with their average earnings each year since 1965. We see that dividends have increased quite steadily against a background of fluctuating earnings. The average level of dividends did not decline much when earnings fell sharply during recessions. This evidence supports Lintner's partial adjustment model in a European context.

---

[2] See E. F. Fama and H. Babiak (1968) "Dividend policy: An empirical analysis," *Journal of the American Statistical Association*, Vol. 63 (December), 1132–1161.

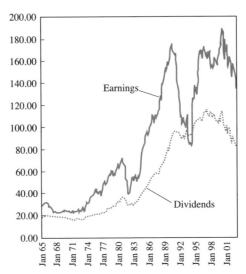

Figure 15.1 Earnings and dividends on the FTSE30 Index.

Although Lintner appears to have discovered the average dividend payment behavior, individual companies can adopt somewhat different dividend policies.

GROWTH COMPANIES

At one extreme, many companies pay no dividends at all. These typically are young growth companies requiring all their earnings to invest in a surfeit of profitable opportunities. Such companies attract shareholders who are content not to receive dividends. These shareholders expect that the resulting growth will yield very large dividends in the future. The share price reflects the present value (PV) of the discounted expected future dividends.

MATURE COMPANIES

At the other extreme, companies in mature industries have greater difficulty finding profitable investment opportunities. Existing earnings can be much more than required for routine reinvestment. Shareholders in such companies rightly demand substantial dividends and usually get them.

CONSTRAINTS ON DIVIDENDS

Most legal jurisdictions, however, limit the amount of dividends a company can pay. A company must not pay dividends out of capital. Although a company can pay more than its current after-tax income as dividends, it cannot do so indefinitely. The cumulative total of dividends paid to date must not exceed the sum of current earnings and all previously retained earnings.

DEFINITIONS

Equity Net worth or shareholder's capital represented by common stock (ordinary shares) and preferred stock.

Expected (mean) Probability-weighted average of all possible outcomes for a random variable.

Partial adjustment model Dividend policy model suggesting companies change dividend payments gradually toward the level implied by their current earnings and their target dividend payout ratios.

Payout ratio Annual dividends divided by annual earnings after tax.

Present value (PV) Value of an investment now as the cost of a comparable investment in the financial market (calculated by multiplying the investment's expected after-tax cash income by the appropriate discount factors).

15-2 DIVIDENDS AS SIGNALS

Shareholders who become accustomed to an established pattern of dividend payments notice when the company appears to deviate from the established pattern. What is management trying to say to investors by making such a change?

DIVIDEND-SIGNALING HYPOTHESIS

The dividend-signaling hypothesis suggests that management can use changes in dividends to signal information to the market without revealing details that could be useful to competitors. This new information would affect the share price.

Indeed, various studies have shown that announcements of increased dividends have increased share prices.[3] Evidence of increases in share prices of several percent near the dates of announced dividend increases lends support to the signaling hypothesis.

DEFINITION

Dividend-signaling hypothesis Proposition that companies use changes in dividends to signal information to the market without revealing details useful to competitors.

15-3 IS DIVIDEND POLICY IRRELEVANT?

MILLER AND MODIGLIANI'S IRRELEVANCE PROPOSITION

In 1961, Miller and Modigliani (MM) published the seminal paper on the theory of dividend policy.[4] Unfortunately, they showed that dividend policy is irrelevant to the value of the firm, which flies in the face of what most company directors and their institutional shareholders appear to believe. The proof seems infallible, nonetheless. The essence of the proof is as follows.

---

[3] P. Healy and K. Palepu (1988) "Earnings information conveyed by dividend initiations and omissions," *Journal of Financial Economics*, Vol. 21, 149–175.

[4] M. H. Miller and F. Modigliani (1961) "Dividend policy, growth and the valuation of shares," *Journal of Business*, Vol. 34 (October), 411–433.

WHY DIVIDENDS MIGHT NOT MATTER

For simplicity, we consider the example of a firm that only uses equity finance and has no debt. Assume that there are no taxes. The premise is that the uses of funds must equal their sources:

$$Uses \ of \ Funds = Sources \ of \ Funds$$

We now split both the uses of the funds and the sources into broad categories. The two categories of uses are the payment of dividends and investment in new assets. The two categories of sources are the cash flow from the already-existing investment and the cash from new capital raised externally. Because the uses must equal the sources, we have:

$$Dividends \ Paid + New \ Investment = Net \ Cash \ Flow \ from \ Existing \ Investment$$
$$+ New \ Capital$$

By rearranging the above equation we get:

$$Dividends \ Paid - New \ Capital = New \ Cash \ Flow \ from \ Existing \ Investment$$
$$- New \ Investment$$

Note that the right-hand side of this equation is fixed. The net cash flow from existing investment was fixed by past investment decisions. Furthermore, the firm's investment policy fixes the cash for new investment. For example, the policy to invest in all projects with positive net present values (NPVs) is a fixed policy.

The right-hand side of the equation represents the firm's free cash flow, which is thus fixed. This also fixes the value of the firm because the value of the firm equals the PV of its free cash flow. Dividends do not appear in the free cash flow on the right-hand side, so they cannot affect the value of the firm. MM argued on this basis that the dividend policy of an individual firm is irrelevant to its market value.

DIVIDEND POLICY AND ISSUES OF NEW CAPITAL

Fixing the cash sources on the right-hand side of the equation also fixes the net value of the left-hand side. Accordingly, if the board of directors decides to increase dividends, they must fund the increase with new capital. At the margin, claims on the firm by the new investors cancel the benefit of the additional dividends to existing shareholders. In this way, the value of the firm to the existing remains unaffected.

FLOTATION COSTS

MM assumed a perfect capital market in which there are no transaction costs involved in raising new capital. Especially for small firms not listed on a stock exchange, the cost of raising external equity can be significant. Therefore, externally funded dividends can reduce the value of a small firm if it can no longer borrow from its bankers. The equity issues of large quoted firms have much lower flotation costs, however. Equity flotation costs do not appear to have affected significantly the dividend policies of large quoted companies.

DIVIDENDS AND FREE CASH FLOW

In essence MM were saying that the value of the firm's equity is equal to the PV of its discounted free cash flow (net of debt payments). The value of the equity is the same regardless of what dividend policy the firm pursues:

$$EQUITY_0 = \frac{C_1}{(1+R)^1} + \frac{C_2}{(1+R)^2} + \cdots$$

Suppose, for example, that the dividend D_1 actually paid in Period 1 is less than the full amount C_1 of the free cash flow in Period 1:

$$D_1 = C_1 - c_1$$

Suppose also that for one period the firm reinvests the unpaid remainder c_1 of the free cash flow. The return on the investment is equal to R. Funds realized from this investment pay for an increase in the dividend D_2 in Period 2. That is:

$$D_2 = C_2 + c_1(1+R)$$

We can now show that discounting the dividends is equivalent algebraically to discounting the free cash flow:

$$
\begin{aligned}
EQUITY_0 &= \frac{D_1}{(1+R)^1} + \frac{D_2}{(1+R)^2} + \cdots \\
&= \frac{C_1 - c_1}{(1+R)^1} + \frac{C_2 + c_1(1+R)}{(1+R)^2} + \cdots \\
&= \frac{C_1}{(1+R)^1} + \frac{C_2}{(1+R)^2} + \cdots
\end{aligned}
$$

which is just where we started. Reinvested free cash flow pays for correspondingly greater dividends subsequently, and the PV of the dividend stream remains unchanged. The firm is still valued as though it pays out all of each period's free cash flow as the dividend for that period.

Of course, the company normally would seek to reinvest for a higher rate than the discount rate R. This fact does not alter the dividend irrelevance argument, however. The argument remains unaltered because the firm could fund the investment equally well with new equity or debt.

MM point out that not paying dividends is equivalent to issuing new external capital (if we ignore transaction and flotation costs). Similarly, paying large dividends is equivalent to reducing the shareholders' investment (negative equity financing). Because external financing does not alter the free cash flow attributable to the existing shareholders, the PV of their stake in the company is not changed.

DEFINITIONS

Capital market   Market for long-term securities. Consists of the banks, insurance companies, and other financial intermediaries (including the stock market) competing to supply companies with financial capital.

Debt   Sum of money or other assets owed by one party to another. Usually, a legally enforceable obligation to pay agreed interest and to repay the principal of a loan to the lender promptly on schedule.

Discount rate   Required rate of return used in the calculation of a discount factor.

Discounting   Multiplying each of an investment's expected cash flow by its present value per unit (discount factor) to obtain the total net present value for the investment.

Flotation costs   Transaction costs associated with the issuance of securities.

Free cash flow   After-tax cash flow from operations net of capital investment and increases in net working capital.

15-4 IS DIVIDEND POLICY AFFECTED BY PERSONAL TAXES?

From the MM standpoint, dividend policy is neutral before tax. This picture could alter after tax when the personal tax rates on dividends are different from the rates on capital gains. Would not shareholders prefer to receive their returns in the form that attracts the lowest tax?

THE DIVIDEND PUZZLE

The well-known dividend puzzle is the curious fact that companies continued to pay substantial dividends when personal taxes were much higher on dividend income than on capital gains.

CLASSICAL TAX SYSTEMS

The tax question issue arises most particularly in countries that operate a classical tax system. The USA and a number of other countries operate a classical tax system. In this system, the Government taxes corporate income three times. First, it taxes the income directly at the corporate tax rate. Second, it taxes the income indirectly by taxing the dividends to shareholders at the relevant personal tax rates. Finally, it taxes again at the personal capital gains tax rate if there are capital gains when the investor sells her shares. When the personal tax rate is higher on dividends than on capital gains, the system appears to discriminate against paying any dividends.

IMPUTATION TAX SYSTEMS

The UK is among a number of European countries that operate an imputation tax system. In the UK system, corporations pay a tax (at the basic rate) on the grossed up dividend to the Inland Revenue. (Higher rate taxpayers pay additional tax on the dividend.) The Government treats this withholding tax as part of the company's Corporation Tax, however. Therefore, from the perspective of the basic rate taxpayer, there are only two taxes on corporate income, Corporation Tax and the Capital Gains Tax. In this way, the system aims to eliminate some of the tax consequences of dividend policy.

BRENNAN'S PROPOSITION

In the context of the US classical tax system, Brennan (1970) suggested an interesting proposition.[5] He proposed that when the rate of personal tax is higher on dividends than on capital gains, companies that pay high dividends must try to earn more before tax than do low-dividend-paying companies. They need to earn more before tax to compensate investors for the higher taxes they must pay on the dividends. This handicap would make high-dividend-paying companies relatively uncompetitive. Brennan's proposition underlines the dividend puzzle.

EXAMPLE 15.2

Table 15.2 illustrates Brennan's proposition for two identical firms differing only in their dividend policies. The first column in the table illustrates a zero dividend payout policy (Policy A). The second column of figures illustrates a policy to pay out all earnings as dividends (Policy B).

Consider first the figures for Policy A in which the company pays no dividends. The earnings per share are $12.50 after corporate taxes, and the initial share price is $100. Because no dividends are paid, the retained earnings add to the value of the company. So, we would expect the share price to increase to $100 + 12.50 = \$112.50$ as indicated in the table.

Because Policy A pays no dividends, shareholders have no taxes to pay on dividend income. Instead, they have a taxable capital gain. Assume that shareholders realize the capital gain in the same year, and the tax on the gain is only 20%. The capital gains tax under Policy A thus comes to $0.20 \times 12.50 = \$2.50$.

Therefore, the after-tax income to the shareholders is $12.50 - 2.50 = \$10.00$ as indicated. Treating this income as a perpetuity discounted at 10%, we obtain the initial share price of $10.00/0.10 = \$100$ as shown in the table.

Table 15.2 Example illustrating Brennan's proposition.

	Policy A (no payout)	Policy B (100% payout)
Earnings per share	$12.50	$12.50
Current share price	$100.00	P_0
Next year's share price	$112.50	P_1
Dividend	0	$12.50
Tax on dividend at 40%	0	$5.00
Capital gain	$12.50	0
Tax on capital gain at 20%	$2.50	0
After-tax income	$10.00	$7.50
After-tax required rate of return	10%	10%
Current share price	$P_1 = \$100.00$	$P_1 = \$75.00$

[5] M. Brennan (1970) "Taxes, market valuation and corporate financial policy," *National Tax Journal*, Vol. 23 (December), 417–427.

How does Policy B compare in which an identical company pays out all its earnings as dividends? We do not yet know the share price P_0 for this policy. Nevertheless, we would expect the share price to remain unchanged because the company retains no earnings under the 100% payout for Policy B. The dividend is equal to the earnings of $12.50 under Policy B.

Unfortunately, the Government in this example taxes dividends at a higher rate than for capital gains. We assume a tax rate of 40% on the dividends. The tax is thus $0.40 \times 12.50 = \$5.00$. Consequently, the net after-tax income to the shareholder is only $12.50 - 5.00 = \$7.50$ compared with $10 if no dividends had been paid. Treating this income of $7.50 as a perpetuity discounted at 10%, we obtain the initial share price of only $7.50/0.10 = \$75.00$. Consequently, the share price of $75 under Policy B compares unfavorably with the price of $100 under Policy A.

Therefore, according to Brennan, the company's share price is lower if it pays dividends. To make the shareholders no worse off, the company paying high dividends would have to earn more before tax than would an identical company paying smaller dividends.

DEFINITIONS

Dividend puzzle   That companies continued to pay substantial dividends when personal taxes were much higher on dividend income than on capital gains.

Classical tax system   Tax system in which the Government taxes corporate income at the corporate tax rate and then taxes shareholders for dividends received and for capital gains at the relevant personal rates of tax.

Imputation tax system   Tax system in which corporations pay a tax on dividends on behalf of shareholders and then offset this tax payment against their Corporation Tax liability.

Perpetuity   Equal sum of money paid in each period for ever.

15-5 DIVIDEND POLICY AND SHAREHOLDER TAX CLIENTELES

Empirical evidence for Brennan's proposition is inconclusive. The answer is not entirely clear, but here is one possible reason. If you were managing the portfolio of a non-taxpaying pension fund, which of the two company's shares in Table 15.2 would you want to hold?

ARBITRAGE

The answer to this question should be clear. You would buy the cheaper shares priced at $75.00 and receive the dividend income of $12.50 on which you would pay no tax. The rate of return $12.50/75.00 = 16.7\%$ compares very favorably with the assumed required rate of return of only 10%.

Therefore, low-tax payers will keep buying the dividend-paying shares, pushing up the price. Eventually, the Policy B shares will end up in the portfolios of low-tax payers, leaving the Policy A shares in the portfolios of the high-tax payers. Accordingly, we need to reduce the assumed tax rates in Table 15.2 for the shareholders attracted to Policy B.

In equilibrium, the taxes actually paid by the respective shareholders under the two policies need not be very different. Therefore, if each dividend policy attracts a different shareholder taxpaying clientele, companies paying high dividends need not suffer a significant disadvantage because of a difference in the tax rates on dividends and capital gains.

TAX CLIENTELE EFFECT

MM had already suggested that there would be a tax clientele effect. Companies paying high dividends would attract low-tax payers like pension funds, leaving the shares of the low-dividend-paying companies in the hands of the high-tax payers. Therefore, the actual personal taxes paid would be little different under high- or low-dividend policies. This undermines Brennan's proposition and supports dividend irrelevance.

If clientele effects were important, the existing shareholder clientele would object to any drastic change of dividend policy. Casual observation suggests that management does encounter such protests from activist shareholders when changing dividend policy too rapidly.

EMPIRICAL EVIDENCE

Pettit (1977) published evidence that low-dividend yields were preferred by investors with high income, by younger investors, by investors whose ordinary and capital gains tax rates differed substantially, and by investors whose portfolios had high systematic risk. These results support the intuitions of most people concerning shareholder clienteles.[6]

Nevertheless, just one year later Lewellen et al. (1978) reported much weaker results using the same data. Therefore, the evidence for a tax clientele effect is not conclusive. We need to find a further possible reason for the lack of strong evidence for dividend tax effects.[7]

DEFINITIONS

Portfolio   Collection of investments in financial securities and other assets.

Rate of return   After-tax cash income and capital gain divided by the investment.

Systematic risk   Risk that portfolio diversification cannot eliminate.

Tax clientele effect   Proposition that companies paying high dividends would attract low-tax payers leaving the shares of low-dividend-paying companies in the hands of the high-tax payers.

15-6 DIVIDEND POLICY AND PORTFOLIO DIVERSIFICATION

Shareholders do not invest in just one company. Diversified shareholders are concerned about portfolio risk as well as dividend income. These shareholders see differences in the dividend policies of individual companies in a larger, portfolio context.

---

[6] R. R. Pettit (1977) "Taxes, transactions costs and clientele effects of dividends," *Journal of Financial Economics* (December), 419–436.
[7] W. Lewellen, K. L. Stanley, R. C. Lease, and G. G. Schlarbaum (1978) "Some direct evidence of the dividend clientele phenomenon," *Journal of Finance*, Vol. 33 (December), 1385–1399.

DIVERSIFICATION AND TAXES

Most high-tax-paying investors wish to hold widely diversified portfolios that reduce risk. Narrow, tax-based arguments such as Brennan's appear not to have persuaded them to focus their investment on low-dividend-paying companies. Similarly, low-taxpaying institutions resist investing exclusively in high-dividend-paying shares. So, a policy of paying either high or low dividends would not affect much the demand for a company's shares if shareholder diversification requirements dominate tax considerations.

While the undoubted importance of portfolio diversification weakens the shareholder clientele explanation, both explanations favor dividend policy irrelevance. So, there are no strong theoretical reasons for large quoted companies to let tax considerations dominate their dividend policies.

DEFINITION

Risk   Probability of an unacceptable loss. In portfolio theory, the standard deviation of holding period returns.

15-7 ALTERNATIVES TO PAYING CASH DIVIDENDS

Companies have several alternatives to paying cash dividends.

STOCK DIVIDENDS

A company finding it inconvenient to pay a cash dividend might choose to pay a stock dividend (scrip issue) instead. For every 100 shares that a stockholder owns she receives one or more additional shares in lieu of cash. The shareholder actually is no better off. Apart from signaling effects, the total market value of her shareholding after the stock dividend remains the same. She holds more shares, but with a correspondingly lower price. In this respect, a stock dividend resembles a stock split. The accounting treatment of a stock dividend is different, but the accounting treatment has virtually no economic significance for the shareholder.

BUYBACKS

Many companies use a part of their earnings to buy back some of their own shares. This puts cash into the hands of shareholders in the form of a realized capital gain instead of a dividend. For some shareholders this could save taxes. In addition, the buyback can signal to investors that the company believes the market has underpriced its shares.

CASH MOUNTAINS

Another alternative is to build a cash mountain invested in Treasury bills or other liquid securities. This seems pointless (and may not be tax-efficient) unless the company intends the funds for a specific purpose such as an acquisition.

TAKEOVERS

Finally, buying stocks of other companies in preparation, perhaps, for a takeover bid is another possible use for the cash.

Shareholders generally do not approve of managers hoarding cash, however. They know that an embarrassment of riches can lead to the squandering of shareholders' funds on unprofitable ventures.

DEFINITIONS

Acquisition   Transfer of control of a company from one group of shareholders to another.

Buyback   Buying the company's shares from its shareholders instead of using the cash to pay them dividends.

Liquidity   Ease with which cash is recoverable from an investment.

Security   Bond or a share certifying legal ownership of a financial asset or a claim on the assets or cash flow of a company. Also denotes collateral for a loan.

Share (stock)   Security legally certifying that its registered holder is a part-owner of the corporation.

Treasury bill   Short-term security sold by a central bank to meet a government's short-term financial requirements. Also used as an instrument of monetary policy, influencing credit and the money supply. The bills sell at a discount because the central bank pays no cash interest on Treasury bills.

15-8 MACROECONOMIC CONSIDERATIONS

The MM dividend irrelevance proposition is a microeconomic theory. That is, it concerns the behavior of individual companies without reference to the wider economy. Nonetheless, a diversified shareholder needs to adopt a macroeconomic perspective reflecting the economy-wide breadth of her portfolio holdings.

WHAT TO DO WITH THE CORPORATE SECTOR SURPLUS

The corporate sector as a whole earns a surplus. Surplus is that part of output not required for reinvestment. Consumption and stockpiling are the two obvious ways to dispose of surplus product. Stockpiling is not consistent with economic growth. Therefore, it is necessary to consume the surplus product.

The surplus belongs to the owners of the corporate sector who need to consume it. The consumption cannot take place unless the owners receive the cash equivalent of the surplus enabling them to purchase the products in the open market. The corporate sector transfers the necessary cash to its owners in at least three ways: by paying dividends, by buying back shares, and by buying the shares of other companies. All three of these transactions put cash into the hands of owners, enabling them to consume the corporate sector surplus.

While the microeconomic theory of dividend policy shows that each individual company can go its own way with respect to the use of its surplus cash, ultimately there is a constraint on the corporate sector as a whole. The aggregate of all companies must distribute the cash equivalent of its surplus regardless of tax considerations.[8]

MARKET FORCES

This fact suggests that market forces would pressure companies to distribute surplus cash to shareholders. One such force is the market for corporate control. A company seen by its shareholders to be squandering its surplus cash on inappropriate strategies and unprofitable investment is vulnerable to takeover by another company. One of the standard defenses against a takeover bid is to increase dividends. Just the potential of a bid from some unknown predator is enough to keep boards of directors of many public companies on the path of regular if not always generous dividend payments.

15-9 CONCLUSIONS

Dividend policy has puzzled finance theorists for decades. The puzzle is that differential tax rates on dividends versus capital gains appear to have had little effect on the dividend policies of companies.

Most company directors feel that they should be paying steadily growing dividends that signal their expectations concerning earnings growth.[9] This policy appears to reflect what shareholders want. If dividend policy truly is neutral as suggested by MM, then conforming to shareholders' wishes can do no harm. Moreover, generous dividends appear to be one good way of avoiding shareholder dissatisfaction that could result in their agreeing to a takeover bid.

How should a company choose a sensible dividend policy? If the dividend payout ratio is set too high and earnings fluctuate, maintaining the dividend can require more frequent external financing and unnecessary flotation costs. Therefore, highly variable earnings call for a low-dividend-payout ratio for the regular dividend. High earnings variability also calls for a slow speed of adjustment of the regular dividend to changes in earnings. The resulting dividend policy is conservative, and thus results in an accumulation of excess cash. The company can distribute this excess cash from time to time as an extra dividend or a special dividend. Investors who understand that these additional dividends are likely to be one-off are less likely to interpret their subsequent omission as an unfavorable signal. Alternatively, excess cash can be used to buy back some of the company's outstanding shares or to invest in suitable acquisitions.

---

[8] J. Broyles and M. Aczel (1996) "The dividend puzzle: Why pay dividends and why receive them?" *Warwick Business School Research Bureau*, No. 211.

[9] An apparent trend toward a smaller proportion of companies paying dividends is attributable at least in part to the large number of new companies established during the 1990s. New companies typically pay little or no dividends.

FURTHER READING

F. Black (1976) "The dividend puzzle," *Journal of Portfolio Management* (Winter).

R. H. Litzenberger and K. Ramaswamy (1982) "The effects of dividends on stock prices: Tax effects or information effects," *Journal of Finance*, Vol. 37 (May), 429–443.

M. H. Miller and F. Modigliani (1961) "Dividend policy, growth and the valuation of shares," *Journal of Business*, Vol. 34 (October), 411–433.

M. H. Miller (1986) "Behavioural rationality in finance: The case of dividends," *Journal of Business*, Vol. 59 (October), 451–468.

QUESTIONS AND PROBLEMS

1   Suppose that a company forecasts after-tax earnings of €100 million net of depreciation equal to €25 million per year. Suppose also that it requires financing to the amount of €60 million.

      (a)   What would be its maximum dividend payout ratio if its forecast investment were:

           (i)

           €135 million; or

           (ii)

           €115 million?

      (b)   What would the company have to do if it wants a dividend payout ratio of 20%, and to invest £135 million?

2   LINTNER PLC declared dividends in a predictable pattern. Its target dividend payout ratio averaged 55% of annual earnings. When earnings changed, however, the company usually changed its dividend only half way toward the level that the target payout ratio would imply. The last dividend was 10c per share, and the company has just announced after-tax annual earnings of 30c per share.

      (a)   What level of dividend per share would the market now expect?

      (b)   The company announces that total dividends for the year will be 10p per share. How would the market react to this announcement? Why would it react in this way?

3   FAMACO PLC announces an increase in its annual dividend. The percentage increase is the same as the percentage increase in annual earnings announced at the same time. The market had correctly anticipated the percentage increase in earnings (but not the amount of the increase in the dividend). Previous dividend changes had been well described by the Lintner model. If the stock market is efficient, which of the following describes the most likely stock market reaction to the dividend announcement?

      (a)   The share price increases.

      (b)   The share price declines.

      (c)   The share price remains about the same.

4   GROWTHTEC PLC expects after tax earnings this year to equal approximately €10 million. The expected earnings are net of depreciation equaling €3 million annually. The company expects earnings to keep growing at a rate of 20% per year. It will finance this growth by reinvesting €10 million from earnings next year. The company has no debt. Investors consider GROWTHTEC risky, and they want a 30% return on their investment in the company's equity.

(a)   Forecast GROWTHTEC's free cash flow for next year.

(b)   What is the total value of this enterprise at the discount rate of 30%? State your assumptions.

(c)   If the company decides to pay a dividend of €2 million next year, what effect, if any, would this have on its financing?

(d)   If this level of dividend payout were to continue indefinitely, what would be the net impact on the value of the enterprise? State your assumptions.

5   YIELDCO is subject to a jurisdiction operating a classical tax system. The company pays taxes on its income at the 35% corporate tax rate. The company's shareholder clientele pays taxes on dividends at 40% and on capital gains at 28%.

(a)   Suppose that the company's taxable income is €1.00 per share and it pays out all after-tax income to its shareholders. What proportion of the taxable income would shareholders receive net of all taxes? Assume that the realization of any capital gains is in the same year.

(b)   If the company pays no dividends and the shareholders realize the resulting capital gains in the same year, what proportion of the taxable income net of all taxes do the shareholders enjoy?

(c)   In the circumstances, which of the two dividend policies would be preferable?

6   PAYOUT PLC is subject to a jurisdiction operating an imputation tax system. The company pays taxes on its income at the 30% corporate tax rate. The company's shareholder clientele pays taxes on both dividends and capital gains at the marginal personal tax rate of 40%.

(a)   Suppose that the company's taxable income is €1.00 per share and it pays out all after-tax income to its shareholders. What proportion of the taxable income would shareholders receive net of all taxes? Assume that the company withholds a tax of 10% on the grossed-up dividend used as an offset against Corporation Tax. Assume that the realization of any capital gains is in the same year.

(b)   If the company pays no dividends and the shareholders realize the resulting capital gains in the same year, what proportion of the taxable income net of all taxes do the shareholders enjoy?

(c)   In the circumstances, which of the two dividend policies would be preferable? State your assumptions.

7   SENIOR CITIZEN'S PENSION FUND paid no taxes on dividend income or on capital gains. The fund operated in a classical tax jurisdiction. The tax rate on dividends was somewhat higher than on realized capital gains. The fund was highly risk-averse, and the investment manager wanted to increase the fund's excess return per unit of risk. This ratio is the Sharpe ratio. The numerator of the ratio is the difference between the expected annual return on the fund and the risk-free rate. The denominator is the standard deviation of the fund's annual return.

Previously, the fund's policy was to invest primarily for income, not capital gains. As the fund paid no tax, management thought it had an advantage in holding shares in companies that pay relatively high dividends. Shares that paid no dividends would be best left in the hands of high-tax payers. There were two problems with this strategy. First, it meant that the portfolio's holdings were concentrated on mature companies with low-growth prospects. Second, this policy left the fund less diversified than was felt to be desirable.

In her preliminary analysis, the investment manager analyzed two hypothetical portfolios. The first portfolio was similar to the existing portfolio, consisting of shares in companies with high-dividend-payout ratios. The second portfolio consisted of shares in companies that paid no dividends. Initially, she considered just three strategies:

(a)   hold only the high-dividend portfolio;
(b)   hold only the zero-dividend portfolio;
(c)   invest half of the fund in each of the two portfolios.

The relevant data are the following:

	Expected return $E(R)$	Standard deviation σ	Correlation $\rho_{1,2}$	Sharpe ratio
Portfolio 1	0.12	0.20	0.3	0.25
Portfolio 2	0.10	0.22	0.3	0.19

The following formulas from Chapter 12 are relevant:

Expected return $\qquad\qquad\qquad E(R_p) = x_1 E(R_1) + x_2 E(R_2)$

Variance $\qquad\qquad\qquad\qquad \sigma_3^2 = (x_1\sigma_1)^2 + (x_2\sigma_2)^2 + 2\rho_{1,2}(x_1\sigma_1)(x_2\sigma_2)$

Return per unit of risk $Sharpe\ Ratio = \dfrac{E(R) - R_f}{\sigma}$

where the proportions $x_1 + x_2 = 1$. The risk-free rate was equal to 5%.

Was the fund doing the right thing to focus its investment only on high-dividend-paying companies? What should the investment manager do?

8   A company has 500 million shares outstanding at 90c per share.

(a)   Calculate the company's market capitalization (the value of its equity).
(b)   Suddenly, the company announces an unexpected €50 million one-off increase in the year's after-tax earnings. What should be the effect of the announcement on the market capitalization and on the share price?
(c)   The company pays the entire 50 million as a special dividend. What will be the ex-dividend value of the equity and the ex-dividend share price?

(d)   Suppose that, instead of paying the special dividend, the company buys back €50 million worth of the company's shares from the shareholders. How many shares does this leave outstanding? What would be the resulting market capitalization? How will the resulting share price compare with the alternative of paying the dividend?

(e)   The company is subject to a classical tax system. All the company's shareholders pay taxes at the 40% rate on dividends and at the 20% rate on capital gains. How much better or worse off are the shareholders if the company buys back the shares rather than paying the special dividend?

DEFINITIONS

Market capitalization   The stock market value of a company's equity. The market price per share multiplied by the number of shares issued.

Risk-averse   Describes an investor who prefers less risk to greater risk associated with an expected return. Implies that the investor requires higher expected return as a reward for taking greater risk.

Standard deviation   Square root of the variance.

16 Capital Structure

Debt and equity represent somewhat different sources of funds for a company, and the Chief Financial Officer (CFO) would like to know the best combination of debt and equity funding to use. That is, what should be the company's capital structure. Should the apparent differences between debt and equity make any difference? Which combination of debt and equity might have the lowest cost? What influence do taxes and the costs of raising new debt and equity capital have on the capital structure decision? How can one quantify the effects of bankruptcy risk? Put another way, what combination of debt and equity financing would help to maximize the market value of the firm?

These issues represent the capital structure puzzle and have vexed finance thinkers for decades. Fortunately, evolving theory is beginning to show how a company can find its optimum capital structure.

TOPICS

This chapter considers the following:

- why capital structure matters;
- the effect of capital structure on financial risk;
- the Weighted Average Cost of Capital;
- differing views on the relevance of capital structure;
- the role of arbitrage;
- the debate concerning the effect of taxes on capital structure;
- the existence of optimum capital structures;
- the effect of flotation costs;
- a combined approach to optimizing a firm's capital structure.

16-1 WHAT IS CAPITAL STRUCTURE AND WHY DOES IT MATTER?

CAPITAL STRUCTURE

A company's capital structure is the mix of different sources of capital the company uses to finance its activities. At the broadest level, capital structure concerns the relative proportions of debt and equity financing. Debt financing consists largely of bank borrowing, financial leasing, and issues of bonds in the bond market. Equity consists largely of retained earnings and issues of additional shares in the stock market.[1] In this chapter, we are concerned with capital structure at the broadest level. That is, we would like to determine what the balance of a company's debt and equity financing should be.

IMPORTANCE

Capital structure is important for at least two reasons. First, debt and equity have different costs. These include differences between interest rates and equity required rates of return. They also include differences in securities' flotation costs, in tax treatments, and in costs associated with financial risk. Maximizing the value of the firm requires minimizing the overall cost of capital. So, an optimum capital structure must represent the combination of debt and equity financing that minimizes the sum of these different costs.

The second reason capital structure is important is that the extent to which a firm borrows affects its financial risk. Interest payments represent an additional fixed expense that increases the volatility of net income and of earnings per share. This increased level of risk increases the interest payable on bond issues. Borrowing also increases the cost of equity capital in the stock market. Furthermore, it increases the likelihood that the company could find itself in financial distress or even bankruptcy.

DEFINITIONS

Bond   An interest-bearing security with usually long-term maturity. Interest payments may be fixed or variable (floating).

Capital structure   The proportions of different forms of debt and equity constituting a company's total capital.

Capital structure puzzle   Issue concerning why companies adopt capital structures that do not make maximum use of interest payments as deductions from taxable income.

Chief Financial Officer (CFO)   A company's most senior financial manager.

Convertibles   Bonds or preferred stocks that give the holder the option (effectively a warrant) to convert the security into the issuing company's ordinary shares (common stock) according to specified terms during some stated period of years.

Debt   Sum of money or other assets owed by one party to another. Usually, a legally enforceable obligation to pay agreed interest and to repay the principal of a loan to the lender promptly on schedule.

Equity   Net worth or shareholder's capital represented by common stock (ordinary shares) and preferred stock.

---

[1] To a lesser extent companies use hybrid forms of debt and equity such as convertible bonds, preference shares, and convertible preference shares.

Financial distress   Condition in which a company might not be able to meet its obligations to creditors; that is, in danger of becoming insolvent or technically bankrupt.

Financial lease   Lease contract committing the lessee to rental payments for the economic life of the leased asset.

Financial risk   Increase in the volatility of a company's earnings due to borrowing.

Flotation costs   Transaction costs associated with the issuance of securities.

Preference shares (preferred stock)   Equity security that pays a (normally fixed) dividend. The issuer must pay the preference dividend before paying any dividends on common stock (ordinary shares). Cumulative preference shares carry forward entitlement to unpaid preference dividends. Participating preference shares also entitle holders to a share of profit.

Rate of return   After-tax cash income and capital gain divided by the investment.

Security   Bond or a share certifying legal ownership of a financial asset or a claim on the assets or cash flow of a company. Also denotes collateral for a loan.

Volatility   Standard deviation of percentage changes in the asset price. More precisely, standard deviation of changes in the natural logarithm of the asset price.

16-2 HOW CAPITAL STRUCTURE AFFECTS FINANCIAL RISK

Let us consider a simple example of how borrowing creates financial risk.

EXAMPLE 16.1

Compare the following two alternative balance sheets for the same firm. In the first case, its capital structure is entirely equity financed. In the second case, the firm borrows half its financing requirements. That is, its capital structure consists of 50% debt and 50% equity.

BALANCE SHEET WITH ALL-EQUITY FINANCING

	Assets		Liabilities
Fixed assets	1,000	Debt	0
		Equity	1,000
1,000		1,000	

BALANCE SHEET WITH 50% DEBT IN THE CAPITAL STRUCTURE

	Assets		Liabilities
Fixed assets	1,000	Debt	500
		Equity	500
1,000		1,000	

DEBT FINANCING AND RISK

Now let us consider how this difference in capital structure would affect the firm's financial risk. We can do this by comparing the ways in which its net income and earnings per share respond to changes in the business environment. Table 16.1 compares the firm's financial performance under two different scenarios. The left half of the table shows the performance of the firm without borrowing. The right half of the table shows the corresponding performance of the firm if it has borrowed 50% of its capital requirements, as in the balance sheet above. For simplicity, we ignore taxes.

Table 16.1   Operating and financial risk.

	Unlevered firm		Levered firm	
	Scenario 1	Scenario 2	Scenario 1	Scenario 2
1. Operating income	100	80	100	80
2. Interest	0	0	50	50
3. Net operating income	100	80	50	30
4. Number of shares	200	200	100	100
5. Earnings per share (EPS)	50	40	50	30
6. Change		−20%		−40%

RISK OF THE UNLEVERED FIRM

Consider first the unlevered firm in the left half of the table, which has no debt. We use two scenarios to show the performance of the firm. In Scenario 1, the firm's net operating income is 100. In Scenario 2, the net operating income falls 20% to only 80, as shown in the first row of the table. Because the firm has no debt, interest is equal to zero in the second row under both scenarios. Therefore, in Row 3, net income is still equal to 100 and 80, respectively, for Scenarios 1 and 2. Row 4 of the table indicates that the firm has issued 200 shares of equity. Dividing net income in Row 3 by the number of shares in Row 4, we obtain the corresponding EPS of 50c (€0.50) and 40c, respectively, for the two scenarios in Row 5. Finally, in Row 6 we note that both the net income and the EPS fall 20%. This decline corresponds to the 20% drop in net operating income (Row 1) between Scenarios 1 and 2.

RISK OF THE LEVERED FIRM

On the right half of the table, we have the financial performance of the same firm for the same two scenarios, but in this case, the firm uses 50% debt financing (levered firm). The calculations on this side of the table are the same as for the left side. Most of the numbers are different, however. Now the firm has interest of 50 to pay under both scenarios. This reduces net income to only 50 and 30, respectively. In Row 4, we note that the number of shares is only 100 with 50% borrowing compared with 200 for the same firm without borrowing. The reason, of course, is that with 50% borrowing we need only half as much equity. As a result, the EPSs are 50c and 30c, respectively, for the two scenarios. Therefore, we find that both net income and EPS fall 40%. This is much greater than the corresponding drop of only 20% for the all-equity financed firm.

FINANCIAL RISK

Note that the underlying business risk is the same in both halves of the table. Net operating income falls just 20% between Scenarios 1 and 2. In response to this change, the firm's financial performance also declines 20% if it is all-equity financed. If the firm borrows half its capital needs, however, the decline in its financial performance is twice as great between the same two scenarios. The difference between these two reflects financial risk due to borrowing.

SOME CONCLUSIONS

We can draw a number of important conclusions from this simple example:

1.   Borrowing requires interest payments that reduce a firm's net income.

2.   Interest expense is a fixed cost that increases the volatility of net income.

3.   Borrowing reduces the need to issue additional equity and thus reduces the number of shares outstanding.

4.   The fact that the reduced number of shares affects the EPS is a matter of simple arithmetic and therefore has no economic significance.

5.   Interest expense is a fixed cost that increases the volatility of the EPS as a direct consequence of the resulting increase in the volatility of net income.

It is also worth noting the effect of financial risk on the cost of equity capital. Increased borrowing increases the volatility of net income and thus makes the shareholders' stake in the firm more risky. Portfolio diversification eliminates part of this additional risk for shareholders. The remaining nondiversifiable risk due to borrowing increases the beta factor for the equity. The Capital Asset Pricing Model (CAPM) suggests that an increase in the value of the beta factor increases the shareholders' required rate of return. In this way, borrowing has an implicit or "hidden" cost: it increases the cost of equity. This implicit cost of debt is in addition to the explicit cost of having to pay interest.

DEFINITIONS

Beta factor   A measure of the market risk of an asset. The factor by which mean returns on the asset reflect returns on the market portfolio.

Capital Asset Pricing Model (CAPM)   Linear model attempting to explain the expected return on a risky asset in terms of the risk-free rate, its beta factor (systematic risk), and the risk premium on the market portfolio.

Diversification   Reduction of a portfolio's risk by holding a collection of assets having returns that are not perfectly positively correlated.

Financial risk   Increase in the volatility of a company's earnings due to borrowing.

Implicit cost of debt   Increase in the cost of equity attributable to the increased borrowing.

Levered (geared) company   Company partially financed by debt.

Net operating income   Profit before deduction of interest or other (nonequity) costs of finance.

Nondiversifiable risk   Systematic risk. Market risk. Risk that portfolio diversification cannot eliminate.

Portfolio   Collection of investments in financial securities and other assets.

Scenario   Plausible sequence of events.

Share (stock)   Security legally certifying that its registered holder is a part-owner of the corporation.

Unlevered (ungeared) company   Company that has no debt.

16-3 THE WEIGHTED AVERAGE COST OF CAPITAL

VALUE MAXIMIZATION

The value of a security relates inversely to the cost of capital associated with it. For example, if the cost of equity goes up, share prices must go down (the higher the discount rate the lower the present value (PV) of dividends). A similar relationship applies to the relationship between interest rates and bond prices. The minimum cost of capital for a firm would reflect the optimum combination of the costs of its debt and equity. Getting the combination right should thus minimize the market's discount rate and maximize the market value of the firm. Believing this, the CFO and the Treasurer attempt to minimize the weighted average cost of capital (WACC).

WEIGHTED AVERAGE COST OF CAPITAL

As discussed in more detail in Chapter 13, the WACC is just the weighted average of the after-tax costs of debt and equity. The weights are the target proportions of debt and equity financing for the relevant period.

Interest is tax-deductible in most countries, and the cost of debt in the WACC would be the expected average corporate borrowing rate net of corporate taxes.

The internal rate of return (IRR) on investment in the company's shares provides one means of estimating the cost of equity. The cash flows in this IRR calculation are the investment (share price) and the income per share (dividends and equity buybacks). Another useful method is to use the CAPM.

EXPLICIT COST OF DEBT

The explicit (interest) cost of debt is low because lenders bear less risk and thus require a lower rate of return than do shareholders. Risk is less for a lender because the interest payments and repayments agreed in the loan contract are legally enforceable by the lender. The contract may also impose restrictive covenants and specify assets as security for the loan. Covenants stipulate circumstances in which the lender can demand immediate repayment of the entire loan. These obligations contribute to the firm's financial risk mentioned earlier. Financial risk due to increased borrowing increases the probability and thus the expected costs of financial distress and bankruptcy. Therefore, a company that incurs more financial risk with increased borrowing reduces its credit rating in the bond market and has to pay a higher rate of interest to compensate the lenders for their share of these expected extra costs.

IMPLICIT COST OF DEBT

In addition, the nondiversifiable part of the financial risk from increased borrowing increases the shareholders' required rate of return. This increase in the cost of equity represents the additional, implicit cost of debt.

In addition to the extra risk, equity shareholders bear the cost if the company finds itself in distress and has to forgo valuable investment opportunities. Additional costs falling in part on the debt holders are the legal and administrative costs associated with receivership and bankruptcy and losses on forced sales of assets.

WHY CAPITAL STRUCTURE IS CONTENTIOUS

Due to increased financial risk, the costs of both debt and equity increase with increased borrowing. So, it is not clear that additional borrowing offers any net advantage. Increased borrowing need not reduce the weighted average cost of debt and equity. Without clarification of this issue, we do not really know whether capital structure has any relevance for the value of the firm.

DEFINITIONS

Buyback   Buying the company's shares from its shareholders instead of using the cash to pay them dividends.

Cost of capital   Cost of funds used by a company for investment.

Cost of debt   Internal rate of return on the after-tax cash flows (interest and repayments) of the company's borrowings and debt securities.

Discount rate   Required rate of return used in the calculation of a discount factor.

Expected (mean)   Probability-weighted average of all possible outcomes for a random variable.

Internal rate of return (IRR)   Discount rate that would make the net present value for an investment equal to zero.

Present value (PV)   Value of an investment now as the cost of a comparable investment in the financial market (calculated by multiplying the investment's expected after-tax cash income by the appropriate discount factors).

Treasurer   Senior financial manager reporting directly to the Chief Financial Officer. Primarily responsible for funding and cash management.

Weighted Average Cost of Capital (WACC)   Value-weighted average of expected after-tax costs of debt and equity financing.

16-4 CONTRASTING VIEWS ON THE RELEVANCE OF CAPITAL STRUCTURE

There have been three main views concerning the relevance of capital structure: the net income view, the net operating income view, and the traditional view. We consider the net income view first.

NET INCOME VIEW

The net income view suggests that companies should borrow as much as possible in order to take full advantage of the lower cost of debt. The assumption is that the costs of debt and equity remain constant as borrowing is increased. On this basis, it would be best to borrow as much as possible in order to minimize the WACC.

EXAMPLE 16.2

Table 16.2 provides a simple example of the net income view. In the table, the after-tax cost of borrowing is 5%, and we keep the cost of equity constant at 10%. As a result, the WACC declines with increasing debt as shown in the fifth column of the table. Figure 16.1 graphs the corresponding relationships between the costs of debt and equity and the WACC for the example in the table.

This view assumes that the costs of debt and equity remain constant. Therefore, the WACC declines as the lower cost debt receives greater weight. For example, in the second row of the table, the calculation of the value of the WACC is:

$$WACC = Proportion\ of\ Debt \times Cost\ of\ Debt\ after\ Tax$$
$$+ Proportion\ of\ Equity \times Cost\ of\ Equity \quad actually$$
$$= 0.25 \times 0.05 + 0.75 \times 0.10 = 0.088 \approx 0,0875$$

The table also assumes that the net operating income is a perpetuity equal to €1 per year. So, the value of the firm in this row is equal to 1 / 0.0875 = €11.4.

In the bottom row, the firm's financing is entirely debt. So, the WACC falls to just 5%. As a result, the value of the firm rises to the maximum of 1 /0.05 = €20. This looks like an easy way to maximize the value of the firm. Do you believe it? (NO)

Table 16.2 Net income view.

Cost of debt (1)	Cost of equity (2)	Proportion of debt (3)	Proportion of equity (4)	WACC (5)	Value of the firm (6)
0.05	0.10	0	1	0.100	10.0
0.05	0.10	0.25	0.75	0.088	11.4
0.10	0.50	0.50	0.50	0.075	13.3
0.05	0.10	0.75	0.25	0.063	16.0
0.05	0.10	1	0	0.050	20.0

mistake   but   no matter

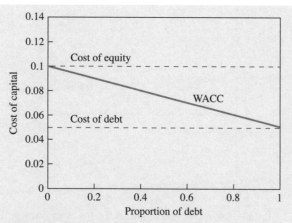

Figure 16.1 WACC according to the net income view.

The net income view is the naive view because it ignores the effect of increased borrowing on the cost of equity. We cannot know the behavior of the WACC without first knowing how changes in the capital structure affect the cost of equity. Although the net income view seems superficially plausible, it has no firm economic foundation.

NET OPERATING INCOME VIEW

Net operating income differs from net income in that it omits deduction of interest expense. The net operating income view asserts that the value of the firm depends only on its net operating income. It does not depend on the division of the net operating income between the company's shareholders and lenders.

Let X represent the net operating income per period and R represent the market's required rate of return for this income given its perceived risk. If the operating income X is a perpetuity, then the value of the firm is:

$$V = \frac{X}{R}$$

So, if V only depends on X and R only depends on the risk of X, then capital structure is irrelevant to the value of the firm. In the absence of bankruptcy costs, leverage affects neither the operating income nor its risk and discount rate. The reason financial leverage has no effect is that the operating income is the firm's income before deduction of interest expense.

Figure 16.2 illustrates the net operating income view. If the value of the firm remains unchanged as shown in the figure, then the WACC cannot change either. This implies that:

$$WACC = R$$

Therefore, the value of the WACC only depends on the risk of X, the net operating income. If the WACC remains unchanged, the cost of equity must increase. The increase must be just sufficient to keep the WACC constant when the proportion of debt increases. So, according to this view, firms do not have optimum capital structures.

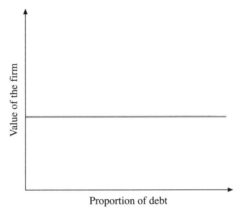

Figure 16.2   Value of the firm according to the net operating income view.

TRADITIONAL VIEW

The traditional view holds that a moderate amount of leverage is beneficial. The view asserts that small amounts of borrowing do not cause the cost of equity to increase fast enough in the WACC to offset fully the lower after-tax cost of the additional debt. If the operating income X is a perpetuity, then the value of the firm is:

$$V = \frac{X}{WACC}$$

As the proportion of debt increases from zero, the WACC falls at first, increasing the value of the firm. As the proportion of debt increases further, however, the cost of equity rises more rapidly. The cost of equity rises for two reasons. First, increasing debt increases financial risk and the resulting beta factor. Second, increased debt increases the likelihood and expected costs of financial distress. Therefore, at some point the cost of equity rises so quickly that the WACC starts increasing. The optimum level of debt that maximizes the value of the firm is at the point where the WACC stops falling and starts increasing.

Figure 16.3 illustrates the traditional view. At the top of the curve, the increased cost of equity fully

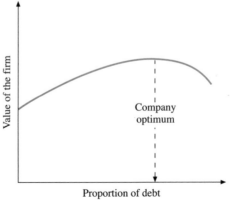

Figure 16.3   Value of the firm according to the traditional view.

offsets the benefit of borrowing. At this optimum level of debt indicated by the dashed line, the WACC is at its minimum, thus maximizing the value of the firm.

Clearly, it is not possible for all three views to be correct simultaneously. How shall we resolve these differing views?

DEFINITIONS

Net income view (naive view)   Contention that a company can reduce its weighted average cost of capital by increasing its borrowing to take advantage of a lower explicit cost of debt.

Net operating income view   Contention that the value of the firm only depends on its net operating income and is not affected by the division of the income between equity and debt holders.

Perpetuity   Equal sum of money paid in each period for ever.

Traditional view   Contention that a moderate amount of borrowing is beneficial.

16-5 ARBITRAGE AND THE NET OPERATING INCOME VIEW

MODIGLIANI AND MILLER'S PROPOSITION I

Modigliani and Miller's Proposition I (1958) is the starting point for the modern theory of capital structure.[2] The proposition states that the value of a firm only depends on its capitalized operating cash flow and not on the division of the company's funding between the providers of its capital. So, the proposition asserts that the net operating income view is correct. According to Proposition I, firms do not have optimum capital structures.

ARBITRAGE PROOF

Modigliani and Miller's (1958, 1969) famous arbitrage proof of Proposition I provides strong support for the view that capital structure is irrelevant to the value of the firm.[3] Their contributions to the theory of capital structure were responsible in part for an award of a Nobel Prize in economics for each of them.

The 1969 arbitrage proof used the following argument. An investor could obtain, for example, 10% of an unlevered firm's net operating income by buying 10% of its equity. Suppose now that debt partly finances an identical firm with the same net operating income. Suppose also that the market gives a higher value to the second firm simply because it borrowed.

---

[2] F. Modigliani and M. H. Miller (1958) "The cost of capital, corporation finance and the theory of investment," *American Economic Review*, Vol. 48 (June), 261–297.

[3] F. Modigliani and M. H. Miller (1969) "Reply to Heins and Sprenkle," *American Economic Review*, Vol. 59 (September), 592–595.

The investor could buy 10% of the levered firm's debt (bonds) and 10% of its equity. By doing so, the investor can obtain the same income as from taking a 10% holding in the unlevered firm's equity. Unfortunately, it would cost him more to obtain this income from the levered firm because the prices of its securities reflect the higher market value of the firm.

What would you do in this situation? No doubt, you would sell the high-priced securities in the levered firm and buy the cheaper equity in the unlevered firm, and you would still be getting the same income. This is arbitrage, simultaneously selling one asset for more and buying virtually the same asset for less. Arbitrage yields an immediate profit with no net investment and virtually no risk.[4] Others would arbitrage in the same way until the two firms have identical market values.

IMPLICATIONS OF ARBITRAGE

The implication is that arbitrage does not permit the value of a firm to change as the proportion of the firm's debt increases. This means that the WACC cannot change. For example, if the operating income X were a perpetuity, then the value of the firm would be:

$$V = \frac{X}{WACC}$$

Therefore, if V and X remain unchanged by debt, the WACC must also remain unchanged. This implies that the cost of equity must rise just sufficiently to keep the WACC constant as the proportion of debt in the WACC increases.

EFFECT OF BORROWING ON THE COST OF EQUITY

We can derive this effect on the cost of equity from the WACC equation (before tax):

$$WACC = \text{Proportion of Debt} \times \text{Cost of Debt} + \text{Proportion of Equity} \times \text{Cost of Equity}$$

With a little algebra we have Modigliani and Miller's Proposition II:

$$\text{Cost of Equity} = WACC + \frac{\text{Proportion of Debt}}{\text{Proportion of Equity}} (WACC - \text{Cost of Debt})$$

$$= WACC + \frac{\text{Debt}}{\text{Equity}} (WACC - \text{Cost of Debt})$$

Proposition II says that a company's cost of equity is directly proportional to the ratio of its debt financing to its equity financing.

---

[4] Perfect arbitrage is difficult to achieve in practice. The assets bought and sold must be similar but rarely are identical. Imperfect correlation between the market values of the assets in an arbitrage results in basis risk. Additional exposure to risk arises from not being able to execute the buying and selling transactions simultaneously. Even imperfect arbitrage still provides a persuasive argument in favor of the Modigliani and Miller Theorem, however.

Table 16.3 Net income view.

Proportion of debt	Proportion of equity	Cost of debt	WACC	Cost of equity
0	1	0.05	0.10	0.10
0.25	0.75	0.05	0.10	0.12
0.50	0.50	0.05	0.10	0.15
0.75	0.25	0.05	0.10	0.25
0.90	0.10	0.05	0.10	0.55

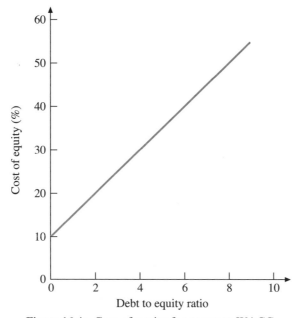

Figure 16.4 Cost of equity for constant WACC.

Table 16.3 shows calculations based on this equation if the cost of debt after tax equals 5%, and the WACC remains constant at 10%. Figure 16.4 plots the resulting costs of equity. For example, in the bottom row of the table the proportion of debt rises to 90% and the proportion of equity falls to only 10%. The cost of debt is still 5% and the WACC remains constant at 10%. The cost of equity in the final row must rise to:

$$Cost\ of\ Equity = 0.10 + \frac{0.90}{0.10}(0.10 - 0.05) = 0.55 \quad or \quad 55\%$$

Figure 16.4 based on this table shows the way the cost of equity changes with increased debt as implied by Modigliani and Miller's Proposition II.

MODIGLIANI AND MILLER'S ASSUMPTIONS

The purpose of a theory such as Modigliani and Miller's is to abstract a simplified picture of the real world to help us understand more clearly the essence of what we observe. Formulating a theory requires simplifying assumptions, and thus the nature of the simplifications determines the limitations of the theory. Modigliani and Miller made the following assumptions:

1.   The capital market is frictionless.

2.   Investors can borrow on the same terms as a corporation.

3.   There are no costs to bankruptcy and financial distress.

4.   Firms issue only two types of claim, debt and equity.

5.   All firms are in the same risk class.

6.   There are no taxes.

7.   All cash flow streams are perpetuities.

8.   Investors possess all relevant information.

9.   Managers maximize shareholder's wealth.

Potentially the most serious limitations of the original Modigliani and Miller position are the assumptions that there are no transaction costs or taxes. Because interest payments are tax-deductible by corporations in virtually all countries, the Modigliani and Miller Propositions first came in for criticism mainly on the zero-tax assumption.

DEFINITIONS

Correlation   Association between two random variables.

Transaction costs   Stockbroker's commission plus the bid-offer spread plus the adverse effect of the transaction on the market price (plus stamp duty on stock purchases in the UK).

16-6 TAXES IN A CLASSICAL TAX SYSTEM

A two-tier classical tax system was the context of the capital structure debate. In the assumed tax system, the corporate tax on net income is the first tier. The second tier is the personal tax on dividends. For simplicity, authors usually lump together the taxes on dividends and capital gains as one combined personal tax when analyzing the capital structure problem.

AFTER-TAX INCOME TO DEBT AND EQUITY INVESTORS

Shareholders receive a company's net income after both corporate and personal taxes, and the debt holders receive interest income after tax. Thus, the total income after tax to both shareholders and debt holders is:

Total Income after Tax to Equity and Debt Holders = (Operating Income − Interest)

$$\times (1 - T_C)(1 - T_E) + Interest \times (1 - T_B)$$

where T_C, T_E, and T_B are the tax rates being paid on corporate net income, shareholders' equity income, and debt holders' interest income, respectively.

ANNUAL TAX BENEFIT FROM CORPORATE BORROWING

By rearranging terms, we can write the equation as:

Total Income after Tax to Equity and Debt Holders = Operating Income

$$\times (1 - T_C)(1 - T_E) + Interest$$
$$\times [(1 - T_B) - (1 - T_C)(1 - T_E)]$$

The last term on the right-hand side represents the annual tax benefit from corporate borrowing. If we assume a constant level of borrowing, this annual benefit is a perpetuity.

VALUE OF THE TAX BENEFIT

In order to obtain the value added to the firm by this perpetuity, we need its PV. The PV of a perpetuity is the annual cash flow divided by the discount rate. In this case, we divide by the after-tax interest rate:

$$\frac{Interest\ Rate \times Amount\ Borrowed \times [(1 - T_B) - (1 - T_C)(1 - T_E)]}{Interest\ Rate \times (1 - T_B)}$$

$$= Amount\ Borrowed \times \left[1 - \frac{(1 - T_C)(1 - T_E)}{(1 - T_B)}\right]$$

Note that the interest rate cancels in this formulation, and thus the result is the same for any nonzero rate of interest.

HOW TAXES AFFECT THE VALUE OF THE FIRM

Consequently, the total value V of a levered firm is the unlevered value V_U plus the additional PV $G \times B$ of the tax benefit from borrowing a constant amount B:

$$V = V_U + G \times B$$

where

$$G = 1 - \frac{(1 - T_C)(1 - T_E)}{(1 - T_B)}$$

Therefore, the answer to the question whether the tax effects of borrowing add any value to the firm depends on whether the value of G is greater than zero. It is easy to see that the answer depends on what we believe should be the relative values of the three different tax rates in the formula for G. Different authors used differing assumptions for these tax rates and therefore reached different conclusions.

DEFINITION

Classical tax system   Tax system in which the Government taxes corporate income at the corporate tax rate and then taxes shareholders for dividends received and for capital gains at the relevant personal rates of tax.

16-7 TAX EFFECTS IN MODIGLIANI AND MILLER'S EQUILIBRIUM

Unfortunately for their famous theorem, Modigliani and Miller had assumed a world without taxes ($G = 0$). In most countries, interest is tax-deductible for companies, however. Five years later in 1963, they introduced corporate taxes into the picture.[5]

MODIGLIANI AND MILLER WITH CORPORATE TAXES

Implicitly, Modigliani and Miller assumed that financial market rates reflect a before-tax equilibrium in which taxes have no effect on the relationship between market rates of interest on corporate borrowing and the cost of equity. Furthermore, they only considered corporate taxes. On this basis the factor G becomes:

$$G = 1 - \frac{(1 - T_C)(1 - T_E)}{(1 - T_B)}$$

$$= 1 - \frac{(1 - T_C)(1 - 0)}{(1 - 0)}$$

$$G = T_C$$

Because G is now equal to T_C, it is greater than zero. Therefore, they concluded that a firm could increase its value by borrowing more. That is:

$$V_G = V_U + G \times B$$

$$= V_U + T_C B$$

Modigliani and Miller concluded that the value added by the tax benefit of borrowing equals the amount borrowed multiplied by the corporate tax rate. This value remains unchanged for any interest rate greater than zero. Accordingly, since the corporate tax rate T_C is a large percentage (historically 30–50% in various countries) a firm could add much value simply by increasing its borrowing B.

This result implies that a company should attempt to borrow sufficiently to exhaust all its taxable income. Modigliani and Miller suggested borrowing up to the limit frequently imposed by lenders or by the company's Articles of Association.

Well, not many companies borrow in this extreme manner so something seems to be wrong in practice with this equally famous conclusion! One cannot really get away with ignoring the effect of taxes on the relationship between the market costs of debt and equity capital. For example, if the effect of taxes is to increase the market rate of interest relative to the cost of equity, then borrowing at this higher interest rate might not be quite such a good thing after all.

[5] F. Modigliani and M. Miller (1963) "Taxes and the cost of capital: A correction," *American Economic Review*, Vol. 53 (June), 433–443.

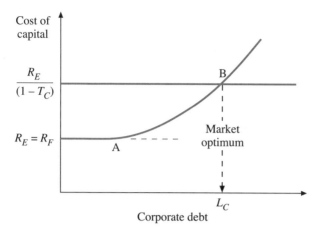

Figure 16.5 Miller's equilibrium.

16-8 TAX EFFECTS IN MILLER'S AFTER-TAX EQUILIBRIUM

In 1977, Merton Miller had second thoughts.[6] He changed a crucial assumption. The new assumption is that financial market rates reflect an after-tax equilibrium. Miller's equilibrium reflects the effects of both corporate taxes on net income and personal taxes on interest income.

SUPPLY OF CORPORATE DEBT

An after-tax equilibrium changes the corporate borrowing interest rate relative to the cost of equity. In Miller's world, the advantage of the deduction of interest from taxable income increases the supply of corporate debt by all companies, thus driving down corporate bond prices and driving up the corresponding borrowing rates relative to the cost of equity.

Figure 16.5 illustrates this process. The horizontal axis represents the total amount of borrowing by the corporate sector in the financial market. The vertical axis measures the costs of debt and equity. The upper horizontal line in the figure represents the highest before-tax interest rate that corporations are willing to pay relative to the risk-free rate on equity. The dashed horizontal line represents the risk-free rate on equity. In Miller's world, all companies pay Corporation Tax at the full rate T_C. Therefore, the relationship between these two rates is governed by:

$$Borrowing\ Rate \times (1 - T_C) \leq Risk\text{-}free\ Rate\ on\ Equity$$

Thus

$$Borrowing\ Rate \leq \frac{Risk\text{-}free\ Rate\ on\ Equity}{(1 - T_C)}$$

---

[6] M. Miller (1977) "Debt and taxes," *Journal of Finance*, Vol. 32 (May), 261–276.

DEMAND FOR CORPORATE DEBT

That is, firms are willing to pay no more interest after tax than the cost of equivalent equity. If the borrowing rate were to be higher than this, they would issue new equity capital instead of issuing bonds.

The curve in the figure represents the lowest lending rate of interest that individual lenders would be willing to accept, depending on the tax rates T_B that they pay. The smallest after-tax rate of interest that each lender would accept must be no less than the equivalent risk-free rate on equity:

$$Lending\ Rate \times (1 - T_B) \geq Risk\text{-}free\ Rate\ on\ Equity$$

If the lending rate after tax were less than this, the lender would prefer to invest in comparable equity.[7]

Potentially, corporate borrowers can get the best deal from non-taxpaying lenders such as pension funds. Because pension funds pay no tax, they can accept a relatively low lending rate and still have income greater than from comparable equity. The lowest lending rate the zero taxpayer can accept is at Point A on the curve and is equal to the risk-free rate on equity. Corporations would want to borrow as much as possible from the zero-rate taxpayers to get the low interest rate these lenders can accept.

Unfortunately, the zero-tax payers have a limited appetite for corporate bonds. They like to maintain balanced portfolios that include other financial assets as well. At Point A in Figure 16.5, the corporate sector has sold all the bonds it can to the zero-taxpayers. It can sell more bonds to low taxpayers on the right of A, however. The minimum rate that these additional lenders would be willing to accept can still be attractive to corporations:

$$\frac{Risk\text{-}free\ Rate\ on\ Equity}{(1 - T_B)} \leq Lending\ Rate < \frac{Risk\text{-}free\ Rate\ on\ Equity}{(1 - T_C)}$$

It is evident that a higher tax rate T_B requires a correspondingly higher interest rate to satisfy lenders in this tax bracket.

MILLER'S EQUILIBRIUM

Any lender who pays tax at a lower rate than the corporations do can offer a lending rate that is attractive to both the lender and to corporate borrowers. So, corporations continue to sell bonds at higher rates of interest to lenders paying ever-higher rates of tax as we move to the right in the figure.

This advantageous process has to end somewhere, and it does so at Point B, Miller's equilibrium. At Point B, the only remaining lenders are those, such as banks, that pay the same rate of tax T_C as corporations:[8]

$$T_B^* = T_C$$

---

[7] Miller analyzed this question under certainty, and thus his conclusions would relate to zero-risk equity directly comparable with risk-free debt. The required rate of return on zero-risk equity would be the risk-free rate.

[8] Miller treated bond issues as the only source of debt for companies. Therefore Miller's bond equilibrium breaks down in any tax regime in which the highest rate of tax paid by bondholders is less than the corporate tax rate. In the Modified Miller Equilibrium discussed below, this ceases to be a problem.

At this point the interest rate has risen to the point where lending and borrowing are a breakeven proposition for both marginal lenders and marginal borrowers, all of whom pay taxes at the corporate tax rate T_C. Breakeven means that the after-tax cost of borrowing equals the cost of comparable equity. This equilibrium corporate borrowing rate is:

$$Corporate\ Borrowing\ Rate = \frac{Risk\text{-}free\ Rate\ on\ Equity}{(1 - T_C)}$$

OPTIMUM AGGREGATE CAPITAL STRUCTURE

At this equilibrium point, we have the optimum capital structure L_C for the corporate sector as a whole. This point is optimum because the corporations will have minimized their cost of capital. If they tried to borrow more, the interest rate would have to rise above the breakeven level. If they borrowed less, they would lose some of the advantage of borrowing from lenders paying a lower rate of tax.

NO NET TAX BENEFIT TO THE MARGINAL BORROWERS

Once established in this way, the corporate borrowing rate becomes the rate paid on all borrowing. Individual companies that pay the full rate of Corporation Tax do not have an optimal capital structure. There is no optimum for them because the equilibrium corporate borrowing rate in Miller's world is the breakeven borrowing rate for corporations paying the corporation tax rate T_C. No matter how much or how little individual companies choose to borrow, they gain no advantage relative to alternative equity financing.

Miller showed in this way that $T_B^* = T_C$ in his after-tax equilibrium, implying that there is no net tax benefit to borrowing. That is, G equals zero:

$$G = 1 - \frac{(1 - T_C)(1 - T_E)}{(1 - T_B)}$$
$$= 1 - \frac{(1 - T_C)(1 - 0)}{(1 - T_C)}$$
$$G = 0$$

WHO GETS THE TAX BENEFIT?

Nevertheless, the Government loses taxes from companies deducting interest expense from taxable income. So, somebody must be getting the benefit of this subsidy. In Miller's equilibrium, the marginal lenders pay the same rate of tax as the corporate sector, but the other lenders pay less. These other lenders get the tax benefit of corporate borrowing indirectly in the form of the higher interest rate on which they pay little or no tax.

THE CAPITAL STRUCTURE PUZZLE

So, in 1977 Miller returned to the original 1958 Modigliani and Miller view: a company cannot increase its value by adjusting its capital structure.[9] Here we have the capital structure puzzle.

---

[9] M. H. Miller (1977) "Debt and taxes," *Journal of Finance*, Vol. 32 (May), 261–276.

Although most financial managers believe that capital structure affects the value of the firm, two of the world's foremost financial economists were unable to find any satisfactory basis for this claim.

The remainder of this chapter is devoted to the solution of this puzzle.

16-9 THE EXISTENCE OF OPTIMUM CAPITAL STRUCTURES

It should be clear by now that the capital structure puzzle results from the simplifying assumptions employed in theories that assert that capital structure is irrelevant. Assume away key factors, and you cannot solve the puzzle. By introducing significant additional factors of concern to financial managers, we can learn how to obtain a capital structure that minimizes the costs of financing.

TAXABLE INCOME IS UNCERTAIN

The first factor that we shall consider is the effect of uncertain taxable income on the effective tax rates paid by firms.

In 1980, DeAngelo and Masulis argued that debt increases the probability of a firm exhausting all its taxable income with interest and other tax deductions (allowances).[10] The resulting expected delays for deductions means that firms expect to pay effective rates of tax that are less than the full rate T_C of Corporation Tax. They showed that if firms thus pay differing expected effective rates of tax, then they can have optimal capital structures in the resulting equilibrium.

A FIRM'S EFFECTIVE CORPORATE TAX RATE UNDER UNCERTAINTY

Corporate income is subject to chance events that are largely beyond the control of management. If a company finds itself with little or no taxable income in a particular year, it must carry some deductions forward to subsequent, more profitable years. This reduces the PV of the deductions.

EXAMPLE 16.3

Suppose that Firm j expects to have to delay deducting interest expense for three years, and that the rate of interest is 7%. Then in this case its expected effective rate of tax T_j is:

$$T_j = \frac{T_C}{(1+i)^\tau}$$
$$= \frac{T_C}{(1.07)^3} = 0.816 \times T_C$$

where τ represents the number of years it would be necessary to carry forward deductions for additional interest payments and flotation costs. In this example, the effective rate is little more than 80% of the Corporation Tax rate.

---

[10] H. DeAngelo and R. Masulis (1980) "Optimal capital structure under corporate and personal taxation," *Journal of Financial Economics* (March), 3–30.

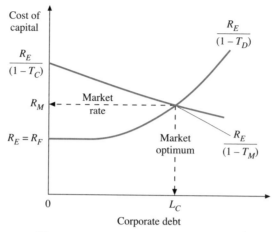

Figure 16.6 Modified Miller equilibrium.

Figure 16.6 illustrates the resulting modified Miller equilibrium when firms pay differing expected effective rates of tax. This figure is a simple but crucial alteration to Figure 16.5. In the earlier figure, the most interest that corporations were willing to pay was the same for all firms and thus represented by a horizontal straight line. This horizontal line becomes a downward sloping curve in Figure 16.6, however. The curve slopes downward now because, when corporations borrow more, they increase the likelihood that they will have to delay getting their deductions for interest expense. The result is that the corporations are unwilling to pay as high a rate of interest. The corporate borrowing rate R_M is now lower in the modified equilibrium because the marginal borrower pays an expected effective tax rate T_m that is less than the Corporation Tax rate. That is, if T_m is less than T_C, then:

$$\text{Acceptable Borrowing Rate for Company} \leq \frac{\text{Risk-free Rate on Equity}}{(1 - T_m)}$$

$$< \frac{\text{Risk-free Rate on Equity}}{(1 - T_C)}$$

AN OPTIMUM CAPITAL STRUCTURE UNDER UNCERTAINTY

Figure 16.7 illustrates why individual firms can have optimum capital structures in this modified Miller equilibrium. The individual firm sees the market rate of interest R_M and considers whether this rate is more or less than the most it is willing to pay. On the left of Point A in the figure, the firm is willing to pay more than the market rate of interest, so it should borrow more. On the right of Point A, it finds that the market rate of interest is more than it is willing to pay. It would use equity financing to repay some of its existing debt. Therefore, the proportion L_j of borrowing at Point A represents the optimum capital structure for the firm under uncertainty, according to DeAngelo and Masulis.

DeAngelo and Masulis made an important contribution to the capital structure debate. They showed that in an uncertain world companies can have optimal capital structures. Unfortunately, the DeAngelo and Masulis framework on its own does not generate the correct equilibrium or the right capital structures. One reason is that they assume along with Miller that there are no

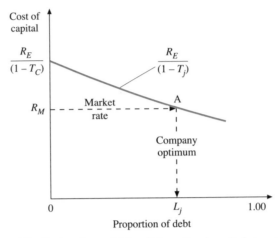

Figure 16.7 DeAngelo and Masulis's optimal capital structure.

transaction costs. The flotation costs of issuing bonds and shares can be significant and need to be included if we want to determine a firm's optimum capital structure.

DEFINITION

Uncertainty   Risk not measurable with historical data.

16-10 THE RELEVANCE OF FLOTATION COSTS

PECKING ORDER THEORY

Myers' Pecking Order Theory (1984) suggests that firms use financing with the lowest flotation cost first. This financing would be retained earnings, followed by debt, then by equity issues.[11] Because retained earnings arise internally, this source of equity does not involve any flotation costs. Therefore, retained earnings are a relatively attractive source of finance compared with issues of debt and equity securities. A debt issue is preferred to an equity issue according to Pecking Order Theory because typically the costs of floating a bond issue are less than the corresponding costs for issuing equity.

OPTIMUM FLOTATION COSTS

An implication of the Pecking Order Theory is that transaction costs are greatest for the extremes of too little and too much borrowing. With too little borrowing, a firm must pay the high costs of issuing equity when retained earnings are insufficient. With too much borrowing, on the other hand, the firm must pay the costs of floating bond issues. Pecking Order Theory suggests that capital structure should minimize the transaction costs associated with issuing securities. Since

---

[11] S. C. Myers (1984) "The capital structure puzzle," *Journal of Finance*, Vol. 39 (July), 581–582.

debt and equity financing are substitutes, the firm should minimize the *net* of equity and debt flotation costs. From a strictly transaction cost perspective, the firm therefore should borrow just sufficiently to minimize the need to issue equity.

The importance of Myers' Pecking Order Theory is that it spotlights the role of net flotation costs on optimum capital structures. Of course, Pecking Order Theory focuses too narrowly on flotation costs to determine a correct optimum capital structure. We need to bring other significant factors such as tax effects and financial risk back into view.

DEFINITION

Pecking Order Theory   Proposition that firms use financing with the lowest flotation cost before using other financing with higher flotation cost.

16-11 A COMBINED APPROACH

Refining the optimum capital structure requires synthesizing the best of recent developments. What we shall call the Combined Approach suggests that individual companies have optimum capital structures that represent the best tradeoff between:

1.   Net tax benefit.

2.   Flotation costs.

3.   Costs due to financial risk.

These three important factors modify the Miller equilibrium of Figure 16.6. The upper supply curve representing the most interest that borrowers are willing to pay must now also reflect the difference between the annualized equity and debt flotation costs. Firms are willing to pay slightly more after-tax interest relative to the cost of comparable equity[12] because the flotation cost is lower for debt.

The lower demand curve represents the lowest interest rate acceptable to lenders. This must now also reflect the credit risk spread. The credit risk spread is the additional interest required by lenders to recompense them for credit risk. For example, if the firm should default, the lenders cannot expect repayment of their loans in full.

The financial market seeks an after-tax equilibrium rate of interest relative to the cost of comparable equity, and this equilibrium implies an optimum amount of borrowing for the corporate sector as a whole. Introduction of flotation costs and the credit risk spread does not alter this broad conclusion. These additional factors increase the rate of interest paid by marginal borrowers and reduce the total amount of borrowing by the corporate sector, however.

---

[12] Comparable equity must have the same risk as debt. While the beta value of variable interest rate debt is likely to be very close to zero, the risk of fixed rate debt is greater. Longer maturity fixed rate debt has larger beta values, but normally less than around 0.30.

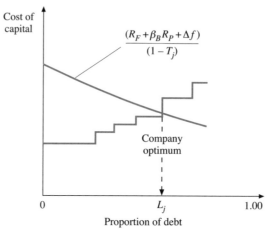

Figure 16.8 Combined optimum capital structure.

OPTIMUM CAPITAL STRUCTURE FOR THE FIRM

We now have the means of identifying optimum capital structures for individual companies reflecting the effects of taxes, flotation costs, and credit risk.

FAVORABLE RATES FOR THE BORROWER

Figure 16.8 is similar to Figure 16.7. The upper curve represents the most interest that a borrower should be willing to pay. In addition to the firm's expected tax position, this must now also reflect the difference between the after-tax difference Δf between the annualized (percentage) flotation costs of equity and debt.[13] The firm should be willing to pay slightly more interest relative to the cost of comparable equity if the annualized flotation cost for a new debt issue is less than for a new equity issue. The curve represents the following:

Acceptable Borrowing Rate for Company $\leq$

$$\frac{Required\ Rate\ on\ Comparable\ Equity + \Delta Flotation\ Cost}{1 - T_j}$$

where

$$T_j = \frac{T_C}{(1 + i)^\tau}$$

where τ represents the number of years it would be necessary to carry forward deductions for additional interest payments and flotation costs. Comparable equity has the same beta value β_B as the bond issue under consideration. Consequently, the CAPM gives:

Rate of Return on Comparable Equity $= R_F + \beta_B \times$ *Risk Premium on the Market Portfolio*

$$= R_F + \beta_B R_P$$

---

[13] The annualized flotation cost for equity equals the flotation cost multiplied by the investors' required rate of return on equity. For debt it is the flotation cost divided by the annuity factor $A_{N,R}$, where N is the number of years until the debt must be refinanced and R is the interest rate on the debt.

FAVORABLE RATES FOR THE LENDER

The lower curve in Figure 16.8 represents the lowest interest rate acceptable to lenders. In addition to the lender's expected tax position, the curve must now reflect the additional interest demanded by lenders for default risk. We cannot write an equation for this curve. It represents the investment banker's views concerning the way in which the company's borrowing would reflect its bond ratings and resulting rates of interest. The steps represent the points at which the firm's bond rating would change. The more the company borrows the greater the risk of default and the lower its bond rating. Bonds with lower ratings must pay higher rates of interest.

Having ascertained the levels of both curves in the figure, one can obtain their intersection. This intersection identifies the optimal level L_j of borrowing that obtains the best combination for the company of the tax advantage to borrowing, net flotation cost, and the credit risk spread. In this way, we have an applicable procedure for obtaining the optimal capital structure with respect to these three important factors.

There are other factors, however. For example, part of the cost of financial distress is the loss of net present value (NPV) from forgone investment opportunities. This opportunity cost is born mostly by the shareholders and has no direct effect on bond ratings. To the extent that additional factors are significant, the firm will borrow less than the maximum L_j represented in Figure 16.8.

DEFINITIONS

Default   Failure to make a payment of interest or a repayment of principal on the due date.

Net present value (NPV)   Difference between the present value of a project's expected after-tax operating cash flows and the present value of its expected after-tax investment expenditures.

Opportunity cost   Income forgone as a result of choosing an alternative course of action.

16-12 CONCLUSIONS

Finance theory is beginning to show how to find a firm's optimum capital structure.

Pecking Order Theory suggests that firms should avoid extremes of too much debt or equity requiring costly security flotations. Firms should borrow just sufficiently to avoid the higher cost of issuing additional equity. If the firm has to issue securities, it should issue bonds rather than shares because flotation costs are much lower for bonds. Flotation costs are not the only consideration, however.

DeAngelo and Masulis directed attention to the differences in tax positions of individual firms. Managers should seek to minimize the PV of taxes when making capital structure decisions. Firms that are most likely to get the full tax benefit of deducting interest from uncertain net income should borrow more than other firms do. Firms that are less likely to get the full benefit should borrow less and perhaps repay some of their debt.

Lenders demand a higher rate of interest when they pay a higher rate of taxes on corporate bond income than on income from shareholdings.

Taxes and flotation costs are not the only considerations, however, because borrowing increases the probability of default. Increased borrowing causes **bond-rating** agencies to lower a borrower's corporate bond rating. Lenders demand higher interest on a lower rated bond because they require additional income to cover expected losses of principal and interest when a high-risk borrower defaults.

The maximum a firm should borrow is at the intersection of the resulting two curves. The first represents the most interest the firm would be willing to pay at different levels of borrowing. This curve reflects the firm's tax position and the difference between its flotation costs for equity and for debt. The second curve represents the least interest lenders can accept. This curve reflects the rate of tax that marginal lenders pay on interest income relative to the rate they pay on income from their shareholdings. The curve also reflects the increasing interest rate premiums that lenders require as the borrower becomes less creditworthy.

The factors represented in these two intersecting curves bring us back to something like the traditional view: a little borrowing can be a good thing, but not too much.

DEFINITION

Bond rating   Rating by an agency of the credit risk of the issuer of the bond.

FURTHER READING

E. A. Altman (1983) *Corporate Financial Distress: A Complete Guide to Predicting, Avoiding and Dealing with Bankruptcy* (Chichester, UK: John Wiley & Sons).

M. J. Barclay, C. W. Smith, and R. L. Watts (1995) "The determinants of corporate leverage and dividend and policies," *Journal of Applied Corporate Finance*, Vol. 7 (Winter), 4–19.

M. C. Jensen and W. H. Meckling (1976) "Theory of the firm: Managerial behavior, agency costs and ownership structure," *Journal of Financial Economics*, Vol. 3 (October), 305–360.

F. Modigliani and M. H. Miller (1958) "The cost of capital, corporation finance and the theory of investment," *American Economic Review*, Vol. 48 (June), 261–297.

M. H. Miller (1977) "Debt and taxes," *Journal of Finance*, Vol. 32 (May), 261–276.

S. C. Myers (1984) "The capital structure puzzle," *Journal of Finance*, Vol. 39 (July), 575–592.

QUESTIONS AND PROBLEMS

I   The CFO of NETINC Ltd. believes that the company's cost of equity is 11%. The company's expected borrowing rate is 7%, and it pays Corporation Tax at 30%. One-half the company's financing is debt.

(a)   What would be the value of NETINC's WACC?

(b)   What would be the net income view of the value of the company's WACC if the company were to reduce its debt financing from one-half to one-quarter?

(c)   What would be the net operating income view of the value of the company's WACC if the company were to reduce its debt financing from one-half to one-quarter?

2   Suppose that the CFO of NETINC Ltd decides to increase the company's debt financing from one-half to three-quarters of its total financing. Based on the data in Problem 1, what would be the effect of this change in capital structure on the company's cost of equity? Assume now that the net operating income view is correct.

3   Suppose that the net income view were to be correct in Problem 1. Describe a profitable investment strategy for investors in the company's bonds and equity if the company were to reduce its debt. What does this strategy imply for the net income view?

4   TRANSNATIONAL POULTRY FARMS expects to invest €240 million in additional capacity next year. The CFO needs to decide how to fund this expansion. She first considers what would be the Pecking Order optimum financing. The company expects operating income to be €100 million next year. Interest on existing debt is €25 million annually. The full corporate rate of tax is 30%. Investors widely expect the company to pay dividends of €20 million next year. The annualized issuing cost for corporate bonds would be 0.2%, and they would then have to pay a fixed rate of interest of 7% annually on the bond. For every euro of retained earnings, the company borrows 50c from banks toward covering short-term net working capital requirements. The expected interest rate on borrowing is 7%.

The CFO felt that the Pecking Order optimum would need to satisfy the following equations:

$$Net\ Income = Net\ Operating\ Income - Interest - Flotation\ Cost$$
$$Retained\ Earnings = Net\ Income \times (1 - Tax\ Rate) - Dividends$$
$$Bank\ Borrowing = 0.5 \times Retained\ Earnings$$
$$Investment = Retained\ Earnings + Bank\ Borrowing + Bond\ Issue$$

What is the Pecking Order optimum financing package to fund this investment (each item to the nearest million euro)? [*Hint:* The Pecking Order optimum avoids unnecessary external equity financing. Find the bond issue required to fund the investment.]

5   The CFO of TRANSNATIONAL POULTRY FARMS is not satisfied with the Pecking Order solution to the company's financing problem. She feels uncomfortable about the large amount of debt in the Pecking Order optimum financing package. For example, if the company borrows too much, it is less likely to be able to deduct all the interest from current year taxable income. Deferment of interest deductions to subsequent years would reduce the PV of the tax benefit of the deductions. The following table contains her initial estimates of how long it would be before she could deduct the incremental interest from increased levels of borrowing.

Borrowing	Time lag for deductions (years)
50	0.25
100	0.50
150	1.00
200	2.00
250	3.00

If the company can borrow at 7%, calculate the effective tax rate applicable to the tax deductions for the incremental interest on each level of borrowing.

6   Suppose that the cost of floating an equity issue for TRANSNATIONAL would be 6%, and the estimated cost of equity would be 12% per year. Suppose also that the issuing cost for corporate bonds would be 2%, and the company would have to pay a fixed rate of interest of 7% annually on the bonds.

(a)   What is the expected annualized flotation cost for an issue of equity?
(b)   What is the expected annualized flotation cost for an issue of zero-coupon bonds repayable in 10 years?
(c)   What would be the net expected annualized flotation cost for equity relative to debt?

[Hint: The investor requires an annual rate of return on the full proceeds of the issue. This requires the company to earn a slightly higher annual rate of return on the net proceeds. The net proceeds are the full proceeds minus the flotation cost.]

7   After revising some of the data used previously, TRANSNATIONAL's CFO compiled the following table.

Borrowing	Effective tax rate for deductions (%)	Cost of comparable equity (%)	Annualized net after-tax flotation cost (%)
50.0	29.50	6.00	0.12
100.0	29.00	6.10	0.12
150.0	27.60	6.20	0.12
200.0	26.20	6.30	0.12
250.0	24.50	6.40	0.12

Calculate the highest level of interest that the company should be willing to pay for each level of borrowing in the table.

8   TRANSNATIONAL's CFO knew that having ascertained the most interest the company should be willing to pay (as in Problem 7), she was well on her way to estimating the optimum combination of debt and equity. Conferring with the company's investment bankers, she was able to put together the following table indicating the likely rates of interest that the company would have to pay for the levels of borrowing shown in the table.

Borrowing	Expected borrowing rate
50	0.07
100	0.07
150	0.09
200	0.09
250	0.11

Using this information together with your answer to Problem 7, obtain an estimate of the optimum borrowing for the company. [Hint: Refer to Figure 16.8.] What qualifications would you add to this result?

17 Lease Finance[1]

Leasing is a major method of financing the use of equipment. The prominence of the leasing industry demonstrates that leasing has advantages that make it competitive with other ways of financing equipment. The timing of cash flows, particularly of tax cash flows, is key to the advantage of financial leasing, while the opportunity afforded to hedge residual value risk explains the use of operating leases. In this chapter, we explain how to obtain the net present value (NPV) of leasing relative to borrowing. We shall examine two methods of lease evaluation, discussing the strengths and weaknesses of each method. Finally, we consider the economics of leasing.

TOPICS

In this chapter, we cover the following topics:

○   *leasing and ownership;*

○   *why companies lease assets;*

○   *how leasing can affect the capital investment decision;*

○   *how to value a financial lease;*

○   *how temporary non-taxpaying affects the leasing decision;*

○   *the after-tax discount rate;*

○   *the loan balance method;*

○   *the internal rate of return approach;*

○   *residual values;*

○   *interactions between leasing and investment decisions;*

○   *lease rates and competition in the leasing market.*

---

[1] Adapted with permission from J. R. Franks, J. E. Broyles, and W. T. Carleton (1985) *Corporate Finance, Concepts and Applications* (Boston: Kent).

17-1 LEASING AND OWNERSHIP

Table 17.1 lists eight ways a company can pay for the use of an asset, ranging from outright purchase at one extreme to short-term rental at another. A lease is a contract between the lessee and a lessor for the rental of a specific asset. The lessee, who is the user of the asset, decides on the kind of asset needed and the length of time it is required. The other party, the lessor, buys the asset and is its legal owner.

Of course, the user of the asset must pay rent to compensate the lessor for the capital cost, for the time value of money, and for risk. The rental payments include a premium for the risk of the lessee defaulting on lease payments. If the lessee defaults, the lessor faces a possible loss when selling the used asset. Alternatively, the lessor might re-lease the asset but usually at a lower rental.

LEASED ASSETS

A wide variety of assets are leased such as:

O *office machinery and equipment;*

O *computers;*

O *transportation equipment;*

O *construction machinery;*

O *production machinery;*

O *agricultural machinery;*

O *medical equipment;*

O *nonconstruction machinery.*

Companies such as railroads and airlines that experience periods of low earnings cannot always take full advantage of the tax shields from depreciation. Such companies that do not expect to pay taxes for some years often find leasing is preferable to buying.

FINANCIAL LEASES

The two main categories of lease are financial leases and operating leases. A financial lease is a rental contract committing the lessee to rental payments for the economic life of the asset. The rental

Table 17.1 Methods of paying for the use of an asset.

Outright purchase	Purchase with the firm's own funds
Unsecured loan	Purchase with borrowed funds not secured by the equipment
Mortgage	Purchase with funds borrowed on the security of the equipment
Conditional sale	Purchase with title passing on completion of instalment payments
Rent with an option to purchase	Rent with option to purchase title at a nominal price
Financial lease	Rent for the economic life of the asset—noncancelable
Operating lease	Rent for some term that is cancelable
Rental	Short-term rental

payments have to cover the lessor's after-tax cost of buying the asset and the lessor's cost of capital.

SALE AND LEASEBACK

A sale and leaseback agreement is similar to a financial lease. The difference is that the lessee already owns the asset but sells it to the lessor as a part of the sale and leaseback agreement. So, the original owner of the asset exchanges it for cash, accepts the liability of the associated lease, and continues to use the asset.

OPERATING LEASES

An operating lease is a rental contract permitting the lessee to terminate before the end of the contract. Accordingly, the rentals do not necessarily include full compensation for the purchase cost. The reason is that the lessor anticipates taking possession of the asset before the end of its useful life and either re-leasing or selling it. The lessor takes responsibility for maintaining the asset. Therefore, the rentals include a service charge. The rentals must also include charges covering the lessor's exposure to the risk of changes in lease rental rates and resale values prevailing at the time the first lease terminates.

LEVERAGED LEASING

With leveraged leasing, the lessor borrows part of the funds to pay for the asset. The loan is secured by the asset and the lease payments. The lessor might borrow, for example, 80% of the funds and still depreciate the full value of the asset for tax purposes.

DEFINITIONS

Default   Failure to make a payment of interest or a repayment of principal on the due date.

Financial lease   Lease contract committing the lessee to rental payments for the economic life of the leased asset.

Lease   Long-term rental agreement.

Lessee   User of the leased asset.

Lessor   Owner of the leased asset.

Leveraged lease   Lease for which the lessor finances part of the cost of the asset with borrowing secured on the asset and the lease payments.

Net present value (NPV)   Difference between the present value of a project's expected after-tax operating cash flows and the present value of its expected after-tax investment expenditures.

Operating lease   Cancelable lease.

Risk   Probability of an unacceptable loss. In portfolio theory, the standard deviation of holding period returns.

Sale and leaseback agreement   Leasing transaction in which the lessee sells an asset to the lessor which is then leased to the lessee.

Time value of money   Rate of return obtainable from comparable alternative investment in the financial market.

17-2 WHY COMPANIES LEASE ASSETS

There are at least three reasons why leasing is often the most attractive way to finance the use of an asset. These are convenience, risk sharing, and taxes.

LEASING CAN BE CONVENIENT

The first reason is that leasing can be convenient. If a company wishes to use an asset for a relatively short time, it will usually lease the asset. For example, a construction company needing the use of a crane for only one day would not waste the effort and expense of buying the crane one day and selling it the next. Lessors are intermediaries that reduce costs by dealing in many such assets and serving numerous customers.

LEASING CAN TRANSFER RISK

The second reason is that a lease can reduce risk for the lessee. If the lessee intends to use the asset for less than its full life, uncertainty about the asset's future second-hand market price becomes important. An operating lease can transfer such risks to the lessor. The lessor owns the asset and therefore bears the risk of re-leasing it at an unknown rental rate or reselling it at an uncertain price. Lessees can protect themselves against the risk of technological obsolescence with operating leases, but the rental payments must be higher to reflect the additional risks taken by the lessor.

LEASING CAN HAVE TAX ADVANTAGES

The third reason is that financial leases provide an effective means of obtaining tax advantages in certain circumstances. A company purchasing an asset can deduct allowable depreciation from taxable income, thereby saving taxes. If the company does not currently have taxable income, it can usually carry the deduction forward to a year when it resumes paying taxes. This postponement of tax deductions, however, reduces the present value (PV) of the tax benefit of the deductions.

If the company leases the asset instead, a lessor with taxable income can enjoy the tax benefits immediately. If the lessee can negotiate a lower rental reflecting a part of this tax timing advantage, both can obtain NPV from the lease. Many lessors are subsidiaries of banks having the current taxable income necessary for tax-efficient leasing transactions.

While lessors attribute many virtues to leasing, the main advantages for lessees continue to be convenience, insurance against risk, and tax timing benefits for current non-taxpayers. These three advantages are sufficient to give leasing a significant role in corporate finance.

DEFINITIONS

Present value (PV)   Value of an investment now as the cost of a comparable investment in the financial market (calculated by multiplying the investment's expected after-tax cash income by the appropriate discount factors).

Uncertainty   Risk not measurable with historical data.

17-3 HOW LEASING CAN AFFECT THE CAPITAL INVESTMENT DECISION

Tax asymmetry between the parties to a lease can create mutual advantage. Although a temporarily non-taxpaying lessee cannot immediately benefit from tax deductions, a taxpaying lessor can do so and thus charge correspondingly lower rentals. The actual rental charged, however, depends upon demand and supply for tax-motivated leasing transactions and the negotiating skills of the participants in the particular leasing transaction.

The question arises as to how the benefits of a lease might influence the investment decision. The financial analyst must answer two questions:

1.   Would the lease offer positive NPV when compared with direct purchase?

2.   Would the project have positive NPV when financed by the lease?

Only when the answer to both questions is affirmative should a company sign a lease contract.

17-4 HOW TO VALUE A FINANCIAL LEASE

Obviously, a company should analyze the terms of a proposed lease contract before signing it. The reasons are several. First, outright purchase might be cheaper than the proposed lease. Second, the precise terms of the lease such as its length and the timing of rental payments need comparison with alternatives. Finally, one needs to know the implied division of the lease's NPV between the lessee and the lessor in order to negotiate lease rentals effectively.

EXAMPLE 17.1

Let us examine an example using a simple lease. Management contemplates lease financing for a machine tool, and a leasing company proposes a financial lease for the machine's five-year economic life. The purchase price of the machine tool is €1 million. The lease contract stipulates ten annual payments of €130,540 per year, each paid one year in advance.

LESSOR'S PERSPECTIVE

Table 17.2 gives an analysis of the proposed lease from the lessor's perspective. The lessor has to pay the €1 million purchase price indicated in the second column but will gain the tax benefits of allowable depreciation in the third column. The fourth

Table 17.2 Analysis of a financial lease from the standpoint of a taxpaying lessor (€ thousands).

End of year	Purchase cost	Tax effect of allowable depreciation	Lease rental receipt	Tax on rentals	Incremental cash flow	Discount factor at 4.9%	Present value
0	−1,000	75.00	130.54	−39.16	−834	1	−833.622
1		56.25	130.54	−39.16	148	0.9533	140.73
2		42.19	130.54	−39.16	134	0.9088	121.38
3		31.64	130.54	−39.16	123	0.8663	106.57
4		23.73	130.54	−39.16	115	0.8258	95.06
5		17.80	130.54	−39.16	109	0.7873	85.95
6		13.35	130.54	−39.16	105	0.7505	78.60
7		10.01	130.54	−39.16	101	0.7154	72.54
8		7.51	130.54	−39.16	99	0.6820	67.44
9		5.63	130.54	−39.16	97	0.6502	63.07
10		16.89			17	0.6198	10.47
						Net present value =	8.19

column shows the lease rental receipts. Column 5 shows the corresponding tax payments of €39,160 on the €130,540 rental income at the assumed 30% corporate tax rate.

The sixth column of the table gives the resulting net incremental cash flow to the lessor. The lessor discounts this net cash flow using its after-tax lending rate. The after-tax rate applies because interest charges are tax-deductible, and the lessor is fully taxpaying. Given the assumed corporate tax rate of 30%, this after-tax interest rate is:

$$7 \times (1 - 0.30) = 4.9\%$$

It is important to appreciate that the lessor would charge this rate on a loan secured on the asset and repayable on the terms implicit in the lease rental schedule. That is, the lessor compares the lease with a hypothetical loan to the lessee secured on the asset.

Discounting the net cash flows in the final column, we find the NPV of the lease to be + €8,190. This positive NPV means that the lease is more profitable for the lessor than lending the funds secured on the machine tool.

We have shown that the proposed lease would be profitable for the lessor. How does the proposed lease appear from the lessee's standpoint, however?

LESSEE'S PERSPECTIVE

Table 17.3 shows the corresponding figures from the point of view of the lessee who also currently pays taxes. Note that the numbers in this table are the same as the corresponding ones in Table 17.2 but with the signs reversed. We discount the lessee's cash flows at the 4.9% interest rate that the company would pay on the equivalent loan secured on the asset. The reason for this symmetry is that the lessor's receipt is the lessee's payment.

Table 17.3 Analysis of a financial lease from the standpoint of a taxpaying lessee (€ thousands).

End of year	Forgone purchase cost	Forgone tax effect of allowable depreciation	Lease rental payment	Tax effect of deducted rental payments	Incremental cash flow	Discount factor at 4.9%	Present value
0	1,000	−75.00	−130.54	39.16	833.62	1	833.622
1		−56.25	−130.54	39.16	−147.63	0.9533	−140.73
2		−42.19	−130.54	39.16	−133.57	0.9088	−121.38
3		−31.64	−130.54	39.16	−123.02	0.8663	−106.57
4		−23.73	−130.54	39.16	−115.11	0.8258	−95.06
5		−17.80	−130.54	39.16	−109.18	0.7873	−85.95
6		−13.35	−130.54	39.16	−104.73	0.7505	−78.60
7		−10.01	−130.54	39.16	−101.39	0.7154	−72.54
8		−7.51	−130.54	39.16	−98.89	0.6820	−67.44
9		−5.63	−130.54	39.16	−97.01	0.6502	−63.07
10		−16.89			−16.89	0.6198	−10.47

Net present value = −8.19

Furthermore, both lessee and the lessor are paying taxes. So, the positive NPV for the lessor implies the identical but negative €8,190 NPV for the lessee.

This example demonstrates that no overall net tax advantage is obtainable when both parties to the lease are in the same taxpaying position.

OTHER BENEFITS

Nevertheless, the company still might wish to sign the lease in order to obtain other benefits. For example, the leasing company might offer quick delivery or a speedy repair and maintenance service, while taking care of insurance premiums. The company can compare its perceived value of the convenience to the NPV of the lease. In this case, the lessee would have to believe that these benefits are worth more than €8,190.

In our simple example, leasing is a zero-sum game unless the lessor can perform services for the lessee at a cheaper rate than the lessee could find elsewhere. The picture could change significantly, however, if the lessee were not paying taxes.

DEFINITIONS

Discounting Multiplying each of an investment's expected cash flow by its present value per unit (disount factor) to obtain the total net present value for the investment.

Net incremental cash flow Difference between a company's expected after-tax cash flows with or without a proposed investment.

17-5 HOW TEMPORARY NON-TAXPAYING AFFECTS THE LEASING DECISION

NON-TAXPAYING

Companies often find themselves in a non-taxpaying position. This happens when a company's current taxable income is insufficient to absorb past losses, or if the income is insufficient to absorb all the allowable depreciation generated by newly purchased assets. Usually the non-taxpaying position will end when future income eventually absorbs the accumulation of unused tax deductions and absorbs the losses carried forward. In order to calculate the NPV of a lease, we must estimate the date when the company will have the taxable income and start paying taxes.

PRESENT VALUE OF THE LEASE

Table 17.4 assumes that the company will not pay taxes for exactly four years and thus will resume paying taxes in the fifth year. Although the lease rental payments are the same as in previous examples, deduction of the lease payments from taxable income will not be possible until the fifth year. In that year the company can deduct $6 \times 130,540 = €783,240$ because it can carry forward unused deductions for the five previous payments. As indicated in the fifth column, the tax effect of deducted rental payments in the fifth year equals $783,240 \times 0.30 = €234,970$. Similarly, the company can also deduct all the allowable depreciation to date from taxable earnings in the fifth year, as in the third column. The value of the lease to the company is now positive at €8,170. So the lease is profitable for both the lessee and the lessor.

Table 17.4 does not reveal the discount rate used in the calculation. The reason is that the discount rate changes with time during the non-taxpaying period. We now turn our attention to this problem.

Table 17.4 Temporarily non-taxpaying lessee.

End of year	Forgone purchase cost	Forgone tax effect of allowable depreciation	Lease rental payment	Tax effect of deducted rental payments	Incremental cash flow
0	1,000		−130.54		869.46
1			−130.54		−130.54
2			−130.54		−130.54
3			−130.54		−130.54
4			−130.54		−130.54
5		−246.61	−130.54	234.97	−142.17
6		−13.35	−130.54	39.16	−104.73
7		−10.01	−130.54	39.16	−101.39
8		−7.51	−130.54	39.16	−98.89
9		−5.63	−130.54	39.16	−97.01
10		−16.89			−16.89

Net present value = 8.17

> **DEFINITION**
>
> **Discount rate**   Required rate of return used in the calculation of a discount factor.

17-6 THE AFTER-TAX DISCOUNT RATE

Companies in some industries, such as the airlines and shipping industries, frequently are temporary taxpayers because of the accumulation of generous tax incentives associated with their investment programs or because of a poor earnings record. We need to be able to analyze financial leases for such companies using the correct discount rate when doing so.

We wish to compare leasing with debt financing. If the company currently pays taxes, the after-tax borrowing rate is the discount rate. If the company is permanently non-taxpaying, the discount rate is the before-tax borrowing rate. When a company is temporarily non-taxpaying, however, the tax adjustment to the discount rate changes with time.

The problem is that for some years the company is non-taxpaying and therefore unable to take immediate advantage of tax deductions for interest payments. You might suggest that we simply use the before-tax discount rate for the cash flows in the non-taxpaying years and the after-tax discount rate for the cash flows in the taxpaying years. This solution is not correct because unused tax credits carry forward to a subsequent year when there will be taxable income. Determining the resulting sequence of discount rates requires dynamic programming. Dynamic programming is efficient but difficult to follow. Fortunately, the loan balance method provides a more transparent approach that is equally valid for this purpose.

> **DEFINITION**
>
> **Loan balance method**   Alternative method of obtaining the present value of a schedule of payments or cash flow. The present value is the initial balance of the equivalent loan leaving a zero balance after the final payment.

17-7 LOAN BALANCE METHOD

In this section, we demonstrate an alternative method of obtaining the NPV of a lease that is entirely consistent with using after-tax discount rates. This alternative is the loan balance method. The loan balance method determines the sum of money deposited in a bank today that would be just sufficient (together with compound interest) to pay all the after-tax lease cash flows. We can use the same procedure for a company in any taxpaying position.

NET PRESENT VALUE OF THE LEASE

The difference between the purchase cost of the asset and the initial sum in the bank equals the NPV of the lease. If the bank deposit is less than the cost of the asset, the NPV of the lease is positive, and the lease therefore would be profitable.

INTEREST PAYMENTS AND TAXES

Fortunately, the loan balance method does not require explicit calculation of the sequence of after-tax discount rates. The method calculates the interest payable if the company borrowed to purchase the asset and then repaid the loan on the schedule implicit in the lease rentals. The loan balance method calculates the interest payments and the corresponding tax savings that occur when the company resumes paying taxes.

CALCULATION

The loan balance method is not difficult for lessees in different non-taxpaying positions. In Table 17.5, we have the equivalent loan balance for the example in Table 17.4, in which the company was non-taxpaying for four years. Column 2 provides the cash obligations of the lease taken from the final column in Table 17.4, except for Year 0. In Year 0 we exclude the purchase cost of €1 million from the cash flow because we wish to estimate the initial bank deposit that will provide for the cost of the lease and to compare this deposit with the €1 million purchase cost of the machine. Column 3 of Table 17.5 shows interest income on each new bank balance. Column 4 shows the tax payments on the interest income starting in Year 5 when the company resumes paying taxes. Column 5, headed "Net change in bank balance," is the sum of all the cash flows in Columns 2, 3, and 4. The final column is the bank balance, which is the sum of the previous year's bank balance less the net change in bank balance in Column 5.

In the final column, we choose an initial loan balance of €991,830. We pay off the first lease rental (in advance) immediately, and the new loan balance is €861,290. We receive interest income of €60,290 at 7% on the outstanding loan balance at the end of Year 1 and make the second lease payment of €130,540. As a result, the bank balance changes by $-$€70,250 $= -$€130,540 + 60,290 to €791,040 at the end of the first year. As we continue this process through the second, third, fourth, and fifth years, we find that, after paying off all obligations of the lease, the bank deposit is exhausted.

Table 17.5   Loan balance method (€ thousands).

End of year	Lease obligation	Interest income at 7%	Tax on interest income	Net change in bank balance	New bank balance
0					991.83
0	−130.54				861.29
1	−130.54	60.29		−70.25	791.04
2	−130.54	55.37		−75.17	715.87
3	−130.54	50.11		−80.43	635.44
4	−130.54	44.48		−86.06	549.39
5	−142.17	38.46	−74.61	−178.33	371.05
6	−104.73	25.97	−7.79	−86.54	284.51
7	−101.39	19.92	−5.97	−87.45	197.06
8	−98.89	13.79	−4.14	−89.23	107.83
9	−97.01	7.55	−2.26	−91.73	16.10
10	−16.89	1.13	−0.34	−16.10	0.00

So, the bank deposit that is just sufficient to pay all the lease cash flows equals €991,830.[2] The NPV of the lease is the difference between the €1 million purchase cost of the asset and the initial loan balance of €991,830 or + €8,170. This NPV very nearly equals the NPV of €8,190 for the lessor. So, the proposed rental divides the tax gains of the lease almost equally between the lessor and the lessee.

SOME CONCLUSIONS

This example demonstrates a number of important points:

1. The loan balance method can provide the NPV of a lease without explicit calculation of after-tax discount rates.

2. The loan balance method is easier than discounting when there are lags in tax payments.

3. Both methods assume that leasing is equivalent to debt financing and that a lease displaces debt in the company's capital structure. This assumption is explicit in the loan balance method, which compares a lease directly with equivalent borrowing. Both lessors and lessees can use the method.

> **DEFINITION**
>
> **Capital structure** The proportions of different forms of debt and equity constituting a company's total capital.

17-8 THE INTERNAL RATE OF RETURN APPROACH

The discounted cash flow (DCF) and loan balance methods are two ways of obtaining the NPV of leasing versus purchase. Many companies, however, prefer to obtain the internal rate of return (IRR) on a lease.

POPULARITY

Surveys show that the majority of companies use the IRR to evaluate a lease. The IRR method is popular because it provides a percentage return on a lease for comparison with the equivalent loan interest rate. In this way, the lessee is able to judge directly whether a lease is cheaper or more expensive than borrowing, and the lessor is able to see whether a lease looks more or less profitable than lending. Although the NPV method uses the equivalent borrowing (or lending) rate to evaluate a lease, the resulting NPV is not directly comparable with market rates of interest. For this reason analysts who like to think like bankers find rates of return more appealing than NPV.

PITFALLS

Recall that in Chapter 6 we showed that the IRR method generally is unsuited for comparison between mutually exclusive alternatives. We found that the IRR can be larger for one of two

---

[2] Finding the right initial balance requires trial and error, carried out by hand, or virtually instantly with your spreadsheet Solver function.

alternatives even though the NPV is smaller. Frequently, comparison is necessary between lease contracts proposed by different lessors or between different leases with different lives. The IRR method can suggest that one lease provides a greater rate of return than another does, even when the NPV is smaller. Therefore, the IRR method can lead to wrong decisions in some circumstances.

A second objection to the IRR method is the choice of the after-tax interest rate for comparison. The IRR calculated on the net cash flows shown in Column 6 of Table 17.4 is 5.02%. This needs comparison with the lessee's after-tax borrowing rate. We argued, however, that there is no single after-tax borrowing rate for this lease. The after-tax interest rates decline with the approach of the return to taxpaying. Because after-tax interest rates in the early years could be higher than 5.02%, it is difficult to know whether the lease is profitable without also calculating the NPV for the lease. For temporary non-taxpayers, consequently, the IRR method has a distinct disadvantage.

The many analysts who use the IRR method should be wary of the pitfalls of the IRR method and should calculate the NPV of each lease as a safeguard.

DEFINITIONS

Discounted cash flow (DCF) method   Comparison of the value of an investment with the cost of a comparable investment in the financial market. Also, comparison of the internal rate of return on a project with its cost of capital.

Internal rate of return (IRR)   Discount rate that would make the net present value for an investment equal to zero.

Rate of return   After-tax cash income and capital gain divided by the investment.

17-9 RESIDUAL VALUES

FINANCIAL LEASE

In our examples, we assumed that the residual value of the leased asset equals zero at the end of the lease. In most lease contracts, the lessee will receive a stipulated proportion (perhaps 80% to 95%) of the resale value of the asset in the form of a rent rebate at the end of the lease. By purchasing the asset instead, the lessee could retain the entire resale value. Therefore, the portion of the residual value kept by the lessor is a negative cash flow in the lessee's analysis of the lease.

OPERATING LEASE

In an operating lease, the lessor keeps the entire residual value of the equipment. Consequently, the residual value of the asset and the tax effects of the asset's disposal are an important part of the net incremental cash flow for both the lessee and the lessor.

Cancellation of the operating lease is an option for the lessee at any time.[3] The lessee exercising this

---

[3] S. R. Grenardier (1995) "Valuing lease contracts: A real options approach," *Journal of Financial Economics*, Vol. 38 (July), 297–331.

option to cancel forfeits the use of the asset but escapes the obligation to continue paying rentals. The lessee captures the most advantage from this option by canceling the operating lease when the resale value of the asset falls below the PV of the remaining rental payments. Future resale values are subject to uncertainty requiring numerical analysis such as the binomial tree method used in Chapter 9. Therefore, valuing an operating lease requires software designed for this type of option. The option to cancel the contract is a benefit to the lessee representing a cost to the lessor recompensed in the contracted rental payments.[4]

RESIDUAL VALUE ESTIMATION

Frequently, estimation of the expected residual value is a difficult exercise. Suppose that the company wishes to lease a car for two years. The company needs to know the residual value in the cash flow at the end of the two-year period when comparing leasing with purchase. The ratio of the current secondhand price for a two-year-old car to its value when new is relevant. Multiplication of this ratio by the price of a new, leased car gives an estimate of its residual value two years hence:

$$Expected\ Residual\ Value\ after\ n\ Years = \left(\frac{Secondhand\ Value\ Now}{Price\ New\ n\ Years\ Ago} \right) \times Price\ New$$

The estimated value obtained in this way requires adjustment for a change in the rate of inflation. Because the estimate of the residual value is uncertain and therefore risky, the discount rate for the residual value in the analysis should include a premium for systematic risk.

Estimation of the expected residual value of technical assets such as computers also needs to reflect any expectation of a change in the rate of obsolescence. For example, if the expected rate of obsolescence increases, the ratio of the secondhand value now to its value when new requires downward adjustment.

If the secondhand value of the equipment at the end of the lease is likely to be financially significant, the contracted proportion of the value kept by the lessor should be included as a negative cash flow for the lessee or as a positive cash flow for the lessor.

DEFINITIONS

Binomial tree   Tree with two branches from each node.

Expected (mean)   Probability-weighted average of all possible outcomes for a random variable.

Residual value   Expected value of an asset at the end of the assumed life of a project or of a lease agreement.

Systematic risk   Risk that portfolio diversification cannot eliminate.

---

[4] For treatment of cancellation as an option, see J. J. McConnell and J. S. Schallheim (1983) "Valuation of asset leasing contracts," *Journal of Financial Economics*, Vol. 12 (August), 237–261.

17-10   INTERACTIONS BETWEEN LEASING AND INVESTMENT DECISIONS

FORECASTING TAX PAYMENT DATES

Leasing analysis requires one to forecast actual tax payment dates. For temporary non-taxpayers the resumption of taxpaying can be difficult to forecast, however. Projects currently under consideration alter the tax position and the non-taxpaying period. Future (possibly unknown) projects do so as well. The question is what incremental difference does the current project (with a lease) make to the expected non-taxpaying period and to the after-tax value of the firm? Having to anticipate future projects and their expected cash flows makes ascertaining this difference more difficult.[5]

ALTERNATIVES TO LEASING

Leasing is only one method of taking advantage of unused tax benefits. The firm could acquire taxpaying companies and combine the taxable income of the acquired company with its own tax-deductible losses. Clearly, there are costs and benefits associated with acquisitions. Whether a company chooses leasing, or acquisition, or some other route to obtaining the tax benefit from unused depreciation allowances depends upon the costs and benefits of each. The existence of such possible strategies adds to the difficulty of forecasting when the company will begin paying taxes.

17-11   LEASE RATES AND COMPETITION IN THE LEASING MARKET

The state of the leasing market is the context of the negotiations between the lessee and potential lessor.

SUPPLY AND DEMAND FOR TAXABLE INCOME

When the amount of taxable income available to lessors is greater than the demand for it by lessees, we can expect lease rental rates to be lower and most of the tax benefit from leasing to go to lessees. Conversely, when relatively large numbers of firms are in non-taxpaying positions and there is a shortage of taxable income among lessors, lease rates rise, leaving lessees with a smaller proportion of the benefit.

GOVERNMENT FISCAL AND MONETARY POLICY

The size of the tax benefits to leasing depends upon two important factors other than the tax positions of the parties involved. The first is the effect of government fiscal policy. Higher corporate tax rates and acceleration of the rate of allowable depreciation make leasing more valuable when the parties to a lease are in different taxpaying positions. The second factor is the effect of monetary policy. If interest rates and the resulting discount rates for the leases were equal

---

[5] The broader problem is that correct valuation of a project requires valuation of the entire portfolio of projects of which it is to be a part. See I. Cooper and J. R. Franks (1983) "The interaction of financial and investment decisions when the firm has unused tax credits," *Journal of Finance*, Vol, 38, No. 2 (May), 571–584.

to zero, the acceleration of tax benefits would not increase the NPV of a lease. High interest rates increase the discount rate and thus increase the NPV of tax benefits accelerated by a lease. Therefore, high interest rates favor leasing.

GOVERNMENT POLICY TOWARD LEASING

You might well ask why governments permit leasing. If a lease is profitable for tax reasons, it provides tax incentives for investments that otherwise might not be undertaken by non-taxpaying companies. Leasing enables companies to recapture some tax benefits even when they are not currently paying taxes. Leasing cannot result in tax losses to the government greater than would be the case if all companies had positive taxable income against which to deduct the allowable depreciation.

17-12 CONCLUSIONS

This chapter describes types of leasing and how to value a lease in different tax situations. It shows that the NPV of a lease changes with different assumptions about the expected taxpaying position of the lessee. We calculated the NPV of a lease using both the discounted cash flow and the loan balance methods. In addition, we compared the NPV and the IRR measures for a lease, noting that although IRR is the more popular method, it can suggest incorrect decisions in some circumstances. Finally, we discussed the economics of leasing, emphasizing some factors that determine the profitability of leasing and the distribution of NPV between lessees and lessors.

FURTHER READING

S. C. Myers, D. Gill, and A. Bautista (1976) "Valuation of financial lease contracts," *Journal of Finance*, Vol. 3 (June), 799–819.

J. R. Franks and S. D. Hodges (1978) "Valuation of financial lease contracts: A note," *Journal of Finance*, Vol. 33 (May), 647–669.

S. R. Grenardier (1995) "Valuing lease contracts: A real options approach," *Journal of Financial Economics*, Vol. 38 (July), 297–331.

QUESTIONS AND PROBLEMS

1   LESSEECO considers leasing an asset costing €1 million for one year. A lessor proposes a one-year lease with just one payment in advance. The current rate of interest on a loan secured on the asset would be 7%. LESSEECO has taxable income and pays corporate taxes annually at 30%. Allowable annual depreciation is 25% taken immediately in Period 0 and 25% per year annually on the reducing balance thereafter. The lease begins just before the company's accounting year-end. What is the largest rental the company can pay without suffering a negative NPV on the lease? Assume that the residual value of the asset equals zero at the end of the lease.

2   As an alternative to the lease proposed in Problem 1, the lessor offers LESSEECO a one-year lease with four quarterly rentals payable in advance.

  (a)   What is the largest quarterly rental the company can pay without suffering a negative NPV on the lease?

  (b)   Calculate the PV of the four rental payments.

  (c)   Why is the sum of the four rental payments greater but their PV less than the single, advance payment on the lease in Problem 1?

3   Assuming the residual value of the asset in Problem 1 will equal €100,000 and the lessor will rebate 90% of the residual value to the lessee at the end of the lease, what is the largest rental the lessee can pay without suffering a negative NPV on the lease?

4   In the following year, a lessor offers LESSEECO a two-year lease on an asset costing €1 million. The lessor proposes eight quarterly rentals of €133,400 payable in advance. The lease begins shortly before the company's accounting year-end. Interest on a loan secured on the asset would be 8%. Allowable depreciation for the asset is 25% annually on the reducing balance, starting immediately in Period 0. The asset's residual value will be zero at the end of the lease.

Early in the next year, LESSEECO expects to acquire another company having accumulated taxable losses. As a result, LESSEECO expects to pay no corporate taxes for the first year of the lease. What is the NPV of the proposed lease from LESSEECO's perspective?

PART 4

Solvency Management

18
Financial Planning and Solvency[1]

Financial planning is the means by which the Corporate Treasurer anticipates the company's cash flow and its funding requirements. Financial planning is necessary to help the company avoid financial distress in adverse business conditions and to ensure adequate financial resources for investment when conditions are favorable. Financial planning is in the obvious interests of management and employees, whose jobs can be at stake in the event of financial distress. Importantly, it also helps protect the interests of shareholders, bondholders, banks, and others who finance the company. We discuss the principal methods of financial planning and the difficulties inherent in making financial forecasts. We show how to organize the assumptions underlying the forecasts. In particular, we provide a method of arranging alternative possible future events into scenarios providing the basis for financial plans.

We use two types of financial plan to illustrate these points. The first type is the pro forma cash budget, which provides the framework for short-term cash management. The second is the long-term financial plan, which is concerned with how changes in the firm's economic environment are likely to affect its cash flow for several years into the future. In the context of both kinds of planning framework, we show how to plan for contingencies arising from events outside the control of management.

TOPICS

In this chapter we consider the following:

○   *the importance of financial planning;*

○   *pro forma cash budgeting and short-term borrowing;*

○   *the funds flow statement and longer term financing;*

○   *breakeven cash flow;*

○   *financial forecasting;*

○   *cash flow implications of financial forecasts;*

○   *scenario-building.*

---

[1] Adapted by permission of J. R. Franks and J. E. Broyles (1979) *Modern Managerial Finance* (Chichester, UK: John Wiley & Sons).

18-1 IMPORTANCE OF FINANCIAL PLANNING AND CONTROL

MAINTAINING SOLVENCY

Piecemeal decision-making is often the road to financial distress and bankruptcy. The complacent assumption that a company's sources of funds will somehow match requirements can be catastrophic.

Appropriate financial planning and working capital management systems are required to keep a company solvent. Financial distress and bankruptcy generate significant costs including legal and administrative fees, not to mention costs to suppliers, customers, employees, and the tax collector. In addition, the opportunity cost of postponed profitable investments while the company is in financial distress and being reorganized should not be overlooked.

FUNDING THE EXERCISE OF REAL OPTIONS

Without assurance that sufficient provision has been made for inevitable financial risk, the board will feel constrained not to exercise all its strategic real options. So, financial planning has an important role to play in laying the financial foundations of strategy.

LIQUIDITY MANAGEMENT

Figure 18.1 helps provide some additional perspective. At the centre of the figure is the fundamental accounting equation asserting that the sources of funds equal their uses. That this accounting equation holds for solvent companies should not provide any sense of security because matching the timing and maturity of the sources and the uses can be crucial. Management is actually concerned with the cash cycle illustrated by the arrows forming the circle in the figure. The lower, solid semicircle represents sources of funds such as borrowing and equity issues that are largely under management's control. The upper, dashed semicircle represents cash generation by existing investments and the resulting effect on subsequent funding. The problem is that this second half of the process is uncertain and largely outside the control of management. It depends upon customers' buying decisions and upon the willingness of investors and lenders to continue providing funds for future investment. Without the confidence and support of customers, suppliers, and investors, the company cannot survive for long.

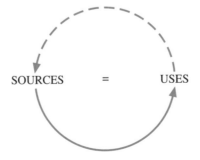

SOURCES   =   USES

Figure 18.1 Cyclic nature of sources and uses of funds.

The role of financial planning in this cycle is to help ensure that management makes advanced arrangements for all plausible funding requirements, helping to build a robust capital structure that can respond to unforseen risks and growth opportunities. In this way, financial planning provides the capacity for management to be more intrepid in the exercise of strategic real options.

WORKING CAPITAL MANAGEMENT

The role of working capital control systems is to signal deviations from financial plans and to ensure that the investment in working capital remains liquid. The control of debtors and of inventories is discussed in subsequent chapters.

PRE-EMPTING RISK

Financial planning enables the decision maker to anticipate the funding implications of new investment opportunities. In addition, financial planning enables management to perceive the associated financial risks and, if appropriate, insure against them. The firm can shift or contract some of the risks to other parties, for example, by:

1. Sharing the risks with partners in joint ventures.

2. Hedging.

3. Entering into insurance agreements.

4. Using contracts incorporating escalation clauses.

5. Negotiating appropriate long-term debt and equity finance.

If by such means management can forestall unnecessary financial risks associated with a more aggressive investment program, shareholders can benefit along with all the company's other stakeholders.

CREDIT MANAGEMENT

The interest groups who finance the enterprise look for competent corporate financial planning. Inadequate planning breeds surprise. Presenting lenders or shareholders with frequent, unanticipated demands for additional funds can result in unnecessarily high transaction costs and an increased cost of capital. Worse still, capital providers can simply refuse to put further capital at risk. Inadequate financial planning is almost certainly the single most important factor in company failure.

DEFINITIONS

Cost of capital   Cost of funds used by a company for investment.

Debt   Sum of money or other assets owed by one party to another. Usually, a legally enforceable obligation to pay agreed interest and to repay the principal of a loan to the lender promptly on schedule.

Equity   Net worth or shareholders' capital represented by common stock (ordinary shares) and preferred stock.

Financial distress Condition in which a company might not be able to meet its obligations to creditors; that is, in danger of becoming insolvent or technically bankrupt.

Financial risk Increase in the volatility of a company's earnings due to borrowing.

Hedging Buying one security and selling another to reduce risk.

Opportunity cost of capital Return forgone when investing in a project instead of the securities market.

Pro forma cash budget Forecast of cash receipts and cash expenditures for a sequence of future periods.

Real option Right to make favorable future choices regarding real asset investments. More precisely, a real option is an opportunity for voluntary future investment in a nonfinancial asset when at least a part of the required investment expenditure is certain or, alternatively, when at least a part of the required investment expenditure is not perfectly positively correlated with the project's present value.

Scenario Plausible sequence of events.

Treasurer Senior financial manager reporting directly to the Chief Financial Officer. Primarily responsible for funding and cash management.

18-2 THE PRO FORMA CASH BUDGET AND SHORT-TERM BORROWING

The pro forma cash budget is one of the chief tools available to management for determining likely financing requirements in the short to intermediate term.

PRO FORMA CASH BUDGET

The pro forma cash budget is a forecast of cash receipts and cash expenditures for each future period. The choice of periods, for example, days, weeks, or months, will depend on the nature and variability of cash flows. Net receipts or expenditures in each period cumulatively adjust the monthly beginning cash balance (or bank overdraft). Cash balances and bank overdrafts projected in this manner can indicate requirements for additional financing.

EXAMPLE 18.1

Table 18.1 illustrates a simplified example of a monthly schedule of cash receipts based in part on an updated sales forecast and an assumed schedule of payments from credit customers.

The essence of credit sales is the lag between sales and actual receipt of payments. Management is forecasting payment of 10% of the credit sales with a delay of only one month, 50% with a delay of two months, and the remaining 40% paid by the end of three months. Therefore, forecast total collections in a given month represent collections for credit sales in several preceding months plus cash sales for that month. Inclusion of other cash receipts is required, such as dividends from trade investments and sales of fixed assets.

We enter the resulting total cash receipts from Table 18.1 on the cash budget in Table 18.3. Also entered in the cash budget in Table 18.3 are total cash payments from Table 18.2.

The ultimate source of the data in Table 18.2 is the operating plan. The purchase of raw materials and subcontracted components in the early months usually represents existing commitments based upon an earlier plan. In subsequent months, purchases will reflect current planning and any necessary adjustments to stocks of raw materials and subcontracted components. Wages paid and other operating expenses depend on the operating plan, affecting personnel levels, salary increases, payments for overtime work, etc. Nonoperating expenses such as expected payments of taxes, dividends and interest, and capital expenditures should be included.

Table 18.3 shows the effect on the net cash position in each period resulting from expected receipts and payments. For example, at the beginning of August the company has €30,000 in cash and an overdraft facility of €20,000. Therefore, the "safety margin" or excess is 30,000 + 20,000 = €50,000. During the month, however, management expects a net negative cash flow of €36,900. This would require an overdraft of €6,900 and reduce the safety margin provided by the overdraft facility to 20,000 − 6,900 = €13,100 euro as indicated. Note that the expected safety margin gets steadily worse until October when an expected shortfall of €21,100 is expected. Obviously, this firm must see its bank immediately to arrange a much larger overdraft facility.

Pro forma cash budgets are for short-term financing and cash planning. The forecast may extend to perhaps 18 months into the future on a rolling basis. The frequency of updating the forecasts depends upon the nature of the business and the speed with which new developments alter the basis of the forecasts. Normally the frequency of updating pro forma cash budgets is no less than once a quarter. In some companies, weekly and even daily forecasts on a computerized basis are required to facilitate money market operations.

UNCERTAINTY

The above procedure often proves entirely inadequate, however. There is nothing in the procedure thus far indicating whether the minimum cash balance or maximum overdraft arranged with bankers is sufficient to meet possible deviations from the forecast.

It is worth noting the points at which uncertainty affects the cash budget, often critically. The sales forecast is usually the least reliable set of data in the budget. Not only might the forecast be inaccurate, but also it often incorporates a systematic bias.

A second source of uncertainty is the promptness with which debtors pay their bills. When business conditions are unfavorable for the company, they are likely to be adverse for customers as well. Therefore, customers (debtors) can be delaying payments when the company is short of cash.

Other cash receipts can also have critical effects; for example, the projected sales of assets might not happen when expected. Frequently, adjustments to purchases and payments to suppliers cannot be made sufficiently or rapidly enough to neutralize the effects of unanticipated changes in cash

Table 18.1 Projected sales and cash receipts (€ thousands).

	May	June	July	August	September	October	November	December
Total sales	83	85	88	101	111	103	109	88
Credit sales	74.7	76.5	79.2	90.9	99.9	92.7	98.1	79.2
Collections:								
1 month 10%		7.5	7.7	7.9	9.1	10.0	9.3	9.8
2 months 50%			37.4	38.3	39.6	45.5	50.0	46.4
3 months 40%				29.9	30.6	31.7	36.4	40.0
Total collections				76.1	79.3	87.1	95.6	96.1
Cash sales				10.1	11.1	10.3	10.9	8.8
Other cash receipts:								
Trade investments				20				
Sales of fixed assets							40	
Other				2	1	1	1	2
Total cash receipts				108.2	91.4	98.4	147.5	106.9

Table 18.2 Projected expenditures.

	May	June	July	August	September	October	November	December
Purchases:								
Raw materials		45	45	45	45	50	50	50
Subcontracted components		20	25	25	25	15	15	20
		65	70	70	70	65	65	70
Cash payments for purchases			65	70	70	70	65	65
Wages			20	22	22	22	18	18
Other operating expenditures			10	13	13	13	7	7
			95	105	105	105	90	90
Other cash payments:								
Tax						14		
Dividends and interest				40				
Capital expenditures							50	
Other								
Total cash payments			95	145	105	119	140	90

Table 18.3 Net cash position.

	August	September	October	November	December
Total receipts	108.2	91.4	98.4	147.5	106.9
Total payments	−145.0	−105.0	−119.0	−140.0	−90.0
Net cash	−36.9	−13.6	−20.6	7.5	16.9
Opening cash	30.0	−6.9	−20.5	−41.1	−33.6
Closing cash	−6.9	−20.5	−41.1	−33.6	−16.7
Maximum overdraft	20.0	20.0	20.0	20.0	20.0
Excess (shortfall)	13.1	−0.5	−21.1	−13.6	3.1

receipts. If the forecast is not sufficiently conservative, the forecast overdraft requirements are unlikely to be sufficient.

For long-term financing, the related funds flow projection provides a more convenient planning format.

DEFINITIONS

Expected (mean)   Probability-weighted average of all possible outcomes for a random variable.

Pro forma cash budget   Forecast of cash receipts and cash expenditures for a sequence of future periods.

Uncertainty   Risk not measurable with historical data.

18-3 THE FUNDS FLOW STATEMENT AND LONGER TERM FINANCING

Longer term financing plans (up to five years into the future) can pave the way for the timely issue of company securities; for example, equity, and long-term debt. The provision of long-term finance must reflect major items such as expected earnings and the acquisition and disposal of fixed assets. Projections of sources and applications of funds in the funds flow statement serve this purpose.

FUNDS FLOW STATEMENT

Table 18.4 illustrates a simplified funds flow statement. This statement begins with a forecast of before-tax profit several years into the future. The table turns the profit forecast into the corresponding cash flow in several steps. The first step is to add back expected depreciation, other cash charges, and expected sales of fixed assets. This results in the forecast of cash income in subtotals (a). The next step is to forecast the net cash outflows in three parts. The three parts are (b) the expected net changes in working capital, (c) dividend payments to existing equity shareholders and taxes, and (d) expected capital investments. Next, the table shows the net of the expected cash income and outflow in subtotals (f).

Table 18.4 A simplified funds flow statement.

Year 0		Year 1 (current)	Year 2	Year 3	Year 4
Profit before tax		95			
Depreciation and noncash charges to profit		20			
Fixed asset realizations (at market value)		5			
	(a)	120			
Less					
Stock increase (decrease)		20			
Debtors increase (decrease)		10			
Creditors decrease (increase)		—			
	(b)	30			
Dividend payments on existing equity		10			
Tax payments		40			
	(c)	50			
Fixed asset expenditure					
Land and buildings		10			
Plant		10			
Vehicles		—			
Other		—			
	(d)	20			
(b)+(c)+(d) =	(e)	100			
Net cash accretion (decrease)					
(a)−(e) =	(f)	20			
Funding					
Loans increase (decrease)		(20)			
Interest					
New equity issued					
Dividends on new equity					
Overdraft increase (decrease)					
Interest					
Tax effects					
Total	(g)	(20)			

The expected net cash flow in subtotals (f) reveals possible negative cash flows suggesting the need for external funding such as short- and long-term borrowing and new equity. Forecast external financing and implications for interest, dividends and taxes can be entered in the next seven rows.

UNCERTAINTY

The problem of uncertainty in the funds flow statement is particularly critical. If profits should turn out to be lower than forecast, the projected requirements for long-term financing will have been inadequate. In this position, the balance of requirements might need covering quickly by short-dated debt instruments and bank borrowing. The firm's ability to obtain the needed funds will be determined not only by the profitability of the company but also by its ability to react to the changed circumstances.

18-4 FINANCIAL MODELING

The pro forma cash budget and the funds flow statement are financial models of the firm implemented with computer spreadsheet software facilitating sensitivity analysis. Such a model can be misleading if its internal structure does not accurately reflect the characteristics of the company's cash flow, however. One of the more important characteristics is the relationship between variable and fixed expenditure.

VARIABLE AND FIXED CASH FLOW

One should be careful to maintain a distinction between those cash flow expenditures that vary with sales volume and those that are independent of volume.[2] In particular, one should focus on expenditure that remains unaffected in the short to intermediate term when sales volume declines.[3] In the presence of high fixed expenditure, net cash will be highly vulnerable to any decline in sales volume below expectations.

Figure 18.2 is a cash flow breakeven chart illustrating the relationship between net cash flow with revenues and fixed and variable expenditure. The figure differs from the usual *profit* breakeven chart by excluding depreciation. Revenue begins at the origin in the figure and rises with a slope equal to the average unit price. Total expenditure begins with fixed expenditure and rises with a slope equal to the average expenditure per unit sold.

SOLVENCY

The net cash flow is the difference between sales revenue and expenditures. The vertical distance between the revenue and total expenditure lines represents net cash flow in the figure. One can clearly see the "scissors action" operating on net cash flow resulting from the presence of fixed expenditure. Fixed expenditure increases the volume of sales (Point A) necessary to break even and increases the volatility of net cash flow for a given change in unit volume. Therefore, fixed expenditure largely determines the vulnerability of the firm to unfavorable business developments. To ensure solvency, the firm must operate quite consistently to the right of the intersection at A. The probability of financial distress reflects the likelihood of sales volume falling below this point.

---

[2] Expenditure is said to be variable when it is proportional to the sales volume. Sales volume cannot vary without limit, however. The spreadsheet MIN function can be used to restrict sales volume to the lesser of demand or capacity, for example.

[3] Expenditure is fixed to the extent that it does not change proportionately to sales. Typically, fixed expenditure does change with the scale of investment in fixed assets, however. A useful modeling device in this case is to let fixed expenditure be proportional to undepreciated fixed assets. So, planned disposal of fixed assets reduces fixed expenditure and planned investment in fixed assets increases it.

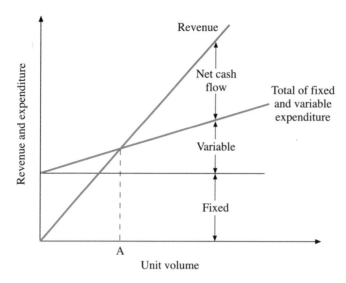

Figure 18.2   Cash flow breakeven chart.

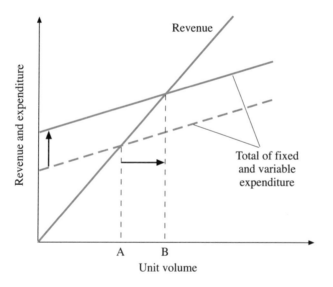

Figure 18.3   Burden of debt.

BORROWING CAPACITY

Increased borrowing increases total fixed expenditure. Figure 18.3 illustrates what happens to net cash flow when the burden of interest charges and loan repayments increase total expenditure. Point A becomes Point B on the right, thus increasing the sales volume needed to break even. Consequently, increased borrowing increases the probability of financial distress. Figures 18.1 and 18.2 illustrate the importance of making a distinction between those expenditures that will change and those that will remain relatively fixed within the planning horizon. These figures illustrate why the financial model needs to incorporate the structure of fixed and variable expenditure to make the forecast cash flow reflect realistically the effects of changes in sales volume. Furthermore, they illustrate the relationship between fixed expenditure and the firm's borrowing capacity.

OPTIONS

When determining which elements of cash flow will change, one must consider what actions management would take in the relevant circumstances. The important questions to ask are: What options are open to management if trading conditions deteriorate? What will be the value of the company's assets (and consequently their value in alternative uses) if such adverse conditions arise?

18-5 FINANCIAL FORECASTING

UNDERLYING ASSUMPTIONS

It would be easy to forecast the elements of the pro forma cash budget and the projected funds flow statement if one knew what assumptions to make about future developments. Existing trends do not just continue. Events intervene: strikes, new competition, and even significant changes in the weather. There are two types of uncertain element in a forecast. First, there are "averaging" kinds of factors such as expected growth, trend, and seasonality. Second, there are discrete events that could intervene to alter the averages; for example, government action or economic collapse.

It can be reasonable to extrapolate or alter averages and trends based on experience and judgment. Unfortunately, foreseeable but ignored discrete events ruin an otherwise plausible forecast. The forecasting problem really divides itself into two parts. The first is defining the economic events and conditions that constitute the underlying assumptions in the financial plan. The second part is the actual forecasts of sales, costs, and other cash flows constituting the plan, which we discussed earlier.

STRUCTURE OF UNCERTAINTY

Many events could undermine existing company plans. These events occur in various combinations over time. The number of possible combinations increases geometrically with the number of such events. A common reaction to this complexity is simply to base forecasts on the most likely sequence of future events and to ignore alternative scenarios that could be more dangerous. The risks of such tunnel vision should be self-evident.

Virtually every forecast is conditional on a whole series of possible events and decisions preceding the future period to which each forecast applies. Who is to say which of these many combinations of relevant events will actually occur? One must be able to judge which of the most plausible combinations of events are significant, and one must prepare for them.

18-6 STRUCTURING UNCERTAINTY

THE TREE DIAGRAM

The tree diagram is a way of structuring alternative sequences of future events upon which financial forecasts depend. In the following section, we illustrate the use of a tree diagram for this purpose.

EXAMPLE 18.2

Consider the problem facing the detergent-manufacturing subsidiary of a national household products company.[4] This subsidiary is responsible for planning its own cash flow needs and obtains funds from its parent company at market rates. The subsidiary is launching a new product but is still considering the decision to launch the product regionally or to launch it nationally during the following year. The company has decided to introduce the product nationally if the outcome of a market test is sufficiently favorable. If not, the company will take the more conservative strategy of introducing the product regionally.

Subsequently, there could be either a favorable or an unfavorable market reception, and at the same time, in this particular case, a strike at the plant could occur. In order to forecast cash flows, management requires a clear picture of the combinations of probable events that could affect the forecasts. Fortunately, a probability tree can represent combinations of uncertain events quite effectively.

PROBABILITY TREE

Figure 18.4 represents such a probability tree. Emerging from the first circle or node are two possibilities or branches: to introduce the product regionally or to introduce it nationally. Management judges that the outcome of the market test will be sufficiently favorable that they would introduce the product nationally with a probability of only 0.25 or one chance in four. The remaining probability is 0.75 or three chances in four that the outcome of the market test would not be sufficiently favourable to warrant the risks of a national campaign.

In any case, within either the national or the regional market the market reception might be unfavorable. Management judged the probability of this as one in five, or a subjective probability of 0.2. If market reception proves favorable (and management assesses this with a probability of 0.8), sales would be vulnerable to the possibility of a strike at the factory. Management judges the chances of a strike as three out of ten or the subjective probability of 0.3. Thus, in Period 2 there are two sets of nodes representing combinations of a favorable and an unfavorable market reception combined with the events of a strike or no strike.

In this case, management felt that the subjective probabilities associated with the market reception and with a strike are independent of whether the product launch is regional or national. This independence need not hold; and, for example, the probability of a favorable market reception might differ on different parts of the tree.

---

[4] See J. R. Franks, C. J. Bunton, and J. E. Broyles (1974) "A decision and analysis approach to cash flow management," *Operational Research Quarterly*, Vol. 25, 573–585.

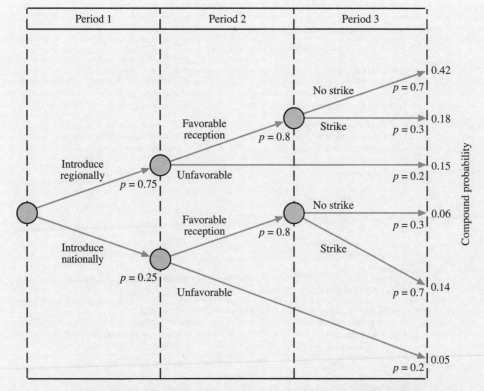

Figure 18.4 Tree of events relating to a new product introduction.

The probability tree provides an analytical framework whereby management can represent those major or significant conditions upon which any well-thought-through forecast must depend. When the knowledgeable manager reveals various caveats, one must seize upon them as useful information. The need to qualify forecasts is warranted, and the probability tree provides a useful way to do so.

When there are many more events to consider, the tree has a large number of branches. So, the main disadvantage of such a probability analysis within a tree framework is the amount of data required and the specialized skills demanded.

18-7 SCENARIOS OF THE FUTURE

A problem with tree diagrams is that frequently there are so many critical uncertain events that the tree develops far too many branches. The number of branches increases geometrically with the number of events incorporated in the tree. This multiplicity of branches simply reflects the complex nature of unfolding reality. Faced with such complexity, what can one do? Resorting to the "educated guess" is inadequate and quite dangerous.

A pragmatic solution is to choose just those paths through the tree that are of most interest for the purpose at hand. For example, when one is preparing forecasts relevant to arranging finance to

Table 18.5   Events and changes.

(a) *Macroeconomic events and changes*
      Inflation   Recession/recovery
      Exchange rates   Credit squeeze
      Interest rates   Birth rates/demography
      GDP growth   Oil prices
      Capital investment   Bank failures
      Consumer spending/saving   Defense policies

(b) *Government interventions*
      Government budget   Taxation of foreign earnings
      Government spending   Import/export restrictions
      Conservation/ecology   Product standards/safety
      Antitrust rulings   Political instability, wars
      Tax rates/fiscal measures
      Investment tax credits

(c) *Industry and regional events and changes*
      Market growth   Labor costs
      Consumer preferences   Transport costs
      Foreign competition   Changes in credit terms
      Technology   Disease
      Energy costs   Weather, floods, draught
      Commodity prices   Infrastructure

(d) *Events and changes affecting relationships between companies*
      New competitor/product   Market share
      New customer   Takeovers and mergers
      Loss of monopoly/patent protection   Loss of supplier
      Security of information   Sources of finance

(e) *Events and changes relating to the company*
      Technology   Cost overruns
      New product   Labor supply
      Loss of managment   Local strikes
      Reorganization   Large negligence claim
      New plant   Accidents, fire
      IT breakdown   Water and electricity supply
                                                          Terrorist attack

meet possible contingencies, one can ask, "Which plausible sequences of events would cause us to seek the most outside funding?" Each such scenario of events implies some immediate actions to forestall financial problems. Only after considering such scenarios can one be reasonably certain that sufficient funding is being made available for contingencies.

A procedure for routine scenario construction follows:

1.   List all future circumstances and significant events for the economy and the industry that could affect the forecast. Table 18.5 lists some events and changes that might be relevant. Please add to this list.

2.   Relist them ranked in order of importance for each future period in the forecast.[5] Table 18.6 provides a format for doing this.

---

[5] Importance is defined in terms of two factors, the likelihood of occurrence and the expected impact on the cash flow should the event occur.

Table 18.6   Scenario construction format

Ranked event or change	Time period

3.   From these ranked items, select a sequence of the more important events and describe the relationships between them through time. This defines the first scenario.

4.   Define two or more further scenarios providing a sufficient range of plausible conditions to test the adequacy of the financial plan. Table 18.6 illustrates two such scenarios.

The resulting scenarios define sets of assumptions on which to base corresponding cash flow forecasts. Can the firm's present financial structure withstand the stress implied by the range of chosen scenarios? What changes in financial structure, insurance, hedging, and other risk-sharing measures are required?

Routinely maintaining and updating a comprehensive list of events and changes such as in Table 18.5 is an integral part of the planning and forecasting process. Management needs to be careful to consider all plausible events that could materially affect the company's cash flow. The actual number of resulting scenarios employed must provide a sufficient sample of conditions to indicate whether the firm's financial plan is robust. One major Europe-based multinational oil company uses three carefully selected scenarios at group level. They elaborate each of the three in more specific detail for each country in which they operate.

SCENARIO BUILDING VERSUS SENSITIVITY ANALYSIS

The use of scenarios in planning differs from sensitivity analysis in that scenarios require defining plausible sequences of events. A common problem with sensitivity analysis is that it does not specify adequately the interrelationship between variables. Therefore, there might be no underlying economic rationale to the numbers. For example, one might assume that wage rates will rise 10% while ignoring the fact that wage forecasts relate to general economic factors. These same factors can also affect exchange rates, for example, that simultaneously affect the cash flow.

The scenario approach eliminates the necessity of analyzing every one of the hundreds of combinations of possible events. It does so by focusing attention on those chains of possible events that are most potentially relevant to the particular forecast. This procedure does not remove the necessity for judgment and economic insight. Although it is possible to err from considering the wrong factors, one is more likely to err from excluding the critical factors.

ADVERSITY

Management should forecast the effect of changes in the economy on the revenues of the industry and of the firm. In addition, estimates should be made of the value of its assets in the existing and alternative uses, given the various scenarios. Deterioration of revenues could necessitate the sale of assets. Therefore, the values of assets in alternative uses require estimation.

Business adversity can materialize in many forms, each having its own implications for liquidity. The most important circumstances fall into the three following important contexts:

1.   Company business deteriorating in relation to the industry.

2.   Industry declining in relation to the economy.

3.   Economy deteriorating.

If the company should suffer in relation to the industry, selling of assets to companies that are being more successful might be possible. However, if the industry is also in decline (but not the economy), assets with alternative uses might find buyers in other industries. If the economy deteriorates as well, alternative uses for assets might be difficult to find, and some assets could realize little more than scrap value. In the best of circumstances, some fixed assets take a very long time to sell. The time lag between the emerging need for cash in an unfolding crisis and actual realization of funds from the sale of these assets could become a critical factor.

DEFINITION

Liquidity   Ease with which cash is recoverable from an investment.

18-8 FINANCIAL PLANNING PROCEDURE

There are, therefore, six basic steps in the financial planning and forecasting procedure:

1.   Use spreadsheet financial forecasts to determine the funding requirements implied by the corporate strategy and the operating plan. This provides the basic financial plan but does not provide for contingencies. Hence, the following steps are also required.

2.   Identify scenarios for the economy, the industry, and the company representative of those that could plausibly affect plans and increase requirements for funds.

3.   Assess the likely speed and nature of management's response to unfolding events when changing operating plans and taking corrective actions.

4.   Ascertain how quickly the sale of various corporate assets could realize cash if the company were to find itself in financial distress.

5.   Test the sensitivity of funding requirements in the financial forecast to the representative scenarios of adverse future events reflecting the implied operating plans and dispositions of assets.

6.   Devise and initiate the appropriate funding program and such measures as hedging and insurance that suffice for all plausible future contingencies.

These six steps enable financial management to determine how much financing is required to meet the strategic requirements of operating management and the additional financing required as a precaution against possible adverse developments.

The amount of financing that will be required to meet contingencies depends very much on the nature of the contingencies that arise and the company's likely response to them. How quickly can the company change its strategy and operating plans in response to events? What would be the response to unfolding scenarios that could spell adversity, and what would be the cash flow implications of such changed strategies and plans? Incorporation of these considerations is necessary to make the funds flow projection and pro forma cash budget relevant for contingency planning purposes.

FINANCIAL PLANNING AND STRATEGIC OPTIONS

Management cannot know how fundamentally sound the company's financial position is until these steps are accomplished. Without assurance that the financial risks are not going to be excessive, the board will feel constrained not to exercise all its strategic real options. In this way, financial management has an important role to play in laying the financial foundations of strategy.

18-9 CONCLUSIONS

We have shown how to structure alternative sets of assumptions for financial forecasts and discussed how to build financial plans on the resulting foundations. Effective financial planning is one of the best means of minimizing the probability of financial distress and bankruptcy with all the resultant costs to customers, suppliers, employees, lenders, and shareholders. By helping management to foresee adverse circumstances, financial planning facilitates defensive financing arrangements and the trading or sharing of excessive risks with partners. By constructing an adequate defensive posture, management can undertake a more aggressive investment program than might otherwise have been thought possible.

FURTHER READING

Simon Benninga (2000) *Financial Modeling*, 2nd edn (London: The MIT Press).

Marie Dolfe and Anna Koritz (1999) *European Cash Management, A Guide to Best Practice* (Chichester, UK: John Wiley & Sons).

Gill Ringland (1997) *Scenario Planning* (Chichester, UK: John Wiley & Sons).

Peter Schwartz (1997) *The Art of the Long View* (Chichester, UK: John Wiley & Sons).

QUESTIONS AND PROBLEMS

1   Describe the reasons for financial planning. What options are available to the firm if forecasts suggest an unacceptable level of risk?

2   What is the method for preparation of the:

    (a)   cash budget?
    (b)   funds flow forecast?

    Describe the principal uses of these two projections and explain their importance.

3   Is financial planning complementary to or inconsistent with the use of the Capital Asset Pricing Model in project appraisal?

4   "A company should accept all profitable investment opportunities." What qualifications would you make to this statement?

5   What importance does the distinction between fixed and variable expenditures have in financial planning?

6   What are the essential elements in a sound financial planning procedure?

7   Construct a scenario for a well-known company, or one with which you are relatively familiar using the following steps:

    (a)   Draw up a list of events and changes that you think could materially affect the company's cash requirements in the next five years. You can select your list from Table 18.5 and add any other items that could be important.
    (b)   Relist the items in a table similar to Table 18.6. List the most important items near the top of the table and the least important ones near the bottom. Then put each item in the time period (or periods) in which it is likely to have the greatest impact on cash flow.
    (c)   Select a scenario from the table. Say why your scenario provides appropriate assumptions for the company's financial plan.

DEFINITION

Capital Asset Pricing Model (CAPM)   Linear model attempting to explain the expected return on a risky asset in terms of the risk-free rate, its beta factor (systematic risk), and the risk premium on the market portfolio.

19 Managing Debtor Risk[1]

Industrial and commercial customers generally avoid paying cash for goods and services. Suppliers usually agree to grant customers a limited amount of credit, permitting them to delay payment, often for months. The choice of customers worthy of trade credit affects the level and the quality of a supplier's sales. Insolvency threatens many suppliers during a recession when their less credit-worthy customers pay late or refuse to pay at all. In this chapter, we consider the implications of credit policy for customers, sales, and collections. In addition, we examine the various aspects of credit policy, the costs and benefits of extending credit, the assessment of creditworthiness, the aging of receivables, and a model of the credit decision.

TOPICS

In this chapter the main areas considered are:

- *credit terms;*
- *the trade credit decision;*
- *trade credit as a lending decision;*
- *trade credit as an investment decision;*
- *the control of trade credit.*

19-1 CREDIT TERMS

RISK

Extending credit to customers is riskier when the cost of goods sold is large in relation to the price, and the credit charges should reflect the risk. So, a supplier might have to charge a different effective rate of interest for credit than it pays to its own bank.

EFFECTIVE RATE OF INTEREST

The price for goods often incorporates an effective rate of interest. Customers who pay promptly might perceive this policy to be unfair, however. Therefore, some companies charge interest

---

[1] Adapted by permission of J. R. Franks and J. E. Broyles (1979) *Modern Managerial Finance* (Chichester, UK: John Wiley & Sons).

explicitly on the credit balance due on the customer's account. The customary method, however, is to offer a specific discount for payment within a specified period.

EXAMPLE 19.1

Table 19.1 illustrates a way to analyze such credit terms. The supplier considers offering a 3% discount for payment within 30 days. The supplier's expected before-tax cost of financing Accounts Receivable (Debtors) is 2% per month. The problem is whether these credit terms can reduce the costs of financing the Accounts Receivable sufficiently to repay the revenues sacrificed by the discount.

The second column shows the average customer payment pattern for €100 of sales. Ten percent of the customers already pay within one month. Of the 30% paying in the second month, the expectation is that 20% will pay in the first month instead if offered the 3% discount. Of the 30% paying in the third month, only 10% would pay earlier when offered the discount. Tardy customers paying after 3 months would not find the discount sufficiently attractive to induce them to pay earlier. Therefore, the expected pattern of payments would change to Pattern B in the third column. The figure 38.80 in the table is net of the discount.

Columns 5 and 6 give the present values (PVs) of each schedule of payments discounted at 2% per month. Since payments Pattern B has a smaller PV, the 3% discount seems insufficiently attractive for the supplier. The expected acceleration of payments would not reduce financing costs sufficiently in this example to justify the expected cost of offering the discount.

CUSTOMER'S OPTION

Those customers who know they are poor credit risks have the option to pay late and are quite likely to do so, unfortunately.

A further consideration not included above is that some late payers insist on paying the discounted price anyway. Incurring hostility by trying to collect the discount from these customers usually is not worthwhile.

Customs and traditions within an industry govern credit terms and affect the feasibility of changing existing credit arrangements.

Table 19.1 Analysis of credit terms: payment lags.

Month	Without discount A	With trade discount* B	PV factor at 2% per month	PV A	PV B
(1)	(2)	(3)	(4)	(5)	(6)
1	10	38.8	0.9804	9.804	38.039
2	30	10	0.9612	28.835	9.612
3	30	20	0.9423	28.270	18.846
4	20	20	0.9238	18.477	18.477
5	10	10	0.9057	9.057	9.057
				94.443	94.032
					−94.443
				PV of savings	−0.411

*Assumes trade discount of 3% for payment within 30 days.

19-2   THE TRADE CREDIT DECISION

LENDING OR INVESTMENT?

Since customers need not accept the terms of credit offered, credit is really a hidden price concession. Greater credit risk implies a larger price concession if the credit terms remain unchanged. As in the pricing decision, three questions are relevant:

1.   Will the terms of credit influence the customer's buying decision?

2.   Is either the supplier or the customer suffering from a shortage of funds?

3.   Is the supplier working below capacity?

Such questions determine whether to treat the decision to offer credit as a lending decision or as an investment decision.

A customer having adequate sources of funds for all its investment opportunities would compare trade credit with other kinds of borrowing opportunity. In addition, the penalties for delaying payments usually are small, and the transaction costs for trade credit often are less than for new borrowing.

Many customers suffer from capital rationing. A supplier refusing to advance trade credit to such customers is likely to lose the sale. In this circumstance, the offering of trade credit is partly a pricing and selling decision and not solely a lending decision.

For a supplier, extension of trade credit may not be a lending decision. It becomes an investment decision if offering credit would increase the use of facilities operating below capacity. In addition, if the supplier's financial resources are limited, providing trade credit to a customer could exclude other profitable investment opportunities. In such situations, trade credit is partly an investment decision for the supplier. Let us now consider trade credit in more detail: first, as a lending decision and, second, as an investment decision.

19-3 TRADE CREDIT AS A LENDING DECISION

If refusal of credit would not influence the supplier's total volume of sales, then its decision whether to offer credit becomes purely a lending decision. In this situation, three questions arise:

1.   What are the principal and the term of the effective loan?

2.   Given the creditworthiness of the customer, what effective rate of interest should be required?

3.   Considering the industry customary terms of trade, how much credit should the supplier extend to a risky customer who might default?

THE EFFECTIVE LOAN

When extending credit does not affect the supplier's total sales, the resulting incremental credit lending is the increase in Accounts Receivable (Debtors) net of discounts. The implied rate of interest on these effective loans has to cover the prevailing rate of interest reflecting the probability of default and the costs of administration including collection.

DISCOUNT FOR EARLY PAYMENT

The supplier could charge interest to the customer's account or, alternatively, include it in the price of the goods. More usually, the discount for early payment reflects an implicit interest charge for credit. For example, if the discount is 10%, the supplier's charge for credit is 10% of the sales price. The expected benefit of early payment resulting from this discount must be sufficient to cover interest on the customer's account.

TERM OF THE EFFECTIVE LOAN

A number of problems arise in the calculation of the cost of credit, however. The first is the exact term of the effective loan provided by the supplier. For example, if the supplier intends to offer a credit limit equivalent to 1 month's sales to a customer for as long as the customer continues in business, the loan approaches a perpetuity. Therefore, the appropriate interest rate to charge for the credit is comparable with prevailing rates on fixed interest long-term loans.

EXAMPLE 19.2

For example, in an industry where a discount of 2% for payment within 30 days is customary, a customer applies for trade credit. Let us assume initially that the credit is risk-free and that the customer will continue making monthly purchases of €1,000 at list price indefinitely.

The customer would save having to pay €980 immediately for each month's purchases, but will have to pay an additional €20 later due to sacrificing the discount for cash purchase. In this way, the principal of the loan reflects the purchase price net of the discount. The actual amount of the principal depends on the number of months' credit granted and used by the customer. If the customer uses two months' credit, the principal of the effective loan is $2 \times 980 = €1,960$.

Since the customer actually purchases only €1,000 worth of goods per month, the monthly interest received on the loan is $1,000 - 980 = €20$. Although the expected amount of sales determines the interest paid, the principal depends upon the amount of credit granted and its expected use by the customer. If the customer takes two months' credit, the interest rate is $20/(2 \times 980) = 1.02\%$ per month. If the customer takes three months' credit, the interest is only $20/(3 \times 980) = 0.68\%$ per month. So, increasing the amount of credit the customer takes, reduces the effective amount of interest received.

For a risk-free customer, the credit decision would consist merely in choosing the amount of credit that would make the effective interest at least the rate available on irredeemable Government securities.

DEFAULT RISK

Trade credit involves some risk, however. The customer might default in any month with some probability p. If the customer defaults, the entire cash value of the credit taken goes unpaid (the cash value of the credit taken reflects only the cost of goods sold). If, with probability $(1 - p)$, the customer does not default, the customer sacrifices the discount but the Credit Department incurs incremental service costs including debtor monitoring, collection, and legal expenses. Therefore, the effective monthly interest rate is:

Effective Monthly Interest Rate

$$= \frac{[(1-p) \times (Discount \times Monthly\ Sales - Service\ Cost) + p \times (-Cash\ Value\ of\ Credit\ Taken)]}{Cash\ Value\ of\ Credit\ Taken}$$

CUSTOMER'S OPTION

Another consideration involves the amount of credit the customer actually takes. By delaying their payments, some customers take more than the granted credit unless prevented by the Credit Department operating strict credit controls. In this manner, the customer could reduce the effective interest rate for the credit. More importantly, the customer could obtain credit in this way when no one else would be willing to lend to him.

CREDIT CONTROL

Therefore, the supplier's investment in the debtor account also reflects the feasible degree of control by the Credit Department in a changing economic environment. The expected amount of credit actually granted and therefore the effective rate of interest depend on the ability of the Credit Department to enforce collections.

If little effective control is possible, the decision becomes whether to grant the particular credit in the first place. If the expectation is that the customer will take more credit than granted, the Credit Department can refuse to grant any credit at all.

EFFECTIVE INTEREST RATE

Another consideration is that trade credit ordinarily represents a risky loan with an effective interest rate needing to reflect the risk of default of the customer. In a liquidation, secured loans rank in front of unsecured creditors. Therefore, a higher interest rate incorporating a larger risk premium is appropriate for trade credit.

Nevertheless, the interest cost for trade credit can sometimes be lower than the equivalent bank loan. If the supplier is in constant touch with industry and company developments, it can get more up-to-date information on credit risks than banks can. In addition, the supplier often can bring more pressure to bear on a customer by cutting off supplies and by influencing the customer's credit standing with other suppliers. In this way, suppliers can often justify offering more favorable terms than banks can. Therefore, the required risk premium might be lower depending on such considerations.

SUMMARY

In summary, the credit decision is a lending decision when the net effect of the decision is merely to change the size of the debtor account. If the refusal of credit would not result in the loss of business, and if the customer is able to turn to alternative sources of funds, the extending of credit is financially equivalent to the granting of a loan facility. Since a fixed trade discount (for early payment) hides hidden implicit interest, however, the time actually taken by the customer to pay determines the effective interest rate. If the Credit Department feels unable to enforce prompt payment, it can refuse credit to customers they believe are unlikely to pay within the time necessary to make the effective rate of interest attractive.

In circumstances where the credit decision is not suitable for treatment as a loan, treatment as an investment decision is usually possible.

DEFINITIONS

Bank loans   Overdrafts and secured loans negotiated with the company's bankers. Normally for a fixed maturity and a specific purpose. Repaid in regular installments. Interest charged at rates varying with the bank's base rate.

Default   Failure to make a payment of interest or a repayment of principal on the due date.

Irredeemables   Government bonds with no fixed maturity.

Perpetuity   Equal sum of money paid in each period for ever.

Risk premium   Extra return expected from a risky asset compared with the return from an alternative risk-free asset.

19-4 TRADE CREDIT AS AN INVESTMENT DECISION

INVESTING IN CUSTOMERS

Frequently, credit decisions have important effects extending beyond the debtor account. Use of trade credit is vital for the survival of some customers. Many companies face a shortage of capital at times, particularly if they have limited access to capital markets. Their assets might not easily be marketable and thus provide poor security for bank loans. If such companies have to forgo profitable projects due to inadequate funding, they are likely to favor suppliers that provide generous trade credit. Therefore, credit policy affects the sales of the supplier by helping some customers to continue operating when the cost of credit from alternative sources is too high. If there are competing suppliers operating below capacity, then extending credit can prevent loss of sales to competitors.

WORKING CAPITAL

The analytical approach can change somewhat when the supplier operates below capacity and the customer requires straight credit. In this situation, credit decisions can affect the volume of business for the supplier. In this position, the credit decision becomes an investment decision because an investment in working capital is required to secure a subsequent positive cash flow from sales.

A new customer account can require a substantial investment of capital to service the account. This can include cash, raw materials, work in progress, and finished goods, as well as an investment in the customer's account. More precisely, the lag between the payment of expenses associated with the new business and the receipt of payments for goods and services provided requires an investment of funds. In return, the supplier must expect an after-tax return commensurate with the risk of the resulting net cash flow stream.

EXAMPLE 19.3

Table 19.2 is an example of a trade credit investment. In order to assess the effect on the business of a new debtor on the business, one needs to consider all the associated incremental cash flows. Table 19.2 includes just some of the expenses that could be relevant. We show investment in cash and stock including raw materials, work in progress, and finished goods. We include variable expense, incremental sales, and administration, including costs of collection and taxes. Not shown are charges for incremental capital expenses on plant or machinery. Not shown as a separate item are incremental handling and warehousing expenses. If the additional business requires more capacity, the decision involves a full capital project appraisal.

Table 19.2 Incremental cash flow for extending credit to new customers.

	Month				
	0	1	2	3	4	...
Cash and stock	−200					
Variable expenditure		−100	−100	−100	−100	...
Sales and administration		−10	−10	−10	−10	...
Revenue		120	120	120	120	...
Taxes*		$\frac{-5}{}$	$\frac{-5}{}$	$\frac{-5}{}$	−5	...
	−200	5	5	5	5	...

*Adjusted for actual lag in payment.

NET PRESENT VALUE

As usual, the analysis must reflect an unbiased estimate of the leads and lags associated with the incremental cash flows from supplying the type of product to the particular category of customer risk. In addition, inclusion of all likely incremental working capital and other net expenditures is necessary. A positive net present value (NPV) at the appropriate monthly discount rate would indicate that the incremental business is profitable, and that the supplier can consider extending the credit terms assumed in the analysis.

A detailed monthly analysis of this nature can uncover profitable business opportunities missed by more conventional rules of thumb that treat the extension of trade credit as a lending decision.

RISK CLASSIFICATION

In order to relieve the company from analyzing every new customer in such detail, one can institute risk classification by customer type and product. The above monthly cash flow analysis can be performed from time to time for each combination of credit class and product. The form of analysis, however, changes depending on whether extending credit is an investment decision or has become a lending decision.

RATE OF RETURN

Because a full investment analysis for individual credit decisions is often not feasible, simple rules of thumb are useful. An example is the following ratio representing the expected return on the investment in extended credit. The numerator of the ratio is the expected incremental cash flow generated by the extension of credit to a customer. The denominator is the expected incremental investment in working capital required to support the additional sales resulting from the extended credit.

In the numerator of the ratio, the symbol p represents the probability of default in the period. Therefore, the expected cash return attributable to granting the credit is the sum of two parts. The first part is the incremental income from the new debtor if, with probability $(1 - p)$, the debtor does not default. The second part is the cash that is recoverable if, with probability p, the debtor defaults. The equation assumes that the incremental investment in working capital is recoverable except for the debtor proportion remaining unpaid in default:

Monthly Rate of Return

$$= \frac{\left[\begin{array}{c} (1 - p) \times (\textit{Net Cash Flow from Sales} - \textit{Service Cost} - \textit{Stock-carrying Cost} - \textit{Taxes}) \\ + p \times (\textit{Net Investment in Working Capital} - \textit{Cash Value of Credit Taken}) \end{array} \right]}{\textit{Net Investment in Working Capital}}$$

In this formula, *Net Cash Flow from Sales* arises from incremental monthly sales minus the cash costs of sales. *Service Cost* covers monthly incremental administrative costs including monitoring, collection, and legal expenses in the Credit Department. *Stock-carrying Cost* includes such items as storage, handling, insurance, and obsolescence expense, but excludes costs of finance. *Net*

Investment in Working Capital treats cash, debtors, and stock at marginal cost and is net of creditors. All items are after tax and should reflect as nearly as possible the items included in Table 19.2.

This ratio is similar to the one used for the lending form of the credit decision, except that the included incremental cash benefits and expenses are more extensive when the granting of credit affects the level of sales. If the after-tax rate of return calculated on this basis exceeds the risk-adjusted required rate of return for this level of risk, granting credit to the customer is profitable.

PROFITABILITY INDEX

A supplier suffering from capital rationing and wishing to compare the credit decision with other investments could use the profitability index (PI). The value of the index in this case equals *Return* in the above formula divided by the required rate of return. One can compare this value with the PI for an alternative project by dividing the PV of the alternative project by its investment.

DEFINITIONS

Capital market   Market for long-term securities. Consists of the banks, insurance companies, and other financial intermediaries (including the stock market) competing to supply companies with financial capital.

Capital project   Investment in a non-financial asset.

Incremental cash flow   Difference between the relevant expected after-tax cash flows of the firm if the project goes forward and if it does not go forward.

Net present value (NPV)   Difference between the present value of a project's expected after-tax operating cash flows and the present value of its expected after-tax investment expenditures.

Profitability index (PI)   Present value of a project divided by the required investment.

Rate of return   After-tax cash income and capital gain divided by the investment.

19-5 THE CONTROL OF TRADE CREDIT

RATIONALE

Trade credit is a flexible source of finance used by most companies. By simply delaying payment to creditors, companies can increase their liabilities without resorting to their banks for further loans. The advantages to users of trade credit represent corresponding disadvantages to its providers. Therefore, control is required to protect against unanticipated financing requirements and other costs of unanticipated increases in Accounts Receivable (Debtors).

CREDIT INFORMATION

The Credit Department can base its decision whether to extend credit to a particular customer using information from a variety of sources including trade references, bank references, credit bureau reports, salesmen's opinions, and published information. In addition, information concerning an existing customer's payment habits is obtainable from the company's sales ledger.

Table 19.3 Age classification of receivables based on monthly sales.

Age classification (days)	Month of sale	Monthly credit sales (€'000)	Value of debtors (€'000)	Debtors as percentage of credit sales
1–30	June	400	360	90
31–60	May	600	360	60
61–90	April	600	180	30
91–120	March	400	40	10
121+	Earlier	—	60	—
		2,000	1,000	

Credit bureau reports or registers include Dun and Bradstreet lists giving financial details and credit ratings of very many companies. Dun and Bradstreet will also prepare special reports on particular companies not included in their lists.

Companies can turn their sales ledgers over to commercial factors that collect money owed to suppliers by their customers. A company using a factor can often obtain information from the factor concerning the payment habits of potential customers.

In one survey of the sources and effectiveness of information used for checking the creditworthiness of new customers, most often identified as being effective were credit registers and trade protection associations whereas least often identified as most effective were reports from sales personnel.

AGE CLASSIFICATION

Age classification is a standard procedure used by companies to spot problems arising within Accounts Receivable (debtors). Table 19.3 illustrates the age classification of receivables based on monthly credit sales. Age classification reveals the percentage of sales for each preceding month still unpaid. Departure from the normal pattern in these percentages can indicate problems requiring a more detailed customer-by-customer analysis of outstanding receivables.

CREDIT COLLECTION PROCEDURE

Most companies operate a standard debt collection procedure. They apply a sequence of collection methods beginning with posted reminders and culminating in court action if necessary. The method most favored by companies is telephone reminders by the credit control department. This method provides informative personal contact helping the credit controller to differentiate between companies habitually paying late and those becoming a credit risk.

19-6 CONCLUSIONS

In summary, there are several costs to extending trade credit. These include the cost of financing the resulting increase in working capital, clerical costs, and the expected costs of bad debts. The benefit from a more liberal credit policy, however, is increased sales. The benefit outweighs the costs when there are adequate credit controls. The amount of credit extended to marginal customers must be limited, however. The sales ledger needs regular monitoring to ensure that customers do not fall significantly behind in their payments. A systematic reminder system helps to make the customer aware that the supplier's credit department is efficient and likely to apply pressure if the customer exceeds granted credit limits.

FURTHER READING

T. S. Maness and J. T. Zeitlow (1993) "Accounts receivable management," *Short-Term Financial Management Text, Cases, and Readings* (New York: West).

QUESTIONS AND PROBLEMS

1   A retail store sells its goods on credit. How should it estimate the cost of credit to its customers?

2   Under what circumstances is the decision to provide credit to a customer solely a financing decision?

3   Why is it difficult to define precisely the period of credit?

4   Under what circumstances should a firm accept a period of credit and reject a discount for early payment?

5   Under what circumstance is it possible for the provision of trade credit to be profitable to both parties?

6   Compute the average debtor collection period for a company with Accounts Receivable (Debtors) outstanding totaling €14,000 and annual sales of €132,000. If the maximum credit period granted by the company is 21 days, what might explain the difference in the average collection period? What questions does this raise and what suggestions could you make to management that might improve the situation?

7   A company forecasts sales totaling €100,000 for the next quarter assuming a 1% discount for payment within seven days. The maximum permitted credit period is 28 days, although some customers take longer to pay. Assuming the customers' cost of borrowing is 15% per annum, should a customer accept the discount for early payment? What difference does it make to your calculations if a customer takes 45 days' credit?

8   A company currently gives 28 days' credit for all sales but experiences the repayments schedule listed in the second column below. The final column shows the forecast collections if the company offered a 1% discount for payment within seven days. Is the proposed credit policy profitable from the company's point of view if the company's borrowing rate is 9% and the customers' average annual borrowing rate is 12%?

Month	Without discount	With trade discount
Within 7 days	0	150
1	400	280
2	100	70
3	50	50
4	10	10
5	10	10
Total sales	€570	€570

9   Customer X purchases €10,000 of goods from Company Y with the usual two months' credit period. In addition, Y offers a 10% discount for immediate payment. Y is aware that X is a risky customer and estimates a 5% probability of default each month. The expected monthly cost of servicing the account is €100. Is the discount a good idea from the seller's point of view? Assume that X can borrow at 20% and Y can borrow at 10% per annum. Show your computations.

10   Both the supplier and its customers are short of funds due to a severe credit squeeze imposed by the Government and the banks. In order to attract customers, however, the supplier considers offering one month's credit rather than the existing terms of cash on delivery. Existing sales are €10,000 per month, and the supplier anticipates an increase in sales to €12,000 per month from the new credit policy. The supplier forecasts that a third of all future sales will be on credit with half on one month's credit and the other half on two months' credit. The expected incremental service costs of the new credit policy total €100 per month, and the gross margin on sales is 50% of the sales price. The company had borrowed funds at 10%. Due to the current credit squeeze, however, offering additional credit requires forgoing profitable projects promising returns of 20% compared with the required rate of return of 15%. Management thinks that the new credit policy is of the same risk as these other projects. Can the supplier expect the new policy to be profitable?

20 Managing Inventory Risk[1]

Inventory investment facilitates smooth functioning of manufacturing, distributing, and retailing operations. Inventories of finished goods assure good customer service and reduce the costly effects on production of fluctuating demand. In addition, raw materials' inventory can prevent shortages due to uncertain timing of deliveries from suppliers. Investment in inventory accounts for as much as 40% of total assets for many manufacturing companies. So, the costs of holding inventory can be significant. An inadequate inventory control system results in unbalanced stocks, thereby reducing both efficiency and customer service. Insolvency can threaten a company producing too much stock that cannot be sold. Accordingly, inventory control deserves the close attention of financial management.

Although specialists carry out the day-to-day operation of inventory control, financial managers exercise influence on inventory investment on at least two levels. First, inventory reporting and other data processing associated with the inventory control system usually are the responsibility of the IT Department, reporting ultimately to the Chief Financial Officer (CFO). Therefore, the choice, design, and subsequent adaptation of the inventory control systems operated throughout the company usually involve financial people. Second, the operation of the system requires periodic monitoring and control. Inventory control systems have severe limitations, and the specialists operating them often do not know current management thinking and strategy concerning working capital targets and priorities. The CFO needs to know the trends in the company's investment in inventory and its salability in order to ensure that the inventory investment does not become excessive and that the company will remain solvent.

TOPICS

The main topics considered in this chapter are:

○   *planning and monitoring inventory levels;*

○   *designing the inventory control system;*

○   *elements of an inventory control system;*

○   *operating at the inventory control system; and*

○   *responsibility for the investment in inventory.*

---

[1] Adapted by permission of J. R. Franks and J. E. Broyles (1979) *Modern Managerial Finance* (Chichester, UK: John Wiley & Sons).

We first discuss methods by which financial management can exercise broad controls on inventory investment. In addition, we describe some inventory control systems that can help inventory managers operate more successfully. Finally, we consider the problems of operating inventory controls within the context of broad targets when several operating departments with conflicting interests share the responsibility for inventory management.

DEFINITION

Inventory control system   Information system and procedures designed to monitor and replenish stock and to maximize the return on investment in inventories.

20-1 PLANNING AND MONITORING INVENTORY LEVELS

Changes in inventory (stock) for a given period are the net of purchasing and production minus sales. Deviations from planned inventory result when purchasing, production, or sales deviate from plans and forecasts.

MONITORING TOTAL INVENTORY INVESTMENT

Each production unit requires an operating plan based on existing orders, forecast sales, and desired changes in inventory. Monitoring of actual production, sales, and inventory relative to the plan enables timely adjustments with changes in market conditions.

Figure 20.1 is an example of a cumulative production, sales, and inventory chart used to facilitate monitoring of total inventory by profit center or by product. The solid line is the cumulative

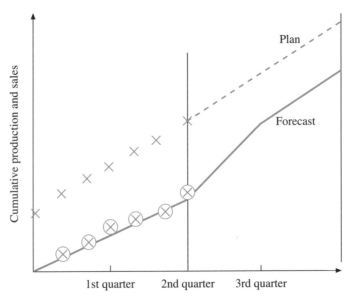

Figure 20.1   Production, sales, and inventory chart.

forecast. The circled points are cumulative sales to date (through June). The first uncircled point (on the vertical axis) is finished goods at the beginning of the year, and subsequent points represent cumulative production. The dashed line represents the cumulative production plan, and the vertical distance between the cumulative sales forecast and the cumulative production plan represents the planned levels of finished goods at each point in time.

For raw materials, we can use a similar chart. In this case, the circled points represent usage in production and the solid line is the forecast usage. The points not circled and the dashed line would represent cumulative purchases and planned purchases, respectively.

Cumulative production, sales (or purchasing), and inventory charts provide financial management with a useful graphical monitor of the trend of requirements for investment in inventory. The charts show the interrelationships between inventory, planned production levels, and seasonal changes in sales. This overview helps to counteract the attempt to maintain a constant number of weeks' stock in every item, requiring unnecessary and costly changes of production levels with each temporary fluctuation in sales activity. Monitoring the aggregate inventory investment also helps prevent excessive investment in inventory contributing to possible insolvency.

MONITORING INVENTORY COMPOSITION

While the interest of financial managers is primarily in the movement in total inventory, they also need to watch the composition of the inventory. Figure 20.2 illustrates a typical distribution of the usage of individual stock items in the inventory. For example, 25% of the items constitute perhaps 60–75% of the total volume. These A category stocks are the most important, deserving individual attention. The next 25% of items, the B category, might account for only 15–20% of the volume of

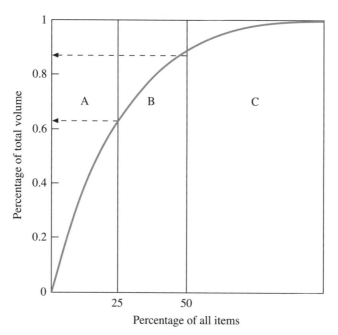

Figure 20.2 ABC analysis.

inventory usage, and the C category comprising the remaining 50% of the items could account for as little as 5% of the usage.

So, possibly 50% of the items are relatively slow-moving and would be held in quantities relatively large compared with anticipated usage. Efforts to reduce inventory quickly can be counterproductive if this merely means selling off the fast-moving A and B items, leaving an unbalanced inventory consisting mostly of C category items.

COSTS OF CARRYING INVENTORY

The costs of carrying inventory are somewhat greater than just the cost of capital for investment in the inventory. At least four items of cost need consideration:

1. *Storage costs, handling, and insurance.* Only incremental costs such as handling and insurance need inclusion when warehouse space has no alternative uses and marginal costing is appropriate.

2. *Obsolescence, deterioration, and theft.* The costs arising from these items depend on the nature of the items in stock.

3. *Clerical costs.* Inventories require recording and controlling. Costs of operating the necessary control systems can be significant.

4. *Financing costs.* Investment in inventory is risky and requires a risk premium.

The total of these stock-carrying costs can range from 10% up to 40% per year of the value of the investment in inventory.

INVENTORY AS CAPITAL INVESTMENT

We can analyze investment in inventory as though it were a capital project. The objective is to maximize the net present value (NPV) of the investment in stock. Consider, for example, finished goods stock. Carrying finished goods enables the company to provide faster service to customers than possible with goods made to order. Shipping and invoicing immediately upon receipt of an order provides better service, can increase sales, and often permit higher prices for the goods. Finished goods inventory also acts as a buffer between production and sales permitting production in efficient batches independent of the sizes of individual customer orders. This reduces production ordering costs and machine setup costs. In this way, it is important to maintain investment in stock at levels consistent with both marketing effectiveness and production efficiency.

We now consider ways to implement inventory control systems balancing the costs of inventory and its benefits.

DEFINITIONS

Capital project   Investment in a non-financial asset.

Chief Financial Officer (CFO)   A company's most senior financial manager.

Cost of capital   Cost of funds used by a company for investment.

Insolvency   Condition in which a company is unable to meet its obligations to creditors when due; that is, being technically bankrupt.

Inventory control system   Procedure to control investment in inventory with the objective of providing acceptable service to customers while minimizing the sum of stock carrying and reordering risks.

Net present value (NPV)   Difference between the present value of a project's expected after-tax operating cash flows and the present value of its expected after-tax investment expenditures.

Risk premium   Extra return expected from a risky asset compared with the return from an alternative risk-free asset.

Risk   Probability of an unacceptable loss. In portfolio theory, the standard deviation of holding period returns.

20-2 DESIGNING THE INVENTORY CONTROL SYSTEM

RATIONALE

Inventory plays an important role in cushioning the various stages of production from short-term changes in supply, and in reducing delivery lead times to customers. Accordingly, the inventory system is crucial to the provision of service to customers efficiently at minimum cost.

The following inventory categories are important:

1.   Raw materials.

2.   Work in process.

3.   Partially processed items including component stocks.

4.   Finished goods.

5.   Distribution stocks.

Within each of these categories the inventory system often must provide:

1.   Inventories in anticipation of seasonal changes in demand.

2.   Inventories arising from quantity ordering and batch production.

3.   Safety stocks serving as a reserve against uncertain demand.

4.   Logistical inventories required to fill the pipeline between stages of production and the distribution system.

The availability of inventories at critical points in the production system can greatly shorten delivery lead times to customers and thus improve the company's competitiveness while reducing manufacturing costs. The inventory control system should seek an optimum balance between these advantages and the costs of carrying inventory within the physical limitations of available space.

We shall now examine in more detail the elements required in an effective inventory control system.

20-3 ELEMENTS OF AN INVENTORY CONTROL SYSTEM

REPLENISHMENT

We can characterize an inventory control system in terms of the method used to replenish stocks. The method chosen depends on (a) the degree of uncertainty associated with demand and (b) the degree of monitoring justifiable in each case. Five basic stock replenishment systems commonly in use are:

1.   Reorder level policy.

2.   Reorder level policy subject to periodic review.

3.   Reorder cycle policy.

4. (s, S) policy.

5.   Materials requirements planning (MRP).

6.   Just in time.

The choice of system depends on the degree of demand uncertainty and on the desired level of monitoring.

DEFINITIONS

Just in time   Integration of information systems of customers and suppliers to facilitate timely supply and efficient inventory control.

Materials requirements planning (MRP)   Production planning and inventory control system designed to exploit predictable patterns in customer orders.

Reorder cycle policy   Reorder policy that reviews stock for replenishment only at fixed points in time and reorders each stock in the quantity necessary to bring the total amount on order and in stock to a predetermined level.

Reorder level policy   Policy of reordering a predefined quantity of a stock as soon as it falls below a specified level.

Reorder level policy subject to periodic review   Reorder level policy that reviews stock for replenishment only at fixed points in time.

(s, S) Policy   Reorder level policy that reviews stock for replenishment only at fixed points in time and reorders each stock in the quantity necessary to bring the total amount on order and in stock to a predetermined level S, but not unless the stock is below a specified level s.

REORDER LEVEL POLICY

The reorder level policy is suitable for real-time monitoring when the arrivals of orders follow no predictable pattern. Therefore, one finds variations of the reorder level policy operating in retail and wholesale outlets or in other parts of the system where many customers can make demands on stock.

A forecast of the average rate of sales is required. The policy also requires an estimate of the *expected* lead time between placement of the replenishment order and the receipt of the goods in stock. For each item in stock, one must calculate a *reorder level*. When stock falls to the reorder level or below, the system immediately places a replenishment order. The reorder level is set equal to expected sales during the lead time so that, on average, stock will not be exhausted before new supplies arrive. In addition, the provision of safety stock helps to meet the additional demand when sales exceed the expected level during the lead time.

One calculates the required safety stock using the statistical distribution of demand for the expected lead time. A computer program determines the probability that exhaustion of stock (a *stockout*) will occur before the arrival of replacement stocks. Larger safety stocks reduce the probability of stock being unavailable when needed.

The system also requires stock-replenishment ordering quantities. The act of reordering can require clerical time, and the opportunity cost of setting up machinery required to satisfy an order for finished goods is costly. Ordering stock in larger quantities requires fewer replenishment orders and thus reduces reordering costs. The size of each batch received in stock influences the size of the resulting inventory, however. The costs of holding this inventory are significant. Economic order quantity formulas minimize the sum of reordering and stockholding costs. Appendix 20.1 gives an example of such a formula.

Thus, the reorder level system requires forecasts of the reordering lead time, the mean and variance of usage during the lead time, reordering and machine setup costs, and the incremental cost of holding stock for one period. The system itself can usually generate all the required data.

The reorder level policy suffers from two quite serious limitations. First, the usual assumption of random arrivals of orders against stock is often inappropriate. When placing replenishment orders, the system takes no advantage of regular patterns in the arrivals. A more serious limitation is that the reorder level policy requires costly, continuous real-time monitoring of every item in stock.

REORDER LEVEL POLICY SUBJECT TO PERIODIC REVIEW

The reorder level policy subject to periodic review is similar to the reorder level policy except that it reviews each item of stock only once per period (e.g., each week or month). Stocks found below their reorder levels generate replacement orders in the same quantities as the reorder level policy with continuous review.

With this system the reorder level must be set higher, however, to allow for expected demand during the sum of the lead time plus one-half the review period. In addition, safety stock must now allow also for the variance of expected demand for one-half the review period.

Although periodic review reduces the clerical and data-processing costs of operating the system, holding costs for the additional inventory are higher. Formulae are available for determining the optimum review cycle. The working cycle of the control department might not conform easily to the theoretically optimum review period, however.

REORDER CYCLE POLICY

The reorder cycle policy is a periodic review system providing a more direct control on stock levels. In each cycle, the system places a replenishment order for the quantity that would bring the total amount on order and already in stock up to a predetermined limit. This limit must be sufficient to cover forecast demand for one full review period plus the lead time. The system includes an additional amount of safety stock to allow for the variability of demand during this total period.

The reorder cycle period chosen minimizes the total of reordering costs and the average lot size stockholding cost.

THE (s, S) POLICY

The (s, S) policy is a hybrid between the reorder cycle policy with periodic review and the reorder cycle policy. The (s, S) policy reviews stocks periodically but does not replenish them unless they fall below their reorder levels s. In this respect, the (s, S) policy is like the reorder level policy with periodic review. The policy does not use economic order quantities, however. Instead, the replenishment order is just sufficient to make the total of goods in stock and goods on order equal to the quantity S. In this latter respect, the method operates like a reorder cycle system.

A problem with the (s, S) method is that calculation of the combination of s, S and the review period minimizing total cost is quite mathematical. A reasonable approach is to make the difference (s, S) equal to the economic order quantity, the reorder level s, equal to the safety stock in the reorder level policy with periodic review, and the review period the same as under the reorder cycle policy.

MATERIALS REQUIREMENTS PLANNING

The four policies reviewed above assume that arrivals of individual demands on stock are unpredictable. As individual demands become more predictable, these policies cease to be optimal and we can get better results using materials requirements planning.

For example, suppose a customer for whom the company holds a stock of finished goods orders the same quantity at the same time virtually every month. An optimal policy needs to take advantage of this information concerning demand. If a replenishment order equal to the customer's monthly demand were placed just over one lead time prior to the expected receipt of the monthly order, virtually no finished stock need be carried because replenishment would be just in time to meet demand.

We know, however, that reordering in larger quantities would reduce machinery setup costs. This implies inventory must meet demand beyond the first month. The decision as to how many months' sales should be included in the replenishment order is a capital investment decision. We need to find the reordering policy that minimizes the present value (PV) of the resulting sequence of setup costs and holding costs.

Therefore, when the pattern of demand is predictable, adapting the ordering policy to take advantage of the pattern is advantageous. Operation of such a system requires close attention to the demand characteristics of each such item of stock, however. It might be necessary to confine such refinements mainly to major items among those categorized as Class A in Figure 20.2 where one might justify the additional costs of the more refined system.

To the extent that the firm manufactures to a backlog of orders, the demand pattern becomes predictable in the short term. Consequently, when there is an order backlog, the various reordering policies discussed earlier are not appropriate. Instead, we can use the known demand to generate orders back through the operating system for the required parts, materials, and components. The resulting *planning* system uses customer orders and resulting lists of parts and quantities to generate factory requirements. These requirements translate into schedules taking into consideration the need to consolidate demand for common components, existing stock, production purchasing lead times, and production batching.

JUST IN TIME

Just in time is the logical extension of materials requirements planning. The difference is that just in time systems are more proactive in generating the information required for optimum production planning and inventory control. Instead of just anticipating the customer order pattern, just in time systems integrate with the internal information systems of both customers and suppliers. Such integrated systems can generate materials requirements information instantly throughout the relevant chain of companies. So, just in time systems represent an attempt to eliminate uncertainty from the whole manufacturing process. The result can be a dramatic reduction in the required investment in inventory.

A criticism of just in time is that some companies use it to eliminate their investment in safety stocks. This can result in a fragile system incapable of adjusting to an unanticipated temporary failure to deliver on time anywhere along the chain of suppliers. An extreme example of such failure was the disastrous effect of the Kobe earthquake on just in time systems throughout Japan.

DEFINITIONS

Expected (mean)   Probability-weighted average of all possible outcomes for a random variable.

Present value (PV)   Value of an investment now as the cost of a comparable investment in the financial market (calculated by multiplying the investment's expected after-tax cash income by the appropriate discount factors).

Variance   Mean squared deviation.

20-4 OPERATING THE INVENTORY CONTROL SYSTEM

MANAGING THE LEVEL OF PRODUCTION

Achieving the optimum overall result requires superimposing the corporate view on the inventory control system. Stock control formulas do not usually consider the costs of sudden changes in the overall level of production. Management must judge how quickly to change production in anticipation of seasonal and other changes in demand, letting inventories serve as the buffer between production and demand changes. In this way, production plans reflect the inventory target and other information underlying the production, sales, and inventory chart of Figure 20.1.

The starting inventory, the sales forecast, and the production plan jointly dictate the planned changes in inventory. Referring to Figure 20.1, at the end of the second quarter, the plan calls for inventory to reach a maximum and then to fall to a minimum three months later.

These planned changes constrain total inventory to levels that are different from the sum of all the theoretically optimum economic order quantities and safety stocks. Therefore, the stock control system must scale the individual order quantities to make the total inventory hit the target level illustrated in Figure 20.1.

CONFLICTS OF INTEREST

A variety of departments control inventories. Each department has an interest in maintaining inventory at a substantial level. Therefore, financial managers need to ensure that conflicts of interest do not bias upward the investment in inventory.

Finished goods stocks are usually required for good customer service. Consequently, marketing managers take an active interest in finished goods, often exercising direct control over individual stock intended for important customers. Marketing personnel often argue for larger inventories to insure against shortages and to maximize sales.

The inventory of finished goods provides a buffer between the market and the production process that facilitates long production runs and minimizes changes in the level of employment. Production managers often push for uninterrupted production runs that minimize unit costs, even though this can result in unbalanced item stocks. Too much of some items implies too little of others. Here again we find an interest in maintaining substantial inventories in excess of what is required.

The Purchasing Department is responsible for providing the raw materials inventories necessary for continuity of production. Therefore, unless the system provides the Purchasing Department with the most up-to-date information about changing requirements, the Department will play safe and order excess stock.

PRODUCTION PLANNING AND CONTROL

In manufacturing companies, a Production Planning and Control Department will normally be responsible for the balancing of the interests of the various departments and for the minimization of the financial and other costs of carrying stock. Production Planning and Control Departments often report to the Director of Production and are frequently located within operating companies of the group. The Production Control Manager is subject to pressures from the other interested departments. If the Production Control Manager does not report to financial management, these pressures can more easily result in suboptimal operating plans and inventories that are inconsistent with corporate strategy and the financial plan.

20-5 CONCLUSIONS

Inventories represent a significant proportion of the assets of manufacturers, wholesalers, and retailers thus requiring the close attention of financial management in such companies. Inventories can become obsolete, and an accumulating excess of unmarketable inventory has led to the bankruptcy of very many companies. Typically, several departments influence the stocks carried in inventory, and thus financial management needs to oversee the inventory control system. Modern information systems provide all the necessary information to manage stock, and financial management has the ultimate responsibility to see that the total inventory investment reflects the right relationship between forecast sales and the costs of capital administration, production, and warehousing. This chapter outlines the tools for managing inventory risk.

FURTHER READING

E. Silver, D. F. Pyke, and R. Peterson (1998) *Inventory Management and Production Planning and Scheduling* (Chichester, UK: John Wiley & Sons).

QUESTIONS AND PROBLEMS

1   What factors make inventory control an important part of the production planning and control system?

2   Describe an effective means of planning and monitoring the aggregate investment in inventories.

3   What are the main costs of carrying stocks? How significant are they in total?

4   What are the principal categories of inventory carried by companies and what types of stock must be provided within each category?

5   What are the characteristics of the six basic inventory replenishment systems in use? In what circumstances is the use of each most appropriate?

6   Describe some of the problems arising in the operation of inventory control systems.

7   LMN Company manufactures Product Line A at the rate of 18,750 per month. The table below gives the quarterly sales forecast.

Quarter	Forecast
1	75,000
2	125,000
3	75,000
4	125,000

Aggregate inventory for Product Line A at the beginning of the year was 200,000 units. If the target inventory for the end of the year is to be 66,667 units, when should normal production resume? Draw the cumulative production, sales, and inventory chart.

8   Identify and label the following on the diagram below: (a) order quantity, (b) reorder level, (c) ordering lead time, and (d) safety stock.

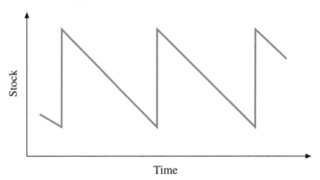

9   For the (s, S) stock control system, identify s and S on the diagram in Problem 8. How would you estimate the values of s and S?

10   The company manufactures stock especially for one industrial customer who regularly orders €1,000 worth (at marginal cost) at the end of each month. If the inventory-carrying cost is 30% per year, and the reordering cost is €100, how many months' stock should be made in each batch, and what average amount of stock will be carried? [*Hint:* use formula derived in Appendix 20.1.]

APPENDIX 20.1   ECONOMIC ORDER QUANTITIES

The economic order quantity (EOQ) formula provides, a basis for obtaining reordering quantities used in some of the inventory control systems described in this chapter. The purpose of the EOQ is to minimize the sum of ordering costs and holding costs for an individual stock.

ORDERING COSTS

Annual ordering costs equal the number of orders multiplied by the cost per order D (typically administrative and any machinery setup costs). The estimated number of orders equals the forecast annual usage S divided by the order quantity Q. Therefore:

$$Annual\ Ordering\ Cost = \frac{SD}{Q}$$

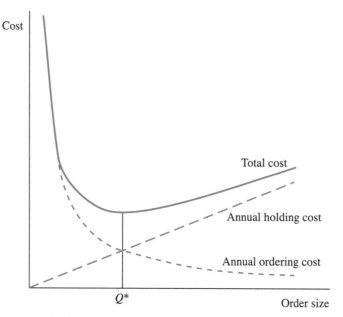

Figure 20.A1   Ordering cost, holding cost, and total cost.

This cost can be reduced by increasing Q as can be seen by the curved line in Figure 20.A1. Increasing the order size Q, however, increases the stock and the resulting stockholding costs.

STOCKHOLDING COSTS

Receipt of a stock replenishment in the amount Q increases stock initially by Q. The stock diminishes to zero on average by the time the next replenishment arrives. Therefore, the *lot size* inventory due to discrete replenishments of stock averages between Q and zero or Q/2. If the cost per unit in stock is V and the annual inventory holding charge is I per unit of value in stock, then the cost of carrying lot size stock is:

$$Stockholding\ Cost = IVQ/2$$

Therefore, stockholding cost increases with the value of Q along the straight line in Figure 20.A1.

MINIMUM TOTAL HOLDING AND ORDERING COSTS

The objective of the EOQ is to minimize the total of holding and ordering costs; that is, to minimize:

$$T = \frac{SD}{Q} + \frac{IVQ}{2}$$

As seen in Figure 20.A1, the minimum occurs at the value of Q where the holding and ordering costs are equal. Consequently, we can solve for the value of Q* where these two terms are the same:

$$Q^* = \sqrt{\frac{2SD}{IV}}$$

This is the *economic order quantity* formula referred to in the chapter. Operations management textbooks give this and other formulas that include more variables.

DEFINITION

Economic order quantity (EOQ)   Stock replenishment order quantity that minimizes the sum of annual stock holding costs and annual ordering costs.

21 Managing Interest and Exchange Rate Risks

Company directors have a legal and moral responsibility to preserve the corporate entity. They must not take unnecessary risks leading to financial distress. Excessive borrowing and foreign exchange exposure entail such risk. The most obvious risk is inability to make loan payments when due. In this chapter, however, we shall be concerned with managing the narrower risks associated with changing rates of interest and with changing foreign exchange rates.

Companies can hedge risks using various options, forwards, futures, and swap transactions. Hedging is about matching assets and liabilities in a manner that makes the matched combination immune to a source of risk. If a company has cash flows, assets, and liabilities denominated in foreign currencies, exposure to unexpected changes in exchange rates can constitute significant risk for the company. Therefore, the Board cannot leave it to shareholders to hedge the company's foreign exchange risk exposure within the context of their own portfolios. Shareholders cannot protect the corporate entity or its creditworthiness in this way. Furthermore, a company cannot keep its shareholders sufficiently informed about the company's current risk exposures for them to hedge their own portfolios effectively. Consequently, it falls to the Corporate Treasurer to hedge at least those risks that plausibly could lead to financial distress.

TOPICS

Consequently, in this chapter we discuss the following topics:

○　　fixed and floating rate debt;

○　　corporate bonds;

○　　interest rate swaps;

○　　forward rate agreements;

○　　interest rate derivatives;

○　　foreign exchange risk management;

○　　behavior of foreign exchange rates;

○　　foreign exchange risk exposure;

○　　foreign exchange risk management methods.

21-1 FIXED AND FLOATING RATE DEBT

If changes in a company's operating income were perfectly, positively correlated with changes in corporate borrowing rates, it would want to borrow at floating rates of interest. The net effect of this would smooth some of the variation in net earnings. For example, when operating income declines, variable interest expense would also fall, thus reducing the corresponding loss of net earnings. Alternatively, if the correlation between changes in a company's operating income and changes in corporate borrowing rates were equal to zero, then the company would need to borrow at fixed rates to minimize variation in net earnings. Virtually all companies fall between these two extremes, suggesting that most companies should consider using a combination of fixed and floating interest rate borrowing to reduce the risk of an unacceptable loss of net income. Alternatively, they can hedge a part of the floating rate risk.

DEFINITIONS

Correlation   Association between two random variables.

Financial distress   Condition in which a company might not be able to meet its obligations to creditors; that is, in danger of becoming insolvent or technically bankrupt.

Floating rate   Variable interest rate changing in response to changes in a specified index of market rates of interest.

Hedging   Buying one security and selling another to reduce risk.

Option   Contract granting the right without obligation to engage in a future transaction on terms specified in the contract.

Portfolio   Collection of investments in financial securities and other assets.

Risk   Probability of an unacceptable loss. In portfolio theory, the standard deviation of holding the period returns.

Swap   Arrangement in which two companies (through the intermediation of a swap bank) agree to exchange loan payments, for example fixed for floating rate payments or payments in different currencies.

Treasurer   Senior financial manager reporting directly to the Chief Financial Officer. Primarily responsible for funding and cash management.

21-2 CORPORATE BONDS

FIXED-RATE CORPORATE BONDS

Fixed-rate corporate bonds, for example X Co., 7.2% loan stock, 2007–10, quote a rate of interest based on a notional £100 face value (par value) and a series of years when the borrower can delay redeeming (repay) the bond. In this case, the bondholder would expect to receive two payments (coupons) of £7.2/2 per year. In addition, the bondholder receives the £100 face value upon redemption of the bond. The borrower makes the redemption payments to a sinking fund administered by the Trustee Department of a bank contracted to represent the interests of the bondholders. The borrower is more likely to want to repay the £100 loan during a period when interest rates fall sufficiently to make the bond's price greater than £100. This would enable the company to borrow again at the lower rate of interest. This choice represents a valuable option for the borrower. The borrower's payment for this option takes the form of a discount in the bond's issue price.

Perpetuals are bonds that have no stated redemption dates but which nevertheless are redeemable (unless the perpetual is an irredeemable bond).

Convertibles are bonds giving the bondholder the option (effectively a warrant) to exchange the bond for a number of the company's shares determined by stated exchange ratios and during a specified period of years.

BOND YIELDS

The redemption yield (yield to maturity) on a bond is its internal rate of return (IRR), treating the current price as the initial investment. The redemption yield is usually greater than the dividend yield on equities. This difference is the well-known yield gap. The reason for the yield gap is that the redemption yield (IRR) includes any expected price appreciation on the bonds, but the dividend yield *excludes* expected price appreciation on the stocks. The time left before the borrower has to redeem the bond is the bond's maturity.

TERM STRUCTURE OF INTEREST RATES

Usually, the bonds with longer maturities (long bonds) have higher redemption yields, and the relationship between yields and maturities is the term structure of interest rates. A declining term structure usually implies that the market believes interest rates and inflation will be lower in the future. However, such forecasts are frequently biased. The reason for the bias is that usually the term structure reflects liquidity preference. That is, the market for short-maturity bonds is more active, making them easier to sell. This greater liquidity increases their relative attractiveness and reduces the yields that investors are willing to accept on shorter maturity bonds. A related proposition is that the longer bonds require higher yields to attract investors when uncertainty about future rates of inflation becomes significant. Therefore, the longer end of the term structure can reflect an inflation risk premium. Such factors usually cause the term structure to rise rather than decline.

Market segmentation theory suggests that long and short bonds appeal to different bondholder clienteles having different preferences (preferred habitats) with respect to maturities and that differences in these preferences help to explain the existence of the term structure of bond yields.

FLOATING RATE CORPORATE BONDS

Floating rate notes (FRNs) are corporate bonds having their interest rates tied to a reference interest rate such as the Euro London Interbank Offered Rate (Euro Libor) plus a quoted margin.

This rate, set daily at 11.00 a.m. UK time, is the average rate of interest at which the largest banks in London lend to each other.[1] The floating interest rate on a bond changes every three months or six months depending on the particular bond. These changes relate to quotations of the reference interest rate by the reference banks at 11.00 a.m. two business days before the change.

INTEREST RATE RISK

This brief review of the corporate bond market reveals sources of interest rate risk for companies. Uncertainty about future rates of inflation increases the variation in bond yields, particularly for long maturities. Corporate treasurers are wary of issuing long-term fixed-interest bonds when they believe that falling rates of inflation could reduce future interest rates in the future. Treasurers can maintain flexibility in this situation by issuing either short-term or floating rate bonds. This strategy can also reduce risk if the company's operating income positively correlates with interest rates and inflation. This particular means of controlling interest rate risk is relatively imprecise, however. Fortunately, corporate treasurers have a number of financial instruments they can use to refine their management of interest rate risk.

DEFINITIONS

Bond   An interest-bearing security with usually long-term maturity. Interest payments may be fixed or variable (floating).

Coupon   When detached from a bond, a coupon serves as evidence of entitlement to an interest payment. The word coupon more usually refers to the rate of interest on an interest-bearing security, however.

Convertibles   Bonds or preferred stocks that give the holder the option (effectively a warrant) to convert the security into the issuing company's ordinary shares (common stock) according to specified terms during some stated period of years.

Dividend yield   Annual dividends per share divided by the current price per share.

Equity   Net worth or shareholder's capital represented by common stock (ordinary shares) and preferred stock.

Euro London Interbank Offered Rate (Euro Libor)   Libor interest rate for euro.

Expected (mean)   Probability-weighted average of all possible outcomes for a random variable.

Face value (par value)   Redemption value printed on a bond or share certificate. The actual market price for the security need not equal its face value.

Floating rate notes (FRNs)   Corporate bonds with interest rates tied to a reference interest rate such as Euro Libor.

Inflation risk premium   Additional yield on long bonds that investors require for risk due to uncertainty about future rates of inflation.

---

[1] Reference interest rates in some other currencies are US$ Libor, £ Libor, Yen Libor and Swiss Frank Libor.

Internal rate of return (IRR)   Discount rate that would make the net present value for an investment equal to zero.

Irredeemables   Government bonds with no fixed maturity.

Libor   Set daily at 11.00 a.m. UK time, the average rate of interest at which the largest banks in London lend to each other.

Liquidity preference   Proposition that shorter-maturity bonds require lower yields to attract investors because the market for them is more active, making them easier to sell.

Loan stock (corporate bonds)   A fixed-interest security (bond) not secured on a specific asset.

Longs   Bonds with dated maturities greater than 15 years.

Market segmentation   Theory of the term structure of interest rates suggesting that different investors prefer different bands of maturities.

Maturity   Period between the creation of a financial claim and the date on which it is to be paid. The final date when a bond is due for repayment.

Perpetuals   Bonds without stated maturities (undated).

Preferred habitat   A band of maturities that may be preferred by particular investors.

Redeem   Repay the face value of a bond.

Redemption yield   Internal rate of return on a bond's interest and redemption payments.

Shorts   Bonds with maturities less than five years.

Sinking fund   An account administered by independent trustees through which the borrower repays outstanding bonds.

Term structure of interest rates   Observed relationship between yields on bonds and their maturities.

Uncertainty   Risk not measureable with historical data.

Warrants   Securities giving the holder the right to buy shares directly from a company at potentially advantageous prices. Warrant terms specify the number of shares, prices, and dates when the warrant may be exercised.

Yield gap   Observed usually positive difference between redemption yields on bonds and dividend yields on equities, explainable because dividend yield omits expected capital growth.

21-3 INTEREST RATE SWAPS

Often a company should borrow at a floating rate but finds that it can get a lower rate compared with other companies if it borrows at a fixed rate. Another company finds it has a comparative advantage borrowing at a floating rate but would rather borrow fixed. Both companies can resolve the problem by engaging in an interest rate swap. In a swap transaction the first company borrows at the relatively advantageous fixed rate and then swaps the fixed payments for the other company's floating payments (via a swap bank acting as an intermediary). No exchange of principal is involved. This way each company achieves the type of interest payment it needs. Furthermore, the resulting rates are more favorable than would have been obtainable if each had acted independently. Of course, the swap bank also shares some of the benefit. The global swaps market is now extremely large.

A fixed rate currency swap involves swapping both interest payments and principal denominated in different currencies. Suppose a French company wants a US dollar fixed rate loan but can get significantly better terms borrowing euros. Similarly, a US company wanting to borrow euro gets better terms borrowing dollars. A swap bank can arrange a currency swap in which each company borrows in its home currency. Then, they exchange the borrowed currency for the preferred currency. Subsequently, the two swap the interest payments as per the swap agreement. The swap transaction enables both companies to pay lower interest rates in their chosen currencies.

DEFINITIONS

Currency swap   Swap of interest payments and principal denominated in different currencies.

Interest rate swap   One company borrows at a relatively advantageous fixed rate and then swaps the fixed payments for another company's floating payments (via a swap bank acting as the intermediary).

21-4 FORWARD RATE AGREEMENTS

Another instrument useful for interest rate management is the Forward Rate Agreement (FRA). The FRA is an over the counter (OTC) agreement between a bank and its corporate customer fixing a rate of interest now for a future notional loan or deposit of a given term. The negotiated rate depends on whether it is for loan or for deposit. Expectations theory suggests that the negotiated rate will closely approximate the forward rate of interest. The forward rate of interest is the interest rate for a period beginning in the future implied by the term structure of interest rates.

EXAMPLE 21.1

For example, what is the forward rate of interest on a one-year loan starting one year from now? Let the quoted spot rate of interest on a two-year loan (starting now) be 12% and for a one-year loan (starting now) be 10%. The implied forward rate of interest $_1f_2$ would be just over 14% found as follows:

$$(1 + 0.1) \times (1 +_1 f_2) = (1 + 0.12)^2$$

$$_1f_2 = \frac{(1 + 0.12)^2}{(1 + 0.10)} - 1 = 0.14036 \quad \text{or} \quad 14.036\%$$

By using FRA's, the Corporate Treasurer can insulate the company from changes in interest rates on an anticipated future borrowing.

DEFINITIONS

Forward Rate Agreement (FRA) Agreement between a bank and its corporate customer fixing a rate of interest now for a future notional loan or deposit of a given term.

Forward rate of interest Interest rate for a period beginning in the future implied by the term structure of interest rates.

Over-the-counter market (OTC) Market in specific securities or currencies conducted by a financial institution in its own offices.

Spot rate of interest Rate of interest for a loan beginning immediately.

21-5 INTEREST RATE DERIVATIVES

Corporate Treasurers can also make use of interest rate derivatives including interest rate options and interest rate futures to manage interest rate risk.

FUTURES

An interest rate futures contract is a "bet" on the three-month interest rate for the three months starting at the end of the contract. Treasurers use futures contracts to hedge changes in interest rates.

EXAMPLE 21.2

Suppose, for example, that on 1 May a Corporate Treasurer expects an equity rights issue in July to raise €40 million. The intention is to invest the €40 million in a euro money market deposit for three months starting in July. The Treasurer's concern is that the money market rate will have fallen by then, however. She buys the same notional value of three-month Euro Time Deposit Futures contracts. If the rate on three-month Euro Time Deposits falls, the futures price will rise to compensate.

HEDGING WITH FUTURES

If a company's operating income is not highly correlated with changes in inflation, it might want to reduce the sensitivity of its floating interest rate payments to changes in the rate of inflation. It can do this by selling interest rate futures contracts to hedge away sufficient of the variability to get a better match with the variability of its operating income.

Interest rate risk is just one of many sources of corporate risk, but active markets such as these permit Treasurers to adjust (at a cost) at least a part of the risk attributable to unexpected changes in interest rates.

CAPS, FLOORS, AND COLLARS

The OTC market operated by the banks for corporate clients offers interest rate options such as caps, floors, and collars. Caps, floors, and collars are options allowing Corporate Treasurers to limit their exposure to interest rate changes on floating rate borrowings and deposits. An interest rate cap is an agreement in which the seller compensates the buyer when an agreed floating rate index rises above the "cap" rate of interest specified in the agreement. The seller writes the contract in terms of a notional amount of principal and for an agreed maturity. A floating rate borrower can buy a cap to keep the hedged floating rate borrowing costs no higher than the cap rate. Likewise, the seller of a floor compensates the buyer when the agreed floating rate index falls below the "floor" rate of interest specified in the agreement. A buyer creates a collar by simultaneously buying a cap and selling a floor, each for the same principal as for its floating rate debt. The collar confines the resulting hedged floating rate on its debt within the limits set by the floor rate and the cap rate.

DEFINITIONS

Collar   Interest rate derivative constructed by simultaneously buying a cap and selling a floor.

Interest rate floor   Agreement in which the seller compensates the buyer when the agreed floating interest rate index falls below the specified floor rate of interest.

Hedging   Buying one security and selling another in order to reduce risk.

Interest rate cap   Agreement in which the seller compensates the buyer when the agreed floating interest rate index rises above the specified cap rate of interest.

Interest rate derivatives   Interest rate agreements and contracts such as interest rate caps, floors, collars, and futures used to manage interest rate risk.

Rights issue   An offer of new shares by a public company to each of its existing shareholders in proportion to the number the shareholder already holds.

21-6 FOREIGN EXCHANGE RISK MANAGEMENT

Interest rates affect changes in foreign exchange rates. If a company has significant cash flows denominated in foreign currencies, exposure to unexpected changes in exchange rates can constitute significant risk to its credit rating and, ultimately, to its survival. Therefore, the Board cannot leave it to shareholders to hedge the foreign exchange risk. Furthermore, a company cannot keep its shareholders sufficiently informed about the company's current risk exposures for them to hedge their own portfolios effectively. So, it falls to the Corporate Treasurer to hedge much of the risk, especially risk that could lead to financial distress.

Consequently, it is important to understand the behavior of foreign exchange rates and how to manage the company's exposure to the risk of changes in foreign exchange-denominated cash flows, assets, and liabilities.

21-7 BEHAVIOR OF FOREIGN EXCHANGE RATES

The spot rate of exchange is the price quoted today for a currency deliverable from banks within two working days. The forward rate of exchange is the price quoted today for a currency to be delivered in the future, for example, in 30, 60, or 90 days. These quotations emanate from banks conducting OTC markets in financial centers such as London and Chicago. Four useful theories helping to explain the behavior of foreign exchange spot and forward rates are the pure expectations hypothesis, interest rate parity, the Fisher open proposition, and Purchasing Power Parity (PPP).

PURE EXPECTATIONS HYPOTHESIS

The pure expectations hypothesis suggests that the currently quoted forward rate of exchange for delivery at future time T equals the expected future spot rate quoted at that time. Thus:

$$Expected\ Spot\ Rate\ at\ Time\ T = Forward\ Rate\ for\ Delivery\ at\ Time\ T$$

If this were not the case, foreign exchange traders could profit systematically. For example, if the spot rate expected to prevail at future time T were less than the forward rate, then traders could expect to profit by selling the currency forward for delivery at time T and buying it in the spot market at that time to deliver against the forward contract.

Although the pure expectations hypothesis is highly inaccurate, empirical tests indicate that it nevertheless represents one of the best ways to forecast future spot rates of exchange.

INTEREST RATE PARITY

Interest rate parity is the proposition that the difference between the interest rates in two currencies explains the difference between their currently quoted forward and spot rates of exchange for the same maturity. Evidence supports this proposition for freely traded currencies unfettered by government exchange controls and central banking interventions.

In such free-market conditions, the actions of foreign exchange traders ensure interest rate parity. When forward and spot rates deviate temporarily from parity, traders engage in covered interest arbitrage. That is, they make risk-free gains by borrowing in the home currency and lending in a foreign currency while selling forward the interest and redemption proceeds in that currency. Alternatively, they lend in the home currency while borrowing in the foreign currency and buying forward the required interest and repayment in that currency. The resulting demand and supply force a rapid return to interest rate parity.

The equilibrium relationship between the euro and a foreign currency implied by covered interest arbitrage is:

$$(1 + Euro\ Interest\ Rate) = \frac{Spot\ Rate \times (1 + Foreign\ Interest\ Rate)}{Forward\ Rate}$$

This equation expresses that the spot and forward transactions necessary for risk-free investment at the foreign rate of interest (right-hand side of the equation) leaves one no better or worse off than investing at the euro rate of interest (left-hand side of the equation).

Solving for the percentage difference between the forward and the spot rate, we obtain:

$$\frac{(Forward\ Rate - Spot\ Rate)}{Spot\ Rate} = \frac{Foreign\ Interest\ Rate - Euro\ Interest\ Rate}{(1 + Euro\ Interest\ Rate)}$$

Foreign exchange traders use small deviations from this formula to find covered interest arbitrage opportunities.

EXAMPLE 21.3

For example, on 8 March 2002, the US$ spot rate against the euro was $0.8762/€1.00, the one-year forward rate was $0.8680/€1.00, the one-year US$ Libor interest rate was 2.78250%, and the one-year Euro Libor rate was 3.77300%. These market data give:

$$\frac{(Forward\ Rate - Spot\ Rate)}{Spot\ Rate} = \frac{0.8680 - 0.8762}{0.8762} = -0.009359 \quad or \quad -0.9359\%$$

and

$$\frac{Foreign\ Interest\ Rate - Euro\ Interest\ Rate}{(1 + Euro\ Interest\ Rate)} = \frac{2.78250 - 3.77300}{1 + 0.03773} = -0.9545\%$$

The difference between these two results $0.9545 - 0.9359 = 0.0186\%$ is small and somewhat less than the transaction costs of arbitrage. Therefore, interest rate parity holds to a very close approximation in this example, offering no opportunity to profit from arbitrage.

FISHER OPEN PROPOSITION

The Fisher effect is the proposition that the nominal rate of interest for a given maturity has two components, the real rate of interest and the expected rate of inflation for the period. The real rate of interest is the rate that would prevail if there were no inflation. More precisely:

$$Nominal\ Interest\ Rate = (1 + Real\ Interest\ Rate)(1 + Expected\ Inflation\ Rate) - 1$$
$$= Real\ Interest\ Rate + Expected\ Inflation\ Rate + Real\ Interest\ Rate$$
$$\times Expected\ Inflation\ Rate$$

Dropping the third term on the right-hand side of the equation, which usually is negligibly small, we have:

$$Nominal\ Interest\ Rate = Real\ Interest\ Rate + Expected\ Inflation\ Rate$$

The Fisher effect holds quite well in practice. Interest rates historically have moved approximately in line with the corresponding rates of inflation.

In the international context, the Fisher effect becomes the Fisher open proposition. Combining the above equation with interest rate parity and pure expectations, we obtain an expression for the expected percentage change in the spot rate of exchange against the euro:[2]

$$Expected\ Percentage\ Change\ of\ Spot\ Rate = \frac{Foreign\ Interest\ Rate - Euro\ Interest\ Rate}{1 + Euro\ Interest\ Rate}$$

Empirical studies provide some support for the Fisher open proposition, although they find significant short-run deviations, as might be expected.

---

[2] This form of the equation assumes indirect quotes for the spot rate. For example, the spot and forward indirect quotes for the US$ against the Euro are dollars per euro, whereas direct quotes would be euros per dollar.

PURCHASING POWER PARITY

Purchasing Power Parity (PPP) suggests that the difference between the expected rates of inflation for two currencies explains the expected change in the spot rate of exchange between the two currencies. The PPP equation for the spot rate of exchange against the euro is:

$$\text{Spot Rate at Time } T = \text{Spot Rate Now} \times \left(\frac{1 + \text{Expected Foreign Inflation Rate}}{1 + \text{Expected Euro Inflation Rate}} \right)^T$$

Evidence supports that PPP is most relevant for long-term exchange rate forecasts and when the difference between the expected rates of inflation is large.

DEFINITIONS

Covered interest arbitrage Making virtually risk-free gains by borrowing in the home currency and lending in a foreign currency while selling forward the interest and redemption proceeds in that currency. Alternatively, lending in the home currency while borrowing in the foreign currency and buying forward the required interest and repayment in that currency.

Fisher effect As originally proposed by Irving Fisher, the hypothesis that interest rates fully reflect expected rates of inflation.

Fisher open proposition Proposition that the expected change of the spot rate of exchange between two currencies reflects the difference between the rate of inflation and therefore also the difference between their interest rates.

Forward rate of exchange Price quoted today for a currency delivered in the future, for example, in 30, 60, or 90 days.

Interest rate parity Proposition that the difference between the interest rates in two currencies explains the difference between their currently quoted forward and spot rates of exchange for the same maturity.

Nominal rate of interest Quoted rate of interest.

Pure expectations hypothesis Proposition that the currently quoted forward rate of exchange for delivery at future time T equals the expected future spot rate quoted at that time.

Purchasing Power Parity (PPP) Proposition that the expected change in the spot rate of exchange reflects the difference between the rates of inflation for the two currencies.

Real rate of interest Rate of interest adjusted for the expected rate of inflation for the same period.

Spot rate of exchange Price quoted today for a currency deliverable from banks within two working days.

21-8 FOREIGN EXCHANGE RISK EXPOSURE

Corporate Treasurers attempt to manage up to four kinds of foreign exchange risk: transaction exposure, operating exposure, translation exposure, and tax exposure.

TRANSACTION EXPOSURE

Transaction exposure arises when a company has expected contractual cash flows such as unpaid accounts receivable, accounts payable, or other obligations denominated in foreign currencies. The corresponding cash flows are at risk as long as they remain unpaid and thus subject to changes in the relevant foreign exchange rates.

OPERATING EXPOSURE

Operating exposure, also called economic exposure, concerns the effects of unexpected exchange rate changes on the company's future cash flow. The effect on the cash flow can be either direct or indirect. If the company expects future income or expenditure in other currencies, changes in the corresponding exchange rates directly affect these cash flows. Risk of an adverse change to the company's competitive position resulting from exchange rate effects on prices and costs is an indirect exposure. A further indirect exposure is the risk of increases in the relative strengths of competitors due to changes in exchange rates.

TRANSLATION EXPOSURE

The necessity to consolidate the accounts of foreign affiliates with Group accounts gives rise to translation exposure. Translation exposure, also called accounting exposure, results from translation of the foreign currency values in affiliates' accounts to the currency of the Group accounts. Translation exposure is the risk that changes in the exchange rates used for translation will have adverse effects on the Group accounts. The risk is not entirely cosmetic. Adverse changes in Group accounting ratios can affect, for example, the company's bond and credit ratings and could trigger default of covenants in some of the company's borrowing agreements.

TAX EXPOSURE

Translation also affects the calculation of taxable income. Tax exposure is the risk that such translation effects could increase tax liabilities.

DEFINITIONS

Operating exposure (economic exposure)   Risk resulting from the direct or indirect effects of unexpected exchange rate changes on the company's future cash flow.

Tax exposure   Risk that translation effects of unexpected changes in exchange rates could increase tax liabilities.

Transaction exposure (accounting exposure)   Risk that unexpected changes in exchange rates will cause losses in contractual cash flows such as unpaid accounts receivable, accounts payable, or other obligations denominated in foreign currencies.

Translation exposure   Risk that changes in the exchange rates used to consolidate the accounts of foreign affiliates with Group accounts will have adverse effects on the Group accounts.

21-9 FOREIGN EXCHANGE RISK MANAGEMENT METHODS

Companies usually centralize the Group's foreign exchange risk exposure management. This permits Group Treasury to manage the Group's net exposure to each foreign currency without costly duplication by companies within the Group. Hedging is the Corporate Treasurer's principal means of managing foreign exchange rate risk. Hedging foreign exchange risk is about matching foreign currency-denominated assets and liabilities in a manner that makes the value of the matched combination immune to unexpected changes in exchange rates. For example, if a non-US company holds a US dollar asset, it also needs a matching US dollar liability of the same maturity if it is to be immune to changes in the dollar exchange rate.

In accordance with this principle, the following are some measures used by companies to manage their net exposures.

FINANCE FOREIGN OPERATIONS IN THE HOST COUNTRY CURRENCY

European companies generating US$ income, for example, often finance the asset with US$ debt. They use the US$ income to pay the interest and repayments on the dollar debt.

SWAP THE CURRENCIES TO MEET THE OBLIGATIONS ON TERM LOANS

When the company's long-term exposure to a particular currency such as the US$ increases significantly, its Treasurer can attempt to neutralize the risk with a currency swap. The Treasurer can arrange with a swap bank to exchange payment obligations on existing debt for the obligations denominated in US dollars. The dollar cash income pays the swapped obligations, thus neutralizing much of the exposure to the dollar exchange rate.

RISK SHARING

A company waiting for payment of an invoice denominated in a foreign currency risks adverse changes in the exchange rate in the meantime. A company can sometimes eliminate the risk by invoicing in its home currency. This practice shifts the exchange risk to the customer and does not please many of them. A compromise available to firms with continuing buyer–supplier relationships is to share the foreign exchange risk. In a risk-sharing arrangement, the buyer and the seller contract to divide the effects of currency movements on payments between them.

More frequently, companies issue a separate price list in each currency and invoice accordingly. This forces them to use other means of managing the resulting foreign exchange risk exposure.

SELL FOREIGN ACCOUNTS RECEIVABLE

An alternative is for the exporter to employ an international factor to collect the payments from overseas customers. Factors are service companies specializing in collecting trade debt. An international factor usually provides the additional service of bearing the foreign exchange risk exposure. Either the factor buys the invoices at a discount or it lends the exporter a proportion of the value of the unpaid invoices. Either way, the exporter receives an immediate payment in the home currency, thus eliminating a large proportion of the foreign exchange risk associated with the unpaid invoices.

BORROW FOREIGN EXCHANGE MATCHED TO A RECEIVABLE AND CONVERT TO HOME CURRENCY

If a company already has a department capable of collecting payments from its various overseas customers, it need not use an international factor to do so. Instead, it can match the foreign currency-denominated receivables with bank borrowing.

For example, a French company owed $100 million by a US customer borrowed $100 million from a New York bank and exchanged it immediately for euro. Later, the French company used the $100 million payment from the US customer to repay the $100 million bank loan.

BUY OR SELL FORWARD FOREIGN EXCHANGE

For the many smaller, short-term transactions, companies use the interbank forward exchange market to reduce the associated foreign exchange risk exposures. Banks routinely quote one-month, three-month, and one-year forward exchange rates. A European exporter owed $1 million payable in 30 days, for example, sold the dollars to its bank for euro at the currently quoted one-month forward rate. The company did not have to deliver the dollars to the bank until the end of the 30 days. By this means, the exporter eliminated the foreign exchange risk for 30 days. Late payment by the customer would still expose the exporter to foreign exchange rate risk while waiting for payment beyond the initial 30-day period, however.

Similarly, a European importer expecting to pay $1 million in 30 days can fix the exchange rate for the period by buying the dollars at the currently quoted forward rate. Thirty days later, the company exchanges euros for dollars at the prearranged forward rate and pays the dollar invoice.

BUY OR SELL FOREIGN EXCHANGE FUTURES

Foreign exchange futures contracts offer alternatives to forward market transactions. A foreign currency futures contract is an exchange-traded contract for future delivery of a standard amount of foreign exchange on a specified date and at a specified price and place. An exporter expecting to receive payment on a foreign currency-denominated invoice can hedge the resulting exposure by selling the appropriate number of futures contracts with maturities nearest to the expected date of receipt of payment. Similarly, an importer expecting to make a future payment of foreign exchange can hedge the payment by buying the appropriate futures contracts.

Features of foreign exchange futures contracts include the following: a standard amount for each currency, standard calendar maturity dates, a specified last day for trading each contract, requirement for collateral, the clearinghouse acting as the counter party to the contract, and commission payment to brokers for dealing on the exchange.[3]

Companies often find that the standardized nature of futures contracts makes it difficult to construct a sufficiently well-matched hedge. Consequently, commercial organizations make less use of futures contracts than do foreign exchange dealers and speculators.

BUY OR SELL FOREIGN EXCHANGE OPTIONS

A foreign currency option contract gives the option buyer the right, but not the obligation, to buy or sell a specified amount of foreign exchange at a fixed price per unit until the option expires. The two kinds of option are **calls** and **puts**. A call is an option to buy foreign currency, and a put is an option to sell foreign currency.[4] Use of foreign currency options as a hedging tool and for speculation has become widespread. In the OTC market, banks offer tailor-made options on the major trading currencies with maturities up to several years. In addition, standardized currency options trade on a number of exchanges worldwide, including the Philadelphia Stock Exchange (PHLX) and the London International Financial Futures Exchange (LIFFE). The exchange clearing-house settles the option contracts so that buyers do not deal directly with sellers. The clearinghouse is the counter party to every option contract and guarantees fulfillment of all contracts.

Foreign exchange options provide a useful alternative to forward and futures contracts for hedging foreign exchange risk on commercial transactions. They permit companies to speculate on favorable exchange rate movements while hedging unfavorable movements. Of course, option writers (sellers) demand a fair price for such advantages, and the resulting costs to option buyers is significant.[5]

DEFINITIONS

American option Type of option that may be exercised before its maturity.

Call option Option giving the holder the right without obligation to buy the option's underlying asset at a specified price on or before a specified date.

Debt Sum of money or other assets owed by one party to another. Usually, a legally

---

[3] Futures contracts are marked to market. That is, at the end of each day, the broker credits or debits the contract holder's account for the day's market gains or losses on the contracts. For this reason, there is no need to take delivery of the underlying currency, and thus holders of the futures contracts usually cancel them before maturity.

[4] An **American option** gives the buyer the right to exercise the option at any time before the option expires, that is, before its maturity date. Holders of **European options**, on the other hand can exercise them only on their expiration dates, not before.

[5] Currency option dealers use the Garman and Kohlhagen model to estimate the fair price of a currency call option. In this model, the foreign rate of interest is analogous to the dividend yield in the dividend-adjusted Black and Scholes equity call option valuation model. The Put Call Parity Formula, which is also adjusted for the foreign rate of interest, determines the value of the currency put. See Mark Garman and Steven Kohlhagen (1983) "Foreign currency option values," *Journal of International Money and Finance* (December), 231–237.

enforceable obligation to pay agreed interest and to repay the principal of a loan to the lender promptly on schedule.

European option   Type of option that may be exercised only on its date of maturity.

Put option   Option giving the holder the right without obligation to sell the option's underlying asset at a specified price on or before a specified date.

21-10   CONCLUSIONS

Company directors have many means to help them ensure the company's survival. Primarily, they must operate the company with a robust financial plan providing sufficient funding for contingencies. At a more detailed level, they need efficient systems for monitoring and controlling risk. These include systems for planning, controlling, and monitoring working capital. In this context, we concern ourselves in this chapter with the management of interest rate and foreign exchange risks.

Because interest payments directly affect the company's net earnings, interest rate management is one of the essential functions of Corporate Treasury. Keeping the right balance between fixed and floating rate debt is an important means of smoothing net earnings and reducing the cost of capital. Assisting in this are many financial market instruments such as FRNs, swaps, FRAs, caps, floors, collars, and interest rate futures contracts.

Because foreign exchange rates directly affect the company's cash flow, earnings, and taxes due to overseas operations, Corporate Treasurers have to manage the company's exposure to possible changes in the relevant foreign exchange rates. Hedging is the principal means of managing foreign exchange rate risk. Hedging foreign exchange risk requires matching foreign currency-denominated assets and liabilities, making the value of the matched combination immune to unexpected changes in exchange rates.

Corporate Treasurers have many means to help them implement the matching principle. These include financing foreign operations in the host country currency and swapping the currencies required to meet the obligations on term loans. They also include sharing foreign exchange risk with suppliers and customers, selling foreign accounts receivable, borrowing foreign exchange matched to a receivable, buying or selling forward foreign exchange to hedge payables or receivables, and buying or selling foreign exchange futures and foreign exchange options.

The Board cannot leave it to the shareholders to hedge the company's interest rate and foreign exchange risk exposure in their own portfolios. Shareholders cannot protect the corporate entity or its creditworthiness in this way. Furthermore, a company cannot keep its shareholders sufficiently informed about the company's current risk exposures for them to hedge their own portfolios effectively. Therefore, it falls to the Corporate Treasurer to hedge on behalf of shareholders, including the risks that collectively could threaten company survival.

DEFINITION

Cost of capital   Cost of funds used by a company for investment.

FURTHER READING

David Blake (1999) *Financial Market Analysis*, 2nd edn (Chichester, UK: John Wiley & Sons).

Bruno H. Solnik (1999) *International Investments*, 4th edn (London: Addison-Wesley).

K. Clinton (1988) "Transaction costs and covered interest arbitrage: Theory and evidence," *Journal of Political Economy*, Vol. 83 (April), 325-338.

C. W. Smith, C. H. Smithson, and D. S. Wilford (1990) *Managing Financial Risk*, 3rd edn (New York: McGraw-Hill).

QUESTIONS AND PROBLEMS

1 SMOOTHING Corporation's Treasurer is trying to ascertain what proportion of the company's borrowing should be floating rate debt. His immediate objective is to minimize the variance of the company's net income before tax. He knew that the variance of net income reflects a combination of the variances of operating income, floating rate interest, and the correlation between the operating income and floating rate interest. The following are his estimates for the relevant data:

Operating Income (O)	€10 million
Interest payments (I)	€5 million
Net income (NI)	€5 million
Total debt (B)	€100 million
Standard deviation of Operating Income (σ_O)	0.20
Standard deviation of floating rate interest payments (σ_F)	0.20
Correlation between Operating Income and the floating rate ($\rho_{O,F}$)	0.25
Floating rate (f)	5%

(a) Plot the relationship between the variance of net income and the proportion of floating rate borrowing. *Hint:* The equation is:

$$NI\sigma_{NI}^2 = (O\sigma_0)^2 + (xfB\sigma_F)^2 - 2\rho_{O,F}(O\sigma_0)(xfB\sigma_F)^2$$

in which x equals the proportion of interest paid represented by floating rate payments.

(b) Demonstrate graphically or otherwise that the optimum proportion x^* of floating rate debt payments is given by:

$$x^* = \rho_{O,F}\frac{O\sigma_0}{fB\sigma_F}$$

2 SMOOTHING Corporation's Treasurer finds that he should increase the existing proportion of the company's floating rate interest payments. An interest rate swap appears to be a good way of doing so while achieving the lowest possible floating rate. The company has an AAA credit rating and pays fixed rate interest at only 5.50% and floating rate interest at six-month Euro Libor +0.25%. If SMOOTHING enters into a swap deal exchanging fixed rate for floating rate obligations with the right company, it could achieve an even lower effective floating rate.

For example, Company X could be such a candidate even though its credit rating is only BBB. Company X must pay 6.5% on its fixed rate borrowing and would like to reduce this by means of a swap. It pays Euro Libor + 0.75% on floating rate debt. If Company X is the right candidate, SMOOTHING could achieve a lower floating rate and Company X could obtain a lower fixed rate, and both would therefore gain from the swap transaction.

(a)   Calculate the combined gain for the two companies if SMOOTHING and Company X transact the swap.

(b)   What floating rate would SMOOTHING pay Company X and what fixed rate must Company X pay SMOOTHING to make the division of the combined gain equal?

(c)   A swap bank intermediates such transactions. What is the maximum the swap bank could charge for this service without making the proposed swap unattractive?

3   The Treasurer of Company X intends borrowing fixed rate one year from now. The particular loan is to have a one-year maturity. Unfortunately, interest rates on fixed rate loans could rise before then. The solution could be to negotiate an FRA covering the interim year. The currently quoted two-year fixed rate is 6% and the one-year rate is 7%. What would be a fair rate of interest on the FRA?

4   In April 2002, the Treasurer of Company X also intends to borrow euros in the London money market toward the end of June. The loan will have a three-month maturity ending in September. In the meantime, the interest rate on the intended borrowing could increase. She could hedge this risk by selling an interest rate future. Using the following data, estimate the fair market value and the quoted price for the appropriate interest rate future.

Contract	Maturity	Libor	Rate
		One-month Euro Libor	3.320 00%
June	65 days	Three-month Euro Libor	3.400 00%
September	155 days	Six-month Euro Libor	3.521 75%

5   On 16 April 2002, a German investor could invest in a two-year German Government bond yielding 4.19%. At the same time, she could invest in a comparable one-year US Government bond yielding 3.31%. The US dollar–euro spot rate of exchange on that day was $0.8829/€. At what one-year forward rate of exchange would the investor be indifferent between the two bonds if she paid no taxes?

6   The rate of inflation in Country A is 10% and in Country B is 30%. The real rate of interest in Country A is 2% and in B is 5%. The spot rate of exchange is 1.5 units of B's currency for each unit of A's currency.

(a)   Estimate the yield on one-year Government bonds in both countries.
(b)   Estimate the one-year forward rate of exchange.
(c)   Estimate the spot rate of exchange at the end of one year.
(d)   Can you reconcile the answers to (b) and (c)?

In each case, name the theories that you use to obtain your answers.

7   On 16 April 2002, the US$–euro exchange rate was $0.8829/€. At the same time, the yen–US$ exchange rate was Y131.105/$. What yen–euro (Y/€) exchange rate would eliminate opportunities for arbitrage between these three currencies on that date?

8   A French company exporting to the USA expects $1 million from various customers in 30 days' time. The company's Treasurer seeks to eliminate the resulting exposure to changes in the US$–euro exchange rate. There are at least two possibilities. The first is to sell the dollars in the forward exchange market at $0.8817/€. The second is to borrow the dollars immediately at $1\frac{7}{8}$% (divide by 12 for the 30-day rate) and convert them to euros at the current spot rate $0.8829/€. The corresponding one-month euro rate is $3\frac{1}{4}$%. Which of the two methods of hedging the exposure has the least cost?

9   The Treasurer in Problem 8 is considering selling foreign exchange futures contracts as an alternative to borrowing US dollars or selling the dollars in the forward foreign exchange market. Using the following data, estimate the fair market price for the futures contract.

One-month forward rate	$0.8817/€
One-month US$ rate	$1\frac{7}{8}$%
One-month euro rate	$3\frac{1}{4}$%

(a)   Why might selling these contracts fail to constitute a perfect hedge?
(b)   Are there any means by which an exporter could hedge foreign exchange-denominated receivables perfectly? If not, why not?

PART 5

International Investment

22 Appraising International Capital Projects[1]

An international project is an investment in real assets involving cash flows in more than one currency.[2] The international aspect introduces at least two important problems for us to consider. The first is how to analyze a project in the context of changing foreign exchange rates. The second is how to analyze effects of being subject simultaneously to both domestic and foreign tax jurisdictions.

We shall consider two related methods of valuing the multicurrency cash flows for an international capital project. Comparison of the methods in their simplest form reveals how we can obtain the net present value (NPV) of after-tax multicurrency cash flows without introducing distortion from biased foreign exchange rate forecasts. This enables us to make a financial assessment on the basis purely of the commercial and fiscal merits of the project. In our initial analysis, we assume a foreign subsidiary operates the project and remits all net cash flows to the parent company. Subsequently, we discuss situations in which altering this remittance assumption can affect a foreign project's NPV.

TOPICS

We cover the following topics:

- *appraisal of international projects;*
- *differential rates of inflation and foreign currency cash flows;*
- *differential rates of inflation and required rates of return;*
- *Valuation Method 1;*
- *differential rates of inflation and expected future exchange rates;*
- *Valuation Method 2: before tax and after tax;*
- *unremitted funds;*
- *international required rates of return.*

---

[1] Adapted by permission of J. R. Franks, J. E. Broyles, and W. T. Carleton (1985) *Corporate Finance, Concepts and Applications* (Boston: Kent).

[2] So, except for taxation, we treat projects spanning different countries in the euro zone as domestic projects.

This chapter serves as a bridge between the customary treatment of project appraisal in a purely domestic setting and project appraisal in the multicurrency, multitaxation international environment of contemporary business.

22-1 APPRAISAL OF INTERNATIONAL PROJECTS

An international capital project involves cash flows in more than one currency. Therefore, valuation of an international capital project requires an understanding of how inflation affects different currency cash flows, interest rates, and foreign exchange rates and often in more than one tax jurisdiction. The relationship between inflation and interest rates in different countries is important because interest rates together with risk premiums determine the discount rates we use for the foreign currency cash flows. Inflation affects these cash flows and the exchange rates used for translating the different foreign currency cash flows into the currency of the project's NPV. We consider the relationship between inflation and cash flows first.

DEFINITIONS

Discount rate   Required rate of return used in the calculation of a discount factor.

International capital project   Real (nonfinancial) investment with cash flows denominated in more than one currency.

Net present value (NPV)   Difference between the present value of a project's expected after-tax operating cash flows and the present value of its expected after-tax investment expenditures.

Risk premium   Extra return expected from a risky asset compared with the return from an alternative risk-free asset.

22-2 DIFFERENTIAL RATES OF INFLATION AND FOREIGN CURRENCY CASH FLOWS

The procedure for forecasting the cash flows of international projects is much the same as for domestic projects.

REAL AND NOMINAL CASH FLOW

Usually, we forecast the before-tax cash flows in real terms and then inflate them at the expected rate of inflation. By definition, the cash flows of an international project are denominated in more than one currency. Accordingly, we must inflate each such real cash flow at the relevant rate for its currency. The formula for each currency is:

$$\textit{Nominal Cash Flow in Period } t = \textit{Real Cash Flow} \times (1 + \textit{Rate of inflation})^t$$

where *Real Cash Flow* is the forecast in terms of current prices and **Nominal Cash Flow** in Period *t* is the corresponding forecast reflecting inflation between now and time *t*. This requires obtaining from reputable economic forecasters the forecasts of the relevant rates of inflation for the relevant currencies.

Companies usually resist trying to use different rates of inflation for product prices, materials, and labor unless they happen to be denominated in different currencies. The reason is that the NPV is very sensitive to errors in differences between the inflation forecasts.

We cannot avoid using different expected rates of inflation for cash flows denominated in different currencies, however, because required rates of return and exchange rates also depend upon the expected rates of inflation for each currency. We must be consistent in our assumptions about inflation for the cash flow, the required rate of return, and the expected exchange rate in each currency.

DEFINITIONS

Expected (mean)   Probability-weighted average of all possible outcomes for a random variable.

Nominal cash flow   Expected future cash flow in terms of future prices reflecting intervening expected inflation.

Rate of return   After-tax cash income and capital gain divided by the investment.

Real cash flow   Expected future cash flow in terms of current prices; that is, unadjusted for intervening expected inflation.

22-3 DIFFERENTIAL RATES OF INFLATION AND REQUIRED RATES OF RETURN

INTEREST RATES

When the expected rate of inflation for a currency is low, the nominal (money) rate of interest quoted in the financial market is approximately equal to the sum of the real (purchasing power) rate of interest and the rate of inflation. The real rate of interest is "real" in the sense that it reflects the additional real goods one can buy as a reward for saving.

EXAMPLE 22.1

For example, if the nominal rate of interest is just over 5% and the rate of inflation is 3%, then the real rate of interest is roughly $5 - 3 = 2\%$. That is, by saving 1 euro, we can only buy about 2% more goods at the end of the year. More precisely, the equation for the Fisher effect predicts the relationship to be:

$$Nominal\ Rate\ of\ Interest = (1 + Real\ Rate) \times (1 + Inflation\ Rate) - 1$$

Thus,

$$Real\ Rate\ of\ Interest = \frac{1 + Nominal\ Rate}{1 + Inflation\ Rate} - 1$$

$$= \frac{1 + 0.05}{1 + 0.03} - 1 = 0.1942 \quad or \quad 1.942\%$$

REQUIRED RATES OF RETURN

For capital projects, the required rate of return found on the Securities Market Line (SML) has the corresponding relationship to inflation:

$$Required\ Rate\ of\ Return = (1 + Real\ Required\ Rate) \times (1 + Inflation\ Rate) - 1$$

where

$$Real\ Required\ Rate\ of\ Return = Real\ Risk\text{-}free\ Rate + Real\ Risk\ Premium$$

These equations express the observed fact that a higher expected rate of inflation results in a higher nominal interest rate. Similarly, the higher expected rate of inflation implies a higher required rate of return for capital projects.

Each of a project's foreign currency cash flows requires a discount rate relevant to the currency. The different currency discount rates collectively must relate to the required rate of return for the whole project. Suppose that the euro is the home currency. Therefore, we intend to calculate the project's NPV in euros. Management's required rate of return for the project in euros is, say, 12%. Suppose also that economists expect a 3% rate of inflation for the euro. The Fisher effect implies that:

$$Required\ Rate\ of\ Return = (1 + Real\ Required\ Rate) \times (1 + Inflation\ Rate) - 1$$
$$0.12 = (1 + Real\ Required\ Rate) \times (1 + 0.03) - 1$$

Solving for the real required rate of return we have:

$$Real\ Required\ Rate = \frac{1 + 0.12}{1 + 0.03} - 1 = 0.087\,38 \quad or \quad 8.738\%$$

This gives the required real rate of return for the project. From this, we can derive the corresponding discount rates for the project's different foreign currency cash flows.

EXAMPLE 22.2

Suppose, for example, the project's expected sales revenues are denominated in Currency C and its investment and operating costs are in Currency D. We simply use Fisher's equation to translate the project's required real rate into the corresponding required nominal rate for each currency, reflecting the currencies' respective expected rates of inflation:

Currency	Real rate (%)	Inflation (%)	Nominal rate (%)
C	8.738	20	30.486
D	8.738	15	25.049

For example, the calculation for currency C is:

$$Required\ Rate\ of\ Return = (1 + Real\ Required\ Rate) \times (1 + Inflation\ Rate) - 1$$
$$= (1 + 0.087\,38) \times (1 + 0.20) - 1 = 0.304\,86 \quad or \quad 30.486\%$$

Fisher's equation provides an elegant way to convert a project's required rate of return to the corresponding required rate for project cash flows denominated in foreign currencies. This provides the basis for obtaining the NPV of the project in Valuation Method 1.

DEFINITIONS

Capital project   Investment in a nonfinancial asset.

Fisher effect   As originally proposed by Irving Fisher, the hypothesis that interest rates fully reflect expected rates of inflation.

Nominal rate of interest   Quoted rate of interest.

Real rate of interest   Rate of interest adjusted for the expected rate of inflation for the same period.

Securities Market Line (SML)   Hypothesized linear relationship in the Capital Asset Pricing Model between the expected return on a security and its systematic risk.

22-4 VALUATION METHOD 1

The purpose of Valuation Method 1 is to show in a world without taxes that valuation of foreign currency cash flows does not require explicit forecasts of future rates of exchange. Method 2 will then show how we can introduce taxes.

METHOD 1

Method 1 requires just three steps:

1. Forecast each of the project's net incremental cash flows in its respective foreign currency.

2. Discount the foreign currency cash flows using the appropriate nominal discount rate for each currency.

3. Translate the resulting foreign currency present values (PVs) to the home currency PV using the relevant current spot rates of exchange between the respective foreign currencies and the home currency.

The resulting sum of the translated PVs gives the project's home currency NPV.

EXAMPLE 22.3

Table 22.1 demonstrates the application of Method 1 to a project with cash flows in the two foreign currencies C and D considered above. The home currency is the euro. The project's nominal required rate of return is 12%. The expected rates of inflation in Currencies C, D, and € are 20%, 15%, and 3%, respectively. As shown earlier, these data imply discount rates of 30.486% and 25.049% for Currency C and D cash flows, respectively, if the euro required rate is 12%.

Row 1 in Table 22.1 shows the project's expected nominal revenues denominated in Currency C. The project's discount rate in Currency C is 30.486%, and the resulting PV is C3,263.50 million as indicated in Row 2. The current rate of exchange between C and the euro is C1.3333/€1.00.

Table 22.1 Method 1: valuation of an international project without taxes (millions).

	End of year					
	0	1	2	3	4	5
Revenue (Currency C)		1,000.00	1,200.00	1,440.00	1,728.00	2,073.60
PV at 30.486% (Currency C)	3,263.50					
Exchange rate (C/€1.00)	1.3333					
PV (translated)	2,447.69					2,447.69
Investment (Currency D)	−1,000.00					
Operating expenditure (Currency D)		−690.00	−793.50	−912.53	−1,049.40	−1,206.81
PV at 25.049% (Currency D)	−3,349.73					
Exchange rate (D/€1.00)	2.0000					
PV (translated)	−1,674.86					−1,674.86
NPV (euro)						772.83

That is, C1.3333 buys only one euro. Therefore, the PV of the revenues translates to only €2,447.69 million as indicated in Row 4.

The next four rows concern the investment and the operating expenditures denominated in Currency D. The PV of these discounted at the project's Currency D required rate of return of 25.049% is D3,349.73 million. The current exchange rate between D and the euro is D2.0000/€1.00. That is, D2.0000 buys only one euro. So, the PV of the investment and the operating expenditures translate to only €1,674.86 million, as indicated.

The final column of the table shows the calculation of the resulting euro NPV of €772.83 million for the project as the sum of the translated PVs.

Method 1 would appear to be a simple and straightforward method of obtaining the NPV of an international project in the absence of taxes. The advantage of Method 1 is that it does not require explicit forecasts of future rates of exchange. In this way, it gives an NPV that is unaffected by bias in foreign exchange rate forecasts. Method 1 does not lend itself to tax calculations, however. We need a method that is equivalent to Method 1 but permits incorporation of international tax effects. Incorporating taxes requires us to forecast exchange rates, however.

DEFINITIONS

Net incremental cash flows Difference between a company's expected after-tax cash flows with or without a proposed investment.

Present value (PV) Value of an investment now as the cost of a comparable investment in the financial market (calculated by multiplying the investment's expected after-tax cash income by the appropriate discount factors).

Spot rate of exchange   Price quoted today for a currency deliverable from banks within two working days.

22-5 DIFFERENTIAL RATES OF INFLATION AND EXPECTED FUTURE EXCHANGE RATES

Valuation of the after-tax cash flows of international projects requires us to forecast the relevant rates of exchange. Multiyear projects need multiyear exchange rate forecasts. The best available method of forecasting exchange rates in the longer term is Purchasing Power Parity (PPP).

PURCHASING POWER PARITY

Purchasing Power Parity (PPP) derives from the notion that the demand and supply effects of foreign trade maintain constant relationships between the real prices of baskets of tradable goods in different countries. Maintaining such constant price relationships requires that foreign exchange rates adjust to reflect the differences in the rates of inflation between the currencies. PPP implies that currencies subject to the highest rates of inflation are the weakest currencies.

EXAMPLE 22.4

In our example, the current rate of exchange between Currency C and the euro is C1.3333/€1.00, and the expected rates of inflation are 20% and 3% for C and the euro, respectively. Suppose we want to forecast the expected exchange rate two years hence. The PPP forecast is:

$$\text{Exchange Rate in Year 2} = \text{Current Exchange Rate} \times \left(\frac{1 + C \text{ Inflation Rate}}{1 + € \text{ Inflation Rate}} \right)^2$$

$$= 1.3333 \times \left(\frac{1 + 0.20}{1 + 0.03} \right)^2 = C1.8097/€1.00$$

If the expected rates of inflation had been the same for the two currencies, the expected future exchange rate would have equaled today's rate. Because we expect a higher rate of inflation for Currency C than for the euro, however, we expect to have to pay more of C to buy the same amount of euros. Whereas currently C1.3333 buys one euro, we expect to have to pay C1.8097 for just one euro two years later. Therefore, PPP implies that the euro will be the stronger currency in this example.

PPP allows us in this way to obtain expected future exchange rates for all a project's foreign currency-denominated cash flows. In addition, PPP has the desirable feature of maintaining equivalence between Method 2 and Method 1. This feature is attractive because we wish to use methods unaffected by biased foreign exchange rate forecasts.

DEFINITION

Purchasing Power Parity (PPP)   Proposition that the expected change in the spot rate of exchange reflects the difference between the rates of inflation for the two currencies.

22-6 VALUATION METHOD 2

Valuation Method 2 permits us to incorporate international tax effects in project appraisal. First, however, we shall consider the method without taxes. This permits us to make a direct before-tax comparison between Methods 1 and 2 to see if they are equivalent. Subsequently, we show how to introduce international tax effects.

METHOD 2 WITHOUT TAXES

For clarity, we first consider Method 2 without taxes. We can then see how to incorporate the tax effects. Method 2 without taxes requires four steps:

1.   Forecast each of the project's nominal net incremental cash flows in its respective currency.

2.   Translate each expected future cash flow into the home currency using PPP-expected future exchange rates.

3.   Combine the translated cash flows.

4.   Discount the translated net cash flows at the appropriate home currency nominal required rate of return reflecting the project's systematic risk.

Table 22.2 shows the relevant figures for Method 2. Row 1 shows the project's revenues denominated in Currency C. Row 2 shows the PPP-expected exchange rates for Currency C. Row 3 gives the revenue cash flows translated into euros. For example, in Year 1 the expected exchange rate is C1.5534/€1.00. If C1.5534 buys only one euro, then C1,000 million buys only 1,000/1.5534 = €643.77 million. Similarly, the next four rows translate the Currency D-denominated investment and operating expenditure cash flows into euros using the indicated PPP-expected exchange future rates.

Table 22.2 Method 2: valuation of an international project without taxes (millions).

		End of year				
	0	1	2	3	4	5
Revenue (Currency C)		1,000.00	1,200.00	1,440.00	1,728.00	2,073.60
Exchange rate (C/€1.00)	1.3333	1.5534	1.8097	2.1084	2.4564	2.8619
Revenue (translated)		643.77	663.08	682.97	703.46	724.56
Investment (Currency D)	−1,000.00					
Operating expenditure (Currency D)		−690.00	−793.50	−912.53	−1,049.40	−1,206.81
Exchange rate (D/€1.00)	2.0000	2.2330	2.4932	2.7836	3.1079	3.4700
Investment and operating expenditure (translated)	−500.00	−309.00	−318.27	−327.82	−337.65	−347.78
Net cash flow (euro)	−500.00	334.77	344.81	355.15	365.81	376.78
NPV at 12% (euro)	772.84					

The expected euro revenues together with the expected euro investment and operating expenditures give the project's before-tax euro net cash flow. Recall that the project's nominal euro required rate of return is 12%. Discounting the net cash flows at this rate gives the NPV of €772.84 million for the project.

EQUIVALENCE

Allowing for rounding error, this is the same result we obtained earlier using Method 1. This reflects that the PPP formula makes Method 2 equivalent algebraically to Method 1. Therefore, as with Method 1, Method 2 gives an NPV undistorted by the possibility of foreign exchange gains or losses. Consequently, the method permits evaluation of the project on its commercial and financial merits separately from issues concerning whether the company's Corporate Treasurer needs to hedge the foreign exchange risks generated by this together with other foreign activities of the company.

METHOD 2 WITH TAXES

Now we can demonstrate how Method 2 facilitates the incorporation of taxes. Method 2 with taxes requires the same four basic steps used above in Table 22.2 but with host country and home country taxes introduced at the appropriate stages. The project belongs to a wholly owned subsidiary paying taxes in Currency D to host Country D. The parent is also taxed in home Country E on the income of its subsidiary in Country D. Fortunately, the parent's home country grants tax credits to domestic companies for taxes paid to host Country D. We wish to see how to obtain the NPV in euros of the project's resulting after-tax multicurrency cash flows.

EXAMPLE 22.5

Tables 22.3 and 22.4 apply Method 2 to this problem. Table 22.3 begins with the calculation of the project's after-tax cash flows from the standpoint of the subsidiary operating the project in host Country D. The project's revenues are foreign Currency C cash flows. We have to translate these to Currency D before estimating taxes payable to the host country. Row 1 of the table shows the expected Currency C revenues, and Row 2 gives the corresponding PPP-expected exchange rates between Currencies C and D. Note that in this case the rate is in terms D per unit of C. So, we translate to D by multiplying the C cash flow by the expected D/C1.00 exchange rate. For example, in Year 1 we expect the exchange rate to be D1.4375/C1.00. Consequently, each unit of C buys 1.4375 of D. The first-year revenue of C1,000 thus translates to D1,437.50 million, as indicated in Row 3.

Row 4 shows the corresponding operating expenditure, and Row 5 gives the resulting before-tax net cash flow in Currency D. These revenues and expenditures together with allowable depreciation and other noncash expenses imply taxable income calculated according to rules imposed by the government of Country D. This taxable income generates the tax liabilities payable in the years indicated in Row 6. Row 7 gives the project's resulting Currency D after-tax net cash flow. We assume for the moment that the subsidiary pays the entire net cash income from the project as dividends remitted to the parent company in home country E. The host country

Table 22.3 Method 2: after-tax remittances to parent company (millions).

		End of year				
	0	1	2	3	4	5
Revenue (Currency C)		1,000.00	1,200.00	1,440.00	1,728.00	2,073.60
Exchange rate (D/C1.00)	1.5000	1.4375	1.3776	1.3202	1.2652	1.2121
Revenue (translated		1,437.50	1,653.13	1,901.09	2,186.26	2,514.20
Operating expenditure (Currency D)		−690.00	−793.50	−912.53	−1.049.40	−1,206.81
Net cash flow before tax		747.50	859.63	988.56	1,136.86	1,307.39
Tax .		−191.63	−230.87	−276.00	−327.90	−387.58
After-tax net cash flow (Currency D)		555.87	628.76	712.56	808.96	919.81
Remitted cash flow (Currency D)		555.87	628.76	712.56	808.96	919.81
Witholding tax at 10%		−55.59	−62.88	−71.26	−80.90	−91.98
Remittance after tax (Currency D)		500.28	565.88	641.31	728.06	827.83

Table 22.4 Method 2: parent company taxes and NPV of project (millions).

		End of year				
	0	1	2	3	4	5
Investment (Currency D)	−1,000.00					
Dividends received (Currency D)		500.28	565.88	641.31	728.06	827.83
Exchange rate (D/€1.00)	2.0000	2.2330	2.4932	2.7836	3.1079	3.4700
Cash flow (translated)	−500.00	224.04	226.97	230.39	234.26	238.56
Estimated taxable income (translated)		245.19	264.57	283.29	301.44	319.12
Corporate tax at 30%		−73.56	−79.37	−84.99	−90.43	−95.74
Foreign tax credit (translated)		110.71	117.82	124.75	131.53	138.20
After-tax cash flow (euro)	−500.00	224.04	226.97	230.39	234.26	238.56
NPV at 12% (euro)	329.20					

charges a 10% withholding tax on dividends, however. The final row in the table shows the resulting after-tax currency D dividend remitted to the parent.

Table 22.4 shows the corresponding cash flows from the standpoint of the parent company in Country E. The parent invests D1,000 million (€500 million) in the project in Row 1 and receives the after-foreign-tax dividend income in Row 2. The PPP-expected exchange rates in Row 3 translate these to the expected euro-denominated cash flow shown in Row 4.

The Country D-taxable income attracts taxes also in the home country that, however, qualifies for tax credits. Row 5 shows the project's Country D-taxable income translated to euros. The next row gives the taxes on this at the home country's corporate tax rate of 30%.[3]

The foreign tax credit in Row 7 is the sum of the project's Country D corporate taxes and withholding taxes translated into euros. The next row gives the project's resulting nominal after-tax cash flow in euros. The project's nominal euro discount rate is 12%, and the resulting NPV for the project is €329.20 million as indicated at the bottom of the table.

INTERRELATED TAX EFFECTS

The distinction made in Method 2 between the estimated taxes in the foreign and home countries can be important if taxes payable in the home country on project earnings do not match the tax credits allowable on the project's foreign taxes. If taxes incurred in the home country on a project's foreign earnings exceed the available tax credits for foreign taxes paid, the after-tax incremental cash flow of the project must reflect the additional tax payable in the home country. On the other hand, if tax credits exceed home country taxes payable on the project and if the parent company is already in a non-taxpaying position, unused tax credits (if they are permitted to be carried forward) could extend the parent company's non-taxpaying period. We require the framework of Method 2 in order to evaluate such net incremental effects of the foreign project on the parent company's taxes.

DEFINITION

Systematic risk   Risk that portfolio diversification cannot eliminate.

22-7 UNREMITTED INCOME

So far, we have assumed payment of all after-tax incremental cash flows from the project to the parent company. A parent company often chooses to reinvest some of the net cash flow in the foreign country generating it, however. In addition, some countries require foreign corporations to reinvest locally a specified proportion of the reported profits.

FAVORABLE REINVESTMENT OPPORTUNITIES

Suppose that the parent company can expect plentiful investment opportunities in the host country. In the short term, reinvestment reduces the dividends to the parent. In the longer term, however, the additional investments increase the dividend income. If the rates of return earned by the resulting additional foreign projects are no less than their required rates of return, there is no net loss of PV. This conclusion is a direct algebraic consequence of the theory of dividend policy discussed further in Chapter 15. In practice, this means that if the parent company can expect to

---

[3] We assume that the home country accepts the host country method of calculating taxable income in this example.

receive dividends on all the additional projects, the parent does not lose any PV as a result of the additional foreign investment.

UNFAVORABLE REINVESTMENT OPPORTUNITIES

A problem arises if there should be insufficient attractive investment opportunities in the host country, or if expropriation of the assets by the host country is a risk. In this case, nonremittance could reduce the NPV of the project. The returns expected on the reinvested funds must compensate for the probability of expropriation but cannot do so unless they can earn somewhat more than the parent company's required rate of return for the host country. The rate of return expected from a project must be greater than the project's required rate of return plus the expected annual probability of expropriation.

A conservative approach often used is to include only those expected cash flows to be remitted through normal channels. Discounting separately the benefits of possible circumvention of host country restrictions (e.g., through transfer prices between divisions in different countries) is one approach.[4] Other items that could merit separate treatment include the ability to reduce or defer taxes by combining profits from operations in countries with relatively low and high taxes or to move expenses and revenues from one affiliated company to another and reinvest profits in low-tax countries. Method 2 can facilitate the required analysis.

22-8 INTERNATIONAL REQUIRED RATES OF RETURN

Our examples assumed that the real rate of interest remains constant and equal for the different currencies. We used the same real discount rate throughout. We also assumed constant expected rates of inflation for each currency. Incorporation of expected differences and changes in these rates in the Fisher and PPP formulas is straightforward, however.

TERM STRUCTURE

While it is not always necessary to use a different discount rate for each future period in the life of the project, it is desirable to do so when there are significant expected changes in either or both the real rate of interest and the rate of inflation for the foreign currency. The discount factor for a Year 5 cash flow, for example, is simply the product of the one-period discount factors for each of the five years. The PPP formula requires a similar multiperiod treatment. The overriding principle is consistency. Consistency requires that the discount rates are calculated using the same assumptions regarding the foreign rates of inflation and real rates of interest that are used when forecasting the foreign cash flows and exchange rates.

RISK PREMIUM

International projects involve a degree of diversification for shareholders not possible from domestic investment alone. Therefore, we could ask whether the resulting lower risk would

---

[4] Attempts by host countries to police such circumventions meet with varying degrees of success.

justify smaller risk premiums in the discount rates for foreign projects. The answer depends upon the degree of international diversification of the shareholders' portfolios because international diversification by companies need not reduce the risk of portfolios that are internationally diversified already. For a variety of reasons, including information costs, shareholders still invest disproportionately in domestically traded securities, and thus financial markets across the world are not fully integrated. From the point of view of shareholders who perceive risk in relation to their own domestic markets, a foreign capital project has lower systematic risk if its performance tends not to relate to the domestic economy. Accordingly, the Capital Asset Pricing Model (CAPM) implies that the discount rate for such an international project is lower than for the equivalent domestic project, assuming that the company can diversify or hedge sufficiently the project's foreign exchange risk.

DEFINITIONS

Capital Asset Pricing Model (CAPM)   Linear model attempting to explain the expected return on a risky asset in terms of the risk-free rate, its beta factor (systematic risk), and the risk premium on the market portfolio.

Diversification   Reduction of a portfolio's risk by holding a collection of assets having returns that are not perfectly positively correlated.

Hedging   Buying one security and selling another to reduce risk.

Portfolio   Collection of investments in financial securities and other assets.

22-9 CONCLUSIONS

We have shown two equivalent methods for obtaining the NPV of a multicurrency international capital project. The first method does not require any forecasts of future foreign exchange rates and thus exchange rate forecasts cannot bias the NPV in this method. The method does not facilitate computation of interrelated tax effects between different national tax jurisdictions, however. The second method facilitates analysis of interrelated taxation by introducing exchange rate forecasts in a form that maintains mathematical equivalence to the first method. The second method thus permits the financial analysis of a multicurrency project's commercial and fiscal merits without introducing the effects of biased exchange rate forecasts. The question as to whether it is possible or desirable to hedge fully the exchange rates is a Corporate Treasury issue that should be taken seriously but can be treated separately.

Reinvestment of a part of a project's cash flows in the host country need not reduce the project's NPV. If the rates of return on the reinvested funds equal or exceed the relevant required rate of return and if expropriation risks are negligible, then reinvestment in the host country is no different in principle from reinvestment in the home country.

FURTHER READING

David K. Eiteman, Arthur I. Stonehill, and Michael H. Moffett (1998) *Multinational Business Finance*, 8th edn (Wokingham, UK: Addison-Wesley).

Alan Shapiro (1983) "International capital budgeting," *Midland and Corporate Finance Journal*, Vol. I (Spring), 26–45.

Alan Shapiro (2001) *Foundations of Multinational Financial Management*, 4th edn (Chichester, UK: John Wiley & Sons).

QUESTIONS AND PROBLEMS

1   GLOBAL ENTERPRISE plc is an international manufacturing company domiciled within the EU. The company plans the Ventgo project for manufacturing in Anderia, a sovereign nation outside the euro zone. So, the manufacturing costs will be denominated in Anderian dollars (A). Labor costs in Anderia are low, but the country exacts a relatively high 50% rate of Corporation Tax. The country does not tax dividends remitted by inward investors to foreign countries, however. Given below are the expected (real) manufacturing cash flows in Anderian dollars (millions) for the five-year project.

0	1	2	3	4	5
−15	−5	−5	−5	−5	−5

Economic forecasters predict a 17% annual rate of inflation for Anderia. Calculate the expected nominal annual before-tax manufacturing cash flow in Anderian dollars for the Ventgo project.

2   GLOBAL'S real required rate of return for the Ventgo project is 15%. Referring to the previous problem, what is the corresponding nominal discount rate for the project's Anderian cash flow?

3   GLOBAL will sell the Ventgo product in the EU. The following is the expected real before-tax net cash flow (€ million) resulting from selling the product.

0	1	2	3	4	5
	12	12	12	12	12

Problem 1 gives the corresponding manufacturing cash flows in Anderian dollars (millions) before tax. The current spot rate of exchange is A1.2222/€1.00. Using Method 1, find the NPV of the project's before-tax cash flows.

4   Economic forecasters predict a 17% annual rate of inflation for Anderia and a rate of only 3% for the euro zone during the next five years. The current spot rate of exchange is A1.2222/€1.00. Use PPP to give an unbiased forecast of the exchange rate for each of the next five years.

5   Referring to the problems above, use Method 2 to find the before-tax NPV in euros for GLOBAL'S project in Anderia.

6   The Anderian subsidiary is to sell the entire Ventgo product in the euro zone. Expected sales are 150,000 units per year. The proposed price will be €80, rising at the euro zone rate of inflation. The subsidiary will pay GLOBAL a 20% commission for marketing the product. The subsidiary will also pay GLOBAL a 5.0% royalty for patents and proprietary services. Allowable depreciation and other noncash charges should be A5 million per year. Anderia levies Corporation Tax at 50% but withholds no taxes on dividends remitted to the parent company. Assume that the subsidiary remits all net cash flow as dividends to the parent company. GLOBAL pays taxes at 30% in the home country on income from foreign subsidiaries and on dividend income. Use Method 2 to calculate the NPV of the Ventgo project's after-tax cash flow.

7   Suppose expected dividends from GLOBAL's Anderian subsidiary are A5 million per year (unadjusted for inflation) during the next 10 years. GLOBAL's real discount rate for these dividends is 15%. Suppose the company decides to forgo any dividend income from Anderia for one year and reinvest the funds in promising commercial projects in that country. The company expected an after-tax 15% real rate of return on these additional investments in Anderia. If the company continues to reinvest the income from the investment for five years and subsequently uses all the principal and income from the investments to increase the dividend in Year 6, what will be the dividend in that year? Show the effect of the forgone dividend on the PV of the Anderian dividend stream.

Present Value Tables

DISCOUNT FACTORS

Present value of €1 received after t periods discounted at R per period $= 1/(1 + R)^t$:

Periods t	Discount rate R														
	1%	2%	3%	4%	5%	6%	7%	8%	9%	10%	11%	12%	13%	14%	15%
1	0.9901	0.9804	0.9709	0.9615	0.9524	0.9434	0.9346	0.9259	0.9174	0.9091	0.9009	0.8929	0.8850	0.8772	0.8696
2	0.9803	0.9612	0.9426	0.9246	0.9070	0.8900	0.8734	0.8573	0.8417	0.8264	0.8116	0.7972	0.7831	0.7695	0.7561
3	0.9706	0.9423	0.9151	0.8890	0.8638	0.8396	0.8163	0.7938	0.7722	0.7513	0.7312	0.7118	0.6931	0.6750	0.6575
4	0.9610	0.9238	0.8885	0.8548	0.8227	0.7921	0.7629	0.7350	0.7084	0.6830	0.6587	0.6355	0.6133	0.5921	0.5718
5	0.9515	0.9057	0.8626	0.8219	0.7835	0.7473	0.7130	0.6806	0.6499	0.6209	0.5935	0.5674	0.5428	0.5194	0.4972
6	0.9420	0.8880	0.8375	0.7903	0.7462	0.7050	0.6663	0.6302	0.5963	0.5645	0.5346	0.5066	0.4803	0.4556	0.4323
7	0.9327	0.8706	0.8131	0.7599	0.7107	0.6651	0.6227	0.5835	0.5470	0.5132	0.4817	0.4523	0.4251	0.3996	0.3759
8	0.9235	0.8535	0.7894	0.7307	0.6768	0.6274	0.5820	0.5403	0.5019	0.4665	0.4339	0.4039	0.3762	0.3506	0.3269
9	0.9143	0.8368	0.7664	0.7026	0.6446	0.5919	0.5439	0.5002	0.4604	0.4241	0.3909	0.3606	0.3329	0.3075	0.2843
10	0.9053	0.8203	0.7441	0.6756	0.6139	0.5584	0.5083	0.4632	0.4224	0.3855	0.3522	0.3220	0.2946	0.2697	0.2472
11	0.8963	0.8043	0.7224	0.6496	0.5847	0.5268	0.4751	0.4289	0.3875	0.3505	0.3173	0.2875	0.2607	0.2366	0.2149
12	0.8874	0.7885	0.7014	0.6246	0.5568	0.4970	0.4440	0.3971	0.3555	0.3186	0.2858	0.2567	0.2307	0.2076	0.1869
13	0.8787	0.7730	0.6810	0.6006	0.5303	0.4688	0.4150	0.3677	0.3262	0.2897	0.2575	0.2292	0.2042	0.1821	0.1625
14	0.8700	0.7579	0.6611	0.5775	0.5051	0.4423	0.3878	0.3405	0.2992	0.2633	0.2320	0.2046	0.1807	0.1597	0.1413
15	0.8613	0.7430	0.6419	0.5553	0.4810	0.4173	0.3624	0.3152	0.2745	0.2394	0.2090	0.1827	0.1599	0.1401	0.1229
16	0.8528	0.7284	0.6232	0.5339	0.4581	0.3936	0.3387	0.2919	0.2519	0.2176	0.1883	0.1631	0.1415	0.1229	0.1069
17	0.8444	0.7142	0.6050	0.5134	0.4363	0.3714	0.3166	0.2703	0.2311	0.1978	0.1696	0.1456	0.1252	0.1078	0.0929
18	0.8360	0.7002	0.5874	0.4936	0.4155	0.3503	0.2959	0.2502	0.2120	0.1799	0.1528	0.1300	0.1108	0.0946	0.0808
19	0.8277	0.6864	0.5703	0.4746	0.3957	0.3305	0.2765	0.2317	0.1945	0.1635	0.1377	0.1161	0.0981	0.0829	0.0703
20	0.8195	0.6730	0.5537	0.4564	0.3769	0.3118	0.2584	0.2145	0.1784	0.1486	0.1240	0.1037	0.0868	0.0728	0.0611

DISCOUNT FACTORS

Present value of €1 received after t periods discounted at R per period $= 1/(1 + R)^t$:

Discount rate R

Periods t	16%	17%	18%	19%	20%	21%	22%	23%	24%	25%	26%	27%	28%	29%	30%
1	0.8621	0.8547	0.8475	0.8403	0.8333	0.8264	0.8197	0.8130	0.8065	0.8000	0.7937	0.7874	0.7813	0.7752	0.7692
2	0.7432	0.7305	0.7182	0.7062	0.6944	0.6830	0.6719	0.6610	0.6504	0.6400	0.6299	0.6200	0.6104	0.6009	0.5917
3	0.6407	0.6244	0.6086	0.5934	0.5787	0.5645	0.5507	0.5374	0.5245	0.5120	0.4999	0.4882	0.4768	0.4658	0.4552
4	0.5523	0.5337	0.5158	0.4987	0.4823	0.4665	0.4514	0.4369	0.4230	0.4096	0.3968	0.3844	0.3725	0.3611	0.3501
5	0.4761	0.4561	0.4371	0.4190	0.4019	0.3855	0.3700	0.3552	0.3411	0.3277	0.3149	0.3027	0.2910	0.2799	0.2693
6	0.4104	0.3898	0.3704	0.3521	0.3349	0.3186	0.3033	0.2888	0.2751	0.2621	0.2499	0.2383	0.2274	0.2170	0.2072
7	0.3538	0.3332	0.3139	0.2959	0.2791	0.2633	0.2486	0.2348	0.2218	0.2097	0.1983	0.1877	0.1776	0.1682	0.1594
8	0.3050	0.2848	0.2660	0.2487	0.2326	0.2176	0.2038	0.1909	0.1789	0.1678	0.1574	0.1478	0.1388	0.1304	0.1226
9	0.2630	0.2434	0.2255	0.2090	0.1938	0.1799	0.1670	0.1552	0.1443	0.1342	0.1249	0.1164	0.1084	0.1011	0.0943
10	0.2267	0.2080	0.1911	0.1756	0.1615	0.1486	0.1369	0.1262	0.1164	0.1074	0.0992	0.0916	0.0847	0.0784	0.0725
11	0.1954	0.1778	0.1619	0.1476	0.1346	0.1228	0.1122	0.1026	0.0938	0.0859	0.0787	0.0721	0.0662	0.0607	0.0558
12	0.1685	0.1520	0.1372	0.1240	0.1122	0.1015	0.0920	0.0834	0.0757	0.0687	0.0625	0.0568	0.0517	0.0471	0.0429
13	0.1452	0.1299	0.1163	0.1042	0.0935	0.0839	0.0754	0.0678	0.0610	0.0550	0.0496	0.0447	0.0404	0.0365	0.0330
14	0.1252	0.1110	0.0985	0.0876	0.0779	0.0693	0.0618	0.0551	0.0492	0.0440	0.0393	0.0352	0.0316	0.0283	0.0254
15	0.1079	0.0949	0.0835	0.0736	0.0649	0.0573	0.0507	0.0448	0.0397	0.0352	0.0312	0.0277	0.0247	0.0219	0.0195
16	0.0930	0.0811	0.0708	0.0618	0.0541	0.0474	0.0415	0.0364	0.0320	0.0281	0.0248	0.0218	0.0193	0.0170	0.0150
17	0.0802	0.0693	0.0600	0.0520	0.0451	0.0391	0.0340	0.0296	0.0258	0.0225	0.0197	0.0172	0.0150	0.0132	0.0116
18	0.0691	0.0592	0.0508	0.0437	0.0376	0.0323	0.0279	0.0241	0.0208	0.0180	0.0156	0.0135	0.0118	0.0102	0.0089
19	0.0596	0.0506	0.0431	0.0367	0.0313	0.0267	0.0229	0.0196	0.0168	0.0144	0.0124	0.0107	0.0092	0.0079	0.0068
20	0.0514	0.0433	0.0365	0.0308	0.0261	0.0221	0.0187	0.0159	0.0135	0.0115	0.0098	0.0084	0.0072	0.0061	0.0053

ANNUITY FACTORS

Present value of €1 received for each of t periods discounted at R per period $= (1/R)[1 - 1/(1+R)^t]$:

| Periods t | \multicolumn{15}{c}{Discount rate R} |

Periods t	1%	2%	3%	4%	5%	6%	7%	8%	9%	10%	11%	12%	13%	14%	15%
1	0.9901	0.9804	0.7909	0.9615	0.9524	0.9434	0.9346	0.9259	0.9174	0.9091	0.9009	0.8929	0.8850	0.8772	0.8696
2	1.9704	1.9416	0.9135	1.8861	1.8594	1.8334	1.8080	1.7833	1.7591	1.7355	1.7125	1.6901	1.6681	1.6467	1.6257
3	2.9410	2.8839	2.8286	2.7751	2.7232	2.6730	2.6243	2.5771	2.5313	2.4869	2.4437	2.4018	2.3612	2.3216	2.2832
4	3.9020	3.8077	3.7171	3.6299	3.5460	3.4651	3.3872	3.3121	3.2397	3.1699	3.1024	3.0373	2.9745	2.9137	2.8550
5	4.8534	4.7135	4.5797	4.4518	4.3295	4.2124	4.1002	3.9927	3.8897	3.7908	3.6959	3.6048	3.5172	3.4331	3.3522
6	5.7955	5.6014	5.4172	5.2421	5.0757	4.9173	4.7665	4.6229	4.4859	4.3553	4.2305	4.1114	3.9975	3.8887	3.7845
7	6.7282	6.4720	6.2303	6.0021	5.7864	5.5824	5.3893	5.2064	5.0330	4.8684	4.7122	4.5638	4.4226	4.2883	4.1604
8	7.6517	7.3255	7.0197	6.7327	6.4632	6.2098	5.9713	5.7466	5.5348	5.3349	5.1461	4.9676	4.7988	4.6389	4.4873
9	8.5660	8.1622	7.7861	7.4353	7.1078	6.8017	6.5152	6.2469	5.9952	5.7590	5.5370	5.3282	5.1317	4.9464	4.7716
10	9.4713	8.9826	8.5302	8.1109	7.7217	7.3601	7.0236	6.7101	6.4177	6.1446	5.8892	5.6502	5.4262	5.2161	5.0188
11	10.3676	9.7868	9.2526	8.7605	8.3064	7.8869	7.4987	7.1390	6.8052	6.4951	6.2065	5.9377	5.6869	5.4527	5.2337
12	11.2551	10.5753	9.9540	9.3851	8.8633	8.3838	7.9427	7.5361	7.1607	6.8137	6.4924	6.1944	5.9176	5.6603	5.4206
13	12.1337	11.3484	10.6350	9.9856	9.3936	8.8527	8.3577	7.9038	7.4869	7.1034	6.7499	6.4235	6.1218	5.8424	5.5831
14	13.0037	12.1062	11.2961	10.5631	9.8986	9.2950	8.7455	8.2442	7.7862	7.3667	6.9819	6.6282	6.3025	6.0021	5.7245
15	13.8651	12.8493	11.9379	11.1184	10.3797	9.7122	9.1079	8.5595	8.0607	7.6061	7.1909	6.8109	6.4624	6.1422	5.8474
16	14.7179	13.5777	12.5611	11.6523	10.8378	10.1059	9.4466	8.8514	8.3126	7.8237	7.3792	6.9740	6.6039	6.2651	5.9542
17	15.5623	14.2919	13.1661	12.1657	11.2741	10.4773	9.7632	9.1216	8.5436	8.0216	7.5488	7.1196	6.7291	6.3729	6.0472
18	16.3983	14.9920	13.7535	12.6593	11.6896	10.8276	10.0591	9.3719	8.7556	8.2014	7.7016	7.2497	6.8399	6.4674	6.1280
19	17.2260	15.6785	14.3238	13.1339	12.0853	11.1581	10.3356	9.6036	8.9501	8.3649	7.8393	7.3658	6.9380	6.5504	6.1982
20	18.0456	16.3514	14.8775	13.5903	12.4622	11.4699	10.5940	9.8181	9.1285	8.5136	7.9633	7.4694	7.0248	6.6231	6.2593

ANNUITY FACTORS

Present value €1 received for each of t periods discounted at R per period = $(1/R)[1 - 1/(1 + R)^t]$:

Periods t	Discount rate R														
	16%	17%	18%	19%	20%	21%	22%	23%	24%	25%	26%	27%	28%	29%	30%
1	0.8621	0.8547	0.8475	0.8403	0.8333	0.8264	0.8197	0.8130	0.8065	0.8000	0.7937	0.7874	0.7813	0.7752	0.7692
2	1.6052	1.5852	1.5656	1.5465	1.5278	1.5095	1.4915	1.4740	1.4568	1.4400	1.4235	1.4074	1.3916	1.3761	1.3609
3	2.2459	2.2096	2.1743	2.1399	2.1065	2.0739	2.0422	2.0114	1.9813	1.9520	1.9234	1.8956	1.8684	1.8420	1.8161
4	2.7982	2.7432	2.6901	2.6386	2.5887	2.5404	2.4936	2.4483	2.4043	2.3616	2.3203	2.2800	2.2410	2.2031	2.1662
5	3.2743	3.1993	3.1272	3.0576	2.9906	2.9260	2.8636	2.8035	2.7454	2.6893	2.6351	2.5827	2.5320	2.4830	2.4356
6	3.6847	3.5892	3.4976	3.4098	3.3255	3.2446	3.1669	3.0923	3.0205	2.9514	2.8850	2.8210	2.7594	2.7000	2.6427
7	4.0386	3.9224	3.8115	3.7057	3.6046	3.5079	3.4155	3.3270	3.2423	3.1611	3.0833	3.0087	2.9370	2.8682	2.8021
8	4.3436	4.2072	4.0776	3.9544	3.8372	3.7256	3.6193	3.5179	3.4212	3.3289	3.2407	3.1564	3.0758	2.9986	2.9247
9	4.6065	4.4506	4.3030	4.1633	4.0310	3.9054	3.7863	3.6731	3.5655	3.4631	3.3657	3.2728	3.1842	3.0997	3.0190
10	4.8332	4.6586	4.4941	4.3389	4.1925	4.0541	3.9232	3.7993	3.6819	3.5705	3.4648	3.3644	3.2689	3.1781	3.0915
11	5.0286	4.8364	4.6560	4.4865	4.3271	4.1769	4.0354	3.9018	3.7757	3.6564	3.5435	3.4365	3.3351	3.2388	3.1473
12	5.1971	4.9884	4.7932	4.6105	4.4392	4.2784	4.1274	3.9852	3.8514	3.7251	3.6059	3.4933	3.3868	3.2859	3.1903
13	5.3423	5.1183	4.9095	4.7147	4.5327	4.3624	4.2028	4.0530	3.9124	3.7801	3.6555	3.5381	3.4272	3.3224	3.2233
14	5.4675	5.2293	5.0081	4.8023	4.6106	4.4317	4.2646	4.1082	3.9616	3.8241	3.6949	3.5733	3.4587	3.3507	3.2487
15	5.5755	5.3242	5.0916	4.8759	4.6755	4.4890	4.3152	4.1530	4.0013	3.8593	3.7261	3.6010	3.4834	3.3726	3.2682
16	5.6685	5.4053	5.1624	4.9377	4.7296	4.5364	4.3567	4.1894	4.0333	3.8874	3.7509	3.6228	3.5026	3.3896	3.2832
17	5.7487	5.4746	5.2223	4.9897	4.7746	4.5755	4.3908	4.2190	4.0591	3.9099	3.7705	3.6400	3.5177	3.4028	3.2948
18	5.8178	5.5339	5.2732	5.0333	4.8122	4.6079	4.4187	4.2431	4.0799	3.9279	3.7861	3.6536	3.5294	3.4130	3.3037
19	5.8775	5.5845	5.3162	5.0700	4.8435	4.6346	4.4415	4.2627	4.0967	3.9424	3.7985	3.6642	3.5386	3.4210	3.3105
20	5.9288	5.6278	5.3527	5.1009	4.8696	4.6567	4.4603	4.2786	4.1103	3.9539	3.8083	3.6726	3.5458	3.4271	3.3158

Probability Table

Cumulative probability $N(d)$ that a normally distributed random variable is less than d standard deviations above the mean:

d	0	0.010	0.020	0.030	0.040	0.050	0.060	0.070	0.080	0.090
0	0.500 00	0.503 99	0.507 98	0.511 97	0.515 95	0.519 94	0.523 92	0.527 90	0.531 88	0.535 86
0.1	0.539 83	0.543 80	0.547 76	0.551 72	0.555 67	0.559 62	0.563 56	0.567 49	0.571 42	0.575 35
0.2	0.579 26	0.583 17	0.587 06	0.590 95	0.594 83	0.598 71	0.602 57	0.606 42	0.610 26	0.614 09
0.3	0.617 91	0.621 72	0.625 52	0.629 30	0.633 07	0.636 83	0.640 58	0.644 31	0.648 03	0.651 73
0.4	0.655 42	0.659 10	0.662 76	0.666 40	0.670 03	0.673 64	0.677 24	0.680 82	0.684 39	0.687 93
0.5	0.691 46	0.694 97	0.698 47	0.701 94	0.705 40	0.708 84	0.712 26	0.715 66	0.719 04	0.722 40
0.6	0.725 75	0.729 07	0.732 37	0.735 65	0.738 91	0.742 15	0.745 37	0.748 57	0.751 75	0.754 90
0.7	0.758 04	0.761 15	0.764 24	0.767 30	0.770 35	0.773 37	0.776 37	0.779 35	0.782 30	0.785 24
0.8	0.788 14	0.791 03	0.793 89	0.796 73	0.799 55	0.802 34	0.805 11	0.807 85	0.810 57	0.813 27
0.9	0.815 94	0.818 59	0.821 21	0.823 81	0.826 39	0.828 94	0.831 47	0.833 98	0.836 46	0.838 91
1	0.841 34	0.843 75	0.846 14	0.848 49	0.850 83	0.853 14	0.855 43	0.857 69	0.859 93	0.862 14
1.1	0.864 33	0.866 50	0.868 64	0.870 76	0.872 86	0.874 93	0.876 98	0.879 00	0.881 00	0.882 98
1.2	0.884 93	0.886 86	0.888 77	0.890 65	0.892 51	0.894 35	0.896 17	0.897 96	0.899 73	0.901 47
1.3	0.903 20	0.904 90	0.906 58	0.908 24	0.909 88	0.911 49	0.913 08	0.914 66	0.916 21	0.917 74
1.4	0.919 24	0.920 73	0.922 20	0.923 64	0.925 07	0.926 47	0.927 85	0.929 22	0.930 56	0.931 89
1.5	0.933 19	0.934 48	0.935 74	0.936 99	0.938 22	0.939 43	0.940 62	0.941 79	0.942 95	0.944 08
1.6	0.945 20	0.946 30	0.947 38	0.948 45	0.949 50	0.950 53	0.951 54	0.952 54	0.953 52	0.954 49
1.7	0.955 43	0.956 37	0.957 28	0.958 18	0.959 07	0.959 94	0.960 80	0.961 64	0.962 46	0.963 27
1.8	0.964 07	0.964 85	0.965 62	0.966 38	0.967 12	0.967 84	0.968 56	0.969 26	0.969 95	0.970 62
1.9	0.971 28	0.971 93	0.972 57	0.973 20	0.973 81	0.974 41	0.975 00	0.975 58	0.976 15	0.976 70
2	0.977 25	0.977 78	0.978 31	0.978 82	0.979 32	0.979 82	0.980 30	0.980 77	0.981 24	0.981 69
2.1	0.982 14	0.982 57	0.983 00	0.983 41	0.983 82	0.984 22	0.984 61	0.985 00	0.985 37	0.985 74
2.2	0.986 10	0.986 45	0.986 79	0.987 13	0.987 45	0.987 78	0.988 09	0.988 40	0.988 70	0.988 99
2.3	0.989 28	0.989 56	0.989 83	0.990 10	0.990 36	0.990 61	0.990 86	0.991 11	0.991 34	0.991 58
2.4	0.991 80	0.992 02	0.992 24	0.992 45	0.992 66	0.992 86	0.993 05	0.993 24	0.993 43	0.993 61
2.5	0.993 79	0.993 96	0.994 13	0.994 30	0.994 46	0.994 61	0.994 77	0.994 92	0.995 06	0.995 20

Index